Long Ago and Far Away...

An Encyclopedia for Successfully Using Literature with Intermediate Readers

by Carol Otis Hurst

with
Margaret Sullivan Ahearn
Leslie Jacquelin Clark
Lynn Otis Palmer
James Neill Yvon

One DLM Park • Allen, Texas 75002

Edited by Tracy Moncure
Cover designed and illustrated by Vicki Langeliers

2 3 4 5 6 7 8 9   96 95 94 93 92 91

Table of Contents

Preface

Just as no athlete is *born* wanting to play football, no one is *born* wanting to read. The desire must be instilled by others—parents, uncles, siblings, coaches, teachers, or neighbors. As the great *New York Times* critic Orville Prescott observed years ago, "Few children learn to love books by themselves. Someone has to lure them into the wonderful world of the written word; someone has to show them the way."

And that is what this book is all about—luring, leading, and awakening children's minds.

If the last twenty-five years of reading research has confirmed anything, it is that reading is an accrued skill, like swimming. True, there are rules and strokes to learn, but that doesn't take much time. What really counts is what comes after the basic strokes or rules. The only way to "get good" at swimming is to jump into the water and swim. And the only way to get good at reading is to jump into a book and read. The more you do it, the better you get. The better you get, the more you like it. The more you like it, the more you do it, *ad infinitum.* But children will never get better at reading without doing it, and they won't do it if they hate it.

We must also teach them to *want* to read. And that is what this book is about: whetting their appetites for this delicious thing called reading; bringing them books that excite and amuse and inform in a way that will not kill the love of learning. The best educators have long known that a book, like a teacher or librarian, need not be dull in order to instruct.

Back in the 1950s, Nathan Pusey, the president of Harvard, defined the role of the teacher: "The close observer soon discovers that the teacher's task is not to implant facts but to place the subject to be learned in front of the learner and, through sympathy, emotion, imagination, and patience, to awaken in the learner the restless drive for answers and insights which enlarge the personal life and give it meaning."

That kind of teaching requires neither the mind of a Rhodes scholar nor the emotive skills of a Katharine Hepburn or Laurence Olivier. It does require more involvement than simply passing out a stack of workbook pages. Involvement is also what this book is about. In recent decades, students have spent less time with real books—books written by real authors, not curriculum committees. Spread this regimen through several generations and you have a crop of teachers and parents who view reading as something dry and artificial, to be learned by rote, filling in the blanks, circling the correct answer. You have generations of young teachers who do not know their folktales or tall tales, who have never heard of Peter Spier or Robert McCloskey, who can't tell a trade book from a textbook.

Ever since I stumbled uninvited into Carol Otis Hurst's elementary school library more than 15 years ago, she has epitomized for me what a children's librarian and teacher can be. She and her team have accomplished with this volume as thorough and practical a course in children's literature as you'll find in any college classroom. And it's written by people who have been in the trenches, on the floor, atop the desks, in the sandbox, behind the easel, and around the bookcase with children.

The ultimate objective, of course, is to create *life*time readers, not just *school*time readers—readers who are still reading and educating themselves twenty-five years after graduation.

Lifetime readers always remind me of Dr. Max Cowan of the Hughes Medical Institute. He was preparing to testify in Washington on behalf of brain research when he realized that most of the Congressional aides attending the briefings might not have seen a real brain. Because he had access to post-mortem specimens, he quickly wrapped one up, tucked it into his briefcase, and headed across the Potomac to the hearings.

He hadn't figured on the security measures he would encouter at the Senate building entrance nor on the frightened look on the guard's face when he opened the briefcase.

"What's that?" he was asked.

"It's a brain," he answered, only to be asked immediately what he planned to do with it. Tongue in cheek, Dr. Cowan explained that most of his colleagues come from "sophisticated places like Boston and New York. But I come from the Midwest, and whenever I come to Washington I feel I need all the help I can get, so I always carry a spare."

That's funny only when you take it literally. If you take it figuratively, it's a serious possiblity. The woman reading her book on the plane, the student reading a paperback on the bus, the passenger reading his newspaper on the subway—isn't each of them traveling with a spare brain? Aren't they all tapping into an extra reservoir of ideas or facts, plugging into the author's heart or soul or intelligence?

Think of all the spare brains resting on our bookshelves, waiting patiently to be connected to future readers. That also is what this book offers—connections that create future readers. If we are to become a nation of thinkers and doers instead of a nation of shoppers and watchers, it is the readers who will make the difference.

Jim Trelease
author of *The New Read-Aloud Handbook*

Introduction

Rationale

With so much of the current research supporting a literature-based curriculum or, at least, suggesting a greater emphasis on the reading of "real" books in the classroom, there comes a sometimes overwhelming responsibility for a teacher. A teacher must not only know the child and the method, but the books as well. It's hard enough to be acquainted with the vast numbers of picture books that would be of use in a classroom; they, at least, can be read in a few minutes. Novels, however, are another matter entirely. With more depth, more intricacies, not to mention more pages, the pile of unread novels grows higher and higher on a teacher's bookshelf. And then, when they are read, so many seem mediocre at best: the plots contrived, the characterization poor, and the writing pedestrian. A teacher often gives up in frustration. A large part of that frustration is the knowledge that there are surely better books. This book will try to point the way to some of those better choices for you, the teacher.

Using This Book

This book is not an attempt to allow you to use novels as a basis for a reading/writing program without reading them yourself. That's an impossibility. If you haven't read the book a child has finished, the only honest question you can ask is "Did you like it?" and then "Tell me about it." Such an approach does not allow much in-depth discussion. You'll never know whether the child has missed the main point or any of the niceties of the writing and you cannot use the book as a means for encouraging the child to read like a writer and write like a reader. Such analysis takes digging—and neither you nor the child can do it without reading first. You must dig in yourself, discovering with the children the richness of the literature that has been written for them.

What this book may do is point your reading, and that of your class, in some of the best directions. We've read and reread hundreds of books in an attempt to weed out the chaff and allow you to see rather quickly what books may be of interest to you and the readers with whom you work. We've summarized the plots to refresh your memory of a book you haven't read for a while. We've listed related books and points of departure for discussion and activities.

Because this book is intended for those working with children from about third grade to about sixth grade, the books have a wide range of difficulty. Whenever possible, we have indicated with a bar continuum the level of sophistication we believe is necessary to understand the book.

■■■■■■■■□□□□□□

Remember this is not a reading level indicator, although difficulty and sophistication often go hand in hand. We think that a reading level or grade level indicator would be chancy and inconsistent with the whole language approach. So much depends on what the child has read previously and what his or her life experiences have been that level of sophistication seems most realistic, albeit equally subjective.

It's possible to bring children's literature into the classroom through a variety of avenues, and this book tries to address some of those avenues.

The book is divided into four sections: Themes, Books at a Glance, Authors and Illustrators, and Special Pages. Start any place you want and go where you will.

Themes

The Themes section covers a variety of subjects, logical and slightly less logical, through which you can bring works of fiction and non-fiction to the attention of young readers.

Books at a Glance

In this section you will find many special books that will start your creative mind branching out to many activities and areas of interest. When you see a check mark, ✔, beside a title, check the Index for other pages where the book is mentioned and/or summarized. Titles marked with a boxed check mark, ☑, are covered in *Once Upon a Time,* the first volume of this series.

Authors and Illustrators

Many authors and illustrators have contributed immeasurably to the storehouse of children's literature and it is impossible to cover all of them. In this volume, we have included studies of more than forty people whose major contributions have been to young children's literature. These studies include information about those people's lives, their works and awards, and, when possible, photographs and addresses where they can be reached.

As you look over the list of authors and illustrators covered in this volume, you will probably notice that a few favorites are missing. More than likely, those authors and illustrators are covered in *Once Upon a Time,* because the bulk of their work is for younger children. *Once Upon a Time* covers such people as Verna Aardema, Janet and Allan Ahlberg, Jan Brett, Eric Carle, Lucille Clifton, Tomie dePaola, Dr. Seuss, Particia Reilly Giff, Peggy Parish, Maurice Sendak, James Stevenson, and Judith Viorst.

Special Pages

Here is the hall closet where we've put the important stuff that doesn't fit anywhere else: annotated lists of books by categories, a calendar of authors' and illustrators' birthdays, writing techniques, a list of publishers and their addresses, and, of course, the Index.

Don't stop here. New books are being published as this one is being printed. This book was put together by a group that includes two administrators, a special education person, a classroom teacher, and a children's literature specialist. We learned a lot while writing it. Each of us had his or her own strengths and we needed them all. We came up with our best ideas when we were together, calling out titles and activities. There was much laughter and not a little frustration. We suggest that you put together your own similarly disparate group of people whose interest in children's books is as keen as yours. No one can do it alone.

Themes

Introduction

☐ While searching for worthwhile books for children, we discovered that most lists of children's books fall into common categories or themes. The themes presented in this book parallel those themes. These themes focus groups of books intended to help young readers place one book into a context of other books with a similar subject. Although many of the themes could and should be woven into social studies, science, and arts units, they can remain simply the thread that binds a group of books so that readers of different books have a base for discussion and activities.

☐ We usually start the theme with a picture book. A picture book quickly sets the subject in its most colorful light; it's a nonthreatening experience for both you and the children; and it establishes that picture books are not "just for little kids." After you have read the picture book aloud and the children have examined the illustrations, begin to set up an area in your classroom that focuses on the theme.

☐ Theme-related bulletin boards and displays of interesting objects stimulate attention and discussion. Encourage the children to bring reading and supplementary materials that relate to the theme.

☐ Choose one of the most interesting books from among those listed for each theme; or, better yet, choose one you've always liked. Read the book aloud, a chapter a day, giving the children a chance to discuss the reading when appropriate.

☐ We have also suggested several activities that the children might do after or concurrent with your oral reading or as follow-up activities to books they have read on their own. The activities suggested are those we've used with kids and are intended to serve as springboards for your own creative ideas. However, don't go overboard with activities. Don't use so many that a book lies dead on the floor when you're finished. Sometimes in our zeal to use good literature in the classroom, we succeed only in making good literature dull.

☐ Supply paperback and hardbound copies of other books related to the theme. Provide multiple copies of some of the titles if possible. If you've read a few of the books, it's very effective to present them as a salesperson might, tantalizing the children by reading a tiny bit from some exciting parts without giving away the story. If you have several copies of three or more titles, let children choose their books without regard to reading level. Your reading groups are then made up of the children reading a specific title. Even though you might have only single copies of several titles, the theme will keep the discussions and activities going.

☐ It is very important that you be as much a part of the reading, writing, and discussing as the children are, so choose a book you haven't read and start reading.

Waltzing Matilda

Rationale

It is possible to build a unit around any region or country using its folklore, history, and customs. We chose Australia because of the wealth of children's material set in that country.

Picture Book Starter

☐ Base, Graeme. *My Grandmother Lived in Gooligulch.* The Australian Book Source, 1988.

Grandma's adventures with Australian wildlife are told in humorous verse. Vivid, realistic illustrations alternate with pen and ink drawings.

☐ Vaughan, Marcia. *Wombat Stew.* Silver Burdett, 1986.

A dingo is outfoxed by a platypus, an emu, a lizard, an echidna, and a koala who "help" him make the perfect wombat stew.

☐ Wagner, Jenny. *The Bunyip of Berkeley's Creek.* Bradbury, 1977.

The Bunyip, a monster that may look like a refugee from the land of the Wild Things, knows he's a bunyip but can't convince anyone else.

Bulletin Board

☐ Display a map of Australia. Let the children add pictures as they gather information.

Museum

☐ Display books and objects from Australia: boomerangs, nonfiction picture books about Australia and its wildlife, an opal, a sheepskin, a shark tooth, and a piece of coral.

Discussions, Projects, and Activities

☐ Sing the song "Waltzing Matilda" and find out what's going on in the song.
☐ Make a Traveler's Guide to Australia using the information you gather in your reading.
☐ Make a videotape using illustrations from *National Geographic* magazine and nonfiction books as visual material while you tell a story about Australia.
☐ On a map of Australia, mark the settings of some of the suggested novels.
☐ Find out about the early history of Australia and its use as a penal colony.

☐ Find out about famous Australians such as Paul Hogan, Evonne Goolagong Cawley, Dame Judith Anderson, Rod Laver, John Newcombe, Rick Springfield, Joan Sutherland, Jan Ormerod, Mary Gilmore, Colin Thiele, A. B. Paterson, and the Bee Gees.
☐ Write to the tourist bureau of Australia for more information: Australian Tourist Commission, 459 Fifth Avenue, New York, NY 10017.
☐ Find pictures of the opera house at Sydney, the Parliament House in Canberra, Ayers Rock in central Australia, the Great Barrier Reef, and other Australian landmarks.

Books

Fiction

Carr, Roger. *The Clinker.* Houghton, 1989.

An American boy visits his great-grandparents in Australia and becomes involved in shipbuilding.

Coleridge, Ann. *Stranded.* Delacorte, 1989.

A coastal community in Australia joins together in an effort to save a group of marooned whales.

Gleeson, Libby. *Eleanor Elizabeth.* Holiday, 1990.

Eleanor Wheeler is a misfit. She resents moving to the family farm in Australia and she resents her inability to fit in. After she discovers her grandmother's diary, she forges a bond with the woman she never knew.

Kelleher, Victor. *Baily's Bones.* Dial, 1989.

Alex and Dee's vacation in Australia is a nightmare as tragedies of the past intrude upon the present.

Klein, Robin. *Penny Pollard's Diary.* Oxford, 1983.

■■■■□□□□□□□□□□□

This is an excellent account of life in Australia in the early 1900s and today. Penny Pollard is a little girl who visits a nursing home under protest but finds a friend.

Park, Ruth. *Playing Beatie Bow.* Atheneum, 1982.

■■■■■■■□□□□□□□

Beatie Bow is an Australian children's game. As Abigail watches young children at play, she sees another pale child watching the game, but not joining in. When Abigail discovers that the child is Beatie Bow, a child from another time, she and Beatie travel back in time to an earlier Sydney, Australia, and find out why the game is called Beatie Bow.

Pople, Maureen. *The Other Side of the Family.* Holt, 1986.

■■■■■■■□□□□□□

Kate Tucker is sent to Sydney to escape the London bombing and then, when the Japanese navy is seen in Sydney Harbour, to rural Australia to stay with her grandmother, a mildly eccentric but incredibly strong and wonderful woman. The glimpses of Australia are limited but informative.

Scholes, Katherine. *The Landing: A Night of Birds.* Doubleday, 1989.

■■■■■■■□□□□□□

When a flock of birds is driven onto their property in remote Australia, Annie and her grandfather help save them. Slowly Annie realizes that she can understand the birds' language.

Southall, Ivan. *Ash Road.* Greenwillow, 1978.

■■■■■■■□□□□□□

In the Australian foothills, a brushfire is a dangerous thing. When this one starts, a group of children find themselves in its path.

Thiele, Colin. *The Hammerhead Light.* Harper, 1977.

■■■■■■■□□□□□□

A lighthouse endangered by winter storms is scheduled for demolition. Twelve-year-old Tessa and her seventy-year-old friend Alex are determined to save the lighthouse. When his own home is destroyed in a storm, Alex moves into the lighthouse where he and Tessa contrive to save Tessa's father.

———. *The Shadow on the Hills.* Harper, 1978.

■■■■■■■□□□□□□

Bodo Schneider is an Australian Tom Sawyer, full of tricks and spunk as well as compassion.

Wrightson, Patricia. *The Ice Is Coming.* Atheneum, 1977.

■■■■■■■■■□□□□□

The Ninya, ice creatures, are coming and only Wirrun, a young Aboriginal man living among the white inhabitants of the coastal town, realizes it. Before the battle is over, all the forces of the land are mustered to turn back the cold.

———. *A Little Fear.* Atheneum, 1983.

■■■■■■■■■□□□□

Mrs. Tucker, an elderly refugee from a retirement home, battles the Njimbin, a gnome, in an isolated cottage in the outback.

Poetry

Fatchen, Max. *The Country Mail Is Coming: Poems from Down Under.* Little, 1990.

McCord, David. "Up from Down Under" from *One at a Time.* Little, 1986.

Paterson, A. B. "The Man from Snowy River" from *The Poetry of Horses,* edited by William Cole. Scribner, 1979.

Prelutsky, Jack. "The Wallaby" from *Zoo Doings.* Greenwillow, 1984.

Sladen, D. "A Summer Christmas in Australia" from *The Oxford Book of Christmas Poems,* edited by M. Harrison. Oxford, 1984.

Varday, M. "In North-West Australia Where the Iron Ore Grows" from *Stuff and Nonsense,* edited by M. Dugan. Philomel, 1977.

Music

"Botany Bay" from *The Fireside Book of Favorite American Songs.* Girl Scouts of America.

"Australia" from *Sing Together.* Girl Scouts of America, 1957.

"Honey Ant Song of Ljaba" from *Folk Songs of the World.* Day, 1966.

"The Kangaroo" from *The Fireside Song Book of Fun and Game Songs.* Simon & Schuster, 1974.

"Kookaburra." Available in many collections.

"The Overlander" from *Folk Songs of the World.* Day, 1966.

Paterson, A. B. "Waltzing Matilda." Available in many collections.

"The Shearer's Dream" from *The Gambit Book of Children's Songs.* Gambit, 1970.

The Cat Walks Alone

Rationale

Animals, particularly pets, are the subject of many novels. Cats, with their distinctive personalities, evoke strong feelings and make them perfect characters for books that range from trivial to soul-searching.

Picture Book Starter

☐ Griffith, Helen V. *Alex and the Cat.* Greenwillow, 1982.

Alex, a dog, and the cat are good friends in these three short stories. Each animal sees the world and events from its own perspective.

☐ King, Deborah. *Cloudy.* Philomel, 1990.

A simple text combined with beautiful illustrations tells the story of Cloudy, a smoky gray cat who used to be wild.

☐ Segal, Lore. *The Story of Mrs. Lovewright and Purrless Her Cat.* Knopf, 1985.

All Mrs. Lovewright needs to feel cozy is a cute little cat that will sit on her lap and purr. What she gets is a cat with a mind of its own who is anything but cuddly.

Bulletin Board

☐ Display cat silhouettes, statues, and stuffed animals all around the room: on top of bookcases, on the teacher's desk, on top of and around, but not on, the bulletin board. Label the bulletin board with a phrase like "Now, where's that cat?"

Museum

☐ Display objects related to cats and to the word *cat*, such as catnip, catsup, pictures of catastrophes, catalogs, picture of a catwalk, cat's cradles, catapult, cattail, catamaran, cat's eye marbles, tiger eye, cat o'nine tails, Arctic cat, Mercury lynx, Mercury cougar, Exxon tiger, box of Frosted Flakes, lasagne (Garfield's favorite food), Garfield, Heathcliff, Cat Woman, and Sylvester. Let the children figure out what the objects are and what they have in common.

Discussions, Projects, and Activities

☐ Distribute silhouettes of a variety of breeds of cats. On the front and back of each silhouette leave space for each child to name it, tell where it sleeps best, what really bothers it about people, what it will eat, what it will not eat, and its favorite toy, least favorite dog, and favorite season.

☐ Write a story in which a picture book cat meets a picture book mouse; for example, Purrless meets Frederick.

☐ Hold a debate between dog and cat lovers. Which makes the better pet and why?

☐ Tell or sing one of the stories from the musical *Cats.* Dress in cat costumes in the style that they use in the musical.

☐ Make a videotape of your cat and then set it to music.

☐ Critique cat food commercials in terms of accuracy, comic value, and drama. Hold a cat commercial awards ceremony. Award prizes in such categories as most aloof cat, most distraught cat owner, most dramatic cat, and most comic cat.

☐ Write to pet food companies to find out how they test products.

☐ Hold a photo contest of classmates' cats. Put the cat's name and a short description on each photo and see who can match the most cats and owners.

☐ Make posters showing facts about your cats. Include pictures, names, food preferences, etc.

☐ Write a diary for your cat.

☐ Choose a holiday and list reasons that it's your cat's favorite.

☐ Explore the role of cats in Egyptian mythology.

☐ Find out about the cats of the Roman Coliseum.

☐ Find and examine superstitions about cats.

☐ Hold an awards ceremony for the cat characters in novels. Give the acceptance speeches as the cat characters would.

☐ Talk about the way any of the novels would be different if the animals were not cats, but dogs or other animals.

Books

Fiction

Alexander, Lloyd. *The Town Cats and Other Tales.* Dutton, 1977.

■■■■■■■□□□□□□□

These are eight short stories about cats. Each cat is devoted, loyal, and independent.

Chambers, John W. *Fritzi's Winter.* Atheneum, 1979.

■■■■■■■□□□□□□□

Left on Fire Island by his family, Fritzi, a Siamese cat, has to fend for himself. Befriended first by a gray cat and later by a hermit, Fritzi gets by fairly well. His family is overjoyed to find him when they return the next year, but you have the feeling that Fritzi will be fine no matter what.

Fosburgh, Liza. *Bella Arabella.* Four Winds, 1985.

■■■■■■■■□□□□□

Miranda the cat has long been Arabella's best friend. Arabella is overwhelmed by life as a girl so she turns into a cat to join Miranda's world. Life as a cat, however, produces other problems.

Lawson, Robert. *Captain Kidd's Cat.* Little, 1956, 1984.

■■■■■■■□□□□□□□

Get the real story of Captain Kidd, notorious pirate, from the one nearest and dearest to him, his cat McDermott, a dapper feline with a ruby in one ear. The troubles and adventures aboard the Adventure Galley are given a pet's eye view.

LeGuin, Ursula K. *Catwings.* Orchard, 1988.
———. *Catwings Return.* Orchard, 1989.

■■■□□□□□□□□□□□

Mrs. Jane Tabby can't explain why her kittens have wings; she only knows that they have a chance to escape the dangerous world of the slums and she unselfishly sends them off. (See page 106.)

Parsons, Elizabeth. *The Upside-Down Cat.* Atheneum, 1981.

■■■■■■■□□□□□□□

Named for her penchant of lying on the hot-air register with her legs up, the upside-down cat Lily Black is loved by Joe, the child who owns her. She is left behind when the family has to leave Maine for their winter quarters, and she survives mostly through the kindness of an elderly fisherman who takes her in. The family returns the next year and is overjoyed to find her. The question is: To whom does she belong?

Stolz, Mary. *Cat Walk.* Harper, 1983.

■■■■■■■■■□□□□

This anthropomorphic story tells of a black kitten who wishes for a name. After his mother explains that only cats who are pets have names, the kitten is taken in by the farmer's daughter who names him Tootsy-Wootsy. He finds life with her confining and runs away to a service station whose owner names him Snowshoes. When the owner's son abuses Snowshoes, the cat is taken to an animal shelter where he is named Max by Mr. and Mrs. Jaffee who own the shelter. They give him to their grandchildren who name him Mistletoe and confine him to one room in the house. Escaping confinement means living homeless and nameless until he finds his way back to the Jaffees.

Poetry

Coatsworth, Elizabeth. "The Two Cats" from *I Like You, If You Like Me: Poems of Friendship,* edited by Myra Cohn Livingston. Atheneum, 1987.

Worth, Valerie. "Kitten" from *All the Small Poems.* Farrar, 1987.

A Kid and a Dog

Rationale
There are more books about dogs than about any animal, including cats.

Picture Book Starter
☐ Day, Alexandra. *Good Dog, Carl.* Green Tiger, 1985.

——. *Carl Goes Shopping.* Green Tiger, 1989.

In the first of these wordless books, Carl the rottweiler is left in charge of the baby while the mother goes out; in the second, Carl is placed in charge of the baby in a large department store.

☐ Weller, Frances Ward. *Riptide.* Philomel, 1990.

Rip is a dog who loves the sea and believes that the beach is his to guard. That's all right until summer comes and the "No Dogs Allowed" signs appear on the beach. Rip's family is called again and again to come get their dog. Tying him up does no good and Rip runs to the beach every time he escapes. When he rescues a drowning person, the lifeguards decide it's not so bad to have a dog on the beach after all.

Bulletin Board
☐ Display stories and articles about dogs.

Museum
☐ Display objects such as dog collars, bowls, and other accoutrements for real and imaginary dogs.

Discussions, Projects, and Activities
☐ List and describe as many breeds as possible and pick your favorite.
☐ Find out how dogs are used for work today and how they were used in the past. What has changed?
☐ Many people fear pit bull dogs and in some places it's against the law to own one. Hold a debate about the law.
☐ Find out about other breeds of animals related to our domestic dogs: wolves, dingos, and wild dogs of Africa.
☐ Are prairie dogs really dogs?
☐ Find out why dogs circle before they lie down.
☐ What do you think dogs dream about?
☐ Find out about expressions related to dogs such as: Doggone it! It's a dog's life. Dog days. You can't teach an old dog new tricks. Three dog night.
☐ Compare dog behavior to the behavior of the wolves in *Julie of the Wolves* by Jean Craighead George (Harper, 1972) and *The Jungle Book* by Rudyard Kipling (many versions).
☐ Make a chart of the dog heroes in the suggested books. Compare them to their owners.
☐ Contact the local humane society and find out how many unwanted dogs are turned in each year. What can we do with unwanted dogs?
☐ Discuss how you feel about animals, particularly dogs, being used for medical experiments.
☐ Find and sing such dog songs as "How Much Is That Doggie in the Window?" "You Ain't Nothin' But a Hound Dog," and "Old Blue."

Books
Fiction
Angell, Judie. *A Home Is to Share and Share and Share.* Bradbury, 1984.

■■■■■■■■☐☐☐☐☐

Sparky is a pregnant stray that the neighborhood children have rescued and adopted. When nobody's parents will allow them to keep the dog, they take it to the animal shelter only to find that the shelter is slated to be closed down and the animals in it will be put to sleep. The children must find homes for six dogs, eight cats, and a monkey.

Armstrong, William H. *Sounder.* Harper, 1969.

■■■■■■■■■■☐☐☐

More than the story of a dog's devotion to his master, this novel is the story of a black sharecropper family's attempt to survive the violence and prejudice of the people in the town.

Burnford, Sheila. *The Incredible Journey.* Little, 1961.

■■■■■■■□□□□□□□

Two dogs and a cat join ranks to find their lost master, traveling hundreds of miles and facing great dangers.

Gardiner, John Reynolds. *Stone Fox.* Crowell, 1980.

■■■■■□□□□□□□□□

Searchlight is a splendid dog and one of the best sled dogs ever, but Stone Fox's dogs are perfectly trained and have never lost a race.

Gipson, Fred. *Old Yeller.* Harper, 1956.

■■■■■■■■■□□□□□

Travis is "the man of the family" on a Texas farm while his father is away, and his only help is Old Yeller, a stray dog. Old Yeller proves himself a valiant friend when forced into battle with a rattlesnake and a rabid wolf.

Griffith, Helen. *Grip, A Dog Story.* Holiday, 1978.

■■■■■■■■■□□□□□

Bill Kershaw's bull terrier, Madman, is a champion fighting dog. At times Bill seems to care more for Madman than he does for his son, Dudley. Grip, son of Madman, is given to Dudley to train and, to his surprise, Dudley loves that puppy with all his heart. However, if Dudley does not teach Grip to fight and win, Grip will be drowned.

Jukes, Mavis. *No One Is Going to Nashville.* Knopf, 1983.

■■■■■■■□□□□□□□

Sonia finds Max munching radishes in the yard and claims him as her own. Because she lives with her mother in an apartment during the week, her father and stepmother will have to care for the dog. It's the stepmother who comes to the rescue in this one.

Little, Jean. *Lost and Found.* Viking, 1986.

■■■■■■■□□□□□□□

Lucy finds a little dog who soothes her loneliness in the new town, but her parents insist that she try to find the dog's rightful owners.

O'Dell, Scott. *Island of the Blue Dolphins.* Houghton, 1960.

■■■■■■■□□□□□□□

Karana, the chief's daughter, lives with her father, brother, and older sister in a village on the Island of the Blue Dolphins. The new chief decides to relocate the village on the far away mainland and so the island is evacuated. Karana's younger brother, Ramo, is left behind and Karana jumps overboard to be with him, convinced that the ship will return for them soon. Ramo is killed by wild dogs and Karana is left to survive there alone. She first wounds and then befriends the leader of the pack of wild dogs. (See page 127.)

Rawls, Wilson. *Where the Red Fern Grows.* Doubleday, 1961, 1986.

■■■■■■■□□□□□□□

Old Dan and Little Ann are more than just fine coon hounds, they are the pride and joy of Billy and his entire family, especially his grandfather. Their love for the dogs is surpassed only by the hounds' love for each other.

Smith, Doris Buchanan. *Moonshadow of Cherry Mountain.* Four Winds, 1982.

■■■■■■■■■□□□□□

Exiled from the house because a child is allergic to dogs, Moonshadow has the run of the mountain. That existence is threatened. A hippie couple moves onto the mountain, but they prove their worth when Moonshine is sprayed by a skunk. It is the Katz family (who, of course, own lots of cats) who really threatens Moonshadow.

Somerlott, Robert. *Blaze.* Viking, 1981.

■■■■■■■■■□□□□□

David has been living with his aunt and uncle in San Francisco when his grandfather, Cappy, whom he hardly knows, sends him a shepherd pup named Blaze. Unfortunately, the aunt and uncle immediately give the dog away. When Cappy discovers the dog months later in the hands of abusive owners, he takes the now-vicious dog back to his ranch. He is unaware that David has stowed away in the truck, perilously close to the dog. Bound together by their love for Blaze, David and Cappy begin the harrowing job of bringing Blaze back from viciousness.

Thomas, Jane Resh. *The Comeback Dog.* Houghton, 1981.

■■■■■■■■■□□□□□

After Captain dies, Daniel doesn't want another dog. Then he finds Lady, half-starved and scared, in a culvert. The vet warns him that survival is unlikely, but Daniel has to try to nurse Lady back to health. Her body heals but she doesn't trust Daniel. He can't show her the warmth he showered on Captain. When Lady runs away, Daniel's anger surfaces.

Poetry
Cole, William. *Good Dog Poems.* Scribner, 1981.
Littledale, Freya. "When My Dog Died" from *A New Treasury of Children's Poetry,* edited by Joanna Cole. Doubleday, 1984.
Livingston, Myra Cohn. *I Like You, If You Like Me: Poems of Friendship.* Atheneum, 1987.
   Brooks, Gwendolyn. "Vern."
   Norris, Leslie. "Buying a Puppy."
Worth, Valerie. "Dog" from *All the Small Poems.* Farrar, 1987.

Into the World of Dolls and Toys

Rationale

This theme often appeals to younger or less sophisticated readers, but even older readers can be intrigued by the more malicious personalities of toys.

Picture Book Starter

☐ Waddell, Martin and Barrett, Angela. *The Hidden House.* Philomel, 1990.

Three dolls are made by a man in a little house in the woods. When the house is abandoned, so are the dolls; when the house is rediscovered, so are the dolls.

Bulletin Board

☐ Display characters from books in and around a dollhouse, a picture of a dollhouse, or a toy chest.

Museum

☐ Display a variety of toys that are not battery operated.

Discussions, Projects, and Activities

☐ Visit a store that sells miniatures, especially dollhouse miniatures.
☐ Visit a doll collection. Notice how dolls have changed over the years.
☐ Bring in favorite dolls. Create a doll display.
☐ Write a journal for one of the dolls.
☐ Make dollhouses out of cardboard cartons. Decorate and furnish them.
☐ Design costumes for dolls.

Books

Fiction

Adler, C. S. *Goodbye, Pink Pig.* Putnam, 1985.

■■■■■□□□□□□□□□

Amanda leaves her unhappy world when she enters the world of her miniature collection. There she finds the friends the real world lacks. Her best friend is a rose quartz Pink Pig. The real world intrudes when Amanda reaches middle school and finds that the janitor is her grandmother.

Banks, Lynne Reid. *The Indian in the Cupboard.* Doubleday, 1981.

■■■■■■■■■□□□□□□□

Omri is given an old, locked cupboard. He discovers that when a toy is placed in the cupboard, the toy comes to life. (See also page 126.)

Cassedy, Sylvia. *Behind the Attic Wall.* Crowell, 1983.

■■■■■■■■■□□□□□□□

Maggie, an orphan who is difficult to love, is sent to live with her equally unlovable aunt and uncle. She manages to alienate not only her relatives, but also everyone at school. Mysterious noises issue from the walls of the old, gloomy house and Maggie eventually discovers their source: two dolls who are capable of speech and thought.

———. *Lucie Babbidge's House.* Crowell, 1989.

■■■■■□□□□□□□□□□

Lucie's life is unbearable at Norwood Hall, so she invents a rich fantasy world in which her dollhouse becomes more interesting than the real world.

Field, Rachel. *Hitty, Her First Hundred Years.* Macmillan, 1969.

■■■■■□□□□□□□□□

Hitty, a wooden doll made for a girl in 19th century New England, has many adventures: she's left in a church, carried off by a crow, meets Charles Dickens, and, finally, lands in an antique shop ready for the next hundred years.

Godden, Rumer. *Four Dolls.* Greenwillow, 1984.

■■■■■□□□□□□□□□□

Here are four of Godden's favorite doll stories in one volume.

Hahn, Mary Downing. *The Doll in the Garden: A Ghost Story.* Clarion, 1989.

■■■■■■□□□□□□□

A shadowless cat and a child crying in the night bother Ashley who has just moved into a new apartment with her mom. Ashley and a friend dig up an old-fashioned doll that was buried in the garden. This leads them back in time to an encounter with a dying little girl.

Kennedy, Richard. *Amy's Eyes.* Harper, 1985.

■■■■■■■■■□□□□

There are two transformations: A girl changes into a doll and then the doll changes into a sea captain with a crew from Mother Goose in search of a treasure. It's a zany way to create a vital sense of life, but that's what the book does.

MacLachlan, Patricia. *Cassie Binegar.* Harper, 1982.

■■■■■■■■□□□□□

Cassie's family has recently moved and they are now living on the shore where her father and two big brothers are commercial fishermen. Everyone else in the family seems to love the new life, but Cassie hates it. Cassie, a budding writer, is embarrassed by her eccentric, messy family. (See also page 105.)

Milne, A. A. *Winnie the Pooh* and *The House at Pooh Corner.* Many editions available.

■■■■■□□□□□□□□

Read one or both of these whimsical stories of Christopher Robin's toys. If all children know is the Walt Disney cartoons and books, they are impoverished.

O'Connell, Jean S. *The Dollhouse Caper.* Crowell, 1976.

■■■■■■■□□□□□□

The dolls and their house belong to three young humans: Kevin, Peter, and Harry. Mrs. Dollhouse worries about being neglected by the boys now that they are growing up, about the robbery they overheard being planned, and about Mr. Dollhouse who spends most of his time with his head in the toilet where the children put him.

Sachs, Marilyn. *The Bears' House.* Dutton, 1961, 1987.

■■■■■■■□□□□□□

Fran Ellen's mother is ill and Fran Ellen bears the responsibility for the family. The kids at school, however, don't know this. All they know is that Fran Ellen smells bad and sucks her thumb. They tease her constantly. The only thing Fran Ellen has going for her is the class dollhouse that is inhabited by a family of toy bears. Just sitting beside it allows Fran Ellen to escape into their world.

Shura, Mary Francis. *The Sunday Doll.* Avon, 1988.

■■■■■■■□□□□□□

Emmy has several problems as she faces her thirteenth birthday. She dreads becoming a teenager because many nice people she knew turned creepy when they turned thirteen. Then she receives a doll with no face for her birthday. Because her beloved and feisty Aunt Harriott sent it, she is even more troubled. She may not like turning thirteen, but a baby gift seems very strange. Most importantly, something awful seems to be going on at home. The trouble has something to do with Emmy's older sister and her boyfriend. Emmy's parents won't tell her anything and ship her off to Aunt Harriott's to get her out of the way. Aunt Harriott has a way of cutting through nonsense, however, and she helps Emmy through a very difficult time.

Sleator, William. *Among the Dolls.* Dutton, 1975.

■■■■■■■■□□□□□□□

A young girl gets a dollhouse for her birthday and the dolls in it seem harmless enough even when she mistreats them. However, the dolls exact their revenge and the girl is helplessly drawn into their world.

Williams, Margery. *The Velveteen Rabbit.* Many versions available.

■■■■■■■■■□□□□□□

This is a familiar classic of how a boy's love for his toy makes it real.

Wright, Betty R. *The Dollhouse Murders.* Holiday, 1983.

■■■■■■■■■□□□□□□

Amy and her retarded sister must unravel a mystery that took place years ago or they'll never get rid of the sinister presence of the dollhouse or of its ghostly light.

Zhitkov, Boris. *How I Hunted the Little Fellows.* Dodd, 1979.

■■■■■■■■■□□□□□□

The narrator visits his grandmother in Russia who, although she is ordinarily kind and permissive, forbids him to touch her miniature steamship. The boy is convinced that inside the ship there are tiny sailors and he pulls the ship apart to find out.

Poetry
Livingston, Myra Cohn. "My Cousin's Dollhouse" from *Worlds I Know and Other Poems,* edited by Nancy Larrick. Atheneum, 1985.

Quirks and Foibles

Rationale

In a good movie, the supporting cast is at least as interesting as the major players. Often the minor characters are eccentric or comic and provide relief from a heavy plot line or give the major characters someone to relate to. The same is true in books; but when writing their own stories, children often overlook the possibilities such roles offer. Looking at eccentric characters also provides opportunities to consider our society's treatment of differences.

Picture Book Starter

☐ Fleischman, Sid. *The Scarebird.* Greenwillow, 1987.

A farmer, Lonesome John, makes a scarecrow and relates to it as though it were a person. When a real person shows up, it takes Lonesome John a while to abandon the scarebird and relate to the real human.

Bulletin Board

☐ Let the children make and display Rube Goldberg-type inventions: bizarre ways of accomplishing simple tasks.

Museum

☐ Display unusual toys and games.

Discussions, Projects, and Activities

☐ Discuss people who dare to be different and those who are different in ways they can't change.
☐ Talk about our fears of people who are different.
☐ Find out about eccentric people and the contributions they made: Henry David Thoreau, Albert Einstein, Amelia Earhart, Eleanor Roosevelt.
☐ Discuss the need for conformity: Who sets styles or behaviors in your crowd?
☐ Do you have to be eccentric to be a genius?
☐ List odd characters on television. How are they different? Why are they on the show? Do such people serve the same purpose in the real world?
☐ Discover the slight differences in meaning in these words: *strange, odd, peculiar, bizarre, exotic, offbeat, unconventional, oddball.* Add other words to the list. Use the words to describe the characters in some of the books you read.
☐ Find old photographs and pretend the people were eccentric. Write their biographies.

☐ On an index card, write one secret quirk you have. Post it on the bulletin board without signing your name. Can anyone figure out who this strange person is?
☐ Look at changing styles in hairdos and clothing. Which styles could you get away with now?
☐ Design a home for an eccentric person.

Books

Fiction: Picture Books

Blos, Joan W. *Old Henry.* Morrow, 1987.

Henry likes the deserted old house. It suits him just fine. The neighbors are pleased at first because they think he'll fix up the house, but Henry has no intention of fixing anything.

Dr. Seuss. *The Sneetches and Other Stories.* Random, 1961.

Sylvester McMonkey McBean is a con artist and an eccentric character who he talks the Sneetches into and out of wearing stars on their bellies. In the same book, Mrs. McCabe, who has forty-nine sons she calls "Dave," is also a candidate for the list of weird ones.

Gackenbach, Dick. *King Wacky.* Crown, 1984.

King Wacky's head is on backwards and so he's a little wacky. This is fine with the people of the kingdom, but it leads to trouble when an outsider appears.

Gammell, Stephen. *Once Upon MacDonald's Farm.* Macmillan, 1981.

This is not more of the same old stuff about MacDonald's farm. This MacDonald puts animals on his farm, all right, but he can't seem to choose the right animals for the right task.

Kellogg, Steven. *The Mysterious Tadpole.* Dial, 1977.

Older audiences will get the most out of the humor here. Children will probably enjoy the story of a tadpole who just doesn't stop growing.

Kimmel, Eric. *Charlie Drives the Stage.* Holiday, 1989.

When Charlie says the stage will make it to the train on time, it does. It isn't until the end that you find out that Charlie is Charlene.

Rylant, Cynthia. *Miss Maggie.* Dutton, 1983.

Miss Maggie is old and lives in a tumble-down house. The children think she's a witch. When Miss Maggie falls ill, it's a child who helps her.

Van Allsburg, Chris. *The Garden of Abdul Gasazi.* Houghton, 1979

Alan is supposed to watch the neighbor's dog, Fritz. When it wanders into the garden, the mysterious Abdul Gasazi changes Fritz into a duck.

———. *The Stranger.* Houghton, 1986.

A farmer accidentally hits a stranger with his car and takes him home to recuperate. The stranger seems to have little memory and summer lasts longer than usual. After the stranger remembers who he is, he leaves and autumn comes.

Wood, Audrey. *King Bidgood's in the Bathtub.* Harcourt, 1985.

The king refuses to leave his bathtub. One by one each member of the court tries to coax him out.

Yorinks, Arthur. *It Happened in Pinsk.* Farrar, 1983.

It isn't just Irv Irving who is bizarre, but he certainly stands out in this crowd of oddballs. One morning his wife discovers that Irv's head is missing. She quickly fashions a substitute head out of a paper bag and Irv sets off in search of his real head—and no one seems to notice the bag.

Fiction: Novels

Carrick, Carol. *The Elephant in the Dark.* Clarion, 1988.

■■■■■■■■□□□□□□

Will doesn't mind too much being an outcast at school and in the village as long as his whimsical and beautiful mother is alive. However, when she dies of consumption and Will has to leave the only home he has ever known, he feels alone and completely vulnerable.

Cresswell, Helen. *The Bagthorpe Saga.* Macmillan, 1979.

■■■■■■□□□□□□□

This is a series of books about a zany, talented family who are the epitome of eccentricity.

Gardiner, John Reynolds. *Stone Fox.* Crowell, 1980.

■■■■□□□□□□□□□

See page 9.

Konigsburg, E. L. *From the Mixed-Up Files of Mrs. Basil E. Frankweiler.* Macmillan, 1967.

■■■■■■■□□□□□□

Claudia believes that she is unappreciated at home and decides to run away. Mrs. Frankweiler is eccentric; however, she's not the dominant character in the book. (See page 119.)

MacLachlan, Patricia. *Cassie Binegar.* Harper, 1982.

■■■■■■■■□□□□□

See page 12.

Pople, Maureen. *The Other Side of the Family.* Holt, 1988.

■■■■□□□□□□□□□

See page 4.

Rylant, Cynthia. *Children of Christmas.* Orchard, 1987.

■■■■□□□□□□□□□

Although each of these short stories is set at Christmas, it is the people who dominate the book: people who are outside the stream of lives most of us live, especially at that time of year.

van de Wetering, Janwillem. *Hugh Pine and the Good Place.* Houghton, 1986.

■■■■□□□□□□□□□

This book is about porcupines, one in particular: Hugh Pine. Unlike the other porcupines, Hugh has the happy facility of looking almost human and so can mingle with and communicate with them. In this book, Hugh wants a place to get away from it all and finds it on an island. Ah, solitude—for a while.

One Potato, Two Potato

Rationale

Folklore is a big category that includes street rhymes and games, Mother Goose, superstitions and customs, folk medicine, folk songs, jokes, riddles, puzzles, legends, myths, ghost stories, folktales and fairy tales. We've kept most of it together, taking out only mythology as a separate theme, but any of its parts could make up a fascinating theme.

Picture Book Starter

Ahlberg, Janet and Ahlberg, Allan. *The Jolly Postman*. Little, 1986.

- This is not a fairy tale but a series of letters delivered by a postman to the characters of fairy tale and nursery rhyme fame. In addition to being a riot in and of itself, the book makes an ideal model for children's writing.

Bulletin Board

- Let the children illustrate common superstitions and folk rhymes.

Museum

- Display objects related to folklore such as good luck pieces, fortunetelling cards, crystal balls, and magic wands.

Discussions, Projects, and Activities

Folk Rhymes

- Write any rhymes you know for bouncing balls, jumping rope, clapping, or deciding who is "it."
- Ask your parents and grandparents to tell you rhymes they know.
- Make a class book of folk rhymes.
- Compare your ways of choosing "it" to those of other neighborhoods and towns. Ask a pen pal in another area of the country or world what rituals they have for choosing.
- Make up jump rope rhymes. The test is whether you can jump to them.
- Compare different versions of Mother Goose rhymes. Decide which rhymes are best for children of different ages. Which rhymes are included in each collection of Mother Goose rhymes? Why do you think there are differences among the collections?
- Find out about the real Mother Goose.

- Find one Mother Goose rhyme you don't know. Use a thesaurus and dictionary to translate each word in the rhyme to a harder word that means the same thing. For example,

    Minuscule John Horner
    Seated himself at the junction of two opposing
      walls,
    Ingesting a yuletide pastry.
    He inserted his opposable digit,
    Withdrew a purple fruit,
    And exclaimed,
    "What an estimable young human being I am."

- Mother Goose rhymes are often criticized for being too violent. Find all of the violence in one collection of rhymes.
- Hold a trial for the criminals in Mother Goose rhymes.
- Write newspaper accounts of the stories in Mother Goose rhymes.
- Do a television interview of one of the Mother Goose characters.

Superstitions and Customs

- More folklore is attached to weddings than to any of our modern customs. Research the origins of such things as: throwing the bouquet and garter; wearing something old, something new, something borrowed, and something blue; giving the bride away; wedding gifts; bridal showers; music; receptions; and bridesmaids, ushers, maids of honor, and best men.
- List holiday customs and find out their origins.
- Write down all the superstitions you can think of. Find out whether any are based on logic.
- Take a survey at school and home to find out who believes in which superstitions.
- Compile a list of superstitions and sort them into categories: weather, gestures, good and bad luck, objects, and animals.

Folk Songs

- Analyze folk songs to find out what they have in common.
- Trace one of the folk songs back to its origins.
- Find picture books of folk songs and see how the artist conceived the action and characters.
- Make your own storybooks of some of the songs.
- Write new verses to folk songs.

☐ Bring folk instruments and learn how to play a song on them.

☐ Invite a folk singer to conduct a sing-along.

Tall Tales

Tall tales are usually regional or concern a specific area and often are about a superhero: Pecos Bill, super cowboy; Mike Fink, super boatman; Paul Bunyan, super lumberjack.

The Paul Bunyan tales did not originate as did the other tall tales. He was the brainstorm of a publicist for a lumber company, but so many tales have been created about him that we've included him here.

Some so-called tall tales are really legends. The best definition of a legend I have found is that either the teller or the listener believes it is true. George Washington's cherry tree, Lincoln's walking a mile to return a penny, and Johnny Appleseed's being responsible for every apple tree in the Midwest are all really legends.

☐ Read several tall tales about one character. Write a newspaper article about him or her.

☐ Read several tall tales. Decide which, if any, might be true.

☐ Make a giant map of the United States showing the tall tale characters, the regional origins, and their actions.

☐ Make up a tall tale about yourself.

☐ Make up a tall-tale character: super student, sportsperson, and so on

☐ Make up endings to statements like: How hot was it? It was so hot that. . . . Decide which endings are the most imaginative.

Fairy Tales and Folktales

☐ Find and compare tales with the following themes or motifs: the theft of a magic object, helpful characters with super powers, or circle stories.

☐ Find and compare as many versions of "Cinderella" as possible. Remember that every civilization has at least one Cinderella story. The Cornish version is "Tattercoats"; one Native American version is "Little Burnt Face." Decide why they are classified as Cinderella stories.

☐ Trace one tale other than "Cinderella" through as many versions as possible and decide which was the earliest version.

☐ Create a fairy tale museum, displaying Cinderella's slipper, Snow White's apple, Jack's beanstalk, and so on.

☐ Read the tales from the area of the world that most or all of your ancestors came from. Retell your favorite.

☐ Use *The Jolly Postman* by Janet and Allan Ahlberg (Little, 1986) as an inspiration to make mailboxes for story characters.

☐ Use the chart below to record information about the fairy tales you read.

Title
Version
Country of Origin
Hero
Heroine
First line
Last line
Three Feats or Tasks Required

Books

Fiction

Aardema, Verna. *Why Mosquitoes Buzz in People's Ears.* Dial, 1975.

■☐☐☐☐☐☐☐☐☐☐☐☐

This cumulative African story is brilliantly retold and illustrated. The author has published many excellenet African tales as picture books.

Bang, Molly. *Dawn.* Morrow, 1983.

■■■■□□□□□□□□□□

This tale of the young woman weaving magic and then leaving is beautifully retold and illustrated.

Baring-Gould, William S. and Baring-Gould, Cecil. *The Annotated Mother Goose: Nursery Rhymes Old and New, Arranged and Explained.* Bramhall House, 1962.

■■■■■■■□□□□□□□

This large and rather scholarly book provides a great deal of information that will be helpful to researchers of any age who are interested in the realm of Mother Goose.

Bierhorst, John. *The Girl Who Married a Ghost and Other Tales from the North American Indians.* Four Winds, 1978.

■■■■■■■□□□□□□□

This collection provides a good representation of Native American folklore.

Briggs, Raymond. *Jim and the Beanstalk.* Coward, 1970.

■□□□□□□□□□□□□□

This is an extension of the Jack-tale in which the giant has grown old and now needs help.

———. *Mother Goose Treasury.* Dell, 1986.

■□□□□□□□□□□□□□

The usual rhymes are vividly and rather comically illustrated.

Chase, Richard. *Grandfather Tales.* Houghton, 1948.
———. *Jack Tales.* Houghton, 1943.

■■■■□□□□□□□□□□

These are Appalachian Mountain tales, lovingly collected and retold. When Mr. Chase was asked to read these books, he always refused, claiming that the tales were meant to be told, not read. He would, however, tell them enthusiastically.

Cole, Brock. *The Giant's Toe.* Farrar, 1986.

■□□□□□□□□□□□□□

This is a prequel to "Jack and the Beanstalk" in which the giant is spared a visit from Jack because of the not-always-welcome presence of a boy who came from the giant's toe.

De Angeli, Marguerite. *Book of Nursery and Mother Goose Rhymes.* Doubleday, 1954.

■□□□□□□□□□□□□□

These rhymes are illustrated with a delicate and old-fashioned charm.

dePaola, Tomie. *Big Anthony and the Magic Ring.* Harcourt, 1979.

■□□□□□□□□□□□□□

This time the magic is in a ring that makes the wearer irresistible to the opposite sex. Big Anthony is the victim/wearer.

———. *Strega Nona.* Prentice, 1975.

■□□□□□□□□□□□□□

This is a southern Italian version of the tale about the pot that wouldn't stop cooking, similar to "The Sorcerer's Apprentice." In this case, the pot makes pasta and the dumb servant is Big Anthony.

Grimm, Jacob and Grimm, Wilhelm. *Little Red Riding Hood.* Illustrated by Trina Hyman. Holiday, 1982.

■□□□□□□□□□□□□□

Here's the traditional tale with just the right illustrations by Trina Schart Hyman who has loved the story since she was little.

———. *Snow White and the Seven Dwarfs.* Illustrated by Nancy Burkert. Farrar, 1972.
———. *Snow White.* Illustrated by Trina Hyman. Little, 1979.

■■■■□□□□□□□□□□

Walt Disney's version can't hold a candle to these beautiful versions of the original tale of youth and age locked in deadly battle. Each of these versions is differently, but exquisitely, illustrated.

Hamilton, Virginia. *The People Could Fly: American Black Folktales.* Knopf, 1985.

■■■■□□□□□□□□□□

Here are twenty-four stories from Black-American folklore with great illustrations by Leo and Diane Dillon.

Knapp, Mary and Knapp, Herbert. *One Potato, Two Potato: The Folklore of American Children.* Norton, 1976.

■■■■■■■■■□□□□□

A folklorist's look at children's play, this book is for the adult audience. However, there is a great deal of information for children investigating American folklore.

Lester, Julius. *The Tales of Uncle Remus: The Adventures of Brer Rabbit.* Dial, 1987.

■■■■■■■□□□□□□□

These tales have been the subject of controversy over the years. Julius Lester, an eloquent black writer, tells some of their history and then retells them with his own special twists.

Lobel, Arnold. *The Random House Book of Mother Goose.* Random, 1986.

■□□□□□□□□□□□□□

Here is a Lobelish look at Mother Goose.

Marshall, James. *Red Riding Hood.* Dial, 1987.

■□□□□□□□□□□□□□

This is the traditional story, but the conversations are hilarious. Grandmother, a dedicated reader, has only one complaint when rescued from inside the wolf: "It was so dark in there I couldn't read a word."

Schwartz, Alvin. *All of Our Noses Are Here and Other Noodle Tales.* Harper, 1985.

———. *Busy Buzzing Bumblebees.* Harper, 1982.

———. *The Cat's Elbow and Other Secret Languages.* Farrar, 1982.

———. *Chin Music: Tall Talk and Other Talk.* Harper, 1979.

———. *Cross Your Fingers, Spit in Your Hat.* Harper, 1974.

———. *Fat Man in a Fur Coat and Other Bear Stories.* Farrar, 1984.

———. *Flapdoodle: Pure Nonsense from American Folklore.* Harper, 1980.

———. *Gold and Silver: Tales of Hidden Treasure.* Farrar, 1988.

———. *I Saw You in the Bathtub and Other Folk Rhymes.* Harper, 1989.

———. *In a Dark, Dark Room and Other Scary Stories.* Harper, 1985.

———. *Kickle Snifters and Other Fearsome Critters.* Harper, 1976.

———. *Love Magic: Dream Signs and Other Ways to Learn the Future.* Lippincott, 1987.

———. *More Scary Stories to Tell in the Dark.* Harper, 1984.

———. *Scary Stories to Tell in the Dark.* Harper, 1981.

———. *Tales of Trickery from the Land of Spoof.* Farrar, 1988.

———. *Ten Copycats in a Boat and Other Riddles.* Harper, 1980.

———. *There Is a Carrot in My Ear and Other Noodle Tales.* Harper, 1982.

———. *Tomfoolery: Trickery and Foolery with Words.* Lippincott, 1973.

———. *A Twister of Twists, A Tangler of Tongues.* Harper, 1972.

———. *Unriddling.* Lippincott, 1983.

———. *When I Grew Up Long Ago.* Harper, 1978.

———. *Whoppers: Tall Tales & Other Lies.* Harper, 1975.

———. *Witcracks: Jokes and Jests from American Folklore.* Harper, 1973.

Each of these books by Alvin Schwartz is based on folklore and each of them could launch its own theme. The tales and rhymes are retold by a folklorist who knows exactly what children like.

Stanton, Will. *Once Upon a Time Is Enough.* Lippincott. Out of print.

■■■■■■■■■■□□□□

Here is a satirical look at many old favorites. Every inconsistency and stereotype in fairy tales is held up and viewed hilariously. You can find this book in many libraries and used book stores.

Stoutenberg, Adrien. *American Tall Tales.* Viking, 1966.

■■■■■■■■■□□□□□

This book tells of eight tall-tale heroes: Paul Bunyan, Pecos Bill, Captain Stormalong, Davy Crockett, Johnny Appleseed, John Henry, and Mike Fink.

Tripp, Wallace. *Grandfa' Grig Had a Pig.* Little, 1976.
———. *A Great Big Ugly Man Came Up and Tied His Horse to Me.* Little, 1973.

■□□□□□□□□□□□□

There are surprises in these books. The illustrations contain some traditional characters that bear a striking resemblance to people you might recognize. The books are loaded with puns, antics, and delight.

Zemach, Harve. *Duffy and the Devil.* Farrar, 1973.

■■■■□□□□□□□□□

Rumplestiltskin's familiar story is told from the Cornish tradition. The magic is clothing, not gold, and the action is wonderful.

———. *A Penny a Look.* Farrar, 1971.

■■■■■■□□□□□□□

This rendition of an old story is such fun. The redheaded fellow and his lazy good-for-nothing brother are looking for a one-eyed fellow so they can form a circus act. The trouble is, there seems to be more than one one-eyed fellow.

Poetry

Hunter, Robert. "Casey Jones" from *Rhythm Road: Poems to Move To,* edited by Lillian Morrison. Lothrop, 1988

Viorst, Judith. "And The Princess Was Astonished to See the Ugly Frog Turn into a Handsome Prince," "And Then the Prince Knelt Down and Tried to Put the Glass Slipper On Cinderella's Foot," "And Although the Little Mermaid Sacrificed Everything to Win the Love of the Prince, the Prince (alas) Decided to Wed Another" from *If I Were In Charge of the World.* Atheneum, 1981.

I'm Coming to Get You

Rationale

Ghost stories have intrigued and frightened humans since the beginning of communication. Approaching literature through this genre is almost sure to bring interest and controversy. Everyone knows a ghost story, and most people like that shivery feeling you get when you almost believe it to be true.

Picture Book Starter

☐ Ross, Tony. *I'm Coming to Get You.* Dial, 1984.

From deep in another galaxy comes a howling, nasty monster. After pillaging one planet, it sets its sights on Earth and little Tommy Brown, but there's a surprise in store for the monster and for the reader.

Bulletin Board

☐ Let the children collect and post newspaper and magazine articles about ghosts.

Museum

☐ Collect and display objects that might inspire a ghost story: books, bones, clothing, or jewelry.

Discussions, Projects, and Activities

☐ Conduct a survey among friends and relatives to see how many believe in ghosts. Chart the results. Does age or religion influence their beliefs?

☐ Ask friends and relatives to tell you of any ghostly encounters they've had. Record their stories.

☐ Write letters to residents of old or eerie houses in your town. Ask for permission to interview them about ghosts. Record the interviews.

☐ Talk to clergy about whether they believe in ghosts.

☐ Visit or find out about a building believed to be haunted.

☐ Plot the action of a ghost story.

☐ Darken a room and tell ghost stories.

☐ Read aloud from the spookiest sections of a book. Decide how, or whether, an author makes you believe in a ghost. Does the author believe in ghosts? What makes you think that?

☐ Describe a haunted house.

☐ Categorize the ghost books: those about real things and those about the supernatural.

☐ Find riddles about ghosts and supernatural creatures or events. Make up some more.

Books

Fiction

Alcock, Vivien. *The Stonewalkers.* Delacorte, 1983.

■■■■■■■■■■■■☐

When Poppy, a lonely, twelve-year-old girl, strikes up a friendship with the statue of a girl she names Belladonna, she doesn't expect it to come to life. Nor does she expect it to become a force for evil.

Arthur, Ruth. *Miss Ghost.* Atheneum, 1979.

■■■■■■■■■■☐☐☐☐

Elphie is a hard child to like, but she's had a hard life. Her mother left, taking Elphie's baby brother; her father fell into an unshakable depression; her grandmother was killed; and, finally, Elphie goes to a foster home. Even there she is unhappy because her foster parents think she's possessed. Then there's the ghost in the tower, Miss Ghost, who never answers but seems to understand Elphie.

Brittain, Bill. *Who Knew There'd Be Ghosts?* Harper, 1985.

■■■■■■■☐☐☐☐☐☐

The men want the house because of the valuable document they are sure it contains. Everything is fine until the children discover two ghosts; the ghosts and children join ranks against the men.

Bunting, Eve. *The Ghosts of Departure Point.* Lippincott, 1982.

■■■■■■■■■■■■☐

Teenagers who were killed in an auto accident come back to haunt the living.

Cresswell, Helen. *The Secret World of Polly Flint.* Macmillan, 1984.

■■■■■■■■☐☐☐☐☐☐

When Polly's father is injured, the family moves in with his domineering sister Aunt Em. It isn't long before Polly discovers a village where ghostly dancers dance the May Pole Dance and a boy, his father, and his grandmother come out of the lake.

Garfield, Leon. *Mister Corbett's Ghost.* Viking, 1968.

■■■■■■■■■■■■□

In Highgate, London, the locale of many of Mr. Garfield's novels, Benjamin Partridge, an apprentice to Mr. Corbett the apothecary, wishes his master dead—and his wish comes true.

———. *The Wedding Ghost.* Oxford, 1987.

■■■■■■■■■■■□

Five days before Jack and Gillian's wedding, Jack takes a nap during which he is told to awaken Sleeping Beauty. He has no choice but to do so, even though it jeopardizes his marriage.

Hahn, Mary Downing. *Wait Till Helen Comes.* Clarion, 1986.

■■■■■■■□□□□□□

Molly and Michael dislike their new stepsister Heather almost as much as she dislikes them. When Heather is convinced that she must follow Helen, a ghost child, to her death, Molly and Michael must save her—but how hard do you try to save someone you hate?

Hearne, Betsy. *Eli's Ghost.* Atheneum, 1987.

■■■■■■■□□□□□□

Eli's life is not happy. His father barely tolerates him and his mother left him. As Eli searches for his mother, he nearly dies and his ghost is released.

Levitin, Sonia. *Beyond Another Door.* Atheneum, 1977.

■■■■■■■■■■□□□□

Daria has precognitive powers that frighten her mother. After her grandmother's ghost appears, Daria understands these fears. Her grandmother was a medium, which caused a rift between her and her daughter. Daria's mother fears a similar rift with Daria.

Mahy, Margaret. *The Haunting.* Atheneum, 1982.

■■■■■■■■■□□□□

Eight-year-old Barney is haunted by his great-uncle Cole. Barney's sister Tabitha takes notes on the haunting and the family's reactions. After an astounding round of revelations, we discover that Tabitha is the only normal one.

Norton, Andre and Miller, Phyllis. *House of Shadows.* Atheneum, 1984.

■■■■■■■■■□□□□

Great-aunt Hendrika's house holds a tangled family history and Tucky has nightmares there. Susan gets a set of paper dolls that represent four generations of the family, and their ghosts haunt the children.

Peck, Richard. *The Ghost Belonged to Me.* Viking, 1975.

■■■■■■■■■■□□□□

Alexander Armsworth's good friend is Blossom Culp. Her mother, who has Gypsy blood, is not surprised when Alexander sees a ghost in the barn. Convinced that Blossom is behind it, Alexander is not upset until he sees a young girl wearing a damp dress who warns him about a train and a man with one hand.

———. *Voices After Midnight.* Delacorte, 1989.

■■■■■■■■■□□□□□

Two weeks in New York City sounds like fun to this California family. After they move into a town house, the children hear voices of people from the past who are desperately in need of help. Only by traveling back in time can the children save two young people from an untimely death.

Westall, Robert. *The Watch House.* Greenwillow, 1978.

■■■■■■■■■■□□□□□

Anne is left with her mother's old nanny for a summer on the English coast. Soon, however, Anne discovers that she is being haunted. With two new friends, Anne investigates the Watch House, a storage site for mementoes of a lifesaving brigade. The person who operated the Watch House is now a ghost who needs help.

Nonfiction
Jaspersohn, William. *The Ghost Book.* Watts, 1989.

■■□□□□□□□□□□□□□

Here is a beginner's book with lots of illustrations about famous ghosts and phenomena.

Poetry
Bodecker, N. M. "The Lady in White" from *Hurry, Hurry, Mary Dear.* Atheneum, 1976, 1987.
cummings, e. e. "Hist wist." Available in many collections.
Guiterman, A. "The Superstitious Ghost" from *In the Witch's Kitchen,* edited by John E. Brewton. Crowell, 1980.
Kennedy, X. J. "Attic Ghosts" from *The Phantom Ice-Cream Man.* Atheneum, 1979.
Lindsay, Vachel. "Abraham Lincoln Walks at Midnight." Available in many collections.
Prelutsky, Jack. "Ghost" from *It's Halloween.* Greenwillow, 1977.
———. "The Haunted House" from *Nightmares.* Greenwillow, 1976.

Music
Bley, Edgar. "My Old Man" from *The Best Singing Games for Children.* Sterling, 1959.
Quackenbush, Robert. "Little Ghost" from *The Holiday Song Book.* Lothrop, 1977.
Yolen, Jane. "The Ghost of John" from *Rounds About Rounds.* Watts, 1977.

Oh, That's Funny

Rationale

Analyzing humor is often dangerous and humorless. These books are just plain funny and worth reading and talking about.

Picture Book Starter

☐ Nixon, Joan Lowry. *Beats Me, Claude.* Viking, 1986.

Shirley and Claude settle in a peaceful spot in East Texas. Claude's happy with the solitude, but Shirley is lonely. When they have a chance to adopt Tom, Shirley is delighted; Claude is concerned that their peace will be disturbed. A series of hilarious encounters between Shirley and Tom and some visitors changes everybody's mind.

Bulletin Board

☐ Post jokes, riddles, and cartoons.

Museum

☐ Display sight gags and tricks.

Discussions, Projects, and Activities

☐ Hold a "Can You Top This?" session in which people tell jokes.
☐ Pick a topic and find as many jokes and riddles as you can that fit the topic.
☐ Watch or listen to some of the great old comedians of movies, radio, and TV, such as Red Skelton, Jack Benny, Abbott and Costello, Bob and Ray, George Burns and Gracie Allen, the Three Stooges, Laurel and Hardy, and Lewis and Martin. Compare their humor to that of Bill Cosby, Robin Williams, and other modern comedians.
☐ Watch a cartoon that is supposed to be funny and categorize the jokes or humorous action. Is it all slapstick? Is there wordplay? Miscommunication?
☐ Make a funny picture book into a comic strip.
☐ Watch a situation comedy on TV and analyze its humor.
☐ Look at the Sunday funny papers. Which ones make you smile? Why?

Books

Fiction

Blume, Judy. *Freckle Juice.* Four Winds, 1971.

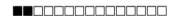

Andrew wants freckles like his best friend, Nicky. When Sharon offers a freckle recipe for fifty cents, Andrew can't wait to try it.

———. *Superfudge.* Dutton, 1980.

Fudge is no longer the youngest in the Hatcher family, Tootsie is. Determined to get rid of her, Fudge tries selling and trading Tootsie.

———. *Tales of a Fourth Grade Nothing.* Dutton, 1972.

Pete's little brother, Fudge, has been a pain in the neck for a long time. When he gets hold of Pete's pet turtle, things draw quickly to a climax.

Brown, Alan. *Lost Boys Never Say Die.* Delacorte, 1989.

Lewis leads a miserable life because he stutters. It's not until he meets Max, an equally miserable child who has a weight problem, that he finds solace. Together the two decide to take part in a production of *Peter Pan* with hilarious results.

Byars, Betsy. *The 18th Emergency.* Viking, 1973.

Cartooning is fun and Benjie, otherwise known as "Mouse," can't resist drawing cartoons of people. When he does one of Hammerman, the strongest and meanest kid in school, his troubles really begin.

Conford, Ellen. *Lenny Kandell, Smart Aleck.* Little, 1983.

■■■■■■□□□□□□□□

Lenny's father was killed in World War II. Now, a year later, Lenny dreams of becoming a professional comedian. His best friend thinks Lenny's a riot, but Mousie Blatner is not amused. Because Mousie is the toughest kid around, he makes a dangerous enemy for Lenny.

Cresswell, Helen. *The Bagthorpe Saga.* Macmillan, 1979.

■■■■■■■□□□□□□□

See page 15.

Danziger, Paula. *Everyone Else's Parents Said Yes.* Delacorte, 1989.

■■■■■■□□□□□□□□

Matthew loves practical jokes and trading insults with his sister. When Matthew's birthday approaches, the tables are turned.

Gilbreth, Frank and Gilbreth, Ernestine. *Cheaper by the Dozen.* Crowell, 1948, 1966.

■■■■■■■■■□□□□□

The humor centers on a father whose twelve children have inherited his penchant for practical jokes. Mr. Gilbreth, an efficiency expert, is sure that things can be done better, but his plans always go awry. His wife copes with all the shenanigans with dignity.

Greenwald, Sheila. *Will the Real Gertrude Hollings Please Stand Up?* Atlantic, 1983.

■■■■■■□□□□□□□□

Gertrude is dyslexic and school is not her favorite place. When she finds that she must stay three weeks with her uncle and aunt and their super-achieving son Albert, she is totally dismayed.

Hall, Lynn. *Here Comes Zelda Claus and Other Holiday Disasters.* Harcourt, 1989.

■■■■■■□□□□□□□□

Fourth-grader Zelda Hammersmith always has great ideas for holiday celebrations—unfortunately, something goes wrong every time.

Heide, Florence Parry. *Banana Blitz.* Holiday, 1984.

■■■■■■□□□□□□□□

This book is the sequel to the equally funny *Banana Twist* (Holiday, 1978). Both are narrated by Jonah, who in this book wants to win a thousand dollars in a contest that involves counting the number of times the word *banana* is used during a commercial.

Howe, James and Howe, Deborah. *Bunnicula.* Atheneum, 1979.

■■■□□□□□□□□□□□

Harold the dog tells this story of a bunny, found in a movie theater, who exhibits strange fang-like teeth and drains its vegetables.

Lawson, Robert. *Ben and Me.* Little, 1939, 1988.

■■■■□□□□□□□□□□

Amos the mouse grows tired of nibbling at the few things his church home offers and sets up house in Ben Franklin's fur cap. From there it's a short way to becoming central to Dr. Franklin's life. According to Amos, what we had in Ben Franklin was an inept, albeit famous, patriot and inventor. It was Amos who invented bifocals and the stove, discovered that lightning was electricity, and so on.

Levy, Elizabeth. *Frankenstein Moved in on the Fourth Floor.* Harper, 1979.

■■□□□□□□□□□□□□

Sam and Robert are convinced that Mr. Frank, their fourth-floor neighbor, is really Frankenstein. Their attempt to prove their suspicion leads to plenty of suspense and humor.

Peck, Robert Newton. *Soup.* Knopf, 1973.

This is the first of a series of books about two boys growing up in Vermont who outdo each other in thinking up the next trick.

Robinson, Barbara. *The Best Christmas Pageant Ever.* Harper, 1972.

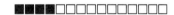

The Herdmans are the meanest kids in town. They set Fred Shoemaker's toolhouse on fire. They smoke cigars. They've never set foot in the church and don't mean to until they hear that there will be free food after the Christmas Pageant at Sunday School. At that point they set about taking over the pageant, using their intimidation skills to drive away any rivals for the parts. (See page 98.)

Rockwell, Thomas. *How to Eat Fried Worms.* Dell, 1975.

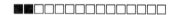

Could you eat them? Maybe if someone bet you fifty dollars you couldn't and you really needed the money. Could you eat fifteen of them?

Take a Closer Look

Rationale

With this theme we highlight the artists of the children's book world. Children in the upper grades can learn a great deal by looking at picture books. For more information on picture books, see *Once Upon a Time. . . An Encyclopedia for Successfully Using Literature with Young Children.*

Picture Book Starter

☐ de Regniers, Beatrice Schenk. *Sing a Song of Popcorn.* Scholastic, 1988.

This collection of poetry is illustrated by nine Caldecott award-winning illustrators. It provides a good base for comparing artists' styles.

Bulletin Board

☐ Display book covers and posters showing the work of some of the illustrators.

Museum

☐ Display paintbrushes, airbrushes, various kinds of paint and other mediums, books on illustration, and biographies or autobiographies of illustrators.

Discussions, Projects, and Activities

☐ Sort picture books according to illustrations: first, by the medium or media used; second, by the style of the illustrator.

☐ Look at one fairy tale as several illustrators conceived it. Which one do you like best and why? Imagine how that illustrator would do a different fairy tale. Which scenes would he/she show?

☐ Imagine what a book you like very much would look like if a different illustrator had done it.

☐ Find out how illustrations are printed in a book.

☐ What media and techniques are used in the books? Why? How does the material used change the look of the book?

☐ Find out how some illustrators got started. What advice do they give new illustrators?

☐ Why do editors sometimes keep illustrators and authors apart when they are working on a book?

☐ Find all the books by one illustrator and put them in the order in which they were published. In what ways has the illustrator's work changed?

☐ Watch a film or filmstrip on the art of illustration, such as those offered by Weston Woods.

Barbara Cooney

☐ Ms. Cooney has illustrated over a hundred children's books. She received the Caldecott Award for *Ox-Cart Man.* Her work is distinguished by the graceful charm of her illustrations and her attention to detail. Her favorite work is *Miss Rumphius,* who she says became her alter ego as she worked.

☐ Barbara Cooney was born in a hotel that her grandfather owned in Brooklyn Heights, New York. She grew up on Long Island and studied art at Smith College and at the Art Students' League in New York. Her mother was an artist and she encouraged Barbara's artwork from the time she was little. After college, she went right to work with children's books because she felt that field would give her the most freedom. She loves cooking, gardening, traveling, and taking photographs. She is married to a doctor, they have four grown children, and they are grandparents. She plans to live to be 100.

Books Written and Illustrated by Barbara Cooney
Christmas. Crowell, 1967.
The Courtship, Merry Marriage, and Feast of Cock Robin and Jenny Wren, to Which Is Added the Doleful Death of Cock Robin. Scribners, 1965.
Island Boy. Viking, 1988. ✔
Little Brother and Sister. Doubleday, 1982.
The Little Juggler. Hastings, 1961.
Little Prayer. Hastings, 1967.
Miss Rumphius. Viking, 1982. ✔

Books Illustrated by Barbara Cooney

American Folk Songs for Children. Seeger, Ruth C. Doubleday, 1980.

Bambi: Life in the Woods. Salten, Felix. Archway, 1982.

The Best Christmas. Kingman, Lee. Peter Smith, 1984.

Burton and Dudley. Sharmat, Marjorie. Avon, 1977.

Chanticleer and the Fox. Chaucer, Geoffrey. Crowell, 1982.

Christmas in the Barn. Brown, Margaret W. Harper, 1985.

The Donkey Prince. Craig, M. Jean. Doubleday, 1977.

Emma. Kesselman, Wendy. Harper, 1985. ✔

How the Hibernators Came to Bethlehem. Farber, Norma. Walker, 1980.

I Am Cherry Alive, the Little Girl Sang. Schwartz, Delmore. Harper, 1979.

Katie's Magic Glasses. Goodsell, Jane. Houghton, 1978.

Kildee House. Montgomery, Rutherford. Doubleday, 1949.

The Little Fir Tree. Brown, Margaret W. Harper, 1985.

Louhi, Witch of North Farm. de Gerez, Toni. Viking, 1986.

The Man Who Didn't Wash His Dishes. Krasilovsky, Phyllis. Doubleday, 1950.

Ox-Cart Man. Hall, Donald. Viking, 1979. ✔

Peter and the Wolf. Prokofiev, Sergei. Viking, 1986.

Seven Little Rabbits. Becker, John. Scholastic, 1985.

Spirit Child. Bierhorst, John. Morrow, 1984.

Squawk to the Moon, Little Goose. Preston, Edna. Penguin, 1985.

The Story of Holly and Ivy. Godden, Rumer. Viking, 1985.

When the Sky Is Like Lace. Horwitz, Elinor. Lippincott, 1975.

Where Have You Been? Brown, Margaret W. Hastings, 1986.

Wynken, Blynken, and Nod. Field, Eugene. Hastings, 1980.

Stephen Gammell

☐ Stephen Gammell shows people differently than most artists do. His people are lumpy. Their clothes often fit poorly and rolls of flesh are sometimes seen peeking through. The people are often rather ugly, and yet they seem familiar and remind us of people we know. In *The Relatives Came,* he used his own family as models: he is the man playing the guitar, his wife is taking pictures, and his father is cutting hair. He uses pencil and charcoal and several of his books have no added color. He won the 1989 Caldecott Medal for his illustrations in Karen Ackerman's *Song and Dance Man.*

☐ Mr. Gammel was born and raised in the Midwest. He taught himself to draw and began making his living as an editorial illustrator in the early 1970s. He and his wife Linda, a professional photographer, live in Minnesota.

Books Written and Illustrated by Stephen Gammell

Git Along, Old Scudder. Lothrop, 1983.

Once Upon MacDonald's Farm. Macmillan, 1981. ✔

The Story of Mr. and Mrs. Vinegar. Lothrop, 1982.

Wake Up, Bear . . . It's Christmas. Lothrop, 1981.

Books Illustrated by Stephen Gammell

Airmail to the Moon. Birdseye, Tom. Holiday, 1988.

And Then the Mouse. Hall, Malcolm. Macmillan, 1980.

The Best Way to Ripton. Davis, Maggie S. Holiday, 1982.

Blackbird Singing. Bunting, Eve. Scholastic, 1983.

Come a Tide. Lyon, George Ella. Orchard, 1990. ✔

Dancing Teepees: Poems of American Indian Youth. Sneve, Virginia Driving Hawk. Holiday, 1988.

Demo and the Dolphin. Benchley, Nathaniel. Harper, 1981.

Flash and the Swan. Brophy, Ann. Warne, 1981.

A Furl of Fairy Wind. Hunter, Mollie. Harper, 1977. ✔

The Ghost of Tillie Jean Cassaway. Showell, Ellen H. Four Winds, 1978.

The Great Dimpole Oak. Lisle, Janet Taylor. Orchard, 1987.

Halloween Poems. Livingston, Myra C. Holiday, 1989.

The Hawks of Chelmey. Jones, Adrienne. Harper, 1978.

The Kelpie's Pearls. Hunter, Mollie. Harper, 1976.

Let Me Hear You Whisper. Zindel, Paul. Harper, 1974.

Meet the Vampire. McHargue, Georgess. Lippincott, 1979.

More Scary Stories to Tell in the Dark. Schwartz, Alvin. Lippincott, 1984.

A Nutty Business. Chittum, Ida. Putnam, 1972.

The Old Banjo. Haseley, Dennis. Macmillan, 1983. ✔

Old Henry. Blos, Joan W. Morrow, 1987. ✔

The Real Tom Thumb. Cross, Helen R. Macmillan, 1980.

A Regular Rolling Noah. Lyon, George Ella. Bradbury, 1986.

The Relatives Came. Rylant, Cynthia. Bradbury, 1985. ✔

Scary Stories to Tell in the Dark. Schwartz, Alvin. Lippincott, 1981.

Song and Dance Man. Ackerman, Karen. Knopf, 1988. ✔

Thanksgiving Poems. Livingston, Myra Cohn. Holiday, 1985.

Waiting to Waltz. Rylant, Cynthia. Bradbury, 1984. ✔

Where the Buffaloes Begin. Baker, Olaf. Warne, 1981.

Who Kidnapped the Sheriff? Callen, Larry. Atlantic, 1985.

Yesterday's Island. Bunting, Eve. Warne, 1979.

Trina Schart Hyman

☐ Ms. Hyman often illustrates romantic work such as fairy tales. She received the Caldecott Award for *St. George and the Dragon.* She does extensive research before illustrating a book. She went to London and stayed with a historical illustrator before she did her *Canterbury Tales.* She did not visit Canterbury, however, because her friend said that it had changed too much since Chaucer's day. Instead she went to the medieval town of Rye, which has stayed very much the same. She stayed there several weeks sketching and getting the feeling of the town. She studied reproductions of paintings from the original *Canterbury Tales* to see the costumes of the time. That's also where she saw the portrait of Chaucer that she put on the end papers. She used elements from medieval manuscripts for the borders of the pictures and she tried to use the limited number of colors for the book that painters of that time had at their disposal. The quote she put around Chaucer's portrait has been her motto since she was a young girl. It was only when she illustrated the book that she found out it was from Chaucer. It took her a year to illustrate the book.

☐ Trina Schart Hyman lives in a 165-year-old farmhouse in northern New Hampshire. She is divorced and has one daughter, Katrin. She lives with her daughter and a friend, Barbara Rogasky, who is a freelance editor. When Ms. Hyman was getting started as an illustrator, she did illustra-tions for textbooks and then for two Little Golden Books. She was afraid of everything when she was little, she says. She used to dress up like Little Red Riding Hood and wander around the backyard with her dog as the wolf. She says she definitely believes in fairies and she loves kids. She takes a three-mile walk every morning during which she thinks about the work she will do that day.

☐ Once a book reviewer named Virginia Kirkus criticized everything Trina did and that made her very angry. She was illustrating the book *Will You Sign Here, John Hancock* at the time. If you look very carefully in the first edition of the book at the gravestones in one picture, you will see how she got even with Virginia Kirkus.

Books Written and Illustrated by Trina Schart Hyman
The Enchanted Forest. Putnam, 1984.
How Six Found Christmas. Little, 1979.
A Little Alphabet Book. Little, 1980.
Self-Portrait: Trina Schart Hyman. Harper, 1989.
The Sleeping Beauty. Little, 1977.

Books Illustrated by Trina Schart Hyman
Among the Dolls. Sleator, William. Dutton, 1986. ✔
The Bad Times of Irma Baumlein. Brink, Carol R. Macmillan, 1972.
Big Sixteen. Calhoun, Mary. Morrow, 1983.
The Bread Book. Meyer, Carolyn. Harcourt, 1976.
Caddie Woodlawn. Brink, Carol Ryrie. Macmillan, 1973. ✔
Canterbury Tales. Chaucer, Geoffrey. Lothrop, 1988. ✔
The Castle in the Attic. Winthrop, Elizabeth. Holiday, 1985. ✔
Cat Poems. Livingston, Myra Cohn. Holiday, 1987.
The Cat Walked Through the Casserole. Espeland, Pamela and Waniek, Marilyn. Carolrhoda, 1984.
A Child's Christmas in Wales. Thomas, Dylan. Holiday, 1985.
A Christmas Carol. Dickens, Charles. Holiday, 1983.
Christmas Poems. Livingston, Myra Cohn. Holiday, 1984.
A Connecticut Yankee in King Arthur's Court. Twain, Mark. Morrow, 1988.
Fairy Poems. Wallace, Daisy. Holiday, 1980.
Hershel and the Hanukkah Goblins. Kimmel, Eric. Holiday, 1989.
A Hidden Magic. Vande Velde, Vivian. Crown, 1985.

Home. Hearne, Betsy. Macmillan, 1979.

How Does It Feel to Be Old? Farber, Norma. Crown, 1979.

Jane, Wishing. Tobias, Tobi. Viking, 1977.

Joy to the World. Sawyer, Ruth. Little, 1966.

King Stork. Pyle, Howard. Little, 1986.

The Kitchen Knight. Hodges, Margaret. Holiday, 1990.

Let's Steal the Moon. Serwer-Bernstein, Blanche. Shapolsky, 1987.

Little Red Riding Hood. Grimm, Jacob and Grimm, Wilhelm. Holiday, 1982.

Magic in the Mist. Kimmel, Margaret M. Macmillan, 1975.

The Man Who Loved Books. Fritz, Jean. Putnam, 1981. ✔

Moon Eyes. Poole, Josephine. Little, 1967.

Night Journey. Lasky, Kathryn. Penguin, 1986.

Peter Pan. Barrie, James Matthew. Scribners, 1980.

Ranger Rick's Holiday Book. Jones, Elizabeth. National Wildlife, 1980.

Rapunzel. Rogasky, Barbara. Holiday, 1982.

Saint George and the Dragon. Hodges, Margaret. Little, 1984.

The Shy Little Girl. Krasilovsky, Phyllis. Houghton, 1970.

Snow White. Grimm, Jacob and Grimm, Wilhelm. Little, 1974.

Star Mother's Youngest Child. Moeri, Louise. Houghton, 1975. ✔

Tight Times. Hazen, Barbara S. Viking, 1979.

Two Queens of Heaven. Gates, Doris. Viking, 1974.

The Water of Life. Rogasky, Barbara. Holiday, 1986.

Why Don't You Get a Horse, Sam Adams? Fritz, Jean. Putnam, 1974. ✔

Will You Sign Here, John Hancock? Fritz, Jean. Putnam, 1976. ✔

Witch Poems. Wallace, Daisy. Holiday, 1976.

Peter Parnall

☐ Mr. Parnall uses white space well. His illustrations are usually in paint and pen and ink with sparse color. They are often very detailed without appearing to be cluttered. The style is usually realistic. He illustrated most of the books written by Byrd Baylor. He seems to have an affinity for nature without being sentimental about it.

☐ Peter Parnall has illustrated over eighty books. He likes horses, sailing, competitive shooting, and woodland management. He lives on a farm on the coast of Maine where he raises sheep.

Books Written and Illustrated by Peter Parnall
Apple Tree. Macmillan, 1988.
Cats from Away. Macmillan, 1989.
The Daywatchers. Macmillan, 1984.
Feet! Macmillan, 1988.
Winter Barn. Macmillan, 1986.

Books Illustrated by Peter Parnall
Annie and the Old One. Miles, Miska. Little, 1972. ✔
Between Cattails. Williams, Terry Tempest. Scribners, 1985.
Cat Will Rhyme with Hat. Chapman, Jean. Scribners, 1986.
The Desert Is Theirs. Baylor, Byrd. Scribners, 1975. ✔
Desert Voices. Baylor, Byrd. Scribners, 1980.
Everybody Needs a Rock. Baylor, Byrd. Scribners, 1974. ✔
Hawk, I'm Your Brother. Baylor, Byrd. Scribners, 1976. ✔
If You Are a Hunter of Fossils. Baylor, Byrd. Scribners, 1980. ✔
I'm in Charge of Celebrations. Baylor, Byrd. Scribners, 1986.
Kavik, the Wolf Dog. Morey, Walt. Dutton, 1977.
The Other Way to Listen. Baylor, Byrd. Scribners, 1978. ✔
The Way to Start a Day. Baylor, Byrd. Scribners, 1978. ✔
Your Own Best Secret Place. Baylor, Byrd. Scribners, 1979.

Dear Diary

Rationale

If we ask children to keep reading logs and lifetime journals, we need to provide models. Books that are based on journals, that use a journal or diary format, or that stress writing show readers that keeping journals can be important and interesting.

Picture Book Starter

☐ Williams, Vera. *Stringbean's Trip to the Shining Sea.* Greenwillow, 1988.

This collection of postcards and snapshots paints a wonderful picture of a summer trip. Some of the places are not usual tourist attractions, but they are a slice of Americana. Stringbean sends one postcard every day and his family puts them into an album.

Bulletin Board

☐ Display pages that might have been torn from any of the diaries listed below. Use tea to "antique" those that are supposed to be old ones, and vary the handwriting.

Museum

☐ Display real journals and diaries.

Discussions, Projects, and Activities

☐ Read some or all of the books listed below. What did the diary reveal about the writer's personality?
☐ Begin your own diary or journal.
☐ Keep a "special day" diary.
☐ Write a day-by-day account of a trip or vacation, real or imaginary.
☐ Write to authors and ask whether they keep or have kept diaries.
☐ Read an excerpt from a famous person's diary.
☐ How and why were President Nixon's and President Reagan's diaries involved in the courts?
☐ Help a younger friend or relative start a diary.
☐ Keep a scrapbook of postcards, notes, letters, and cards. Write a short account about each item.
☐ Start a photograph album. With each picture write a short description explaining who, where, when, and so on.
☐ For a book report write a journal or diary of one of the characters.
☐ Ask to read an entry in an adult's diary.

Books

Fiction

Anderson, Joan. *Joshua's Westward Journal.* Morrow, 1987.

■■■■□□□□□□□□□□□

Joshua Carpenter's journal is an account of his family's trip west by Conestoga wagon in pioneer days as they endure many hardships. The accompanying photographs were taken at two living-history sites and lend authenticity to the journal.

Cleary, Beverly. *Dear Mr. Henshaw.* Morrow, 1983.

■■■■■■■□□□□□□□□

Leigh Bates began a correspondence with author Henshaw because a teacher made him. When the author refuses to answer dumb, uninteresting questions, Leigh responds more personally. Eventually, he turns to a journal and reveals the pain of his parents' divorce and we see a very real boy.

Conrad, Pam. *Holding Me Here.* Harper, 1986.

■■■■■■■■■■□□□□□

Robin finds a diary in which a young woman tells about the pain she feels because she left her husband and children. Robin tries to bring them back together, unaware that she is dealing with spousal abuse.

Fitzhugh, Louise. *Harriet the Spy.* Harper, 1964.

■■■■■■■■■□□□□□□

Harriet wants to be a writer and knows that close observation is the secret to good writing. So she watches people carefully, evens spying on them, and writes everything in her notebook. When her notebook is read by the people she's been writing about, Harriet's life becomes quite miserable.

Gleeson, Libby. *Eleanor Elizabeth.* Holiday, 1990.

■■■■■■■■□□□□□□□

See page 3.

Harvey, Brett. *My Prairie Year.* Holiday, 1986.

■■■■■□□□□□□□□

Elenore is nine years old in 1889 when this diary begins. She and her family move from Lincoln, Maine, to the Dakota Territory. Their daily life, with its inevitable chores and the freedom of Sundays, moves the plot along. The winter snow and cold and the awesome destruction of a tornado provide the background.

Heinrich, Bernard. *An Owl in the House: A Naturalist's Diary.* Little, 1990.

■■■■■■■■□□□□□□

The diarist finds a baby great horned owl nearly frozen in the Vermont snow. Raising it to maturity requires more than a little adjustment for both. We learn a great deal about nature and raising wild young from this interesting diary.

Holland, Isabelle. *Abbie's God Book.* Westminster, 1982.

■■■■■■■■□□□□□□

Abigail Tyrell is confused about God, so her father encourages her to keep a journal of her religious questions and feelings. The journal tells us about Abigail's life as well as about her quest for God.

Klein, Robin. *Penny Pollard's Diary.* Oxford, 1984.

■■■■■■■□□□□□□

See page 4.

MacLachlan, Patricia. *Arthur, For the Very First Time.* Harper, 1980.

■■■■■□□□□□□□□□

Arthur's parents are about to have another baby, so they send him to visit his great-aunt and great-uncle who have a French-speaking chicken and an about-to-be-mother pig. They also have a neighbor, Moira, a young girl whose parents have deserted her. Arthur's anger at his parents loses its dominance as he begins to take responsibility for the very first time. (See page 94.)

———. *Cassie Binegar.* Harper, 1982.

■■■■■■■■■□□□□□

See page 105.

Mardsen, John. *So Much to Tell You.* Little, 1987.

■■■■■■■■■■■■□□

Fourteen-year-old Marina goes from the hospital to a boarding school. She assumes that it's because she isn't speaking and that her mother can't stand her silent presence. Mr. Lindell, the English teacher, requires that everyone keep a journal. The book, drawn from a true story, outlines Marina's growth through her journal entries.

Paulsen, Gary. *The Island.* Orchard, 1988.

■■■■■■■■□□□□□□

When Wil Neuton moves with his family to upstate Wisconsin, he thinks he'll never be able to adjust to life away from Madison. Once there, he isolates himself further by retreating to an island. On the island he studies the nature around him and tries to become part of it, writing and drawing all that becomes part of him. There are excerpts from his writing before and after the island adventure.

Pfeffer, Susan. *Dear Dad, Love Laurie.* Scholastic, 1989.

■■■■■■■■□□□□□□

Her mother and father are divorced and Laurie keeps in touch with her dad through letters in which she details the ups and downs of life in the sixth grade.

Robertson, Keith. *Henry Reed, Inc.* Viking, 1958.

■■■■■■■□□□□□□□

This is Henry's first-hand account of his visit to his uncle and aunt who live near Princeton University. There he becomes intrigued with the prospect of doing his own research. Setting up a research lab in an old barn, he and a neighbor girl are off on a series of hilarious adventures. This is the first book in the Henry Reed series.

Sharmat, Marjorie. *Chasing After Annie.* Harper, 1981.

■■■■■■■■□□□□□□□

Alternating journals tell the story here. Richie Carr is convinced, and says so in his diary, that Annie likes him. On the contrary, Annie reports in her journal that she hates him more than ever. Then Annie's dog Fritz disappears and Richie brings back the wrong dog.

Smith, Robert Kimmel. *Mostly Michael.* Dell, 1987.

■■■■■□□□□□□□□□□

Michael, a boy in contemporary suburbia, is at first an unwilling diarist. Later, he becomes enthusiastic. The reading level is fairly easy as novels go, probably within reach of most fourth graders. The year of life covered in this diary is not especially traumatic or even terribly eventful for Michael, but his problems will provide many readers with a sense of comradeship. (See page 138.)

Tolles, Martha. *Who's Reading Darci's Diary?* Lodestar, 1984.

■■■■■■■■■□□□□□□

Darci loves to write in her diary. It contains all her innermost thoughts. That's why she is completely devastated when her diary disappears. Darci writes a letter that is published in the school newspaper. Its publication gives Darci a new look at many of her teachers, friends, and classmates.

Turner, Ann. *Nettie's Trip South.* Macmillan, 1987.

■■■■■■■■■□□□□□□

This book is based on the diary of the author's great-grandmother. Nettie, a New Yorker, writes home to her friend Addie about her trip to Virginia in a time when slavery was the law. Black people are called only by their first names. No Black person is allowed to learn to read or own a book. But, of course, worst of all, they can be sold as a possession with no regard for their families or feelings.

Van Leeuwen, Jean. *Dear Mom, You're Ruining My Life.* Dial, 1989.

■■■■■■■■■□□□□□□

She isn't really ruining Samantha's life at all. Sam tends to overstate things, especially in her letters. In fact, this mother is incredibly understanding although unconventional. Sam, like many sixth-grade girls, wants to be just like all the fashionable girls with conventional households. Sam's mother is a writer and her father is a mathematical genius. In Sam's class for gifted children, she is encouraged to make daily journal entries. This light-hearted book includes letters to and from her mother and friends and excerpts from the journal.

Blank Diaries

Blume, Judy. *The Judy Blume Memory Book.* Dell, 1988.

The proceeds of this book go to a special fund established by Ms. Blume to support programs for young people. The book is divided into twelve months with a personal memory from Judy Blume's *Growing Up Days* at the beginning of each section. There are seven Memory Saver activities to help keep memories alive, and there is a section for keeping track of important dates for each month. "Memories in the Making" pages provide space to record current events and feelings.

Cleary, Beverly. *The Beezus and Ramona Diary.* Morrow, 1986.

On a slightly higher level than *The Ramona Quimby Diary*, this diary contains quotes from all the Ramona books to bring back memories. The monthly sections provide space for secret thoughts, feelings about special holidays, school events, and friends that might be inspired by the quotes.

————. *The Ramona Quimby Diary.* Morrow, 1984.

Along with excerpts from the Ramona books, each month features a drawing spot, picture place, special day notation, things to remember for the next month, funny places, and other variations on the usual blank page format. There is also plenty of space for writing personal entries, and a page of stickers to mark special entries.

Knights and Ladies

Rationale

The Middle Ages were colorful and romantic from one point of view, but the harsh reality of life for the have-nots was a direct and awful contrast. It was also the time when many of our fairy tales are loosely set. Because most children have fantasized about knights, castles, and damsels in distress, this theme is an opportunity to bring those fantasies into the foreground for closer examination.

Picture Book Starter

☐ We have included many picture books in this theme. In fact, there are more picture books listed than novels, but the Jonathan Hunt book contains so many ideas for developing the theme that we have started with it.

☐ Hunt, Jonathan. *Illuminations.* Bradbury, 1989.

This alphabet book highlights the clothing, customs, and vocabulary of the Middle Ages with a wealth of information from alchemy to zither.

Bulletin Board

☐ Examine the illuminated letters that begin each page of *Illuminations.* Have the children find other illuminated letters in books of fairy tales and the like. Then ask each child to design one illuminated letter and find a word from the Middle Ages that begins with the letter. Have the children print their words on paper cut and curled to look like a scroll. Place the scroll on a bulletin board with an ornate border.

Museum

☐ Collect and display pictures or reproductions of objects and clothing from the Middle Ages.

Discussions, Projects, and Activities

☐ Plan to hold a medieval festival for one day or one week and involve the whole school. Let individuals and groups of students choose roles for the day: serfs, nobles, witches, dragons, knights, pages, troubadours and other musicians, costumers, magicians, monks, and scribes. Encourage the children to research roles they will assume that day.

In the mornings, play madrigals or other music from the time over the loud speaker. Encourage the music department to produce a choral presentation for the fair.

Design and create: booths for wares and foods, a tournament area for jousting and archery contests, costumes, armor, facades of castles, banners, mock stained-glass windows, stilts, and games.

Every morning announce a "Word of the Day" over the loudspeaker. The person giving a clearly written definition of the word as it applies to the Middle Ages will get tournament points for the festival day. Such points can be used to purchase food or items for sale. Possible words: villein, wattle and daub, portcullis, quintain, troubadour, scribe, signet, psaltery, alchemy, Magna Carta, serf, squire, guild, scutage, turret, longbow, surcoat, crusade, chivalry.

☐ Find out about astrology and fortunetelling. Set up a fortunetelling booth at the fair.

☐ Find out about famous people from that time: King Arthur and his Knights, Robin Hood and his Merry Men, Galileo, Pierre Abelard, Thomas à Becket, Richard the Lion-Hearted, King John, Genghis Khan, Yaqut ibn Abdullah, Francis of Assisi, Roger Bacon, Kublai Khan, Marco Polo, the Pied Piper of Hamelin, William the Conqueror, Robert the Bruce, the Aztecs, the Black Prince, Tamerlane, John Wycliffe, Geoffrey Chaucer, Dick Whittington, Leif Eriksson.

☐ Investigate coats of arms and the symbols used on them. Design a coat of arms for your family.

☐ Perform a science experiment that some people in the Middle Ages would have thought was magic. For example, demonstrate static electricity.

☐ Turn the classroom into a place of the Middle Ages. Try not to use anything in the classroom that did not exist during that time: no electricity, running water, pencils, etc.

☐ Investigate the bubonic plague and find other diseases that were once plagues.

☐ What real things or events might have caused people in the Middle Ages to believe in dragons and witches?

☐ Read about King Arthur, Robin Hood, and the Pied Piper of Hamelin and find out whether there is historical evidence that they existed. What events in these legends might have occurred?

Books

Fiction

Aliki. *A Medieval Feast.* Crowell, 1983.

■□□□□□□□□□□□□

For weeks the serfs and nobility make elaborate preparations for the arrival of the king and queen at the manor house.

Bulla, Clyde Robert. *The Sword in the Tree.* Harper, 1956, 1988.

■■■■□□□□□□□□□

Shan's uncle has made his own brother a prisoner in order to take control of the castle. Shan's only hope is to reach King Arthur.

Burkert, Nancy. *Valentine & Orson.* Farrar, 1989.

■■■■■□□□□□□□□

A fairy tale of knights and magic is cast as a folk play and performed by itinerant players from sixteenth-century Flanders.

Chaucer, Geoffrey. *The Canterbury Tales.* Lothrop, 1988.

■■■■■■■■□□□□□

The most interesting parts of the book are the introduction to each tale and the illustrations, by Trina Hyman, in which the narrators come to life.

De Angeli, Marguerite. *The Door in the Wall.* Doubleday, 1949.

■■■■■□□□□□□□□

Robin is put in the care of Brother Luke at the monastery. There Robin learns skills far different from those he would have needed to become a page; he learns to see "the door in the wall."

Furlong, Monica. *Wise Child.* Knopf, 1987.

■■■■■■■■□□□□□

Wise Child, an abandoned nine-year-old, goes to live with the witch woman and learn the ways of magic in this story set in Great Britain during the Dark Ages. The setting is as much a character in the story as the child and the witch are.

Gray, Elizabeth Janet. *Adam of the Road.* Viking, 1942, 1987.

■■■■■■■■■□□□□

Adam, his minstrel father, and dog Nick are on the way to the fair at St. Giles when Nick is stolen. During the chase, Adam and his father become separated. It is a long winter through disaster and triumph before they are all reunited.

Lasker, Joe. *Merry Ever After: The Story of Two Medieval Weddings.* Viking, 1976.

■□□□□□□□□□□□□

This picture book focuses on two weddings, contrasting the lives of a peasant and a noble family. While witnessing the preparations and the celebrations from these two contrasting lifestyles, we gain information about clothing, food, and customs.

Skurzynski, Gloria. *What Happened in Hamelin.* Four Winds, 1979.

■■■■■■■■■□□□□

Could it be that the real Pied Piper was a traveling minstrel, named Gast, who had diabolical motives and enlisted Geist, the narrator of this tale, in his treachery? This is a fascinating story of gullibility and guile.

35

Sutcliff, Rosemary. *The Light Beyond the Forest: The Quest for the Holy Grail.* Dutton, 1980.

■■■■■■■■■□□□□

This is a retelling of the Arthurian legend of Lancelot and the Knights of the Round Table.

Nonfiction

Anno, Mitsumasa. *Anno's Medieval World.* Putnam, 1980.

With his unmistakable touch, Anno shows us what people knew and thought about during the Middle Ages.

Brooks, Polly. *Queen Eleanor.* Lippincott, 1983.

This is the story of Eleanor of Aquitaine, an independent spirit in the medieval world.

Corbin, Carole Lynn. *Knights.* Watts, 1989.

In this book we follow knights in unromantic reality from training to actual service.

Gee, Robyn. *Living in Castle Times.* EDC, 1982.

Here we see the lives of two medieval children, a tradesman's son and a nobleman's daughter.

Goodall, John S. *The Story of a Castle.* Macmillan, 1986.

This picture book shows the birth of a Norman castle and follows its occupation for eight hundred years.

Hindley, Judy. *Knights and Castles.* Usborne, 1976.

Ms. Hindley shows us the effects of the Crusades on Europe from the 1200s.

Humble, Richard. *The Age of Leif Eriksson.* Watts, 1989.

The Vikings struck terror all over Europe from 790 to about 1050 and rightly so, for they robbed and pillaged much of it. However, they were also explorers, traders, farmers, and artists.

Macauley, David. *Cathedral: The Story of Its Construction.* Houghton, 1973.

Carefully detailed drawings show how craftsmen cooperated in the building of a cathedral.

MacDonald, Fiona. *Everyday Life in the Middle Ages.* Silver, 1984.

This book is just what the title says.

Matthews, Rupert. *Let's Look at Castles.* Bookwright, 1988.

Here is an amply illustrated book of castles.

Wright, Sylvia. *The Age of Chivalry.* Warwick, 1988.

The age of chivalry is not dead in this look at English society from 1200 to 1400.

Bank on It

Rationale

Many novels for children deal with moneymaking enterprises. Using them as a wedge into various classroom activities that deal with economics and money forms a nice bridge from literature to mathematics and social studies.

Picture Book Starter

☐ Noble, Trinka Hakes. *Meanwhile, Back at the Ranch.* Dial, 1987.

Poor Elna stays home while Rancher Hicks goes to town for excitement—and he finds it: turtles crossing the road, an endless checker game, and new items on the menu at the luncheonette. Meanwhile, back at the ranch, Elna strikes oil, inherits money, is discovered by a Hollywood producer, and on and on.

☐ Schwartz, David. *How Much Is a Million?* Lothrop, 1985.

A million, a billion, a trillion! Each super number is explored in funny pictures that are relevant to a child. Even I began to comprehend what is meant by all those zeroes.

☐ ———. *If You Made a Million.* Lothrop, 1989.

Money is the theme. What will it buy? How many bills equal how much money, etc.

Bulletin Board

☐ Let the children write and post want ads for items they want to buy or sell.

Museum

☐ Display coins and currency from around the world.

Discussions, Projects, and Activities

☐ Find the origins and meanings of such business related expressions as: A fool and his money are soon parted. In the money. Funny money. Get one's money's worth. Give someone a run for his/her money. Money to burn. Like money in the bank. Mad money. Make money hand over fist. Money burns a hole in the pocket. Money doesn't grow on trees. See the color of someone's money. They make money the old-fashioned way—they earn it. Throw good money after bad. Feel like two cents. Not one red cent. Put in one's two cents worth. Two cents plain. Cash and carry. Cash on the barrelhead. Cold hard cash.

☐ Find and sing money songs such as: "I've Got Sixpence," "Pennies from Heaven," "We're in the Money," "Side by Side," "Buddy, Can You Spare a Dime," and "If I Were a Rich Man."

☐ Collect cans and bottles and conduct other enterprises to make money for a worthy cause.

☐ Choose one stock from the stock market, pretend you invest a hundred dollars in it, and find out how much money you'll have if you sell the stock in a month.

☐ Talk to a numismatist about his or her collection.

☐ Find out which coins currently in circulation are worth more than face value.

☐ If there is a branch of Junior Achievement in your area, find out more about it. Interview someone who participates.

☐ Figure out why the rewards in fairy tales are gold and castles.

☐ Investigate buried and sunken treasure.

☐ Find out about salvage businesses that have located great treasures.

☐ Investigate famous robberies. Make wanted posters for the unsolved cases.

☐ Form groups of children to inhabit imaginary islands. Have them invent a product to manufacture or grow and set up trade with other islands.

Books

Picture Books

Anno, Mitsumasa. *Anno's Flea Market.* Putnam, 1984.

Tables of wares reflect categories of logical and illogical items for sale.

Bauer, Caroline. *My Mom Travels a Lot.* Warne, 1981.

A traveling mom means everyone in the family has to make adjustments, but there are pluses to the situation as well as minuses.

Blaine, Marge. *The Terrible Thing That Happened At Our House.* Scholastic, 1975.

Mother goes back to work and things deteriorate immediately. It isn't until each member of the family pitches in that life becomes manageable.

Hall, Donald. *Ox-Cart Man.* Viking, 1979.

A colonial farm family has worked hard to produce materials to be bartered at the market. In the fall, the man of the family loads everything into an ox cart he has made and walks his ox and cart to Portsmouth market. There he trades the produce, including the cart and ox, for items the family needs.

Hoban, Lilian. *Arthur's Funny Money.* Harper, 1981.

Arthur and his sister lose money while trying to earn it washing bikes.

Marshall, James. *Willis.* Houghton, 1974.

Willis' friends help him earn money for sunglasses.

Martin, Charles. *For Rent.* Greenwillow, 1986.
———. *Island Rescue.* Greenwillow, 1985.
———. *Island Winter.* Greenwillow, 1984.
———. *Summer Business.* Greenwillow, 1984.

In each of these books, the children who stay on a resort island year round are involved in the economy of the island and their own money-making schemes.

Provensen, Alice and Provensen, Martin. *Shaker Lane.* Viking, 1987.

Shaker Lane is the kind of road almost every community has. The houses aren't very pretty and the yards are full of junk. Most of the people who live ther aren't highly thought of by the people who live in more respectable areas. What happens to Shaker Lane is viewed as progress by some.

Turkle, Brinton. *Rachel and Obadiah.* Dutton, 1978.

Quaker children run errands to earn money.

Vincent, Gabrielle. *Bravo, Ernest and Celestine.* Greenwillow, 1981.

Ernest the bear and Celestine the mouse earn money to fix a leaking roof. However, with a salute to O. Henry, each spends the money to buy gifts for the other.

Viorst, Judith. *Alexander Who Used to Be Rich Last Sunday.* Macmillan, 1978.

All three boys are given the same amount of money by their grandparents. The other boys manage to keep theirs, but Alexander can't resist a bargain, even when he doesn't see one.

Fiction

Bawden, Nina. *Carrie's War.* Dell, 1973.

When Carrie and Nick Willow are evacuated from London during World War II, they are placed with Mr. Evans and his sister Lou in a small town in Wales. Mr. Evans is a strict, strongly religious man who has worked hard and saved his money rather than enjoyed it. He does care for his sisters; however, he bullies one and ignores the other. He is scrupulously honest—he even has Carrie return money to people who were overcharged in his store. (See page 104.)

———. *The Finding.* Lothrop, 1985.

Alex is adopted. He knows that he was abandoned on one of the Sphinxes on London's Embankment. The thing is, others seem to know lots more about Alex's background than they are prepared to admit. When Alex is left a large sum of money by a lady he barely knows, things come to a head, and Alex runs away.

Callen, Larry. *Pinch.* Little, 1976.

Pinch is a trader of the first class. He wants a pig that's for sale at the local store, but he has no money. He captures a bullfrog, trades it for two chickens, and parlays those into enough money for the pig. Even then his troubles aren't over.

Clements, Bruce. *Anywhere Else But Here.* Farrar, 1989.

Molly and her dad have a wonderful relationship, which is fortunate because everything else around them is rotten. Her dad's printing business failed, at least partly because of "Uncle Shel." Molly wants more than anything to go to Willimantic, Connecticut, to start a new life with her dad. She's even willing to sell her most treasured possession, a dollhouse left by her mother, in order to do so. (See page 93.)

Collier, James and Collier, Christopher. *Jump Ship to Freedom.* Delacorte, 1981.

■■■■■■■■■■■■■□

Daniel Arabus needs money to buy his freedom and that of his mother from the household of Captain Ivers. To do so, he must recover the money his father earned during the Revolution. After he steals the money, he runs to Philadelphia where the Continental Congress is trying to decide what to do about slavery.

Estes, Eleanor. *The Hundred Dresses.* Harcourt, 1974.

■■■■■□□□□□□□□□

A very poor child is ridiculed because of her clothing. She insists that she has a hundred dresses at home. The children who ridicule her later regret their insensitivity.

Gardiner, John Reynolds. *Stone Fox.* Crowell, 1980.

■■■■■□□□□□□□□□

See page 9.

McGraw, Eloise Jarvis. *The Money Room.* Atheneum, 1981.

■■■■■■■■□□□□□□

Great Gramp lost his fortune and moved to Oregon. Now Scotty, his mother, and younger sister are looking for the Great Money Room that Gramps told them exists. They're not the only ones determined to get their hands on the fortune and the farm.

Merrill, Jean. *The Toothpaste Millionaire.* Houghton, 1974.

■■■■■■□□□□□□□□

Twelve-year-old Rufus manufactures toothpaste in sixth grade. By the time he's an eighth grader, he's a millionaire and ready to retire. There are allusions to advertising and business malpractice.

Myers, Walter Dean. *The Mouse Rap.* Harper, 1990.

■■■■■■■■■■□□□□

According to rumors, Tiger Moran, a gangster during the 1930s, left a large amount of money in an abandoned building in Harlem. Mouse and his neighborhood gang decide to look for it. Sheri's grandfather says he worked as a mover for Moran, so the kids get him and two of his friends from the nursing home to help locate the cash. Then Mouse's life gets complicated. Mouse's father, who disappeared eight years ago, now wants to return, and Mouse's romance with Beverly takes a few turns. Each chapter begins with a rap by Mouse.

Paterson, Katherine. *The Master Puppeteer.* Crowell, 1976.

■■■■■■■■■■■□□□

Set in eighteenth-century Japan, this story tells of Jiro, a thirteen-year-old boy who becomes an apprentice in a theater owned by a master puppeteer, Yoshida, because he has seen food there. Jiro is the sole surviving child in the family of Isako, and he thinks his mother resents his existence. At the theater, Jiro excels and finds hints of Saburo, a Japanese Robin Hood, who commandeers rice and money from the wealthy to share with the starving masses.

Perl, Lila. *Tybee Trimble's Hard Times.* Clarion, 1984.

■■■■■■□□□□□□□□

More than anything else, Tybee wants to go to the circus, but her parents can't afford a ticket. Tybee turns her creative mind to fund-raising, but when she finally has enough money to go to the circus, she changes her mind and buys something else.

Roberts, Willo Davis. *What Could Go Wrong?* Atheneum, 1989.

■■■■■■■■□□□□□

While waiting for a plane, Gracie, one of three cousins on the trip, discovers a coded message in a newspaper crossword puzzle. This leads the threesome through a mugging and bomb threats to a suitcase full of money and a very suspicious character.

White, E. B. *The Trumpet of the Swan.* Harper, 1970.

■■■■■■■■■□□□□□

Louis doesn't have a beautiful voice like all the other trumpeter swans—he's mute. His father knows that without a voice Louis cannot communicate, so he steals a trumpet for Louis. With it, Louis earns enough money to pay for the trumpet and to win the fair Serena.

Music, Music, Music

Rationale

The connection between music and literature is one that is not often made for children, but it follows logically that one art form should lead to another.

Picture Book Starter

☐ Because of the nature of the theme, there are many picture books that should be used throughout the theme. See the suggested book list that follows the discussion ideas.

Bulletin Board

☐ Display repeated patterns of instruments and notes with the titles of books curving through and around the notes and instruments.

Museum

☐ Display objects that make music—real instruments and homemade ones.

Discussions, Projects, and Activities

☐ Hold a barn dance.

☐ Put on a vaudeville musical.

☐ Compare Broadway musicals of the 1930s and '40s to more recent musicals such as *Cats, A Chorus Line,* and *Phantom of the Opera.* How has the music changed? How about the show itself?

☐ Create a musical history of the United States, starting with colonial songs and music, going through the wars, and up to the present.

☐ Do a dance history of the United States: the minuet, waltz, Charleston, the Twist, break dancing, and everything in between.

☐ Listen to an instrumental piece of music that suggests a story, such as "Peter and the Wolf," and do your own illustrations.

☐ What musical games did you play as a young child? Do kids still play them? What about the ones your parents and grandparents played?

☐ Listen to the recording of the Broadway musical "Really Rosie" based on Maurice Sendak's book *The Sign on Rosie's Door* (Harper, 1975). Then write your own musical based on a book.

☐ Sing a song like "Jingle Bells" as a rock singer, an opera singer, or a jazz singer might sing it.

☐ Make a tape of musical themes of TV shows. See who can identify them.

☐ Make a tape of music from commercials. See who can identify them.

☐ Look for current music that is a remake of older music. Play both versions and compare them.

☐ Make a music trivia game.

☐ Find out the history of recorded music. What were the earliest recordings made on. What changes have been made in recording and playback devices?

☐ Look at *Prairie Home Companion Folk Song Book* by Jon and Marcia Pankake (Viking, 1988). Sing the song parodies and make up others. Find the well-known poems set to familiar music. Set another poem to music.

Books

Fiction: Picture Books

Ackerman, Karen. *Song and Dance Man.* Knopf, 1988.

In this Caldecott Award winner, Grandpa, who used to be a song and dance man, leads the children up to the attic where he keeps a trunkful of costumes and memories. For a little while he's a song and dance man again and the children are a most appreciative audience.

Clement, Claude. *Musician from the Darkness.* Little, 1990.

In the dawn of time while the other members of the tribe hunt for food, a man with sky-blue eyes takes a young boy on a different kind of safari. They hide in the grasses and look and listen to the life around them. Then the man with sky-blue eyes makes a flute from reeds and imitates the birds' songs. This attracts the birds that the hunters shoot. The man is shunned by the tribe when he refuses to play for them again, but at night he plays and drives away their fears.

Fleischman, Paul. *Rondo in C.* Harper, 1988.

As a young girl plays the piano, thoughts and images roam through the minds of her listeners.

Griffith, Helen. *Georgia Music.* Greenwillow, 1986.

The music that the grandfather and his grand-daughter share during this Georgian summer is more than that played by the old man on his mouth organ; it's the music of the birds, the grasshoppers, the katydids, and the crickets. Indeed, the old man says he plays for them. Later, when he is ill and has to go to Baltimore to live with his daughter and granddaughter the grand-daughter makes music for him.

Isadora, Rachel. *Ben's Trumpet.* Greenwillow, 1979.

A boy hears jazz coming from the club near his house and plays his imaginary trumpet along with the band.

Haseley, Dennis. *The Old Banjo.* Macmillan, 1983.

As a man and a boy go about the chores on the farm, the boy hears music and together they find abandoned instruments that play on their own.

Kuskin, Karla. *The Philharmonic Gets Dressed.* Harper, 1982.

Each orchestra member gets ready for the night's performance. We see them first in their everyday clothes and activities and then changing to their performing clothes.

Martin, Bill, Jr and Archambault, John. *Barn Dance.* Holt, 1986.

With a barn dance caller's lilt, the book tells of a young boy "much too full of wonderment to spend the night in bed." The boy is drawn to the barn where the farm creatures are having a dance.

Turkle, Brinton. *The Fiddler of High Lonesome.* Parents.

This beautiful book has been out of print for years, but you can still find it in some libraries. In it, a boy who makes beautiful music can charm the critters on High Lonesome and most of the people around the mountain, but he cannot charm the awful Fogels who claim to be his kin.

Walter, Mildred. *Ty's One-Man Band.* Macmillan, 1987.

Out of the woods comes a peg-legged man who eats by the pond and then drums on his cup with his spoon. He tells young Ty, who has been watching him carefully, that he's a one-man band

and that, if Ty will get him the necessary materials, he will perform that evening. Soon everyone is enjoying the music made with a washboard, two wooden spoons, a pail, and a comb.

Fiction: Novels

Babbitt, Natalie. *Tuck Everlasting.* Farrar, 1975.

■■■■■■■■□□□□□□

This extraordinary novel is about many things including immortality, murder, and life, but there is also music in the form of a music box. It belongs to Mae Tuck and she never goes anywhere without it. Unfortunately, it leads the man in the yellow suit to the Tucks and this leads to tragedy. The music box is heard again in the last line of the book when the Tucks leave Treegap forever. (See page 163.)

Bawden, Nina. *The Outside Child.* Lothrop, 1989.

■■■■■■■■□□□□□□

Jane has always known that her family is unusual. Her mother died soon after Jane was born, her father is at sea most of the time, and she lives with two eccentric but lovable aunts. Aunt Bill is overweight, loud, and brash. She is an artist, often using her garden flowers as models. Aunt Sophie is tiny and musical and teaches piano to supplement her income, but her real pleasure is as a percussionist in a band. Jane says she listens to the music in her head as if she had an invisible radio. (See page 144.)

de Felice, Cynthia. *Weasel.* Macmillan, 1990.

■■■■■■■■■■□□□□

This is a harsh story about a family on the frontier of Ohio trying to cope with evil, hatred, and revenge. Healing comes through music as the children and their father attend a dance and fiddling contest. The boy, who has been almost consumed with hatred, finds himself wanting to become a fiddler. (See page 168.)

MacLachlan, Patricia. *The Facts and Fictions of Minna Pratt.* Harper, 1988.

■■■■■■■□□□□□□□

Minna's mother is a writer who never asks normal questions such as "How was your day?" Minna's brother is offbeat as well. Minna longs for a normal life and to play her violin with vibrato.

Paterson, Katherine. *Come Sing, Jimmy Jo.* Lodestar, 1985.

■■■■■■■□□□□□□□

James's family has always sung in the bluegrass band and, while they travel, James stays with his grandmother who was once part of the band but is now too old to travel. Everything changes when the call comes for Jimmy Jo to join the band and he becomes a star. (See page 109.)

Selden, George. *The Cricket in Times Square.* Farrar, 1960.

■■■■■□□□□□□□□□□

Chester, the cricket, has arrived at Grand Central Station and the station will never be the same. Mario Bellini, a boy whose parents run a newspaper stand, befriends Chester, as do Tucker the mouse and Harry the cat. Chester sings beautifully and entertains the travelers with selections from grand opera.

Showell, Ellen Harvey. *Cecelia and the Blue Mountain Boy.* Lothrop, 1983.

■■■□□□□□□□□□□□

A boy is heading for the music festival at Chester and hears a strange story of a lively girl who changed Chester from a somber town to a music-loving place.

Slepian, Jan. *The Night of the Bozos.* Dutton, 1983.

■■■■■■■■■□□□□□

George's life revolves around music and he isn't interested in the carnival until he and his Uncle Hibbie meet the tattooed girl. She takes them behind the scenes of the carnival where they learn a lot about that world and their own.

Weik, Mary Hays. *The Jazz Man.* Atheneum, 1977.

■■■■■■■□□□□□□□

Young Zeke is often alone and afraid, but the music he hears from the Jazz Man, a pianist in a nearby apartment, comforts him. His mother and his father abandon him, and when the Jazz Man also leaves, Zeke is truly alone.

White, E. B. *The Trumpet of the Swan.* Harper, 1970.

■■■■■■■■■□□□□□

See page 40.

Whodunits

Rationale

Many children are already mystery readers. Often such series as The Hardy Boys and Nancy Drew are their introductions to the genre. Introducing children to other, perhaps better-written, mystery books is a good way to broaden the picture. The children become careful and critical readers as they hunt for clues to unravel mysteries. Because mystery books vary widely in quality, comparing the writing is a natural outcome.

Picture Book Starter

☐ Van Allsburg, Chris. *The Mysteries of Harris Burdick.* Houghton, 1984.

Supposedly, a man named Harris Burdick once went to a publisher with twelve illustrations and captions for twelve stories he intended to write. He then disappeared. The pictures are mysterious and the stories they evoke are invariably spooky.

☐ Read the preface and examine the book with the children. Then go back to the picture titled "Mr. Linden's Library." Brainstorm plot lines and then let the students form groups of two or three to see what stories they can come up with. Let them read or tell their mysteries.

☐ Don't forget that Mr. Burdick himself is a mystery. Where did he go? Why did he never return? Let the children become private detectives and solve the case. They can report his disappearance as Robert Stack does on TV's *Unsolved Mysteries* or as any TV detective might.

Bulletin Board

☐ Display "Wanted" posters for people wanted for questioning in some of the mystery novels. Encourage readers to add to the collection as they read and to write or stamp SOLVED across posters for the books they've read.

Museum

☐ Display clues and weapons from a variety of mystery books.

Discussions, Projects, and Activities

☐ Set up a mystery bulletin board of scary paragraphs from the books.

☐ Make "Wanted" posters for villains of the stories.

☐ Conduct your own version of *Unsolved Mysteries* using crimes from the books.

☐ Find an unsolved mystery in your town.

☐ Talk to a real detective and compare the way he/she works to the way the detectives in the books work.

☐ Read aloud from a book until a crime occurs. Discuss how you would proceed if you were called in on the case.

☐ Make flow charts of the books and decide whether the author plotted the action well.

☐ Group mysteries into categories: whodunit, locked room, hidden treasure, and missing persons.

☐ Write the first few pages of each kind of mystery.

☐ Play the board game or video game Clue®.

☐ Find out about Sherlock Holmes.

☐ Have a Sherlock Holmes costume day.

☐ Role-play with a partner. One person is the detective and the other is a suspect from one of the stories. The detective interrogates the suspect.

☐ Watch a TV mystery or old detective movie together and try to solve the crime.

☐ Compare a TV mystery to one of the books.

☐ Dress as your favorite book detective and defend the claim that you are the best.

☐ Use the information you've gained from reading the books to decide what makes a good mystery.

☐ Read aloud the first lines of several mysteries to see which grabs your attention best. Can you figure out why?

☐ Compare the codes used in several mystery books. In each case, decide whether the code was necessary and/or difficult to decipher. Write messages to each other in code.

☐ Devise a code. Try to crack each other's codes.

☐ Find out how codes are used in real life.

☐ Discuss the methods book detectives use to record information.

Books
Fiction

Avi. *The Man Who Was Poe.* Orchard, 1989.

■■■■■■■■■■■■■□

When Edmund's family disappears, the young boy is without resources to survive, let alone locate his missing relatives. A mysterious alcoholic writer offers to help him. The writer, Edgar Allen Poe, masquerades as Auguste Dupin, the detective in Poe's stories "The Purloined Letter," " The Murders in the Rue Morgue," and "The Mystery of Marie Rogêt." (See page 136.)

———. *Who Stole the Wizard of Oz?* Knopf, 1981.

■■■■■□□□□□□□□

It's not the Wizard that's missing—it's the book. Someone stole it and four other classics given to the library by the ungrateful heir of a very rich woman. Becky is questioned by the police because she was asking for the book just before it disappeared. With her friend Toby, Becky sets out to trap the thief.

Bawden, Nina. *The Outside Child.* Lothrop, 1989.

■■■■■■■■□□□□□

See page 42.

Branscum, Robbie. *The Murder of Hound Dog Bates.* Viking, 1982.

■■■■■□□□□□□□□

Sass's dog is killed, and Sass suspects that one or all of his three aunts murdered him. The same aunts raised Sass and he still lives with them, so there is a certain awkwardness. Kelly O'Kelly promises to help Sass find the murderer. Meanwhile, O'Kelly is courting the youngest aunt. Clem Watts, an old suitor of the other aunts, turns up and they decide to teach him a lesson.

Brenner, Barbara. *Mystery of the Plumed Serpent.* Knopf, 1980.

■■■■■■□□□□□□□

Elena and Michael recognize a mystery, so they follow clues to an ancient Mexican treasure.

Bunting, Eve. *Is Anybody There?* Lippincott, 1988.

■■■■■■■□□□□□□

Marcus Mullen's mother works and his father is dead, so Marcus is a latchkey child. When things begin disappearing from the house, he is understandably concerned. At first he suspects Nick, his mother's friend. When Marcus finds out that the intruder is Nick's estranged son, he decides to bring them together again.

Clifford, Eth. *The Dastardly Murder of Dirty Pete.* Houghton, 1981.

■■■■□□□□□□□□□

Mary Rose and her sister Jo-Beth accompany their father on a leisurely trip to California. They stop for a night in a ghost town that seems to have a real ghost. Someone turns on the record player, cooks up a tasty meal, and locks the father in jail.

———. *I Hate Your Guts, Ben Brooster.* Houghton, 1989.

■■■■□□□□□□□□□

There was a mix-up in luggage on Ben's trip to visit his cousin Charlie. Ben thinks he's carrying his own suitcase, but it actually belongs to Grace Aberdeen. When the boys discover that the suitcase contains a will leaving Grace a hidden treasure, her family becomes involved in helping Grace wrest the treasure from her scheming relatives.

Corcoran, Barbara. *The Person in the Potting Shed.* Atheneum, 1980.

■■■■■■■■■□□□□□

Screams in the night, a disappearance, and an intruder are all happening at Belle Reve where Dorothy and Franklin are staying with their mother and new stepfather. Solving the mystery means investigating a love affair and winning their stepfather's respect.

Curry, Jane. *The Big Smith Snatch.* Macmillan, 1989.

■■■■■■■□□□□□□□

Mrs. Smith is rushed to the hospital while on a trip to Pittsburgh, leaving four of the five children in the care of emergency foster parents. The Dickeys seem kind and eager to take the children. Boo soon discovers that the Dickeys are not what they seem. They intend to force the children into a life of crime, and the children's only hope for rescue lies with Boo.

Garfield, Leon. *The December Rose.* Viking, 1986.

■■■■■■■■■■■□□□

Barnacle is a chimney sweep so his ability to hang on to the inside of a chimney is a useful skill. When he loses his grip and tumbles into a room where a plot is being hatched, he grabs a locket and runs. Unfortunately, the locket is the key to the plot.

Giff, Patricia Reilly. *Have You Seen Hyacinth Macaw?* Delacorte, 1981.

■■□□□□□□□□□□□□

Seeing a sign offering a reward for Hyacinth Macaw is all Abby Jones and her pal Potsie need to start hunting. They have no trouble finding mysteries or suspects, one of whom is Hyacinth's brother Dan.

Hahn, Mary Downing. *The Dead Man of Indian Creek.* Houghton, 1990.

■■■■■■■□□□□□□□

When Parker and Matt camp out on Indian Creek and find a body in the water, Parker is sure the murderer is his mother's boyfriend George Evans. The police clear Evans, but Parker is determined to prove Evan's guilt—and he does. Unfortunately, Parker's mother is also implicated.

——. *Following the Mystery Man.* Avon, 1988.

■■■■□□□□□□□□□□

Madigan and her friend Angie love to play detective. When a stranger, Clint, takes a room in Madigan's grandmother's boarding house, the girls have a field day. Madigan is convinced that Clint is her long-lost father. When she discovers that he is a criminal, her entire value system is turned upside-down.

Howe, James and Howe, Deborah. *Bunnicula.* Atheneum, 1979.

■■■□□□□□□□□□□□

See page 25.

Hutchins, Pat. *Follow That Bus!* Knopf, 1977.

■■■■□□□□□□□□□□

A third-grade class takes a field trip the children will never forget. On this rather routine visit to a farm, the teacher accidentally picks up a satchel identical to hers that belongs to two desperate bank robbers. After a wild bus ride, a fox hunt, disguised robbers, and much more, the children return to a heroes' welcome.

——. *The Mona Lisa Mystery.* Greenwillow, 1981.

■■■■□□□□□□□□□□

On a trip to Paris with Miss Barker, the children become involved in the theft of the *Mona Lisa*. They apprehend the thief, thanks to Morgan's resourcefulness and a lot of champagne corks.

MacLeod, Charlotte. *We Dare Not Go A-Hunting.* Atheneum, 1980.

■■■■■■■■■□□□□□□

Molly Bassett baby-sits for the Truell family on the island of Netaquid. When her charge is kidnapped, the second kidnapping in as many summers, Molly tries to find the child and solve the crimes.

Prince, Alison. *The Sinister Airfield.* Morrow, 1983.

■■■■■■■■■□□□□□□

The airfield is supposed to be haunted by men who died in the war, but when the boys discover a dead man near the field, they have nothing to fear from ghosts. Harrie overhears two men plotting to rustle cattle with the new gamekeeper. When Ian and Harrie try to trap the rustlers, it's Noel who saves them all.

Roberts, Willo Davis. *The View from the Cherry Tree.* Aladdin, 1987.

■■■■■■□□□□□□□□□

Rob witnesses a murder from the cherry tree, but he doesn't see who the murderer is. His household is in turmoil and no one will listen to him when he tells about the murder. It isn't until later that he realizes that the murderer is stalking him.

———. *What Could Go Wrong?* Atheneum, 1989.

■■■■■■□□□□□□□□□

See page 40.

Sachs, Marilyn. *At the Sound of the Beep.* Dutton, 1990.

■■■■■■■■■■■□□□□

When the twins Mathew and Mathilda find out they're about to be separated by their parents' divorce, they run away to San Francisco to live with their Uncle Ben. Unfortunately, he's not home and the children must live in Golden Gate Park while they wait for him. There they become involved in the lives of the homeless and in a murder mystery, and Matilda is nearly killed.

Snyder, Zilpha Keatley. *The Egypt Game.* Atheneum, 1967.

■■■■■■■■□□□□□□

Inspired by a statue of Nefertiti, the girls begin the Egypt Game in which they recreate the world of the ancient Egyptians. When a child in the neighborhood is murdered, the game takes a back seat and April and Melanie stand a real chance of becoming murder victims themselves.

Storey, Margaret. *Ask Me No Questions.* Dutton, 1975.

■■■■■■■□□□□□□□

Imogen wakes up to find herself held captive by a nurse and a man named Keen. Keen is abrupt, taciturn, and often cruel, but Imogen grows to like him in spite of it all.

York, Carol Beach. *Once Upon a Dark November.* Holiday, 1989.

■■■■■■■■■□□□□□□

Katie does housework after school for Mrs. Herron whose husband is Katie's English teacher. The family seems happy enough until Mrs. Herron's cousin Martin arrives. Mrs. Herron has dreaded the visit and Katie can see why when she meets the brooding Martin. When a woman is murdered, the finger of suspicion points to Martin, who has disappeared. But why is he after Katie?

Superheroes

Rationale

The creatures of mythology permeate much of literature. Children should become acquainted with some of the stories from Greek and Roman mythology early in their literary ventures. Myths have been handed down through many cultures, and it is a fairly logical step to go from reading the Greek and Roman myths to those of the Native American, Egyptian, Eastern, and Nordic cultures. Also, most children are familiar with superheroes through comic books, television, and movies; these superheroes often reflect the problems and attributes of ancient mythological characters.

Many myths were told in an attempt to explain a natural phenomenon or human behavior. As such they are related to the *pourquoi,* or why, stories of folklore. Why do we have thunder? What causes the seasons? In mythology, however, these tales are part of a set of cultural beliefs. Approaching myths from this point of view sometimes helps students become more involved than starting with a broad question such as "How did the world begin?" Young children don't often ask this question on their own.

The connection between mythology and superheroes is strong. Superman and Hercules aren't so very far apart, as movies have attempted to show. Approaching mythology through its heroes and their super powers and comparing them to comic book and movie heroes is another successful approach.

Picture Book Starter

☐ Fisher, Leonard Everett. *Theseus and the Minotaur.* Holiday, 1988.

Mr. Fisher's formal illustrations are ideal for this tale from Greek mythology. The story tells about the killing of the beast that guarded the labyrinth and includes references to other gods, humans, and creatures of mythology.

☐ Hodges, Margaret. *The Arrow and the Lamp.* Little, 1989.

This is a handsome edition, illustrated by Donna Diamond, of the tale of love between Psyche and Eros and of Psyche's arrival at Mount Olympus.

Bulletin Board

☐ Make a family tree of the gods and goddesses of Greece. Let the children put the names in place as they learn about the characters. Many children will enjoy adding illustrations of the characters.

Museum

☐ Let the children make and display replicas and illustrations of the objects and characters mentioned in the myths.

Discussions, Projects, and Activities

☐ After you've read a few myths, ask the children to dress as people from ancient Greece or Rome, as ancient Vikings, or as modern scientists, and have them explain a phenomenon from their mythology or beliefs.

☐ Make a comic strip of a mythological hero and his/her deeds.

☐ Create a quest chart for some of the myths. Who is after what and how is the search hampered?

☐ Make constellation patterns by pasting stars on black paper. Tell the stories of the constellations.

☐ Look at a star map and find other combinations of stars that could be combined into constellations. Tell their stories.

☐ Look at a familiar constellation. Do you see something different? Tell the story.

☐ Make posters showing the monsters in the myths. Print its fate across the face of each monster.

☐ Make a board game based on the travels of Ulysses or the labors of Hercules.

☐ Write a journal for Ulysses, Theseus, or Hercules.

☐ Find and tell the stories behind the Signs of the Zodiac. Why were these particular constellations chosen for the Zodiac?

☐ What's your sign? Find out as much as you can about your sign.

☐ Read the riddle of the Sphinx and try to solve it. Ask others for their solutions.

☐ Compare the superheroes of myths to Superman, Captain Marvel, and Batman.

☐ The planets were named for mythological gods and goddesses. How are the names appropriate?

☐ If another planet were discovered beyond Pluto, what would you name it? Why?

☐ Use some of the words from mythology to create a board game.

Words from Mythology

Write the following words on cards. Have the children find out what each word means, discover its source, and write a synonym. Have them find it used in an advertisement or a newspaper or magazine story. Then have the children sort all of the words into groups, such as words that come from a specific mythology, words from a particular myth, words related to a god or goddess.

Achilles heel	graceful	ocean
aeolian harp	gracious	odyssey
Amazon River	hymn	Olympics
ambrosia	hypnosis	Pandora's box
arachnid	hydra	parasol
Argonaut	immortal	phobia
Athens	iridescence	Pluto
Atlanta	iris	psychology
Atlantic	January	python
atlas	June	rhea
aurora borealis	labyrinth	Saturday
calliope	lunatic	scorpion
cereal	March	siren
cosmic	marital	solar
echidna	Mars	solarium
echo	May	Sphinx
eohippus	Medusa jellyfish	syringe
erotic	mercurial	tantalize
Europe	Mercury	Thursday
fate	Midas touch	Titanic
fauna	morphine	Tuesday
flora	mortal	typhoon
florist	music	uranium
Friday	narcissus	Uranus
furious	nectar	Venus
giant	nectarine	vulcanize
gigantic	Neptune	Wednesday
grace	nymph	

Signs of the Gods

Flip the Facts. Put each symbol and the name of a god or goddess on one side of an 8½ x 11″ sheet of oaktag. On the other side number and write several facts about that god or goddess and about stories of the god or goddess. Use pronouns or blanks in place of the subjects' names. (Suggestions for facts follow the symbols.)

Then cut the cards into strips so there is one fact on each strip. Mix the strips together. Have the children sort the facts and place all those pertaining to each god or goddess into a file folder. If they have sorted the facts correctly, they can put the pieces together like a puzzle, flip each set of facts, and find the symbol of the god or goddess.

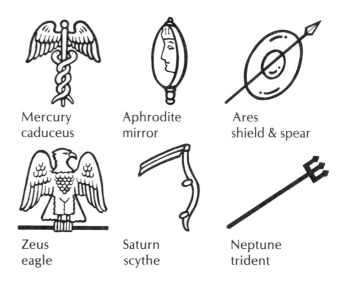

Mercury	Aphrodite	Ares
caduceus	mirror	shield & spear
Zeus	Saturn	Neptune
eagle	scythe	trident

Mercury Roman
(**Hermes** Greek)

He was the son of Jupiter (Zeus) and Maia.

He wore winged sandals.

He was Jupiter's (Zeus's) messenger.

He was shrewd and cunning and a master thief.

He stole Apollo's herds.

He invented the lyre.

He led souls of the dead to Pluto (Pluto or Hades) in the underworld.

He was Jupiter's (Zeus's) favorite traveling companion.

Aphrodite Greek
(**Venus** Roman)
   She was the goddess of love and beauty.
   She sprung from the foam of the sea.
   She was the wife of Hephaestus (Vulcan).
   Her favorite tree was the myrtle.
   She made Psyche sort an enormous pile of seeds.
   She turned Anaxarete to stone.
   She loved Adonis.
   She helped Aeneas escape from Troy.
   She was the mother of Eros (Cupid).
Ares Greek
(**Mars** Roman)
   He was the son of Zeus (Jupiter) and Hera (Juno).
   His mother and father hated him.
   His sister was Eris, the goddess of discord.
   His bird was the vulture.
   When he walked, the goddess of war, Enyo, and Terror, Trembling, and Panic went before him.
   He was the father of the Amazons.
   He was imprisoned by Otus and Ephiates.
   He always sided with Aphrodite (Venus) in arguments on Olympus.
   He fought alongside Hector in the Trojan War.
Zeus Greek
(**Jupiter** Roman)
   He was the ruler of the gods, lord of the sky, the rain god, and the cloud gatherer.
   He wielded thunder and lightning.
   He had greater power than any other god or goddess.
   His bird was the eagle.
   His tree was the oak.
   He killed Asclepius (Aesculapius).
   He was the son of Cronus (Saturn) and Rhea (Ops).
   He led a terrible war against Cronus and the Titans.
   He punished Sisyphus.
Saturn Roman
(**Cronus** Greek)
   He ruled the Titans.
   He was the father of Jupiter (Zeus).
   He was the protector of the sowers and the seed.
   He was the grandfather of Faunus.
   He fled to Italy when Jupiter (Zeus) dethroned him.
   He was the father of Ceres (Demeter).
   He swallowed his children as they were born.

Neptune Roman
(**Poseidon** Greek)
   He was the ruler of the seas.
   He was second in command to Jupiter (Zeus).
   He was the husband of Salacia (Amphitrite).
   He gave the first horse to man.
   He drove a golden chariot over the waters and stilled the waves.
   He sided with the Greeks during the Trojan War.
   He delayed the return of Ulysses (Odysseus).
   He sent a flood to Athens.

Books

Asimov, Isaac. *Words from the Myths.* Houghton, 1961.

Barth, Edna. *Cupid and Psyche.* Clarion, 1976.

Benson, Sally. *Story of the Gods and Heroes.* Dial, 1940.

Birrer, Cynthia and Birrer, William. *Song to Demeter.* Lothrop, 1987.

Colum, Padraic. *The Children of Odin: The Book of Northern Myths.* Macmillan, 1920, 1984.

Coolidge, Olivia. *Greek Myths.* Houghton, 1949.

Crossley-Holland, Kevin. *Axe Age, Wolf Age: A Selection for Children from the Norse Myths.* Andre Deutsch, 1985.

D'Aulair, Ingri and D'Aulair, Edgar. *Book of Greek Myths.* Doubleday, 1962.

Espeland, Pamela. *The Story of Baucis and Philemon.* Carolrhoda, 1981.

———. *The Story of Cadmus.* Carolrhoda, 1980.

———. *The Story of King Midas.* Carolrhoda, 1981.

———. *Theseus and the Road to Athens.* Carolrhoda, 1981.

Evslin, Bernard. *The Greek Gods.* Scholastic, 1984.

———. *Heroes and Monsters of Greek Myth.* Scholastic, 1984.

Gates, Doris. *A Fair Wind for Troy.* Penguin, 1984.

———. *The Golden God: Apollo.* Penguin, 1983.

———. *Lord of the Sky: Zeus.* Penguin, 1982.

———. *Mightiest of Mortals: Heracles.* Penguin, 1984.

———. *Two Queens of Heaven: Aphrodite and Demeter.* Penguin, 1983.

———. *The Warrior Goddess: Athena.* Penguin, 1982.

Green, Richard. *Myths of the Norsemen.* Penguin, 1970.

Green, Roger. *Tales of Greek Heroes.* Penguin, 1974.

Hadley, Eric and Hadley, Tessa. *Legends of Earth, Air, Fire, and Water.* Cambridge University, 1985.

Hamilton, Edith. *Mythology.* Little, 1942.

Hutton, Warwick. *Theseus and the Minotaur.* Macmillan, 1989.

McDermott, Gerald. *Daughter of Earth: A Roman Myth.* Delacorte, 1984.

———. *Sun Flight.* Four Winds, 1980.

McKissack, Patricia and McKissack, Fredrick. *King Midas and His Gold.* Childrens, 1986.

Price, Margaret. *A Child's Book of Myths and Enchantment Tales.* Checkerboard, 1987.

World Book Staff. *Great Myths and Legends.* World Book, 1984.

Poetry

Aiken, Joan. "Apollo and Daphne" from *The Skin Spinners.* Viking, 1976.

Parker, Elinor. *Echoes of the Sea.* Scribners, 1977.
    Campion, T. "In Praise of Neptune."
    Farjeon, Eleanor. "Neptune."

A Sound from the Earth

Rationale

A theme based on characters from novels who are Native Americans quickly and obviously becomes a social studies unit, or at least brings into focus social studies material learned earlier. Because the Native Americans have been treated so poorly throughout this country's history, novels dealing with their plight sometimes make others feel more deeply about the injustices than can more objective views.

Picture Book Starter

☐ Miles, Miska. *Annie and the Old One.* Little, 1971.

Annie's grandmother, the Old One, has said that when the rug that is now on the loom is finished, she will go back to the earth. Annie can't bear to think that her grandmother will die, so she sets about seeing that the rug will not be finished. First, she carefully removes each thread her grandmother has woven each day. Later, she causes trouble at school so that her grandmother will not have time to weave. Her grandmother is wise as well as old, however, and she soon realizes what Annie is doing. She takes Annie to the top of the hill and shows her the sunset, which must happen for each sunrise. Together they go down the hill to face what will happen.

☐ Martin, Bill, Jr and Archambault, John. *Knots on a Counting Rope.* Holt, 1987.

A grandfather passes on the family's history to a blind Native American boy.

Bulletin Board

☐ On a map of the United States, mark each state, city, or landmark with a Native American name. Around the map, display the children's illustrations of homes or costumes of an area's Native American tribes. Use strings, ribbons, or beads to connect the illustrations to the correct area.

Museum

☐ Display Native American artifacts, models, and replicas, carefully labeled.

Discussions, Projects, and Activities

☐ Get in your time machine and take a trip across America in 1790. List the names of each tribe whose land you would pass through.

☐ Research one particular tribe: its customs, language, housing, costume, and history.

☐ Native Americans in the past reared their children differently than did most whites. What were the main differences? Are there still differences?

☐ List Native American foods that are part of most American's diets.

☐ Find out about the forced marches that Native Americans had to endure. Why did white people make them leave their homes? What was the justification?

☐ List Native American names of towns, cities, rivers, and other landmarks in your area.

☐ Find out what happened to the Native Americans who live(d) in your area.

☐ Visit a reservation. Find out why many Native Americans still choose to live there.

☐ Write to children on a reservation.

Books

Fiction

Baker, Betty. *Walk the World's Rim.* Harper, 1965.

■■■■■■■□□□□□□

During the sixteenth century, Chakho, a Native American boy, travels from Texas to Mexico with two Spanish explorers and a Black slave.

Baker, Olaf. *Where the Buffaloes Begin.* Warne, 1981.

■■■■■■□□□□□□□

Little Wolf, a ten-year-old Native American boy, is fascinated by a tribal legend about a sacred spot where the buffaloes were said to have begun. The Native Americans' reverence for the buffalo and for all things of nature is a key point in this beautiful book.

Benchley, Nathaniel. *Only Earth and Sky Last Forever.* Harper, 1972.

■■■■■■■■■■■□□□

Dark Elk joins Crazy Horse's troops to prove himself worthy of Lashuka. After the Battle of Little Big Horn, Dark Elk helps pursue Major Reno and his men.

Goble, Paul. *Buffalo Woman.* Bradbury, 1984.

■■■■□□□□□□□□□□

A buffalo becomes a beautiful woman before the eyes of a great hunter. Sent to him because of his goodness, the woman is to strengthen the ties between the Native American and the buffalo. They marry and have a son, Calf Boy, but the tribe rejects the woman and her son.

Hamilton, Virginia. *Arilla Sun Down.* Greenwillow, 1976.

■■■■■■■■■■■□□□

Arilla, a child with both Black and Native American heritage, has trouble finding her own special talent in her very talented family.

Highwater, Jamake. *Legend Days.* Harper, 1984.

■■■■■■■■■■□□□

Amana sees the buffalo disappearing and her tribe succumbing to white traders, settlers, and governmental regulations. When smallpox strikes, she is told to hide. While in hiding, she has a vision filling her with power and the song of the fox.

O'Dell, Scott. *Island of the Blue Dolphins.* Houghton, 1960.

■■■■■■■□□□□□□□

See page 9.

———. *Sing Down the Moon.* Houghton, 1970.

■■■■■■■□□□□□□□

This is the story of the Navajo's forced "Long Walk" from their homes in the canyons to Fort Sumner where they were held as prisoners for two years. During that time more than fifteen hundred Navajos died. Bright Morning and her husband, Tall Boy, escape and return to the canyon.

———. *Streams to the River, River to the Sea: a Novel of Sacagawea.* Houghton, 1986.

■■■■■■■■□□□□□□

The Shoshone woman who interpreted for the Lewis and Clark expedition narrates, beginning with her capture by the Minnetarees, her marriage to the French trader Toussaint Charbonneau, and the birth of a child before Lewis and Clark arrived.

Rockwood, Joyce. *Groundhog's Horse.* Holt, 1978.

■■■■■■■■□□□□□□

Groundhog's horse Midnight is stolen by the Creeks. His Cherokee tribe refuses to fight for the horse, because they believe that it's a taunting gesture and that one horse isn't worth the risk. Groundhog resolves to get his horse back. The book is especially recommended because of its lack of stereotypes.

Thayer, Marjorie. *Climbing Sun: The Story of a Hopi Indian Boy.* Dodd, 1980.

■■■■■■■□□□□□□□

This is a fictionalized version of the life of a real Hopi whose Anglicized name is Hubert. Sent away to an Indian School in 1928, he is forced to abandon his language and his customs and adopt the white man's ways.

Wolf, Bernard. *Tinker and the Medicine Man: The Story of a Navajo Boy of Monument Valley.* Random, 1973.

■■■■■■■■□□□□□□

This is a simple and serious photodocumentary about a boy who wants to become a medicine man and peyote chief like his father.

Wood, Nancy. *Many Winters: Prose and Poetry of the Pueblos.* Doubleday, 1974.

■■■■■■■■■■■□□□

These are the "old people," the Anasazi, who speak in prose and poetry and reflect on the past.

Nonfiction

Freedman, Russell. *Indian Chiefs.* Holiday, 1987.

■■■■■■□□□□□□□□

Around 1840, Native American leaders made difficult choices about fighting the increasing numbers of white settlers or yielding to their greater numbers and more sophisticated weapons. These are the photos and words of the great leaders.

Fritz, Jean. *The Double Life of Pocahontas.* Putnam, 1983.

■■■■■■□□□□□□□□

This is another of Jean Fritz's longer biographies for children. As always, she brings the character to life without fictionalizing history. We see Pocahontas as the young Native American princess who at first delights in her role as emissary between her people's world and that of the new settlers. (See page 112.)

Kelly, Lawrence C. *Federal Indian Policy.* Chelsea House, 1989.

■■■■■■■■■■■□□□

Here is a look at some of the unfair and inhumane treatment of many Native Americans by the United States government.

Poetry

Larrick, Nancy. *Room for Me and a Mountain Lion.* Evans, 1974.

Lindsay, Vachel. "The Flower-Fed Buffaloes."

Stafford, William. "A Sound from the Earth."

Livingston, Myra Cohn. "Indians of the Plains" from *Worlds I Know and Other Poems,* edited by Nancy Larrick. Atheneum, 1983.

Welcome to the Neighborhood

Rationale

Examining fictional neighborhoods might lead young readers to take a closer look at their own neighborhoods as sources of stories. The interplay among fictional neighbors allows the reader to examine characters in their context.

Picture Book Starter

☐ Blos, Joan. *Old Henry.* Morrow, 1987.

Henry likes the deserted old house. It suits him just fine. The neighbors are pleased because they think he'll fix up the house, but Henry has no intention of fixing anything. He likes it just the way it is. The neighbors begin to exert pressure on him and Henry moves away. Then the neighbors have an empty dilapidated old house and they miss him. They eventually compromise.

Bulletin Board

☐ Divide the board into sections and have the children place buildings and houses in each section to represent a neighborhood different from theirs: country, inner city, suburb, old-time town.

Museum

☐ Display photographs from as many kinds of neighborhoods as possible.

Discussions, Projects, and Activities

☐ Talk about what your neighbors expect of your family. What makes a neighborhood? Where does yours begin and end?

☐ What happens in your neighborhood when someone dies or is in trouble?

☐ What games do you play in your neighborhood?

☐ How do you feel about neighborhood gangs? Are there gangs in your neighborhood? Are they good or bad?

☐ Read the poems about neighborhoods in Jack Prelutsky's *New Kid on the Block* (Greenwillow, 1984).

☐ Without looking, try to describe each building on your street or block. How many families in those buildings do you know? How many buildings did you leave out?

☐ Find out about neighborhoods in your city or town. Is one part of town considered better than another to live in? Why? What could change that?

☐ Investigate such expressions as: Good fences make good neighbors. There goes the neighborhood. Good neighbor policy. Not in my backyard.

☐ Plan and carry out a project to make your neighborhood a little better.

☐ Switch the neighborhoods in two of the suggested books. How would that affect the plots?

☐ Defend the advantages of your neighborhood.

☐ Write an ad to sell a house in your neighborhood.

☐ Go to City Hall and get a topographical map of your neighborhood. Draw in the houses and buildings.

☐ Find out about the architecture of your neighborhood. Take pictures of interesting parts of some of the houses and other buildings.

☐ Find out which are the newest and oldest buildings in your neighborhood and compare them.

☐ Design an ideal neighborhood.

Books

Fiction

Angell, Judie. *A Home Is to Share and Share and Share.* Bradbury, 1984.

■■■■■■☐☐☐☐☐☐

See page 8.

Bunting, Eve. *Is Anybody There?* Lippincott, 1988.

■■■■■■☐☐☐☐☐☐

See page 45.

Cohen, Peter Zachary. *Deadly Game at Stone Creek.* Dial, 1978.

■■■■■■■■☐☐☐☐

When the Brookings family moves to a farm twenty-five miles from town, Cliff is disappointed that he won't be able to play baseball in the summer leagues. When Karla, a young neighbor, is badly injured by a pack of wild dogs, Cliff risks his baseball career to help.

Levy, Elizabeth. *Frankenstein Moved In on the Fourth Floor.* Harper, 1979.

■■□□□□□□□□□□□

See page 25.

Lisle, Janet Taylor. *Afternoon of the Elves.* Orchard, 1989.

■■■■■■■■■□□□□□

The backyards of the two girls are joined, but the contrast between them is stark. Hillary's is trimmed, neat, and full of carefully tended plants; Sara-Kate's is wild, full of poison ivy and junk. However, it's in her yard that the elf village appears. Hillary thinks Sara-Kate might be an elf until she discovers Sara-Kate's desperate situation. (See page 92.)

Lowry, Lois. *Autumn Street.* Houghton, 1980.

■■■■■■■□□□□□□□

Here's life at home, in this case Philadelphia, during World War II. Elizabeth, her sister, and pregnant mother live with her grandparents while her father is fighting in the Pacific. Their next-door neighbors are viewed with suspicion because of their German heritage. There is racial prejudice and even murder in this taut, memorable book.

Myers, Walter Dean. *Mojo and the Russians.* Viking, 1977.

■■■■■■■□□□□□□□

There are Russian diplomats in the neighborhood and the gang in Harlem needs to know why they are there. The interplay between the gang members is what is important in this novel.

———. *The Mouse Rap.* Harper, 1990.

■■■■■■■■■■□□□□

See page 39.

Polseno, Jo. *This Hawk Belongs to Me.* McKay, 1977.

■■■■■■■□□□□□□□

Dino De Angelo knows everyone in his neighborhood. Indeed, most of his neighbors are related to him. With his cousin, Dino frequently skips school to wander around a wildlife refuge on Long Island. It is there that Dino discovers an abandoned kestrel. Helping the kestrel live means keeping it wild and ultimately setting it free.

Snyder, Zilpha Keatley. *The Egypt Game.* Atheneum, 1967.

■■■■■■■■■□□□□□

See page 47.

Talbot, Charlene Joy. *The Sodbuster Venture.* Atheneum, 1982.

■■■■■■■□□□□□□□

Thirteen-year-old Maud is keeping house for Silas Newton until his fiancée Belle arrives. Unfortunately, Silas dies, leaving Maud and Belle to survive on their own, fighting their no-account neighbors who want to lay claim to the land.

Winthrop, Elizabeth. *Belinda's Hurricane.* Dutton, 1984.

■■■■■□□□□□□□□□

When a hurricane threatens, Belinda gets a chance to know her grandmother's reclusive neighbor.

Zimelman, Nathan. *Mean Chickens and Wild Cucumbers.* Macmillan, 1983.

■■□□□□□□□□□□□□

There's a hole in the fence dividing the property of two neighbors. When one neighbor's mean chicken pecks the second neighbor through the hole in the fence and the second neighbor's cucumber vine tweaks the nose of the first through the same hole, a fence war begins. Each man is determined to build a higher fence than the other.

This Land Is Your Land

Rationale

Because the people of history are of more interest to us than dates and military maneuvers, the characters in many children's historical novels create interest in a period. Investigating the pioneer spirit can make for good reading and good writing.

Picture Book Starter

☐ Harvey, Brett. *Cassie's Journey: Going West in the 1860's.* Holiday, 1988.

This picture book is based on the actual accounts of journeys by covered wagon to the Midwest.

Bulletin Board

☐ Display pictures of pioneer homes, vehicles, tools, and foods.

Museum

☐ Display Early American tools and furniture or replicas.

Discussions, Projects, and Activities

☐ Find out about the Homestead Act and what it did to open up new settlements.
☐ Find out about treaties the United States made with the Indians. Did we honor the treaties?
☐ Find out what happened to the Native American tribes who originally lived on the land that is now most populated.
☐ Sing some of the songs the settlers sang.
☐ Hold a square dance and dress as pioneers.
☐ Make models of the homes used by pioneers.
☐ Find out which of our presidents were pioneers.
☐ Find out about gold and silver rushes.
☐ Find out what the pioneers read.
☐ Listen to the music from the Broadway musical *Oklahoma.*
☐ Listen to "Mail Order Annie" by Harry Chapin.
☐ Make a quilt of paper or cloth using the patterns used by pioneers.
☐ Make butter the way pioneers did it.
☐ Get raw wool, prepare it, spin it into yarn using a spindle, dye it, and weave it into cloth.
☐ Find out what games the pioneer children played and play them.
☐ Make cornhusk dolls.

Books

Fiction

Brenner, Barbara. *Wagon Wheels.* Harper, 1978.

Johnny moves with his family from Kentucky to Kansas in the 1870s. There they join the Black community of Nicodemus, Kansas, where Johnny is left to care for his younger brothers while their father goes in search of better land.

Brink, Carol Ryrie. *Caddie Woodlawn.* Macmillan, 1973.

Caddie has been allowed to be a tomboy, riding around on the Wisconsin frontier in search of adventure and challenge. Now trouble with the Native Americans makes Caddie rely on her friendship with one of them to save the settlement.

Collier, James and Collier, Christopher. *The Bloody Country.* Four Winds, 1977.

After the Revolution, Ben Buck and Joe Mountain and their families become part of the Susquehanna Company settling Pennsylvania. The Bucks operate a mill there. After Native American uprisings and a devastating flood, many of the settlers decide to return to Connecticut. After a quarrel with Joe, who is Black and considered a slave by some, Ben leads the settlers back to Connecticut. Ben returns to make the permanent settlement in Pennsylvania near what is now Wilkes-Barre.

Conrad, Pam. *Prairie Songs.* Harper, 1985.

Louisa loves the prairie and so does her father. Her mother seems to have adjusted to it. When the Doctor and Mrs. Berryman arrive, Mrs. Berryman faints when she sees the sod hut she will live in. Louisa tries to get her to see the beauty of the prairie, but Emmeline Berryman misses the city and its refinements. (See page 147.)

Moeri, Louise. *Save Queen of Sheba.* Dutton, 1981.

■■■■■■■■■■□□□□

A twelve-year-old boy and his sister are the only survivors of an attack by Native Americans and must travel to Oregon for help from other settlers.

St. George, Judith. *The Halo Wind.* Putnam, 1978.

■■■■■■■■■■□□□□

This story chronicles the trials of the Oregon Trail as experienced by the Thatcher family, particularly by thirteen-year-old Ella Jane Thatcher and Yvette, a Native American girl about the same age. Ella Jane's aim is to get to the West; Yvette's is to save her people's land from the white settlers.

Talbot, Charlene Joy. *An Orphan for Nebraska.* Atheneum, 1979.

■■■■■■■■□□□□□□

Kevin is sent with other orphans to work on the new farms in Nebraska. The last of the lot to be chosen, Kevin ends up working on a newspaper.

Poetry
Frost, Robert. "The Gift Outright." Available in many collections.
Gildner, G. "Comanche" from *The Poetry of Horses,* edited by William Cole. Scribners, 1979.
Plotz, Helen. *The Gift Outright.* Greenwillow, 1977.
    Berryman, J. "Minnesota Thanksgiving."
    Bishop, J. P. "The Spare Quilt."
    Heyen, W. "The Trail Beside the River Platte."
Sandburg, Carl. "Buffalo Dusk." Available in many collections.
Whitman, Walt. "Night on the Prairie" from *Room for Me and a Mountain Lion: Poetry of Open Space,* edited by Nancy Larrick. Evans, 1974.

Music
"Little Old Sod Shanty" from *Cowboy and Western Songs,* edited by Austin Fife. Potter, 1969.
"Starving to Death on a Government Claim" from *Best Loved American Folk Songs,* edited by John Lomax. Grosset, 1947.
"Sweet Betsy from Pike." Available in many collections.
Walt Disney Productions. "The Ballad of Davy Crockett" from *The Walt Disney Songbook.* Golden, 1971.
"When I First Came to This Land" from *Favorite American Ballads,* edited by Pete Seeger. Oak, 1961.

Quests and Voyages

Rationale

Searching for treasure of one kind or another is an old theme. Although the theme is obvious in some stories, it is more subtle in others. As readers identify the quest and see how the author develops characters and presents obstacles, they might develop the same techniques in their own writing.

Picture Book Starter

☐ Snyder, Zilpha Keatley. *The Changing Maze.* Atheneum, 1985.

An evil king built a maze designed to change constantly. Not only does the maze change, it changes those who dare enter it. Hugh, a young shepherd, dreads the maze but enters it to find his lost lamb. He finds the lamb at the center of the maze but is diverted by a magical chest of gold. Only his love for the lamb keeps him from the chest's evil.

Bulletin Board

☐ On a world map, have the children trace the routes of real and fantasy quests.

Museum

☐ Display a collection of articles that might be in a treasure chest. Choose the articles carefully so they represent a worthwhile quest for each member of the class.

Discussions, Projects, and Activities

☐ Find out about famous quests such as the search for the Titanic, the quest of the Challenger crew, the search for the Holy Grail, the search for the source of the Nile River, the quest to break world records.

☐ Analyze the quest in a novel. Who was searching? What did he/she want? Who or what hindered the search? Was the seeker successful?

☐ Create a short quest story of your own.

☐ Read and tell some tales of King Arthur.

Books

Fiction

Adams, Richard. *Watership Down.* Avon, 1976.

■■■■■■■■■■■■☐

A small group of rabbits leaves their warren to journey to a safe place to establish a new warren. Along the way, they encounter hardships from farm equipment, dogs, wild animals, and other rabbits. (See page 167.)

Babbitt, Natalie. *The Search for Delicious.* Farrar, 1969.

■■■■■■■☐☐☐☐☐☐

Written in fairy tale style, this story concerns a conflict between a king and a queen over the meaning of delicious. Gayland, a young boy, goes out to find out what the people of the kingdom think but is hindered by Hemlock, who cuts off the water supply to each town. Gayland leaves a trail of bickering people everywhere he goes, which helps Hemlock in his attempt to overthrow the king.

Burnford, Sheila. *The Incredible Journey.* Little, 1961.

■■■■■■■☐☐☐☐☐☐

See page 9.

Disch, Thomas M. *The Brave Little Toaster.* Doubleday, 1986.

■■■■■☐☐☐☐☐☐☐☐

A group of appliances abandoned in a summer cottage set out to find their master. The smaller appliances ride on a chair pulled by the vacuum cleaner. They survive all sorts of perils before reaching their goal.

Fleischman, Sid. *By the Great Horn Spoon.* Little, 1953.

■■■■■□□□□□□□□□

To regain the family fortune, an orphaned boy and the family butler stow away on a vessel sailing around the Horn at the height of the gold rush. They are beset with problems and perils before reaching their goal and then losing it.

George, Jean C. *Julie of the Wolves.* Harper, 1972.

■■■■■■■■■■■■■□

Julie, whose Eskimo name is Miyax, is on the tundra where her survival depends on her ability to get a wolf pack to adopt her. She is attempting to reach her pen pal in San Francisco but is unsure whether her happiness lies in forsaking or embracing her Eskimo heritage. (See page 128.)

Hoban, Russell. *The Mouse and His Child.* Harper, 1967.

■■■■■□□□□□□□□□

A wind-up mouse child and father go off in search of happiness armed only with their own courage and love for each other.

Holling, Holling C. *Paddle-to-the-Sea.* Houghton, 1941.

■■■■□□□□□□□□□□

A Native American boy carves a tiny canoe and sets it free to travel to the sea. It survives the journey.

McGraw, Eloise Jarvis. *The Money Room.* Atheneum, 1981.

■■■■■■■■□□□□□□

See page 39.

Paulsen, Gary. *The Voyage of the Frog.* Orchard, 1989.

■■■■■■■■■■□□□□

David Alspeth sets out on a small sailboat, the Frog, to spread the ashes of his favorite uncle. He has food and water but does not check the weather forecast. When a sudden storm comes up, David is hit by the boom and knocked unconscious. He comes to in time to save the boat, but he is far off course. (See page 166.)

Smith, Doris Buchanan. *Voyages.* Viking, 1989.

■■■■■■■■□□□□□□

Janessa is immobilized because of an accident. One day she happens on the key to another world where she is running free. Is it her imagination or the path to reality?

Winthrop, Elizabeth. *The Castle in the Attic.* Bantam, 1985.

■■■■■□□□□□□□□□

William's friend and housekeeper, Mrs. Phillips, gives him a castle as a parting gift. The castle has been in her family for generations and is realistically detailed. In order to keep Mrs. Phillips with him, William miniaturizes her and puts her in the castle. Then he must miniaturize himself to save Mrs. Phillips.

Rebels and Redcoats

Rationale

Conflict creates a good story and our country's conflict with England has been the subject of many. Historical novels can make a period of history seem more real than factual history texts are sometimes able to do.

Picture Book Starter

☐ Fritz, Jean. *And Then What Happened, Paul Revere?* Coward, 1973.

Although not strictly a picture book, this is a short history of Paul Revere, concentrating on his eventful ride. It makes a good introduction to this period in history because it is historically correct and Ms. Fritz breathes life into heroes of our past in a way that few writers are able to do. This book in particular gives us a sense of what Boston must have been like during that turbulent time. Because "that's where it all began," let's start our Revolutionary War theme there as well.

☐ ———. *Can't You Make Them Behave, King George?* Coward, 1977.

We watch the America Revolution from the King's point of view. The humor is considerable but based on fact.

Bulletin Board

☐ Post a map of the Thirteen Colonies. Around the edges of the map, place pictures of characters from books about the Revolution. Use arrows pointing to the areas where the characters lived.

Museum

☐ Dress dolls in Revolutionary War costumes.

Discussions, Projects, and Activities

☐ Find out what, if anything, the people in your town or part of the country were doing during the Revolutionary War.

☐ Compare our revolution to any that are now going on in the world or that have taken place recently. Were the causes the same? What was the outcome? How did other countries react?

☐ Investigate the clothing and music of the time.

☐ Hold a meeting like those held by the Sons of Liberty.

☐ Divide the class into two groups and argue for and against the revolution.

☐ Reenact the Boston Tea Party.

☐ Read a biography of one of the people alive at the time of the American Revolution. What did he/she do during the Revolution?

☐ Read a nonfiction book about the area or time of the Revolution.

☐ Keep a chart such as the one below.

Book Title
Setting
Main Character
Problem
Historical Figures/Events

Books

Fiction

Avi. *The Fighting Ground.* Lippincott, 1984.

■■■■■■■■■□□□□□

This is an account of two days in a boy's life during the American Revolution. Captured in battle by three Hessian soldiers, Jonathan realizes that fighting is a complex adult activity and that informed choices are extremely important. Jonathan is taken by the Hessians to a farmhouse where a little boy is the only survivor of his family. Jonathan finds that he can't kill the sleeping Hessians, so he escapes with the little boy and finds the remnants of the troop he was with in battle. Realizing that the troop must have killed the boy's parents, Jonathan smashes a rifle and heads back to the farm, sadder and less certain about the rights and wrongs of war.

Collier, James and Collier, Christopher. *Jump Ship to Freedom.* Delacorte, 1981.

■■■■■■■■■■■■■□

See page 39.

———. *My Brother Sam Is Dead.* Scholastic, 1977.

■■■■■■■■■■■■■□

Sam is the only member of his family who is not a Tory and he's joined the rebelling army. Falsely accused of stealing cattle, his family's sympathies work against him and he is tried and executed as an example of General Putnam's discipline.

Edwards, Sally. *George Midgett's War.* Macmillan, 1985.

■■■■■■■■■□□□□

The people of Ocracoke Island, off the coast of North Carolina, want no part of the war. Then British Raiders kill the deaf-mute woman who tends their pigs and carry off the pigs. The islanders get their revenge.

Fast, Howard. *April Morning.* Crown, 1961.

■■■■■■■■■■□□□

This is a first person account of April 19, 1776, at the battle of Lexington and Concord. The fifteen-year-old boy who narrates it sees his father shot in the first exchange of gunfire. He flees only to fight back as the Redcoats return to Boston. The horrors of war are graphically portrayed.

Forbes, Esther. *Johnny Tremain.* Houghton, 1943.

■■■■■■■■■■■■□

Johnny Tremain is a silversmith's apprentice in Boston. Another apprentice, jealous of Johnny's skill, causes him to be terribly burned with molten silver. Johnny must look for other work because of his shriveled hand. As a rider for the *Boston Observer,* Johnny becomes interested in the Revolution and participates in the Boston Tea Party and other revolutionary acts. He also learns to accept himself, scars and all.

Fritz, Jean. *Early Thunder.* Coward, 1967.

■■■■■■■■□□□□□

Daniel is a Loyalist, sharing his father's fealty to the King. The Liberty Boys harass the Tories, which strengthens Daniel's feelings until he sees the equal injustices of the British soldiers.

———. *Traitor: The Case of Benedict Arnold.* Putnam, 1981.

■■■■■■□□□□□□□

This is a biography of the man whose name has become synonymous with the word *traitor.* Here is his flamboyant life from his boyhood to his death. (See page 161.)

Gauch, Patricia Lee. *This Time, Tempe Wick?* Coward, 1974.

■■□□□□□□□□□□□

Based on legend, this is the story of a young girl who kept her horse from the Continental Army by hiding it in her bedroom for three days.

Jensen, Dorothea. *The Riddle of Penncroft Farm.* Harcourt, 1989.

■■■■■■■■□□□□□

When Lars moves from his home in Minnesota to Pennsylvania, he is contacted by the ghost of one of his ancestors who gives him the inside story of the Revolution, especially his days at Valley Forge.

O'Dell, Scott. *Sarah Bishop.* Scholastic, 1980.

■■■■■■■■■■■■□

Sarah's father, a Loyalist, was tarred and feathered by the rebels and died. Sarah is arrested as part of the harassment but escapes to survive in the Connecticut wilderness.

Snow, Richard. *Freelon Starbird: Being a Narrative of the Extraordinary Hardships Suffered by an Accidental Soldier in a Beaten Army During the Autumn and Winter of 1776.* Houghton, 1976.

■■■■■■■■■■■■■□

Freelon and his friend volunteered for the army while slightly drunk and found that the Pennsylvania Militia was in a terrible fix. They were up against a well-equipped, well-trained British army and nearly starved or froze to death. The attack on Trenton is a surprising victory.

Wibberly, Leonard. *John Treegate's Musket.* Farrar, 1959.

■■■■■■■■■■■■■□

John Treegate is a Loyalist who fought for the king at the Battle of Quebec. Changing sides is easier for his son, Peter, who quickly joins the Revolutionary forces. John defects just in time for the Battle of Bunker Hill.

Nonfiction
Carter, Alden R. *The American Revolution: At the Forge of Liberty.* Watts, 1988.

Here we begin with the Continental Army's arrival at Philadelphia in 1777 and end when the Revolution does in 1783.

———. *The American Revolution: Birth of the Republic.* Watts, 1988.

This book covers the last days of the Revolution and the forging of the new government.

———. *The American Revolution: Colonies in Revolt.* Watts, 1988.

Beginning with the death of an eleven-year-old boy in the streets of Boston and continuing to full-fledged war, this book uses maps, paintings, lithographs, and a clear text to tell the story.

———. *The American Revolution: The Darkest Hours.* Watts, 1988.

This book begins with the call-to-arms at Concord and ends with the destruction of Burgoyne's army at Saratoga.

Fritz, Jean. *Shh! We're Writing the Constitution.* Putnam, 1987.

The trouble isn't over just because the Revolution is. Representatives must write a constitution that will satisfy each representative from every state. As usual, Ms. Fritz's text is historically accurate and she includes the human details that make us care. The book contains a copy of the Constitution.

Poetry
Benet, Stephen Vincent and Benet, Rosemary. *Book of Americans.* Holt, 1984.

Emerson, Ralph Waldo. "Concord Hymn." Available in many collections.

Hayden, R. "Crispus Attucks" from *Celebrations,* edited by Arnold Adoff. Follet, 1977.

Longfellow, Henry Wadsworth. "Paul Revere's Ride." Available in many collections.

Sandburg, Carl. "Washington's Monument by Night." Available in many collections.

Music
Silber, Irwin. *Songs of Independence.* Stackpole, 1973.

It Could Happen Someday

Rationale

The line between fantasy and science fiction is a thin one. In general, science fiction is supposed to deal with things that might someday be possible and fantasy deals with things that can never happen. Speculating on the human condition in future times or in other worlds can make interesting fiction and spirited discussion.

Picture Book Starter

☐ Yorinks, Arthur. *Company's Coming.* Crown, 1988.

Two outer-space creatures land their spaceship at a suburban home. Their first request is for a bathroom, which makes sense, doesn't it? After that there are the wonders of suburbia to explore.

Bulletin Board

☐ Display articles about space exploration and UFOs and about ecological problems and advances in technology. Also include children's illustrations of scenes from the suggested books.

Museum

☐ Provide materials for building robots: boxes, foil, colored paper, paints, markers, nuts, bolts.

Discussions, Projects, and Activities

☐ Separate the novels into categories of science fiction. In what major ways are they different?
☐ Find the planet in our solar system that could hold a life form and design a civilization for it. Design life forms and space travel equipment for them.
☐ Diagram time/space machines.
☐ Take one of the problems our society has today and design a science fiction solution or a science fiction ending for it.
☐ Watch an episode of *Star Trek* or a *Star Trek* movie. Compare it to any of the novels suggested.
☐ Decide which of the suggested novels is most believable and why.
☐ Identify the weakest point in any of the novels. How could the author have overcome this?

Books

Fiction

Asimov, Janet and Asimov, Isaac. *Norby and Yobo's Great Adventure.* Walker, 1989.

■■■■■■■■□□□□□□

Norby is a robot capable of transporting himself and his companions through time. His usual companion is Jeff Wells, but this time they take Admiral Boris Yobo with them in order to trace an heirloom: a mysterious, carved ivory tusk.

Christopher, John. *The City of Gold and Lead.* Macmillan, 1967.

■■■■■■■■■■□□□

This is the second book of the Tripods Trilogy. The battle against the Tripods comes closer as the boys take part in an athletic contest, in which the winners have the privilege of serving the Tripods.

———. *Empty World.* Dutton, 1978.

■■■■■■■■■■□□□

The Calcutta plague causes its victims to rapidly age and die. The plague quickly spreads worldwide, leaving Neil Miller the only person alive in his area. After traveling to London, he finds and moves in with two girls whose personalities are almost opposite. Neil and Lucy fall in love and Billie tries to kill him.

———. *Fireball.* Dutton, 1981.

■■■■■■■■■■□□□

Transported by a supernatural fireball to a parallel England, Simon and his American cousin, Brad, find themselves in a civilizaton modeled on ancient Rome.

———. *The Guardians.* Macmillan, 1970.

■■■■■■■■■■■□□□

In 2052, England is divided into two societies, and a thirteen-year-old boy rebels against customs.

———. *The Pool of Fire.* Macmillan, 1968.

■■■■■■■■■■■□□□

This is the third book in the Tripods Trilogy. Here we have the defeat of the Tripods as Will and the other boys work with a group of people who are striving for world peace.

———. *The White Mountains.* Macmillan, 1967.

■■■■■■■■■■■□□□

This is the first book in the Tripods Trilogy. In the twenty-first century, people are happy and well cared for. Three boys rebel against the thing that seems to assure their happiness: being capped at the age of fourteen. Creatures called Tripods rule the planet and the boys decide to escape their domination by hiding out in the White Mountains where they discover free people.

Dereske, Jo. *The Lone Sentinel.* Atheneum, 1989.

■■■■■■■□□□□□□□

Erik is a guard on the remote planet Azure and is visited by humans and other alien beings.

Dickinson, Peter. *The Weathermonger.* Little, 1969.

■■■■■■■■■■■□□□

In the near future, the state of feudalism has returned to England. Any mechanical object is forbidden and weather is controlled by magic. Geoffrey escapes to France and then returns to seek the cause of the enchantment.

Engdahl, Sylvia. *Enchantress from the Stars.* Atheneum, 1970.

■■■■■■■■■□□□□□

On the planet Andrecia, the medieval culture is in danger from invaders with an advanced technology. Elana, the narrator, is sent with her family from their highly advanced society with psychic powers and technology to help the natives repel the invaders without revealing their true identity.

———. *This Star Shall Abide.* Atheneum, 1979.

■■■■■■■■□□□□□□

Noren resents being kept from knowledge because of religious taboos on his distant planet. The rural society is governed by Scholars who live in the Inner City and the Technicians who serve them. Noren is determined to enter the Inner City where he is captured and given the opportunity to repent.

Hoover, H. M. *The Delikon.* Viking, 1977.

■■■■■■■■■■■□□□

Varina, a teacher on Delikon, and the two humans she is tutoring become caught up in the revolution of Earthlings against Delikon.

———. *Orvis.* Viking, 1987.

■■■■■■■■■■■□□□

Earth has lost most of its population. Most Terrans live in space ships or colonies. Toby is attending an Earth school and likes it. Her grandmother has decided she'd be better off in a school on Mars. Toby, her friend Thaddeus, and an old robot named Orvis decide to visit her great-grand-mother near Lake Erie.

Karl, Jean. *Beloved Benjamin Is Waiting.* Dutton, 1978.

■■■■■■■□□□□□□□

Lucinda was abandoned by her parents so she takes up residence in a cemetery where something or someone talks to her through the statue of a dead boy. When it turns out that the "something" is a delegation from another galaxy, Lucinda enlightens the space visitors while they, in turn, help her. (See page 97.)

———. *The Turning Place: Stories of a Future Past.* Dutton, 1976.

■■■■■■■□□□□□□□

Each of these short stories deals with a different character after an alien-designed holocaust that causes everyone left on Earth to start over.

Sleator, William. *The Boy Who Reversed Himself.* Dutton, 1986.

■■■■■■■■■■■□□□

When Laura discovers that the unpopular boy living next door can transport himself into the fourth dimension, she decides to go with him. The danger they confront is real and the characters they meet are unusual, to say the least.

———. *House of Stairs.* Dutton, 1974.

■■■■■■■■■■■■■□

Five teenagers are placed against their will in a house with endless stairs where they must take part in psychological experiments.

———. *Strange Attractors.* Dutton, 1990.

■■■■■■■■■■■□□□

When Max wakes up after passing out in Dr. Sylvan's laboratory, he finds himself being chased by two identical teams of fathers and daughters who are after the phaser, a device that can transport objects and humans through time.

Townsend, John Rowe. *Noah's Castle.* Lippincott, 1976.

■■■■■■■■■■□□□□

The world is now so short of food that people commit acts of violence in order to get it. The narrator, Barry, is confused when his father buys a huge house and turns it into a fortress. When his father refuses to admit visitors or share the provisions, Barry joins ranks with a food share group.

———. *The Visitors.* Lippincott, 1977.

■■■■■■■■■■□□□□

There are newcomers to the city who seem to be normal tourists, but John and Alan know they are not. They are spies sent from the future to investigate the civilization, and before they are recalled, John's older brother falls in love with one of them.

Walsh, Jill Paton. *The Green Book.* Farrar, 1982.

■■■■■■■■■■□□□□

The brave Earth colony travels for four years to the distant planet Shine to establish a new colony. They've brought seeds and animals and each passenger has been allowed to bring one book. Hopes quickly fade as the vegetation on Shine proves fatal to the Earth rabbits and the seeds won't grow. Food supplies dwindle and people begin to feel that taking the poison pills they brought with them would be better than slow death by starvation.

Gifts from the Sea

Rationale
The sea is a versatile theme that can be a science or social studies unit with very little stretching.

Picture Book Starter
□ McCloskey, Robert. *Burt Dow, Deep Water Man.* Viking, 1947.

This is a tall tale of an encounter between a deep-sea fisherman and a whale and later a pod of whales. Read aloud until Burt is inside the whale and can't figure out how to get out. The children can offer solutions other than the "Pinocchio solution." They can also make up more Burt Dow adventures.

Bulletin Board
□ Let the children create an underwater scene, relating each object on the board to a picture book or novel.

Museum
□ Display articles associated with the sea: shells, tropical fish, claws, seaweed, egg cases, driftwood, lobster traps, and nets.

Discussions, Projects, and Activities
□ Learn and sing some sea chanteys.
□ Sing Raffi's "Baby Beluga."
□ Bring in shells and sort them into categories.
□ Read books about selkies and mermaids and then write a story about one of them.
□ Make models or drawings of as many kinds of ships and boats as possible.
□ Discover differences between a boat and a ship.
□ Learn to tie sailor's knots.
□ List occupations on sea and on land that have to do with ships.
□ Listen to a recording of the songs of whales.
□ Find out which countries still allow whale killing. Why do these people kill whales? What species are endangered? How do you feel about killing whales? If you disapprove, what can you do to help stop it?
□ Find out about real and imaginary pirates.
□ Learn about signal flags and hoist flags that tell about weather or some other event.
□ Find out about sea serpents. Do you believe in them? Why?
□ Find out about real treasures. Bury a treasure and create a treasure map.
□ Write a diary for an explorer.
□ Learn about sea birds or mammals and share your information in the most interesting way you can think of.
□ Draw pictures to show how bathing attire has changed over the years.
□ Hold a clambake or fish fry.
□ Find paintings of the sea and match them to poems about the sea. Create an exhibit.
□ Listen to music about the sea and its creatures. Paint a picture as you listen.
□ Find out about lighthouses. Which were most famous? Make models of lighthouses.
□ What can you do to clean up and protect the sea?
□ Investigate different kinds of ships. Make models or draw pictures of the ships.
□ Find out about famous shipwrecks: the Titanic, the Arizona, the Thresher, the Andrea Dorea.
□ Investigate Atlantis and the Bermuda Triangle. Do you believe they exist? Why?
□ Compare a schooner to a prairie schooner.

Books
Fiction
Beatty, Patricia. *Sarah and Me and the Lady from the Sea.* Morrow, 1989.

■■■■■■□□□□□□□

After the Abbot's fortune is lost, the children and their mother must learn to survive a winter on the Washington peninsula. When a mysterious lady is washed ashore, tied to a mast and unable to speak any identifiable language, they have a mystery to occupy their thoughts and time.

Buck, Pearl S. *The Big Wave.* Harper, 1947.

■■■■■■■■□□□□□

When a tidal wave wipes out Jiya's family and home, he goes up the mountain to live with his friend Kino where it is safe. Kino is horrified when the village rebuilds in the same place.

Chambers, Aidan. *Seal Secret.* Harper, 1981.

■■■■■■□□□□□□□□

On holiday on the coast of Wales, William meets Gwyn, a local boy. When William discovers that Gwyn is going to keep a seal pup, he rescues the pup and takes it to the sea, only to find that the sea is a formidable foe indeed.

Holling, Holling C. *Paddle-to-the-Sea.* Houghton, 1941.

■■■■□□□□□□□□□□

See page 60.

Hunter, Mollie. *The Mermaid Summer.* Harper, 1988.

■■■■■■■■■■■■□□

The people of Scotland know that the mermaid can cause strange things to happen and so they speak well of her. Eric Anderson, however, speaks ill of her and learns his lesson. He must leave or bring misfortune to the village. His granddaughter Anna and her brother Jon match wits with the mermaid to save their grandfather. (See page 137.)

———. *A Stranger Came Ashore.* Harper, 1975.

■■■■■■■■■□□□□□

Finn Learson appears to be a handsome, ship-wrecked sailor. When it becomes clear that he wants to marry Elspeth, Old Da and Elspeth's brother Robbie are convinced that Finn is the Great Selkie come to lure Elspeth to his crystal kingdom under the sea. (See page 156.)

Jarrell, Randall. *The Animal Family.* Pantheon, 1965.

■■■■■■■■■□□□□□

In this haunting book, a hunter hears the song of a mermaid. He watches her, courts her, and then brings her home to learn from her and to teach her. Their family grows as a bear cub, a lynx, and, finally, a baby boy join the animal family.

Kennedy, Richard. *Amy's Eyes.* Harper, 1985.

■■■■■■■■■■□□□□

See page 12.

MacLachlan, Patricia. *Cassie Binegar.* Harper, 1982.

■■■■■■■■□□□□□□

See page 12.

O'Dell, Scott. *Island of the Blue Dolphins.* Houghton, 1960.

■■■■■■■■□□□□□□

See pages 9 and 127.

Paulsen, Gary. *The Voyage of the Frog.* Orchard, 1989.

■■■■■■■■■■□□□□

See pages 60 and 166.

Sperry, Armstrong. *Call It Courage.* Macmillan, 1940.

■■■■■■■■□□□□□□

Mafatu, son of the great chief, is called a coward because he is afraid of the sea. Life on the island in the South Pacific, where courage is the most respected human quality, becomes unbearable for Mafatu. Alone, he sets out to conquer his fear and the sea. (See page 103.)

Weller, Frances Ward. *Riptide.* Philomel, 1990.

■■□□□□□□□□□□□□

See page 8.

Poetry

Aiken, Joan. "The Fisherman Writes a Letter to the Mermaid" from *The Skin Spinners.* Viking, 1976.

Coatsworth, Elizabeth. "The Sea Gull" from *The Poetry Troupe,* edited by Isabel Wilner. Scribners, 1977.

Moore, Lillian. "Until I Saw the Sea" from *A New Treasury of Children's Poetry,* edited by Joanna Cole. Doubleday, 1984.

Parker, Elinor. *Echoes of the Sea.* Scribners, 1977.

Be a Sport!

Rationale

Although sports books tend to be the most frequently circulated books in the library, they are usually factual books consisting mainly of photographs with captions. There's nothing wrong with this type of books; but if they are the children's steady diet, the children are probably unaware of how good a strong sports story can be. This theme can lead some surface readers into better books.

Picture Book Starter

☐ Kuskin, Karla. *The Dallas Titans Get Ready for Bed.* Harper, 1986.

Here we see what happens after the excitement of the big game, even after the locker room television coverage. What we get is a closer look at football gear and clothing than most spectators ever get.

Bulletin Board

☐ Create a time line of sports uniforms.
☐ On a map of the United States, mark the sites of sports halls of fame and the national headquarters for major league baseball, football, hockey, soccer, and basketball. You might want to use helmets or caps as symbols.

Museum

☐ Display collections of sports cards and other sports paraphernalia.

Discussions, Projects, and Activities

☐ Read a sports biography. Then read newspaper and magazine articles about the same person. Decide whether the biography or the periodical accounts is more accurate.
☐ Talk to baseball card collectors. Find out what you can about the cards.
☐ Hold a debate about the Pete Rose incident or other sports scandals.
☐ Put together the best team of all time for baseball, football, basketball, hockey, or soccer.
☐ Hold a debate about the participation of females in sports.
☐ Which sports should be added to the Olympic Games? Which events should be taken out?

☐ Do research about the Olympic Games. Make a display of the most interesting information found.
☐ Imagine you are the owner of a major league team. Pick your players from any team. Keep records on each player. Do you have a winning team?
☐ Compare baseball or football greats of the past to those of today. How is the game different today than it was in the past? Why?
☐ Do dramatic readings of "Casey at the Bat."
☐ Sing "Take Me Out to the Ballgame." Create new versions about other sports.
☐ Put together a sports hall of fame using characters from sports fiction.
☐ Listen to "Put Me in, Coach" by John Fogarty.
☐ Listen to the song "Playing Right Field" by Peter, Paul, and Mary.

Books

Fiction

Baron, Nancy. *Tuesday's Child.* Atheneum, 1984.

■■■■□□□□□□□□□□

Grace's hero is Mickey Mantle and her greatest desire is to become the first woman in major league baseball. Her mother has other ideas, like ballet. The result is a disaster for baseball, for ballet, for Grace, and for her mother.

Cohen, Barbara. *Thank You, Jackie Robinson.* Lothrop, 1974, 1988.

■■■■■■■□□□□□□□

Sam Green is such an avid Dodger fan that he has memorized every game they've played in his lifetime. This love for the Dodgers cements a friendship between Sam and Davy, the cook at the inn. They go to games at Ebbets Field and to every other ball field within a day's drive of New Jersey. Davy especially admires Jackie Robinson because he was the first black man in major league baseball. When Davy is ill, Sam overcomes his shyness enough to get Jackie Robinson to autograph a baseball for Davy. (See page 158.)

Cohen, Peter Zachary. *Deadly Game at Stone Creek.* Dial, 1978.

■■■■□□□□□□□□□□

See page 55.

Dygard, Thomas J. *Forward Pass.* Morrow, 1989.

■■■■■■ ■□□□□□□□□

The new player has possibilities: great ball-catching and throwing abilities, speed, and enthusiasm. The trouble is that she's a girl, and the high school football team has never had a female player. Everyone wants her to quit, even her father and the coach; but Jill is a determined young lady.

Grossinger, Richard and Kerrane, Kevin. *Into the Temple of Baseball.* Celestial Arts, 1990.

■■■■■■■□□□□□□□

This book is full of stories, poems, and personal narratives about baseball.

Harris, Robie. *Rosie's Double Dare.* Knopf, 1980.

■■■■□□□□□□□□□□

The Willard Street Gang plays baseball and Rosie wants very much to join them, but her baseball skills just don't measure up. The gang makes a deal with her: if she accepts their dare, they'll let her play. She must sneak into Mr. Quirk's apartment and steal his false teeth. She fails when she returns with only his wig. Her second chance is to untie a dog and set him free. The dog runs away, Rosie chases him, and she ends up in the middle of a Red Sox game.

Hurwitz, Johanna. *Baseball Fever.* Morrow, 1981.

■□□□□□□□□□□□□□

Ezra is an avid baseball fan. His father, an intellectual who believes that baseball is a waste of time, is disgusted by his son's preoccupation with the sport. The compromise eventually worked out combines chess and baseball.

Knudson, R. R. *Rinehart Lifts.* Farrar, 1980.

■■■■□□□□□□□□□□

Zan Hagan is a fifth-grade sports freak who, after watching weightlifting on TV, decides that her unathletic friend Arthur Rinehart will become a champion weight lifter. The pair eventually has a fleeting moment of triumph over the class bullies.

Miles, Betty. *The Secret Life of the Underwear Champ.* Knopf, 1981.

■■■■□□□□□□□□□□

Larry takes a job as a model for a sports underwear commercial, hoping his baseball team will never see it. When it airs the night before the first game of the season, everyone sees it, including the opposing team.

Slote, Alfred. *Hang Tough, Paul Mather.* Lippincott, 1973.

■■■■□□□□□□□□□□

Paul has leukemia and his doctors have warned him against playing baseball, but he loves the game and is an excellent pitcher. After pitching a spectacular game, Paul is hospitalized. At the next game, Paul is in a wheelchair, growing steadily weaker, but determined to fight back.

———. *Jake.* Lippincott, 1971.

■■■■■■■□□□□□□□

Jake, an eleven-year-old Black boy who lives with his uncle, is competent enough to run his Little League team. When the league president announces that the team must have an adult male coach at each game and when Jake's principal decides that Jake belongs in a foster home, Jake's world falls apart.

———. *The Trading Game.* Lippincott, 1990.

■■■■■■■□□□□□□□

Andy Harris is a pitcher on his Little League team and he collects baseball cards. Little wonder then that he idolizes his grandfather who used to play in the majors. When his grandfather finally consents to coach Andy's team, trouble begins.

Smith, Robert Kimmel. *Bobby Baseball.* Delacorte, 1989.

■■■□□□□□□□□□□□

Bobby dreams, writes, and plays baseball. His father made it to professional baseball, but, not to the major leagues. Bobby has his own dream all laid out. His father is the little league coach and he does let Bobby pitch, but it's the beginning of the end of Bobby's dream. (See page 99.)

Nonfiction

Anderson, Dave. *The Story of Basketball.* Morrow, 1988.
———. *The Story of Football.* Morrow, 1985.
Hall, Jackie and Jefferis, David. *Skiing and Snow Sports.* Watts, 1990.
Jefferis, David. *Trail Bikes and Motocross.* Watts, 1990.
Ritter, Lawrence. *The Story of Baseball.* Morrow, 1983.
Sullivan, George. *This Is Pro Hockey.* Dodd, 1976.

Poetry

Cole, Joanna, ed. *A New Treasury of Children's Poetry.* Doubleday, 1984.
  Francis, Robert. "The Base Stealer."
  Morrison, Lillian. "The Sidewalk Racer."
Glenn, Mel. "Crystal Rowe Track Star" from *Rhythm Road: Poems to Move To.* Lothrop, 1988.
Kennedy, X. J. "The Abominable Baseball Bat" from *The Phantom Ice-Cream Man.* Atheneum, 1979.
McCord, David. "Little League" from *One at a Time.* Little, 1977.
Swenson, M. "Analysis of Baseball" from *Moments,* edited by Lee Bennett Hopkins. Harcourt, 1980.

Stormy Weather

Rationale

Nature provides us with many dramatic moments, and violent storms create the climax for many works of literature.

Picture Book Starter

☐ Lyon, George Ella. *Come a Tide.* Orchard, 1990.

Grandma says there's going to come a tide. It's been raining for days and the river rises until, indeed, there comes a tide. The family climbs into the pickup for a trip to higher ground. Although there's little spare room in the truck, they offer it to every family they pass but each has a reason to delay. Eventually, the rain is over and the people start the thankless job of cleaning up. The illustrations by Stephen Gammell look as wet and muddy as the people must have been.

Bulletin Board

☐ Display newspaper and magazine articles about floods, tornadoes, hurricanes, earthquakes, and other natural disasters.

Museum

☐ Display objects or newspaper clippings about items that have survived the elements: mittens found after a snow, toys that have been left outdoors too long, and other items that survived floods and storms.

Discussions, Projects, and Activities

☐ Make a volcano.
☐ Interview your local meteorologist.
☐ Graph the weather in your area. Compare the accuracy rates of TV and radio meteorologists.
☐ Interview storm survivors.
☐ Talk about weather superstitions and the folklore of predicting weather.
☐ Describe the worst weather in your area.
☐ Sing weather songs: "Singing in the Rain," "Blue Skies," "Button Up Your Overcoat," "Let It Snow," "Don't Rain on My Parade," "One More River to Cross."
☐ Find out about the blizzard of '88.
☐ Find out about weather-related expressions such as: Take the wind out of someone's sails. Blow against the wind. It's an ill wind that blows nobody good. Cast discretion to the wind. Into each life a little rain must fall. It never rains but it pours. A tempest in a teacup. Take someone by storm. The calm before the storm. Fair-weather friend. Keep a weather-eye out. Weather the storm. Thunderstruck. Steal someone's thunder.
☐ Find out about rain dances.

Books

Picture Books

McCloskey, Robert. *Burt Dow, Deep Water Man.* Viking, 1947.

See page 67.

———. *Time of Wonder.* Viking, 1957.

A family spends the summer on an island in Penobscot Bay. The story is almost a lyric poem.

Murphy, Shirley Rousseau. *Tattie's River Journey.* Dial, 1983.

When a flood picks up Tattie's house with her and her animals in it, Tattie has a wonderful time, at least at first.

Fiction

Buck, Pearl S. *The Big Wave.* Harper, 1947.

■■■■■■■■■□□□□□□

See page 67.

Nelson, Theresa. *Devil Storm.* Orchard, 1987.

■■■■■■■■■□□□□□□

Walter Carroll and his younger sister Alice meet and talk with Old Tom the Tramp, who lives on the fringes of the town. Some say he's the son of the pirate Lafitte and others say he's a chicken thief. After they've warned him about the angry farmers, he warns them of the oncoming hurricane—the one that devastated Galveston, Texas, in 1900.

Paulsen, Gary. *The Voyage of the Frog.* Orchard, 1989.

■■■■■■■■■■□□□□

See pages 60 and 166.

Rogers, Jean. *King Island Christmas.* Greenwillow, 1985.

■■■□□□□□□□□□□□

The people of the Eskimo village are waiting to celebrate Christmas with a new priest who is stranded on a ship in the Bering Sea. In order to rescue the priest, they must carry their boat across the mountainous island to the sea.

Ruckman, Ivy. *Night of the Twisters.* Harper, 1984.

■■■■■□□□□□□□□

Dan Hatch and Arthur Darlington experience the series of tornadoes that devastated Grand Island, Nebraska, in 1980. Cut off from the rest of their families, the boys huddle with Dan's baby brother under a blanket in the cellar while the house is blown away above them. Later, they experience another tornado while being driven to safety in a police car.

Stevens, Carla. *Anna, Grandpa, and the Big Storm.* Clarion, 1982.

■■■■■■■■□□□□□□

The Blizzard of 1888 is experienced by a child and her grandfather stranded on the "El" train.

Nonfiction

Arnold, Caroline. *Coping with Natural Disasters.* Walker, 1987.

Boning, Richard. *Horror Overboard.* B. Loft, 1973.

Coble, Cindy. *Survival Basics for Kids.* Survival, 1980.

East, Ben. *Desperate Search.* Crestwood, 1979.

———. *Forty Days Lost.* Crestwood, 1979.

———. *Found Alive.* Crestwood, 1979.

Fradin, Dennis. *Disaster! Blizzards and Winter Weather.* Childrens, 1983.

———. *Disaster! Droughts.* Childrens, 1983.

———. *Disaster! Tornadoes.* Childrens, 1982.

Geline, Robert. *Trapped in the Deep.* Raintree, 1980.

Gold, Ned. *Eight Who Wrestled Death.* Raintree, 1980.

Irving, Robert. *Hurricanes and Twisters.* Scholastic.

Jennings, Gary. *Killer Storms: Hurricanes, Typhoons, and Tornadoes.* Harper, 1970.

McReynolds, Ginny. *Woman Overboard.* Raintree, 1980.

Stone, Judith. *Minutes to Live.* Raintree, 1980.

Tripp, Jenny. *One Was Left Alive.* Raintree, 1980.

Turner, Susan. *Lost at Sea.* Raintree, 1980.

Alone

Rationale

Many of the best novels for children are based on the need to survive. The survival theme is easy to identify, and, after reading or hearing the books suggested here, children should be able to see how this theme applies to some of their other reading. If a character is in a situation in which he/she must survive alone, there is often very little dialogue. This can make for boring, endless description. When an author has well-developed characters and exciting and believable situations, he/she has created something worth reading.

Picture Book Starter

□ Murphy, Jim. *The Call of the Wolves.* Scholastic, 1989.

A young wolf, wounded and chased by hunters, must find his way back to the pack if he is to survive. The book concludes with a two-page history of the wolf. The illustrator, Mark Alan Weatherby, thanks Wolf Haven in Washington for the use of their wolves as live models for this realistic picture book.

Bulletin Board

□ Encourage the children to post newspaper and magazine articles about real animals and people who survived a variety of situations. Also, post articles the children write based on the survival tales in literature.

Museum

□ Display articles similar to those that story characters made or used to survive their ordeals.

Discussions, Projects, and Activities

□ Chart the setting of each story, the main character, his/her qualities, and the tools and skills required for survival. Indicate whether the characters had those skills and tools when the story began or whether they were acquired.
□ Which of the books are believable and why?
□ Did the situation described in the story you read ever happen? Find documentation of a similar story from real life.
□ How did each character keep track of time? Why?

□ How did the characters cope with loneliness? Was an animal involved? What role did it play?
□ Alter one event in the story. How would this change the outcome?
□ Could a character in one story be put into another situation and still survive?
□ Which of the characters would most enjoy living with you? Why?
□ Decide in which environment you would be most likely to survive. Which would be most difficult?
□ Investigate the latest natural disaster in your area. How did people survive? For how long?
□ Create posters with survival tips.

Books

Fiction

George, Jean C. *Julie of the Wolves.* Harper, 1972.

■■■■■■■■■■■□

See pages 60 and 128.

———. *My Side of the Mountain.* Dutton, 1959.

■■■■■■□□□□□□

Sam Gribley camps out for a year on land abandoned by his ancestors in the Catskills. Readers will get a great deal of information on edible plants, falconry, and many other survival techniques and tools.

———. *The Talking Earth.* Harper, 1983.

■■■■■■■□□□□□

Billy Wind, a young Seminole girl, faces a thirteen week ordeal when she is forced to retreat into a cave as fire engulfs her island.

Holman, Felice. *Slake's Limbo.* Macmillan, 1974.

■■■■■■■□□□□□

Artemis Slake, escaping some bullies, finds a cave in a subway tunnel just outside Grand Central Station. The cave becomes his home and refuge for 121 days. (See page 153.)

Houston, James. *Frozen Fire.* Atheneum, 1977.

■■■■■■■■■■□□□□

Based on a true incident in the Canadian Arctic, this story tells of Matthew Morgan and Kayak, his Eskimo schoolmate. When Matthew's father is lost, Matthew and Kayak set out in a snowmobile to find him.

Konigsburg, E. L. *From the Mixed-Up Files of Mrs. Basil E. Frankweiler.* Macmillan, 1967.

■■■■■■■□□□□□□□

See pages 15 and 119.

Mazer, Harry. *Snowbound: A Story of Raw Survival.* Delacorte, 1973.

■■■■■■■■■■■■■□

Two teenagers are stranded for ten days in a desolate area during a snowstorm.

Moeri, Louise. *Save Queen of Sheba.* Dutton, 1981.

■■■■■■■■■■□□□□

See page 58.

O'Dell, Scott. *Island of the Blue Dolphins.* Houghton, 1960.

■■■■■■■□□□□□□□

See pages 9 and 127.

———. *Sarah Bishop.* Houghton, 1980.

■■■■■■■■■■■■■□

See page 62.

Paulsen, Gary. *Hatchet.* Bradbury, 1987.

■■■■■■■■□□□□□□

Brian is on his way to visit his father in northern Canada when the pilot of the plane dies of a heart attack. Facing the facts that his only survival tool is a hatchet and that he might not be rescued takes all the courage he can muster. (See page 123.)

Roth, Arthur. *Iceberg Hermit.* Scholastic, 1976.

■■■■■■■■■■■■■□

Based on a true story, this book tells of Allan Gordon, a nineteen-year-old boy who survives for seven years in the Arctic; first, alone on an iceberg and in the ruined hulk of a whaling ship, and later, in an Eskimo village. During this time, he learns self-reliance, patience, and the skills of survival.

Ruckman, Ivy. *Night of the Twisters.* Harper, 1984.

■■■■■□□□□□□□□□

See page 73.

———. *No Way Out.* Harper, 1988.

■■■■■■■■■■□□□□

Rick and Amy are camping out with Amy's little brother Ben in the Zion Narrows. The experience is glorious until the rains start and the beautiful canyon becomes a death trap.

Skurzynski, Gloria. *Lost in the Devil's Desert.* Lothrop, 1982.

■■■■■■■■■□□□□□

Kevin's father has returned from a desert survival course and is on his way to the Middle East. Fortunately, he shares some survival tips, because Kevin needs the information when he is kidnapped and must survive three days in the desert.

Speare, Elizabeth George. *The Sign of the Beaver.* Houghton, 1983.

■■■■■■■□□□□□□□

In 1768, Matt Hallowell and his father go to the Maine woods to build a house, leaving the rest of the family in Massachusetts. When the cabin is finished, Mr. Hallowell goes back to get the family and leaves Matt with a rifle, a field of corn, and minimal survival skills. After a fur trapper steals the rifle and Matt is seriously injured, an Indian chief offers to help Matt if Matt will teach the chief's grandson, Attean, to read. (See page 152.)

Sperry, Armstrong. *Call It Courage.* Macmillan, 1940.

■■■■■■■■□□□□□□□

See pages 68 and 103.

Steig, William. *Abel's Island.* Farrar, 1976.

■■■■□□□□□□□□□□□

Abelard Flint, a debonair young mouse, is swept away trying to rescue his wife's scarf during a storm on the river. He lands on an island in the middle of the river and is forced to survive, by using skills he didn't know he had. (See page 91.)

Taylor, Theodore. *The Cay.* Doubleday, 1969.

■■■■■■■■□□□□□□□

When their ship is torpedoed, a spoiled, prejudiced young boy and a Black man are stranded on a deserted island in the Caribbean.

Voigt, Cynthia. *Homecoming.* Atheneum, 1981.

■■■■■■■■■□□□□□□

Dicey is left in charge of her younger siblings when their distraught mother deserts them in a parking lot in Pawtucket, Rhode Island. They set out on foot for Bridgeport, Connecticut, where their rich great-aunt Cilla lives. When they arrive, they find that she has died and their cousin Eunice grudgingly takes them in. After discovering that their mother is in a mental hospital, the children set out for their grandmother's home in Maryland.

Walsh, Jill Paton. *Fireweed.* Farrar, 1970.

■■■■■■■■■■■■■■□

Two children who were supposed to be evacuated from London during the Blitz pool their resources in order to survive there. Bill is older than Julie and comes from a less-privileged family. Before their friendship, too, is destroyed, they set up housekeeping in the ruins. (See page 116.)

Nonfiction

Arnold, Caroline. *Coping with Natural Disasters.* Walker, 1987.

Boning, Richard. *Horror Overboard.* B. Loft, 1973.

Coble, Cindy. *Survival Basics for Kids.* Survival, 1980.

East, Ben. *Desperate Search.* Crestwood, 1979.

———. *Forty Days Lost.* Crestwood, 1979.

———. *Found Alive.* Crestwood, 1979.

Fradin, Dennis. *Disaster! Blizzards and Winter Weather.* Childrens, 1983.

———. *Disaster! Droughts.* Childrens, 1983.

———. *Disaster! Tornadoes.* Childrens, 1982.

Geline, Robert. *Trapped in the Deep.* Raintree, 1980.

Gold, Ned. *Eight Who Wrestled Death.* Raintree, 1980.

Irving, Robert. *Hurricanes and Twisters.* Scholastic.

Jennings, Gary. *Killer Storms: Hurricanes, Typhoons, and Tornadoes.* Harper, 1970.

McReynolds, Ginny. *Woman Overboard.* Raintree, 1980.

Stone, Judith. *Minutes to Live.* Raintree, 1980.

Tripp, Jenny. *One Was Left Alive.* Raintree, 1980.

Turner, Susan. *Lost at Sea.* Raintree, 1980.

Poetry

Holman, Felice. "Loneliness" from *I Like You, If You Like Me: Poems of Friendship,* edited by Myra Cohn Livingston. Macmillan, 1987

———. "Who Am I" from *These Small Stones,* edited by Norma Farber and Myra Cohn Livingston. Harper, 1987.

Larrick, Nancy, ed. *Room for Me and a Mountain Lion: Poetry of Open Space.* Evans, 1974.

Dresbach, Glen W. "The Cave."

Wagoner, David. "Staying Alive."

Foiled Again

Rationale

Like eccentric characters, villains can be more fun than plain vanilla heroes and heroines. A careful look at the way professional writers portray villains can help children incorporate them into their own writing. As you get into this unit, you will see that we have gone beyond the funny, "melodrama" villains to include some people who are really evil. Some children are ready to deal with evil characters and to see, for example, that many of the personality traits of evil people are "good" qualities taken to an extreme or used inappropriately and that most people have both a good and a bad side. The children might look at villains from various points of view: Is there such a thing as pure evil? Do villains have a rationale for their behavior? Is evil, like beauty, in the eyes of the beholder? As with each of the units, you will want to choose those activities and books that are appropriate for your children.

Picture Book Starter

☐ Macaulay, David. *Black and White.* Houghton, 1990.

This intriguing book appears to tell four stories simultaneously, at least one of which is about a masked man. As you read, however, it becomes apparent that the stories are intertwined or perhaps the same story from different points of view. Deciding which story comes first or even which event happens first is quite a task.

Bulletin Board

☐ Let the children make and display wanted posters of real and imagined villains.

Museum

☐ Display criminals' tools: masks, kerchiefs, lock picks, locks, handcuffs. Encourage the children to add other items, even seemingly innocuous ones, label them, and tell how a villain used them for a dastardly deed.

Discussions, Projects, and Activities

☐ Why are there villains in stories?
☐ After reading a story with a villain, discuss whether the villain changed by the end of the book. Why? If the villain changed, did you find it believable?
☐ Does the villain of a particular story have a good side? How did the author show the villain's point of view?
☐ They say that crime does not pay. Does it?
☐ Why do we have laws? Why do most people obey laws even when they would probably not be caught breaking them?
☐ Discuss "white collar" crimes.
☐ Talk about rehabilitation programs for real criminals. Do they work?
☐ Discuss capital punishment.
☐ List cartoon villains and their characteristics.
☐ Find out if, when, and how each of these people were considered villainous and add to the list any others you can think of: Willie Sutton, Jesse James, Billy the Kid, Hitler, Mussolini, Butch Cassidy, Benedict Arnold, Tokyo Rose, Simon Le-Gree, John Wilkes Booth. Would we still find those people villainous? Is there a believable defense for their actions?
☐ Who are today's villains? Does everyone think they are evil?
☐ Which villains would you root for? Why?
☐ Make a list of stereotypical villainous traits: long moustaches, beady eyes. Look at the people on your list of villains and see which of them had any of the traits you listed.
☐ Write or tell about the most villainous thing you ever did.
☐ Find articles in the newspaper about villainous deeds. Find an article about a good deed for every villainous one.

Books

Fiction: Picture Books

Dr. Seuss. *Horton Hears a Who.* Random, 1954.

Horton is intent on rescuing the tiny Whos living on a dust speck. Others, however, are equally intent on putting an end to what they consider to be nonsense.

Kellogg, Steven. *The Island of the Skog.* Dial, 1973.

A boat load of mice discover an island. Unfortunately, the island seems to be inhabited by a very large, very ferocious monster.

Fiction: Novels

Adams, Richard. *Watership Down.* Macmillan, 1974.

■■■■■■■■■■■■■□

See pages 59 and 167.

Aiken, Joan. *The Wolves of Willoughby Chase.* Doubleday, 1964.

■■■■■■■■■■□□□□

This Victorian melodrama is full of villains. It tells of the fortunes and misfortunes of two cousins, Bonnie and Sylvia who, through the villainy of Miss Slighcarp, become wards in an orphanage. Mr. Grimshaw, Mrs. Brisket, and Diana Brisket are equally villainous. (See page 170.)

Bawden, Nina. *Carrie's War.* Lippincott, 1973.

■■■■■■■■■■■■■□

See pages 38 and 104.

Clements, Bruce. *Anywhere Else But Here.* Farrar, 1981, 1989.

■■■■■■■□□□□□□

See pages 38 and 93.

de Felice, Cynthia. *Weasel.* Macmillan, 1990.

■■■■■■■■■■■□□□

See pages 42 and 168.

Fleischman, Sid. *The Ghost in the Noonday Sun.* Little, 1965.

■■■■■■■■ ■□□□□□

Oliver Finch is kidnapped by Captain Scratch, a villain if ever there was one, and young Oliver has no choice but to pursue the ghost of Gentleman Jack and a buried treasure.

Fox, Paula. *The Village by the Sea.* Orchard, 1988.

■■■■■■■■□□□□□□

Aunt Bea is the villainous character in this novel but, because of Emma's strength, Bea is not as damaging as she could be. However, Bea remains a fascinating study in the motivations of a destructive, jealous, and petty person. (See page 165.)

Fritz, Jean. *Brady.* Coward, 1960.

■■■■■■■■□□□□□

There are many villains in this story of one station on the Underground Railroad. All of the slave-hunters are surely villainous, as are Loban and Bill Williams. (See page 100.)

Karl, Jean E. *Beloved Benjamin Is Waiting.* Dutton, 1978.

■■■■■■■■□□□□□

See pages 66 and 97.

Stevenson, Robert Louis. *Treasure Island.* Many versions.

■■■■■■■■■■■■■□

There are several villains in this classic. The most memorable, of course, is Long John Silver.

Way Out West

Rationale

The wild days of the Old West, its colorful villains and heroes, and the ordinary people who were neither can be as fascinating to today's children as they were to the authors of these books.

Picture Book Starter

☐ Kennedy, Richard. *The Contests at Cowlick.* Little, 1975.

The sheriff and his men go fishing after assuring the townspeople that there'll be no trouble while they're gone. Then Hogbone and his men ride into town. Little Wally, hiding under the water trough, is the only one who dares confront them. He challenges them to contests, neatly outsmarting them all. Read it with gusto!

☐ Nixon, Joan Lowry. *Beats Me, Claude.* Viking, 1986.

Shirley and Claude have settled down at last in East Texas, but Shirley is lonely and Claude wants an apple pie. He finally gets one, but only after Shirley has had a few unpleasant visitors and one very nice one. (See page 24.)

☐ ———. *Fat Chance, Claude.* Viking, 1987.

This is the third book in the Shirley and Claude series, but it describes the childhoods of Shirley and Claude, their rivalry, and their eventual love and marriage. Shirley scares off every suitor with her dauntless behavior until she meets Claude, a hard-working responsible soul, who thinks women should be feminine and sweet. Claude's in for some surprises.

☐ ———. *If You Say So, Claude.* Warne, 1980.

Claude and Shirley leave the mining towns of Colorado and set out to find a peaceful place to live. Claude finds several places that suit him, but Shirley's harder to please. Shirley's behavior in this one comes very close to tall-tale behavior.

☐ Purdy, Carol. *Iva Dunnit and the Big Wind.* Dial, 1985.

Iva and her six kids are left on the prairie to cope with nothing but "our wits, our strength and young'uns that knows how to stay put." But that's enough when the big wind comes.

Bulletin Board

☐ Display real or made-up "Wanted" posters for gunmen and robbers from the Old West.

Museum

☐ Display Western artifacts, lariats for practicing rope tricks, and reproductions of Western art.

Discussions, Projects, and Activities

☐ Practice panning for gold by using flecks of glitter in sand. Figure out ways to isolate "the gold."
☐ Sing some mining and cowboy songs: "My Darlin' Clementine," "Oh, Susannah," "Red River Valley," "Streets of Laredo," "Ol' Paint," "Sweet Betsy from Pike," "Git Along, Little Dogies."
☐ Listen to Aaron Copeland's symphony *Rodeo*. This is unlike any other symphony most young people have heard. It's great for dancing.
☐ Find out about women's roles in the Old West.
☐ Make a topographical map of one of the territories.
☐ List the Native American tribes whose land you'd pass through if you were heading west from St. Joseph, Missouri.
☐ Write a journal for one of the Pony Express riders.
☐ Find out about the clothing worn by different types of people in the Old West.
☐ Make a chart listing the reasons people went west.
☐ Write about the settlers from the Native American's point of view.
☐ Find out what happened to travelers stranded in the Donner Pass.
☐ Build models of the different types of housing used during this period.
☐ Build a model of a frontier town.
☐ Ask a quilter to show you different types of quilting patterns and stitches. Hold a real or mock quilting bee.
☐ Hold a barn dance.
☐ Ask a country fiddler to play.
☐ Put on a dance hall show.
☐ Study some of the brands used for cattle then and now and make up a brand you'd use. Put your brand on papers you write.
☐ Which of the roles in the Old West would you prefer? Why?

□ Find out about different occupations required for a frontier town to survive and grow.

□ What has happened to wild horses? What should and could be done to save the mustangs?

□ Find out about Boot Hill. Make up some epitaphs.

□ Find out about firearms used at that time. Were there real gunfights?

□ Find out about barbed wire. Why are there so many different kinds?

□ Listen to the soundtrack of the musical *Annie Get Your Gun*. Find out about the real Annie Oakley.

□ Find out about: Billy the Kid, Kit Carson, Buffalo Bill, Calamity Jane, Doc Holiday, Wyatt Earp, Jesse James, Wild Bill Hickok, and other heroes and villains of the west.

□ Find out about gangs in the Wild West.

□ Learn how to do a rope trick.

□ Watch an old western movie and check it for accuracy against what you have learned.

Books

Fiction

Baker, Betty. *The Spirit Is Willing.* Macmillan, 1974.

■■■■■■■■■■■□□□

Carrie Thatcher and her companion Portia set out to find excitement in Arizona in the days of the Old West. Discovered trying to sneak into the Rough 'n Ready Saloon, they are dragged into some excitement all right, but not quite what they had in mind.

Beatty, Patricia. *Eight Mules from Monterey.* Morrow, 1982.

■■■■■■■■□□□□□

In 1916, Fayette, her younger brother, and her widowed mother set out for the Santa Lucia mountains of California where the mother is setting up library outposts.

Coren, Alan. *Arthur the Kid.* Bantam, 1984.

■■■■□□□□□□□□□

Answering a help wanted ad placed by the Black Hand Gang, Arthur is put in charge of the bungling gang. He changes their routine from unsuccessful bank robbery to successful activities.

Fleischman, Sid. *By the Great Horn Spoon.* Little, 1953.

■■■■■□□□□□□□□

See page 60.

———. *Humbug Mountain.* Little, 1978.

■■■■■□□□□□□□□

Once again the Flints—Pa, Ma, Glorietta, and Wiley—are on the move, but Ma has had enough traveling around the West setting up newspapers. This time they are headed for Sunrise, a new city that Grafter Tuggle had staked out along the Missouri River. The only trouble is that nobody has seen Tuggle for three years and they've only a dim notion of where Sunrise is.

———. *McBroom Tells a Lie.* Little, 1976.

■■■■■□□□□□□□□

Josh McBroom is a teller of tall tales—so tall as to be ridiculous. With his wife and eleven children, he works his wonderful one-acre farm with earth so amazingly rich they could "plant and harvest two-three crops a day with time left over for a game of horseshoes." While his children build a popcornmobile, he attempts to save his farm from Heck Jones, his foxy-eyed neighbor.

Talbot, Charlene Joy. *The Sodbuster Venture.* Atheneum, 1982.

■■■■■■■□□□□□□

See page 56.

Nonfiction

Alter, Judith. *Growing Up in the Old West.* Watts, 1989.

The hard work and danger are carefully recounted but so are the good times.

———. *Women of the Old West.* Watts, 1989.

The old saying "The West was kind to men and dogs but hard on women and horses" is shown to be true in this richly illustrated book.

Collins, James L. *Exploring the American West.* Watts, 1989.

Each of the early expeditions west of the Mississippi is mapped out and described.

————. *Lawmen of the Old West.* Watts, 1990.

It was hard to tell the good guys from the bad guys in those days. This book tells the good and bad of both sides.

Dicerto, Joseph J. *The Pony Express: Hoofbeats in the Wilderness.* Watts, 1989.

Pony Express mail delivery from St. Joseph, Missouri, to Sacramento, California, lasted only a short while, but this book offers as much information as possible with photographs, lithographs, and drawings.

Freedman, Russell. *Cowboys of the Wild West.* Clarion, 1985.

The real cowboys of the old west were hard workers for low pay.

Levine, Ellen. *Ready, Aim, Fire : The Real Adventures of Annie Oakley.* Scholastic, 1989.

After you read about her life, listen to the music from *Annie Get Your Gun.*

Wolf, Bernard. *Cowboy.* Morrow, 1985.

Here is a photo essay about today's cowboys.

Poetry

Dimoff, John. "West of Chicago" from *Room for Me and a Mountain Lion: Poetry of Open Space,* edited by Nancy Larrick. Evans, 1974.

Sandburg, Carl. "Buffalo Dusk." Available in many collections.

A Woman's Work

Rationale

Children's literature has not always done well by its female characters. Traditional fairytales show most females as passive and helpless. Even more modern picture books have more male than female protagonists. Looking at those stories and contrasting them with some of these in which females are more realistically portrayed can make for lively discussion.

Picture Book Starter

☐ Browne, Anthony. *Piggybook.* Knopf, 1986.

Mr. Piggott and the two boys take Mrs. Piggott for granted. She keeps a full-time job and does all the work around the house. When she disappears, leaving only a note saying, "You are pigs!" they gradually change into pigs and are living like pigs when she returns. It's a strong satire on traditional women's roles.

Bulletin Board

☐ Collect photographs of women from various time periods and have the children make up one paragraph biographies of their supposed deeds.

Museum

☐ Display items that represent career choices for women today: hard hat, stethoscope, dentist's mirror, ruler, cradle, etc.

Discussions, Projects, and Activities

☐ Make a list of outstanding women in American history. Find out what each did to achieve fame.
☐ Debate the pros and cons of all-girls and all-boy schools in today's world.
☐ Rewrite picture book stories with strong male characters and change the characters to females: Maxine in the land of the Wild Things, Joanna Appleseed, Pecos Lil, Pauline Bunyan, Michelle in the Night Kitchen.
☐ Investigate the meaning of the following phrases about women and decide which are put-downs: Behind every man there's a good woman. A woman's place is in the home. A woman's place is in the house and the senate. A natural woman. A woman's work is never done. The female of the species is more deadly than the male. Feminine intuition. Women drivers.

☐ Make a display of women's clothing throughout history and decide what it shows about female roles in society.
☐ Look at the strong female characters in the books suggested and decide how and where they got their strength.
☐ Take a survey of children's picture books and determine the percentage of strong female characters in them.
☐ Look at female characters in classic books such as *Little Women, Heidi, Bambi, The Little House on the Prairie.* Decide how they were portrayed and whether or not they'd be portrayed the same way today.
☐ List your favorite male authors. How do they treat female characters in their books?
☐ Find fairy tales with strong female roles. Is Beauty in '"Beauty and the Beast" strong? Why?

Books

Fiction: Picture Books

Cooney, Barbara. *Miss Rumphius.* Viking, 1982.

Miss Rumphius tries to accomplish three things suggested by her grandfather: travel widely, live by the sea, and leave the world more beautiful. She accomplishes the third by planting lupine everywhere she goes.

Hedderwick, Mairi. *Katie Morag and the Two Grandmothers.* Little, 1986.

Two women of the same generation couldn't be more different and Katie loves them both.

Kesselman, Wendy. *Emma.* Harper, 1985.

Emma is seventy-two and lonely. Her family loves her and comes to see her, but most of the time she is alone with her cat and her memories. One day she decides to paint and becomes so good at it that she surprises everyone, even herself.

Miles, Miska. *Annie and the Old One.* Little, 1971.

See page 52.

Murphy, Shirley Rousseau. *Tattie's River Journey.* Dial, 1983.

See page 72.

Nixon, Joan Lowry. *Beats Me, Claude.* Viking, 1986.
See pages 24 and 79.

———. *Fat Chance, Claude.* Viking, 1987.
See page 79.

———. *If You Say So, Claude.* Warne, 1980.
See page 79.

Noble, Trinka Hakes. *Meanwhile, Back at the Ranch.* Dial, 1987.
See page 37.

Purdy, Carol. *Iva Dunnit and the Big Wind.* Dial, 1985.
See page 79.

Williams, Vera B. *Three Days on a River in a Red Canoe.* Greenwillow, 1981.
Two children, their mother, and their aunt, set off on a camping and canoeing trip. The book has several maps and various ways of recounting their exciting travels.

Fiction: Novels
Avi. *Who Stole the Wizard of Oz?* Knopf, 1981.
■■■■■□□□□□□□□□
See page 45.

Babbitt, Natalie. *Tuck Everlasting.* Farrar, 1975.
■■■■■■■■□□□□□□
See pages 42 and 163.

Bawden, Nina. *Carrie's War.* Lippincott, 1973.
■■■■■■■■■■■□□□
See pages 38 and 104.

George, Jean C. *Julie of the Wolves.* Harper, 1972.
■■■■■■■■■■■■■□
See pages 60 and 128.

———. *The Talking Earth.* Harper, 1983.
■■■■■■■■□□□□□□
See page 74.

MacLachlan, Patricia. *The Facts and Fictions of Minna Pratt.* Harper, 1988.
■■■■■■■■□□□□□□
See page 43.

———. *Sarah, Plain and Tall.* Harper, 1985.
■■■■■■■■□□□□□□
A lonely, motherless family on the prairie places an ad in the newspaper. Sarah Elisabeth Wheaton of Maine, describing herself as "plain and tall," arrives and meets the family's needs.

O'Dell, Scott. *Island of the Blue Dolphins.* Houghton, 1960.
■■■■■■■■□□□□□□
See pages 9 and 127.

Pople, Maureen. *The Other Side of the Family.* Holt, 1986.
■■■■□□□□□□□□□□
See page 4.

Voigt, Cynthia. *Homecoming.* Atheneum, 1981.
■■■■■■■■■□□□□□
See page 76.

On a Wing and a Prayer

Rationale

World War II was a dramatic, life-changing time for most people in the world and its effects are still being felt. It has provided the setting for many excellent novels for children. Because many people who lived through that period and many who participated are still alive, children investigating war should have ample sources of first-hand information.

Picture Book Starter

☐ Abells, Chana B. *The Children We Remember.* Greenwillow, 1986.

This book of photographs and memories of children who were victims of the holocaust will haunt anyone who opens it.

Bulletin Board

☐ Display newspaper headlines and pictures of people in service uniforms from World War II.

Museum

☐ Display memorabilia such as medals, postcards, uniforms, military equipment, and letters.

Discussions, Projects, and Activities

☐ Talk to veterans about what they did during the war and how they feel about it now.
☐ Ask grandparents and great-grandparents about rationing, bomb shelters, blackout curtains, volunteer work, victory gardens, V-Mail, and anything else they can remember about the war years in this country.
☐ Play records by the Andrews Sisters, Gracie Moore, Bing Crosby, Kate Smith, Benny Goodman, and other recording artists popular at that time.
☐ Look through books to see what kind of clothing people wore.
☐ Find newspaper accounts of American soldiers' first glimpse of the concentration camps.
☐ Find out what we did with prisoners of war during that time.
☐ Find out how we treated Japanese-American citizens. How did we treat German-Americans?
☐ Find out how many people were killed during the war years.
☐ Find out how the war affected your family.

☐ Find out about Berlin and the Berlin Wall.
☐ Make a map showing which countries were involved in the war. Which countries ceased to exist? Which countries' borders changed?
☐ Read a novel and a nonfiction book about the same place and time. Compare the information.
☐ Make a chart to show the point of view and plot of the war books that the class or individuals read.

Book Title
Author
Main Characters
Country
Problem Faced
Effect of the War on the Plot

Books

Fiction

Bishop, Claire H. *Twenty and Ten.* Viking, 1952.

■■□□□□□□□□□□□□

Twenty French children are safe in the orphanage run by Sister Gabriel until the Jewish children, escaping from the fate Hitler has in mind for them, appear at their door and seek admission. The children agree to let them in and put themselves in very real danger.

Chaikin, Miriam. *Lower! Higher! You're a Liar.* Harper, 1984.

■■■■■■■■□□□□□□

This is a distant view of what's happening to the Jews in Europe as seen through the eyes of a Jewish family living in Brooklyn during World War II. Through the radio news broadcast by Gabriel Heater, Molly's family learns of Hitler's deeds. Meanwhile, Molly is involved with a local dictator, Celia, an old nemesis.

Coerr, Eleanor. *Sadako and the Thousand Paper Cranes.* Dell, 1986.

■■■■□□□□□□□□□□

Sadako is dying of leukemia because she was in Hiroshima when the atom bomb was dropped. She is convinced that if she can fold one thousand paper cranes, the gods will grant her wish for life.

Gillham, Bill. *Home Before Long.* Andre Deutsch, 1984.

■■■■■■■■□□□□□□

When the children are evacuated from London in 1940, Dorothy Turner is admonished by her mother to "Look after Billy." Billy turns out to be a difficult brother. When life with their host family, the Updikes, becomes impossible for Billy, Dorothy decides they must return home.

Haugaard, Erik Christian. *Chase Me, Catch Nobody.* Houghton, 1980.

■■■■■■■■□□□□□□

When Erik Hansen joins his Danish schoolmates on a trip to northern Germany in 1937, he becomes involved with an underground group that helps Jews escape from the Gestapo. Later, he and a schoolmate rescue Nobody, a half-Jewish escapee, in a rowboat bound for Denmark.

Kherdian, David. *The Road from Home.* Greenwillow, 1979.

■■■■■■■■□□□□□□

This biography of the author's grandmother recounts the effect on her family of Hitler's decision to annihilate the Armenians.

Little, Jean. *Listen for the Singing.* Dutton, 1977.

■■■■■■■■□□□□□□

The effects of the war on this Canadian family are multiplied when their son joins the navy and is blinded.

Lowry, Lois. *Autumn Street.* Houghton, 1980.

■■■■■■■□□□□□□□

See page 56.

————— *Number the Stars.* Houghton, 1989.

■■■■■□□□□□□□□□

It's 1944. The Nazis have been in control of Denmark for several years and have been harassing the Jews. The harassment becomes uglier and the Nazis prepare to "relocate" Denmark's Jews to concentration camps or worse. Described here is the heroism of citizens of occupied Denmark who smuggle Jews to Sweden before this can happen. We see the underground battle through the eyes of Annemarie Johansen whose friend, Ellen Rosen, and her family are in grave danger. The courage of the Rosen family and their fellow Jews is shared by the Johansen family and friends.

McSwigan, Marie. *Snow Treasure.* Dutton, 1942; Scholastic, 1986.

■■■■■■□□□□□□□□

Norwegian children, living near the Arctic circle, display great courage during the war. Nazi troops have occupied their village, but the children find a way to get nine million dollars in gold past the unsuspecting Germans.

Magorian, Michelle. *Good Night, Mr. Tom.* Harper, 1982.

■■■■■■■■■■■■□□

William Beech, an abused and terrified child, is evacuated from London to the English countryside where he is taken in by a gruff and lonely man, Tom Oakley. It takes as long for Tom to let go of his grief for his family as it does for Will to feel strong and free. (See page 121.)

Pople, Maureen. *The Other Side of the Family.* Holt, 1986.

■■■■□□□□□□□□□□

See page 4.

Roth-Hano, Renee. *Touch Wood.* Puffin, 1989.

■■■■■■■■■□□□□□□

The terrors of anti-Semitism are experienced by a Jewish child in occupied France.

Smith, Doris Buchanan. *Salted Lemons.* Macmillan, 1980.

■■■■□□□□□□□□□□

Darby and her family move to Atlanta, Georgia, during World War II, and Darby has great difficulty adjusting. When her only friend, Yoko is sent with her Japanese-American family to a relocation camp and the friendly German grocer is called a spy, it's almost too much for Darby.

Streatfeild, Noel. *When the Sirens Wailed.* Random, 1976.

■■■■■■■■■□□□□□□

During the blitz of London, a family is split. The father is in the Navy, the mother works in a weapons factory, and the children are evacuated to Dorset where they live with Colonel Stranger. It's good enough until the Colonel dies and then life for the children becomes almost unbearable.

Suhl, Yuri. *On the Other Side of the Gate.* Watts, 1975.

■■■■■■■■■■■■■□

A Jewish couple must smuggle their infant son out of the Warsaw ghetto where Jews are being starved and/or sent to the prison camps. A Polish Catholic family is asked to "find" the child on their doorstep and save him from his parents' fate.

———. *Uncle Misha's Partisans.* Four Winds, 1973.

■■■■■■■■■□□□□□□

In the Ukraine during the war, a colony of Jewish freedom fighters lives in a forest. Motele's parents are killed by the Nazis, so he joins the group, bringing only his skills with a violin. He yearns to do more than entertain, so he becomes a spy.

Terlouw, Jan. *Winter in Wartime.* McGraw, 1976.

■■■■■■■■■■■■■□

Michiel, a boy in the Netherlands, takes care of a wounded British flyer when his friend is picked up by Nazis. The flyer and his friend had killed a German soldier for whose death Michiel's father is shot. Now Michiel must learn the harsh lessons of the underground.

Uchida, Yoshiko. *Journey Home.* Atheneum, 1978.
———. *Journey to Topaz.* Atheneum, 1977.

■■■■■■■■■□□□□□□

These two perceptive novels tell of Yuki and her family during and after their internment in a Utah prison camp during World War II.

Van Stockum, Hilda. *The Borrowed House.* Farrar, 1975.

■■■■■■■■■□□□□□□

Janna likes being in the Hitler Youth Movement and is not pleased to leave it to join her parents in Amsterdam. It is only then that Janna becomes aware of the cruelty and lies in Germany.

Vander Els, Betty. *The Bombers' Moon.* Farrar, 1985.

■■■■■■■■■□□□□□□

In the light of the moon, the Japanese use the coast of China for bombing practice. Ruth and her brother, separated from their missionary parents, are taken to India where the family is reunited.

Walsh, Jill Paton. *Fireweed.* Farrar, 1970.

■■■■■■■■■■■■■□

See pages 76 and 116.

Westall, Robert. *The Machine Gunners.* Greenwillow, 1976.

■■■■■■■■■□□□□□□

A small town in England is strafed each day by German planes and expects to be invaded. Chas finds a machine gun in a downed plane. With the help of other children and a retarded adult, he hides the gun in preparation for the invasion. When a German soldier arrives, the children take him prisoner.

Wolitzer, Hilma. *Introducing Shirley Braverman.* Farrar, 1975.

■■■■□□□□□□□□□□

World War II is experienced by a Brooklyn family.

Nonfiction
Adler, David A. *We Remember the Holocaust.* Holt, 1989.

The survivors tell their tales of this tragic period in this amply illustrated book for children.

Matthews, Rupert. *Winston Churchill.* Bookwright, 1989.

This book covers the main events, with illustrations, in the life of this charismatic leader.

Takashima, Shizuye. *A Child in Prison Camp.* Tundra, 1974.

The Canadians placed Japanese-Canadians in prison camps during the war. This is the account by a person who was taken from her home in Vancouver and kept behind barbed wire for three years.

Tames, Richard. *Anne Frank.* Watts, 1989.

Intended for a younger audience than the diary itself, this book gives us background, diagrams, and pictures of the tragic life of Anne Frank.

Taylor, Theodore. *Battle in the Arctic Seas: The Story of Convoy PQ.* Crowell, 1976.

This account of a naval disaster during the war is told primarily through the diary excerpts of one young officer.

Other Wars: Fiction
Clark, Ann Nolan. *To Stand Against the Wind.* Viking, 1978.

■■■■■■□□□□□□□□

Em remembers his village in Vietnam before the war: the holidays, the food, the rice paddies. He is determined to keep those memories alive following the war and devastation.

Paterson, Katherine. *Park's Quest.* Lodestar, 1988.

■■■■■■■■■■□□□□

A young boy undertakes a quest for his heritage.

Other Wars: Nonfiction
Garland, Sherry. *Vietnam: Rebuilding a Nation.* Dillon, 1990.

This is a book about the people, geography, and customs of Vietnam.

Warren, James A. *Portrait of a Tragedy: America and the Vietnam War.* Lothrop, 1990.

Here is an in-depth look at what happened in Vietnam and why.

Books at a Glance

Introduction

☐ There are some books that, although they may or may not fit into a theme unit, have enough depth and style to stand on their own. Such books can be read to a group or by individuals; discussed and analyzed for plot, characterization, and literary techniques; and serve as a base for comparison to other books. These books serve as compasses by pointing the way to topics for research and to other reading. On the following pages, you will find books that we found to have substance enough to stand careful reading and follow-up activities and discussions.

☐ Although you'll see some of the old standbys here, we've included many books we hope will be new to you and your students. No teacher's book can be large enough to include all the books we like, but we feel this is a strong collection that exposes the reader to many genres of literature.

☐ We've summarized the plot, characters, setting, and, when identifiable without too much stretching of the imagination, the underlying theme of the book. We've listed other books by the same author and books by other authors that relate to the target book in some way. This will remind you of books you may have forgotten about and point you in new directions for reading. As with every other book listed in *Long Ago and Far Away,* it is important that you, the teacher, read a book before reading or discussing it with the children.

☐ We've outlined some things you might like to bring up for discussion; but, here too, comes a word of warning: If you use the discussion topics just as questions for the children to answer, you will sink the book and the discussion. These discussion ideas are not test questions; they are things the reader may or may not have noticed and they are worth pointing out. Such discussions should be, as much as possible, on the same level that you would discuss an adult book with another adult. In such adult discussions, you are not testing to see whether the other really read the book, you are trying to share the enjoyment and deepen each other's understanding and appreciation. The same should be true with classroom book discussions.

☐ When you are discussing a book with a group of children, stay within the book as long as possible: "Why did he/she behave that way? Were you surprised? Scared? Bored? Why?"

Then step back from the book and relate it to the readers' previous experiences: "Have you ever felt like that? When? Did you find the plot believable? Can we find this place on a map?"

Step back further to the author's view: "What did the author have to know to write this book? How might he/she have come to know that? How did the author make you feel scared? Excited? Sad? Look at the first paragraphs and see how the author drew you into the action and characters. Look at the final paragraphs to see whether the author left any questions unanswered or any problems unresolved. Relate the author's techniques to your own. How can you keep your readers as involved as this author did?"

☐ We've also listed some activities and ideas for extending the book. Again, be careful! Activities that follow the reading of a book should strengthen the understanding of the book and present the book in such a way that others will become interested in reading it. Follow-up activities take literature and reading into other areas of the curriculum. With these activities, as with those from other teacher's books, do them only if you, the teacher, can justify the time and energy they take. That an activity is fun is seldom reason enough to use precious class time away from educational goals.

Abel's Island

Abel's Island
by William Steig. Farrar, 1976.

■■■■□□□□□□□□□□

Theme: Discovering your capabilities in order to survive.

Setting: An island in the middle of a river; 1904.

Characters: *Abel Flint,* a gentlemanly mouse.
Amanda, his loyal wife.
Gower Glackens, an elderly, forgetful frog.

Plot: Abelard Flint, a debonair young mouse, is swept away during a storm on a river while trying to retrieve Amanda's scarf. He lands on an island in the river and is forced to survive, using skills he didn't know he had. He sends messages downstream in pots he makes. The messages promise a substantial reward for his rescue. Companionship arrives with Gower Glackens, a frog who promises to send help but forgets. Abel rescues himself by swimming ashore during the driest part of the summer when the river is low. Yes, he gets home with the scarf.

Awards and Recommendations: American Library Association, Newbery Honor Award

Things to Talk About and Notice

□ Discuss the ways Abel changed while he was on the island.

□ Talk about how the author makes us believe that Abel is real.

□ Discuss the reasons the author used a mouse as his main character.

□ Compare Abel's life on the island to his life on land.

Things to Do

□ Convert measurements to mouse-tail lengths.

□ Make a map of the classroom or other area using units of measure such as mouse tails.

□ Make models of Abel's island.

□ Make models of Abel and Amanda's home.

□ Read more survival stories.

□ Retell part of *Abel's Island,* thinking of Abel as a moose instead of a mouse.

□ Compare Abel to mice in other books, such as *The Great Christmas Kidnapping Caper* by Jean Van Leeuwen (Dial, 1975).

Books

Written by William Steig

The Amazing Bone. Farrar, 1976.☑
Amos and Boris. Farrar, 1971.☑
The Bad Island. Windmill, 1969.
Brave Irene. Farrar, 1986.
Caleb and Kate. Farrar, 1977.☑
CDB. Windmill, 1968.☑
CDC. Farrar, 1986.☑
Doctor De Soto. Farrar, 1982.☑
Dominic. Farrar, 1972.
Farmer Palmer's Wagon Ride. Farrar, 1974.
Gorky Rises. Farrar, 1980.
The Real Thief. Farrar, 1973.
Roland the Minstrel Pig. Windmill, 1968.
Rotten Island. Simon & Schuster, 1984.
Shrek! Farrar, 1989.
Solomon the Rusty Nail. Farrar, 1985.☑
Spinky Sulks. Farrar, 1988.☑
Sylvester and the Magic Pebble. Windmill, 1969.
Tiffky Doofky. Farrar, 1978.
Yellow and Pink. Farrar, 1984.
The Zabajaba Jungle. Farrar, 1987.

Islands

Cooney, Barbara. *Island Boy.* Viking, 1988. ✔
Defoe, Daniel. *Robinson Crusoe.* Many versions.
Kellogg, Steven. *The Island of the Skog.* Dial, 1973.☑
Martin, Charles. Island book series. Greenwillow.☑
Mazer, Harry. *The Island Keeper.* Delacorte, 1981.
O'Dell, Scott. *Island of the Blue Dolphins.* Houghton, 1960. ✔
Roy, Ron. *Nightmare Island.* Dutton, 1981.
Sperry, Armstrong. *Call It Courage.* Macmillan, 1940. ✔
Stevenson, Robert Louis. *Kidnapped.* Many versions.
Verne, Jules. *Mysterious Island.* Many versions.
Wyss, Johann. *The Swiss Family Robinson.* Many versions.

Genteel Animals

"Beauty and the Beast." Many versions.
Dahl, Roald. *Fantastic Mr. Fox.* Knopf, 1970. ✔
Ferguson, Alane. *That New Pet.* Lothrop, 1986.☑
"Frog Went A-Courtin'." Many versions.☑
Grahame, Kenneth. *The Wind in the Willows.* Many versions.
King-Smith, Dick. *Babe, the Gallant Pig.* Crown, 1985.☑
Moore, Lilian. *I'll Meet You at the Cucumbers.* Atheneum, 1988. ✔

Perrault, Charles. *Puss in Boots.* Many versions.
Sewell, Anna. *Black Beauty.* Many versions.
Steig, William. *Doctor De Soto.* Farrar, 1982.☑
———. *Dominic.* Farrar, 1972.
Titus, Eve. Anatole series. McGraw.
White, E. B. *Charlotte's Web.* Harper, 1952.✔

Survival
See pages 74–76.

Poetry
Faber, Norma and Livingston, Myra Cohn. *These Small Stones.* Harper, 1987.
Hoban, Russell. "Small, Smaller."
Kuskin, Karla. "Square As a Mouse."

Afternoon of the Elves

Afternoon of the Elves
by Janet Taylor Lisle. Orchard, 1989.

Theme: Coping with poverty and making magic of harsh reality.

Setting: A suburban neighborhood

Characters: *Sara-Kate,* a thin, strangely dressed young girl, treated as a pariah by the children at school. She creatively explains away differences between herself and other children. She is independent and often angry.
Hillary, Sara-Kate's only friend. She is scorned by her other friends when she is drawn into Sara-Kate's elf world.
Mrs. Lenox, Hillary's mother. It is she who brings an end to Sara-Kate's world.
Mrs. Connelly, Sara-Kate's mother. She is ill and completely dependent on Sara-Kate.

Plot: This is not the outright fantasy the title implies. It's the story of a very real, resourceful, imaginative, and desperate girl, Sara-Kate; her confused but loyal friend, Hillary; the elf village in Sara-Kate's backyard; and Sara-Kate's secret life. The elf village appears with ingenious tiny houses, a well, and a Ferris wheel. Hillary thinks that Sara-Kate might be an elf until she discovers Sara-Kate's desperate situation. Unfortunately, Hillary's mother makes the same discovery.

Awards and Recommendations: Newbery Honor Award

Things to Talk About and Notice
☐ Discuss Sara-Kate's survival skills and why she needed them.
☐ Discuss what was real and what was fantasy in Sara-Kate's world, why she needed the elf village, and why Hillary needed it.
☐ Talk about what Mrs. Lenox did. Consider whether she had other options. Talk about what you might have done. What might your parents have done?
☐ Consider what might happen to Sara-Kate and her mother.

Things to Do
☐ Role-play a meeting between Sara-Kate and Hillary years from now.
☐ Make an elf village in your backyard.
☐ Talk to a psychiatrist or psychologist about the behavior Mrs. Connelly exhibited.
☐ Find out about services in your community that might have helped Sara-Kate.

Books
Written by Janet Taylor Lisle
The Dancing Cats of Applesap. Bradbury, 1984.
The Great Dimpole Oak. Orchard, 1987.
Sirens and Spies. Bradbury, 1985.

Unusual Characters
Burch, Robert. *Queenie Peavy.* Viking, 1966.
Sachs, Marilyn. *The Bears' House.* Dutton, 1987.✔

Poverty

Byars, Betsy. The Blossom family series. ✔

Dahl, Roald. *Charlie and the Chocolate Factory.* Knopf, 1964. ✔

Estes, Eleanor. *The Hundred Dresses.* Harcourt, 1974. ☑

——. *The Moffats.* Harcourt, 1968. ✔

Gardiner, John. *Stone Fox.* Crowell, 1980. ✔

"The Little Match Girl." Many versions available.

Provensen, Alice and Provensen, Martin. *Shaker Lane.* Viking, 1989. ✔ ☑

Rabe, Bernice. *The Girl Who Had No Name.* Dutton, 1977.

Robinson, Barbara. *The Best Christmas Pageant Ever.* Avon, 1973. ✔

Rylant, Cynthia. *Miss Maggie.* Dutton, 1983. ✔

——. *When I Was Young in the Mountains.* Dutton, 1982. ✔

Imaginary Worlds

Byars, Betsy. *The Cartoonist.* Viking, 1978. ✔

Paterson, Katherine. *Bridge to Terabithia.* Crowell, 1977. ✔

Urban Survival

Holman, Felice. *Slake's Limbo.* Scribners, 1974. ✔

Mathis, Sharon. *Teacup Full of Roses.* Avon, 1981.

Poetry

Field, Rachel. "Green Riders" from *These Small Stones* edited by Norma Farber and Myra Cohn Livingston. Harper, 1987.

Anywhere Else But Here

■■■■■■■■■□□□□□□

Anywhere Else But Here
by Bruce Clements. Farrar, 1980, 1989.

Setting: Schenectady and Saratoga, New York.

Characters: *Molly,* a very determined young girl who is not afraid of adult responsibilities. *Mr. Smelter,* Molly's father. He's very trusting and forgiving and includes Molly in most of his decisions and activities. *Aunt Aurora,* Molly's aunt. She has been living with Molly and her father since Molly's mother died. Now she is going to marry Shel. *Uncle Shel,* Aunt Aurora's fiance. He is selfish and underhanded, and he cheated Molly's father out of his business. *Fostra Post,* Aurora's girlhood friend. She is following her guru on what he says is the path of enlightenment. She neglects her son, Claude, and refuses to take responsibility for him, saying that to do so would infringe on his freedom.

Claude, Fostra's eight-year-old son. He is deeply angry, probably because of the way his mother treats him. His father is in Mexico and doesn't seem to care about him either. Molly gets through to him and he loves her. *Walter Potrezeski,* a friend from Poland and Molly's great friend and confidant.

Plot: Molly and her Dad have a wonderful relationship, which is fortunate because everything else around them is awful. Her dad's printing business failed. Aurora's girlhood friend Fostra Lee Post descended on the family, dragging along her son. Fostra has found the secret to life, she says, and is following her own path to glory. Molly wants more than anything else to go to Willimantic, Connecticut, to start a new life with her dad. She even sells her most treasured possession, a dollhouse left to her by her mother, in order to do so.

Awards and Recommendations: School Library Journal

Things to Talk About and Notice

☐ Notice the ways Mr. Clements lets us know how Molly and her father feel about each other.

☐ Discuss Molly's freedom to travel alone and whether it is realistic. Do you have the same freedoms? Why?

☐ Compare Mr. Potrezeski's feelings about the dollhouse to Molly's feelings.

☐ Talk about refugees who hid out during a war.

Things to Do

☐ Compare Molly's feeling about the dollhouse to Fran Ellen's feeling about the bears' house in the book *The Bears' House* by Marilyn Sachs (Dutton, 1961, 1987).

Books

Written by Bruce Clements
Coming About. Farrar, 1984.
Coming Home to a Place You've Never Been Before, with Hanna Clements. Farrar, 1975.
From Ice Set Free. Farrar, 1972.
I Tell a Life Every So Often. Farrar, 1974.
Prison Window, Jerusalem Blue. Farrar, 1977.
The Treasure of Plunderell Manor. Farrar, 1987.
Two Against the Tide. Farrar, 1967.

Dollhouses
See pages 11–13.

Weddings
Roberts, Willo Davis. *The View from the Cherry Tree.* Atheneum, 1975. ✔

Arthur, For the Very First Time

Arthur, For the Very First Time
by Patricia MacLachlan. Harper, 1980.

■■■■■☐☐☐☐☐☐☐☐☐☐

Setting: A farm.

Characters: *Arthur,* a journal-keeping child who has trouble *doing;* he's a watcher. He's a little resentful of his parents and baffled by the behavior of his great-aunt and great-uncle and Moira.

Moira, Arthur's tomboy friend with a sharp wit and tongue. She goads Arthur into experiencing life more fully while she reaches for understanding herself.

Uncle Wrisby, an independent, humorous farmer who loves the people and animals in his life but seldom expresses it in words.

Great Aunt Elda, a daring, religious, no-nonsense woman whose mother died at childbirth. She was raised by her stepmother, a mail-order bride.

Dr. Moreover, named because he says "more-over" a great deal. He's the veterinarian and Moira's guardian.

Plot: Arthur's parents are about to have another baby, so they send him to visit his great aunt and uncle, wonderful, understanding people with a French-speaking chicken and a pregnant pig. They also have a neighbor, Moira, a young girl whose parents have deserted her. Arthur's anger at his parents loses its dominance as he takes responsibility for the very first time.

Awards and Recommendations: American Library Association

Things to Talk About and Notice

☐ Discuss whether Patricia MacLachlan got the idea for the mail-order marriage in this book from *Sarah, Plain and Tall* or vice versa. Why do you think that?

☐ What do the French words used to converse with Pauline the chicken mean.

☐ Discuss the birth of the pigs and why it is probably the climax of the book.

☐ Tell about characters from other stories that are like Great Aunt Elda or Uncle Wrisby.

☐ Discuss whether Moira will ever see her mother and father again.

☐ Discuss the title *Arthur, For the Very First Time.*

☐ Describe the relationship between Arthur and Moira and tell how it effects the story.

☐ Talk about why Arthur refuses to read the letters from his parents.

☐ Compare this book to "The Wizard of Oz." Is Great-Aunt Elda like Auntie Em? Is the Wizard like Yoyo? What about the storm?

☐ Discuss reasons for looking through the large or far away end of binoculars.

Things to Do

☐ Compare this book to other books that emphasize journals. See pages 31–33.

☐ Read Randall Jarrell's poem "The Mockingbird" in *Dusk to Dawn,* edited by H. Hill (Crowell, 1981). How does this poem relate to the book?

Books

Written by Patricia MacLachlan
See page 234.

Pigs
Brooks, Walter R. *Freddy, the Detective.* Dell, 1979.
Browne, Anthony. *Piggybook.* Knopf, 1986. ✔
Cole, Brock. *Nothing But a Pig.* Farrar, 1990.
King-Smith, Dick. *Babe, the Gallant Pig.* Crown, 1985. ☑
Peck, Robert Newton. *A Day No Pigs Would Die.* Knopf, 1972. ✔
White, E. B. *Charlotte's Web.* Harper, 1952. ✔

Living with Relatives
Bawden, Nina. *Kept in the Dark.* Lothrop, 1982.
Burnett, Francis. *Secret Garden.* Many versions.
Cassedy, Sylvia. *Behind the Attic Wall.* Crowell, 1983. ✔
Pople, Maureen. *The Other Side of the Family.* Holt, 1986. ✔

Babe, the Gallant Pig

Babe, the Gallant Pig
by Dick King-Smith. Crown, 1985.

■■■■□□□□□□□□□□

Setting: Rural England.

Characters: *Babe,* an intelligent, ambitious, and loving pig.

Fly, mature black and white collie who has been shepherding her entire life. She's good but not great.

Mr. Hogget. a tall, lanky farmer with a soft heart. He enjoys shepherding because it takes so little conversation, and he loves Babe and Fly.

Mrs. Hogget, a practical woman who loves to talk. In fact, she says everything over and over. She wants Babe for food, and only agrees to let him live after he saves the sheep.

Plot: Farmer Hogget wins Babe at a fair by guessing its weight. He takes Babe home where he is welcomed by his wife for the ham he will one day be. The pig is also welcomed by Fly who is in the final stages of training her litter of pups. She adopts Babe who proves to be an intelligent, polite student. Fly herds the sheep by fear and is convinced that sheep are unintelligent creatures who can understand no other way. Babe, however, finds that he can communicate with them best by treating them civilly. After foiling sheep rustlers and wild dogs, Babe wins the respect of Farmer Hogget and Mrs. Hogget. When he wins the sheep trials, his victory is complete.

Awards and Recommendations: American Library Association, Boston Globe/Horn Book, IRA Children's Choice

Things to Talk About and Notice
□ When Farmer Hogget thinks Babe has killed the sheep, he takes Babe to the barn. What is the tube Babe sees?
□ Discuss Fly's statement "People only eat stupid animals." Is that true? Does any civilization eat animals you would not eat?

Things to Do
□ Find out more about sheep herding.
□ Babe calls himself a Large White. Is that a breed of pigs? What other breeds are there?
□ Compare Fly and Babe to Charlotte and Wilbur in *Charlotte's Web* by E. B. White (Harper, 1952).
□ Find out about training dogs for other jobs.

Books
Written by Dick King-Smith
Ace: The Very Important Pig. Crown, 1990.
Farmer Bungle Forgets. Atheneum, 1987.
The Fox Busters. David & Charles, 1978.
Harry's Mad. Crown, 1987.
Magnus Powermouse. Harper, 1984.
Martin's Mice. Crown, 1989.
The Mouse Butcher. Viking, 1982.
Noah's Brother. ABC-Clio, 1986.
Pigs Might Fly. Viking, 1982.
The Queen's Nose. Harper, 1985.
Saddlebottom. G. K. Hall, 1987.
Sophie's Snail. Delacorte, 1989.

Animals with Unusual Traits
Brooks, Walter R. *Freddy, the Politician.* Knopf, 1932.
Callen, Larry. *Pinch.* Little, 1976. ✔
MacLachlan, Patricia. *Arthur, for the Very First Time.* Harper, 1980. ✔
Peck, Robert Newton. *The Day No Pigs Would Die.* Knopf, 1972. ✔
Peet, Bill. *Chester the Worldly Pig.* Houghton, 1965. ☑
Steig, William. *Roland the Minstrel Pig.* Windmill, 1968.
White, E. B. *Charlotte's Web.* Harper, 1952. ✔
————. *The Trumpet of the Swan.* Harper, 1970. ✔

Poetry
Worth, Valerie. "Pig" from *All the Small Poems.* Farrar, 1987.

Beloved Benjamin Is Waiting

Beloved Benjamin Is Waiting
by Jean E. Karl. Dutton, 1978.

■■■■■■■☐☐☐☐☐☐

Setting: A cemetery.

Characters: *Lucinda Gratz,* an abused and frightened child who, nevertheless, shows resourcefulness and bravery in order to survive on her own.

Benjamin the statue of a child who died in the last century. Lucinda's channel of communication to the distant civilization.

Mr. Simon, the gatekeeper of the cemetery. He takes an interest in Lucinda; however, he has no idea she is living in the cemetery.

Mrs. Gratz, Lucinda's mother. For a while she tries to cope, but she is too caught up in her own problems to care for anyone, even her own children.

Joel Gratz, Lucinda's older brother who worries about her but is involved in his own life at private school.

Cheryl Gratz, Lucinda's older sister who worries about her but is involved in her own life in another household.

Kate, Lucinda's friend who deserts her because she believes Lucinda has gone over to the drug gang.

Rosella, a classmate who is a member of the gang and is out to hurt Lucinda.

Plot: Lucinda Gratz was deserted by everyone she knows. First, her oldest brother was sent to reform school. Her other brother, Joel, went away to private school. Her older sister took a housekeeping job to pay her way through college. Her father and mother also left. Even her best friend Kate refuses to speak to her. Lucinda is fleeing the wrath of the gang her oldest brother was part of. Taking refuge in an abandoned house in the cemetery, Lucinda begins to communicate with the statue of a dead child. It's not ghosts, however, that she talks to, but beings from another galaxy.

Awards and Recommendations: School Library Journal

Things to Talk About and Notice

☐ Read the author's descriptions of the cemetery house and of Lucinda's own home. Discuss which description gets more space and why.

☐ Talk about how Lucinda became so self-sufficient.

☐ Discuss whether Lucinda's mother will return and why.

☐ Compare the education, transportation, and government on the distant planet to ours.

☐ Talk about how the aliens communicate through Benjamin's statue.

☐ Discuss the reasons the author used the broken statue as a channel for communication.

☐ Talk about the significance of the statue's missing hands.

☐ Talk about ways Lucinda and the "others" helped each other.

☐ Discuss Lucinda's reason for not going to the gatekeeper for help earlier.

Things to Do

☐ Pretend that you are one of the aliens. Report on Lucinda to the others.

☐ Draw pictures of the others.

☐ Write a sequel about a revisitation.

Books

Written by Jean E. Karl
But We Are Not of Earth. Dutton, 1981.
Strange Tomorrow. Dutton, 1985.
The Turning Place. Dutton, 1976. ✔

Cemeteries
Rodowsky, Colby. *The Gathering Room.* Farrar, 1981.

Science Fiction
See pages 64–66.

Statues
Alcock, Vivien. *The Stonewalkers.* Delacorte, 1982. ✔
Bellairs, John. *The Curse of the Blue Figurine.* Dial, 1983. ✔
Fleischman, Paul. *Graven Images.* Harper, 1982.
Konigsburg, E. L. *From the Mixed-Up Files of Mrs. Basil E. Frankweiler.* Macmillan, 1967. ✔
Snyder, Zilpha Keatley. *The Egypt Game.* Atheneum, 1967. ✔

The Best Christmas Pageant Ever

The Best Christmas Pageant Ever
by Barbara Robinson. Harper, 1972.

■■■■□□□□□□□□□

Setting: A small town.
Characters: *The Herdman Children,* Ralph, Imogene, Leroy, Claude, Ollie, and Gladys. The big ones teach the little ones what they know, so the meanest is the youngest, Gladys.
Mrs. Herdman, works double shifts at the factory rather than accept welfare and stay home with the children.
Narrator, a young child whose mother is running the Christmas pageant. He/she is a keen observer of the Herdmans and their behavior and an excellent analyst.
Charlie, the narrator's brother.
Narrator's mother, a sincere and overwhelmed woman. She treats the Herdmans with as much dignity as possible. She has a loving and caring relationship with her family.
Narrator's father, reacts to everything his wife says to him with great practicality and becomes the reality check in the story.
Reverend Hopkins, an affable minister who ignores complaints from his congregation and allows the pageant to continue.
Plot: The Herdmans are the meanest kids in town. They didn't intend to set foot in a church until they heard that free food is served after the Christmas pageant. So they set about taking over the pageant. Everyone is aghast until, with their strange brand of innocence, the children restore meaning to the story on which the pageant is based.

Awards and Recommendations: American Library Association

Things to Talk About and Notice
- Talk about how the Herdmans are able to get away with their shenanigans before the pageant.
- Tell how you would react to the Herdmans.
- Are the Herdmans "incorrigible"?
- Discuss the ways in which the author made the Herdmans likeable.
- Why did Mrs. Herdman work two shifts?
- Discuss the general opinion of the Herdmans before and after the pageant.
- What did the Herdmans think about other people before and after the pageant?
- Tell what was important to the Herdmans; to the other children.
- Talk about why the Herdmans understood the Christmas story so well.
- Discuss reasons the author didn't name the narrator and his/her family except Charlie.

Things to Do
- Prepare a script for the Herdmans so they will better understand the Christmas story.
- Find out about the gifts of the Magi.
- Compare the Herdmans to the Moffats in Eleanor Estes' books.

Books
Written by Barbara Robinson
My Brother Louis Measures Worms and Other Louis Stories. Harper, 1988.
Temporary Times, Temporary Places. Harper, 1982.

Christmas
Burch, Robert. *Christmas with Ida Early.* Viking, 1983. ✔
Caudill, Rebecca. *A Certain Small Shepherd.* Holt, 1965.
Houston, Gloria. *The Year of the Perfect Christmas Tree: An Appalachian Tale.* Dial, 1988.
Moeri, Louise. *Star Mother's Youngest Child.* Houghton, 1975. ✔
Rylant, Cynthia. *Children of Christmas.* Orchard, 1987. ✔

Poverty
Estes, Eleanor. *The Hundred Dresses.* Harcourt, 1974. ☑
———. *The Moffats.* Harcourt, 1968. ✔
Gardiner, John. *Stone Fox.* Crowell, 1980. ✔
Lisle, Janet Taylor. *Afternoon of the Elves.* Orchard, 1989. ✔
Provensen, Alice and Provensen, Martin. *Shaker Lane.* Viking, 1989. ✔ ☑
Rabe, Bernice. *The Girl Who Had No Name.* Dutton, 1977.
Rylant, Cynthia. *Miss Maggie.* Dutton, 1983. ✔
———. *When I Was Young in the Mountains.* Dutton, 1982. ✔

Bobby Baseball

Bobby Baseball
by Robert Kimmel Smith. Delacorte, 1989.

■■■■■☐☐☐☐☐☐☐☐☐☐

Theme: Dreams die hard.

Characters: *Bobby Ellis,* a determined, fiercely competitive, hot tempered boy who loves everything about baseball, except losing.
Chuck Ellis, Bobby's father and coach. He, too, loves the game. He gives Bobby a chance but keeps him realistic about his goals.
Grandpa, lives with the family and is a great storyteller. He gives Bobby love and stability.
Sammy Ellis, helps his father coach the team. His little league baseball career was cut short because of failing eyesight.
Mouth, Jane DeMuth. Jane is called Mouth because hers is always going. She's a good second baseperson and eventually becomes a friend to Bobby.
Jason Moss, Bobby's best friend and teammate. His attitude toward baseball is much more laid-back than Bobby's.

Plot: Bobby Ellis calls himself Bobby Baseball. Bobby dreams, writes, and plays baseball. His father is the coach of Bobby's team and he lets Bobby pitch, but it's the beginning of the end of Bobby's dream.

Things to Talk About and Notice
☐ Discuss Grandpa's role in the family. Notice when he tells his stories.
☐ Describe what's in Bobby's father's mind throughout the book.
☐ Discuss the relationship between Bobby's father and mother.

Things to Do
☐ Compare baseball cards.
☐ Follow one player on a professional team throughout a season.
☐ Debate the positive and negative aspects of Little League Baseball.
☐ Talk or write about your baseball experiences.
☐ How do you control your temper?

☐ Read *Thank You, Jackie Robinson* by Barbara Cohen (Atheneum, 1974). Compare Bobby and Sam Greene.
☐ Compare yourself to Bobby.
☐ Talk to a Little League coach about what he or she would do or has done with a kid like Bobby.
☐ Listen to the song "Centerfield" by John Fogarty and compare it to your baseball experiences.

Books
Written by Robert Kimmel Smith
Chocolate Fever. Putnam, 1989.
Jelly Belly. Dell, 1982.
Mostly Michael. Delacorte, 1987. ✔
The War with Grandpa. Delacorte, 1984.

Baseball
Baron, Nancy. *Tuesday's Child.* Atheneum, 1984. ✔
Christopher, Matt. *The Year Mom Won the Pennant.* Little, 1986. ✔
Cohen, Barbara. *Benny.* Lothrop, 1977.
———. *Thank You, Jackie Robinson.* Lothrop, 1974. ✔
Giff, Patricia Reilly. *Left-Handed Shortstop.* Delacorte, 1980.☑
Kalb, Jonah. *The Goof That Won the Pennant.* Houghton, 1987.
Lord, Betty Bao. *In the Year of the Boar and Jackie Robinson.* Harper, 1984. ✔
Slote, Alfred. *Hang Tough, Paul Mather.* Harper, 1973. ✔
———. *Jake.* Lippincott, 1971. ✔
———. *The Trading Game.* Lippincott, 1990. ✔

Poetry
Hayden, Robert. "Those Winter Sundays" from *Crazy to Be Alive in Such a Strange World* edited by Nancy Larrick. Evans, 1977.
Kennedy, X. J. "The Abominable Baseball Bat" from *The Phantom Ice Cream Man.* Atheneum, 1979.
McCord, David. "Little League" from *One at a Time.* Little, 1986.
Prelutsky, Jack. "Mr. Mulligan's Window" from *Rolling Harvey Down the Hill.* Greenwillow, 1980.
Silverstein, Shel. "Play Ball" from *A Light in the Attic.* Harper, 1974.
Swenson, M. "Analysis of Baseball" from *Moments* edited by Lee Bennett Hopkins. Harcourt, 1980.

Brady

Brady
by Jean Fritz. Coward, 1960.

■■■■■■■■□□□□□□

Theme: People become adults when they become concerned with something outside themselves.

Setting: A small town in southwestern Pennsylvania just prior to the Civil War.

Characters: *Brady Minton,* has trouble keeping secrets and thinks that his father has no respect for him because of it. Brady has little self-respect and believes that he is an untrustworthy coward.
Mr. Minton, Brady's father, a minister, is a moderate on the question of abolition of slavery. Although he is against slavery, he believes it should be eliminated gradually.
Mrs. Minton, Brady's mother. From a southern family, her sympathies are with the South. When her husband announces his feelings against slavery from the pulpit of his church, however, she takes a stand beside him.
Matt Minton, Brady's brother, a professor at Washington College and more radical in his antislavery beliefs than his father.
Moss, a runaway slave whom Brady discovers hiding in the Sermon House.
Carl Minton, Brady's uncle, the town's sheriff.
Drover Hull, a hermit who is also a member of the underground railroad.
Tar Adams, a barber who appears to be crippled.
Loban Williams, a malicious boy about Brady's age who is proslavery.
Bill Williams, Loban's father, an ignorant man running for sheriff against Brady's uncle.

Plot: The Minton family is divided on the slavery question. Mrs. Minton believes that Henry Clay is right and Mr. Minton is equally sure that slavery must be abolished. Events cause him to take a stand that alienates some of his parish, including his best friend. Brady discovers a station on the Underground Railroad and can't keep quiet about it. When Brady inadvertently discovers a young slave hiding in the house, he must not only keep the secret, he must act to save him.

Things to Talk About and Notice
☐ Talk about whether Brady shoud have hit Loban.
☐ Discuss what Mr. Minton recorded in the Bible.
☐ Discuss the possibility of compromise on issues such as slavery.
☐ Talk about the roles of people in the household. For example, Mary Dorcas is not expected to do outdoor work. Brady and his uncle are shooed from the kitchen.
☐ What name is used to denote African Americans in this book? Why?
☐ Discuss the difficulties of keeping secrets.
☐ Talk about Brady's strengths and weaknesses.
☐ Brady refused to put a mouth on the scarecrow. Why?
☐ Talk about what caused the laughter at the Fourth of July celebration.
☐ Discuss whether churches should take a stand on political and moral issues.
☐ Mr. Ferguson said that slaves have "no capacity to use freedom." What did he mean?
☐ Talk about why there were laws against teaching slaves to read and write.
☐ Discuss Brady's inability to cope with the idea of slavery and yet understand Moss's plight.
☐ Were Moss's fears justified? Why?
☐ Which characters speak lines that Ms. Fritz probably believes? What makes you think that?
☐ Discuss Brady's telling Range how he feels about hunting. Why did he bring it up at that point?
☐ Read Ms. Fritz's dedication. What does she tell you there?
☐ Look for clues in the book that tell what's going on in the Sermon House.
☐ Mr. McKain talks about shooting passenger pigeons. What were they? Why don't we have them any more?

Things to Do
☐ Some real people are mentioned in the book: William Lloyd Garrison, Henry Clay, and John Quincy Adams. Find out about each of these men and their feelings concerning slavery.
☐ Look for and talk about similes such as "madder than a wet hen" and "keeping a secret was like riding a runaway horse."
☐ Find out about the slavery laws in Pennsylvania just prior to the Civil War.

□ Find out about the Underground Railroad. Where did it begin and end? How long did it operate?

□ Make a continuum showing attitudes toward slavery. At one end is the idea that slavery is necessary and moral and at the other end is the idea that it's unnecessary and immoral. Place each story character along that line according to his/her beliefs.

Books

Written by Jean Fritz
See page 217.

Slavery and the Underground Railroad
Hamilton, Virginia. *Anthony Burns: The Defeat and Triumph of a Fugitive Slave.* Knopf, 1988.
Warner, Lucille Schulberg. *From Slave to Abolitionist: The Life of William Wells Brown.* Dial, 1976.
Winter, Jeanette. *Follow the Drinking Gourd.* Knopf, 1988.

The Civil War
Beatty, Patricia. *Charley Skedaddle.* Morrow, 1987.
———. *Turn Homeward, Hannalee.* Morrow, 1984.
De Angeli, Marguerite. *Thee Hannah.* Doubleday, 1989.
Freedman, Russell. *Lincoln: A Photobiography.* Clarion, 1987. ✔
Haugaard, Erik Christian. *Orphans of the Wind.* Houghton, 1966.
Hunt, Irene. *Across Five Aprils.* Follet, 1967.
Lunn, Janet. *The Root Cellar.* Scribners, 1983.
Meltzer, Milton. *Voices from the Civil War.* Crowell, 1989.
Perez, N. A. *The Slopes of War.* Houghton, 1984.
Reeder, Carolyn. *Shades of Gray.* Macmillan, 1989. ✔

Bridge to Terabithia

Bridge to Terabithia
by Katherine Paterson. Crowel, 1977.

■■■■■■■■□□□□□□

Theme: We must learn the joy of friendship and how to accept death.
Setting: Rural America.
Characters: *Jesse Aarons,* a ten-year-old boy living on a farm near Washington, DC. *Leslie Burke,* Jesse's imaginative friend. *Judy and Bill Burke,* Leslie's understanding mother and father who are writers.
Plot: Jesse and Leslie develop a secret hiding place across a dangerous creek—their imaginary world, Terabithia. When Leslie is killed trying to get to Terabithia, Jesse is filled with guilt. Later he builds a real bridge to Terabithia.

Awards and Recommendations: American Library Association, Newbery Medal, School Library Journal

Things to Talk About and Notice

□ Discuss reasons people might want to escape to imaginary places. What are some other things people do for the same reasons?

□ Talk about why the author called the book *Bridge to Terabithia* rather than just *Terabithia.*

□ Talk about the most dangerous thing you ever did.

Things to Do

□ Set up and name an imaginary place. Decide what rules you will have and what it will look like. Draw a map of your imaginary world.

□ Compare the two sets of parents. Compare them to the parents in *The Facts and Fictions of Minna Pratt* by Patricia MacLachlan (Harper, 1988).

□ Compare Jesse's feelings after Leslie's death to those of the narrator in *A Taste of Blackberries* by Doris Buchanan Smith (Harper, 1973).

□ Find characters like Jesse and Leslie in other books.

Books
Written by Katherine Paterson
See page 237.

Death
Anders, Rebecca. *A Look at Death.* Lerner, 1977. ✔

Bunting, Eve. *The Happy Funeral.* Harper, 1982. ✔

Coerr, Eleanor. *Sadako and the Thousand Paper Cranes.* Dell, 1986. ✔

Coutant, Helen. *First Snow.* Knopf, 1974.

Greene, Constance. *Beat the Turtle Drum.* Viking, 1976. ✔

Hermes, Patricia. *You Shouldn't Have to Say Good-bye.* Harcourt, 1982.

Hyde, Margaret and Hyde, Lawrence. *Meeting Death.* Walker, 1989. ✔

Jukes, Mavis. *Blackberries in the Dark.* Knopf, 1985. ✔

Krementz, Jill. *How It Feels When a Parent Dies.* Knopf, 1981. ✔

Lowry, Lois. *A Summer To Die.* Houghton, 1977. ✔

Mann, Peggy. *There Are Two Kinds of Terrible.* Avon, 1979. ✔

Marino, Jan. *Eighty-Eight Steps to September.* Little, 1989. ✔

Pringle, Laurence. *Death Is Natural.* Four Winds, 1977. ✔

Rofes, Eric, ed. *The Kids' Book about Death and Dying.* Little, 1985. ✔

Smith, Marya. *Across the Creek.* Arcade, 1989.

Steele, Mary Q. *The Life (And Death) of Sarah Elizabeth Harwood.* Greenwillow, 1980. ✔

Child Abuse
Adler, C. S. *Fly Free.* Coward, 1984.

Bawden, Nina. *Squib.* Lothrop, 1982. ✔

Branscum, Robbie. *Toby, Granny and George.* Doubleday, 1976. ✔

Byars, Betsy. *The Pinballs.* Harper, 1977. ✔

Magorian, Michelle. *Good Night, Mr. Tom.* Harper, 1982. ✔

Orr, Rebecca. *Gunner's Run.* Harper, 1980.

Roberts, Willo Davis. *Don't Hurt Laurie!* Atheneum, 1977. ✔

Guilt
Bauer, Marion Dane. *On My Honor.* Clarion, 1986.

Fox, Paula. *The One-Eyed Cat.* Bradbury, 1984. ✔

Smith, Doris Buchanan. *A Taste of Blackberries.* Harper, 1973. ✔

Call It Courage

> ### *Call It Courage*
> by Armstrong Sperry. Macmillan, 1940.
>
> ■■■■■■■■□□□□□□□
>
> **Setting:** An island in the South Pacific.
>
> **Characters:** *Mafatu,* a fifteen-year-old boy, scorned by family and tribe. He is called a coward by the youths because of his fear of the sea.
>
> *Tovana Nui,* the great chief of the Hikueru. He is disappointed in his son and shamed by the way Mafatu is treated by the tribe.
>
> *Kava,* the only boy Mafatu's age who is friendly to Mafatu, but he calls Mafatu a coward behind his back.
>
> *Uri,* a nondescript yellow dog who is Mafatu's inseparable companion. He has faced every terror with his master and has shown his love and devotion throughout.
>
> *Kivi,* Mafatu's pet, an albatross with a deformity who is heckled by other birds.
>
> **Plot:** Mafatu, the chief's son, lost his mother to the sea and he fears it so much that he is scorned by the tribe and a disappointment to his father. He must face the sea god Moana and conquer his fear. He sails his canoe to an isolated island. Facing an unknown terrain, wild boars, cannibals, and other terrors, he creates a shelter, tools, and weapons in preparation for a triumphant return to his people. The crowd assembled on his island sees him, straight and tall against the sea, the spear flashing in his hand, the necklace of boar's teeth on his chest. It is Mafatu who is now called Stout Heart.
>
> **Awards and Recommendations:** American Library Association, Newbery Medal

Things to Talk About and Notice

☐ Discuss how the author maintains excitement without much dialogue.

☐ Talk about why the book has only five chapters.

☐ Discuss Mafatu's reasons for going to the island.

☐ Talk about fears and phobias you have and how they have changed your life.

☐ Discuss what Mafatu knew before his isolation by the tribe. What had he learned by the time he was accepted as a member of the tribe?

☐ Discuss the role of the gods in the lives of ancient peoples and the roles they play today.

☐ What other gods might Mafatu have believed in?

Things to Do

☐ Choose a different locale or time and tell how that changes the action of the story.

☐ Follow Mafatu's journey on a map.

☐ Draw a map of Mafatu's island.

☐ Find out about Polynesia and Polynesians today.

☐ Find out about other sea gods.

Books
Written by Armstrong Sperry
All About the Arctic and Antarctic. Random, 1957.

All Sails Set: A Romance of the Flying Cloud. Winston, 1935.

Bamboo: The Grass Tree. Macmillan, 1942.

The Boy Who Was Afraid. Land, 1942.

Coconut: The Wonder Tree. Macmillan, 1942.

Lost Lagoon. Doubleday, 1939.

One Day with Jambi. Winston, 1934.

One Day with Manu. Winston, 1933.

Pacific Islands Speaking. Macmillan, 1955.

The Rain Forest. Macmillan, 1947.

Thunder Country. Macmillan, 1952.

Survival
See pages 74–76.

Overcoming Fear of Water
Knowles, Anne. *The Halcyon Island.* Harper, 1981.

Paterson, Katherine. *Bridge to Terabithia.* Avon, 1979. ✔

O'Dell, Scott. *Black Pearl.* Houghton, 1967.

Overcoming Other Fears
Aiken, Joan. *Wolves of Willoughby Chase.* Dell, 1987. ✔

Brink, Carol Ryrie. *Caddie Woodlawn.* Macmillan, 1973. ✔

O'Dell, Scott. *Island of the Blue Dolphins.* Houghton, 1960. ✔

Smith, Doris Buchanan. *Voyages.* Viking, 1989. ✔

Speare, Elizabeth George. *The Sign of the Beaver.* Houghton, 1983. ✔

Carrie's War

Carrie's War
by Nina Bawden. Lippincott, 1973.

■■■■■■■■■■■■■□

Setting: Wales during World War II.

Characters: *Carrie,* a spirited young girl with a strong sense of right and wrong. She has spent most of her life feeling guilty for throwing the skull into the lake.

Mr. Evans, a strict, strongly religious man who has worked hard and saved his money but not enjoyed it. He is scrupulously honest, even having Carrie return money to people who were overcharged in his store.

Nick, Carrie's brother. He hates Mr. Evans, but he loves Carrie, the people of Druid's Bottom, and food.

Louisa Evans, Mr. Evans' sister. She has the courage to fall in love with an American soldier and escape Evans' domination.

Mister Johnny, a shy, retarded young man whose speech is so garbled that only Nick can understand him. He is very sensitive and has a violent temper when he is teased.

Dilys Gotobed, Mr. Evans' sister who married a mine owner. She has lived what Mr. Evans' thinks is a wasteful life, going to balls and enjoying luxuries.

Albert Sandwich, a bright boy billeted at Druid's Bottom. He is bookish and is delighted with his assignment because of the library there. He loves Carrie.

Plot: Carrie and Nick Willow are evacuated from London during World War II and placed with Mr. Evans and his sister Lou in a small town in Wales. Mr. Evans and the children have difficulties because he is harsh and unforgiving. He browbeats his sister Lou. His sister Dilys and he are estranged. He believes that Dilys is under the spell of Hepzibah, a woman caring for Dilys in her old age. After Dilys dies, the children think that Mr. Evans has stolen her will so he can turn Hepzibah and Mr. Johnny out of her home.

Awards and Recommendations: American Library Association, School Library Journal

Things to Talk About and Notice
☐ Discuss the way the flashback, the last scene, and the Afterword create a framework for the book.
☐ Discuss Lois Lowry's comments in the Afterword. Do you agree? What would you have written for an Afterword?
☐ Talk about what Mr. Evans' life was like after the children left.
☐ Discuss how you think you would feel if you were separated from your family and sent to live with strangers in a strange town.
☐ At the beginning of the book, Carrie tells her son, "I did a dreadful thing, the worst thing of my life, when I was twelve-and-a-half years old." Discuss what she did, how it made you feel, and whether you agree with her assessment.
☐ Talk about guilt and the way it must have changed Carrie's life.

Things to Do
☐ Compare this story to *Goodnight, Mr. Tom* by Michelle Magorian (Harper, 1982).

Books
Written by Nina Bawden
See page 183.

Children during World War II
Gillham, Bill. *Home Before Long.* Andre Deutsch, 1984. ✔
Magorian, Michelle. *Good Night, Mr. Tom.* Harper, 1982. ✔
Pople, Maureen. *The Other Side of the Family.* Holt, 1986. ✔
Streatfeild, Noel. *When the Sirens Wailed.* Random, 1976. ✔
Walsh, Jill Paton. *Fireweed.* Farrar, 1970. ✔

Cassie Binegar

Cassie Binegar
by Patricia MacLachlan. Harper, 1982.

■■■■■■■■□□□□□□

Theme: Things do not stay the same forever.
Setting: The seashore.
Characters: *Cassie Binegar,* a sensitive, precocious young girl who wants answers to everything. She is certain that she caused her grandfather's death. She writes poetry and wants to become a professional writer.
Gran, a wise, fun-loving grandmother who refuses to stop experiencing life to its fullest.
Mrs. Binegar, Cassie's mother, worries about her husband and sons when they are at sea, loves her family, and works hard getting the old cottages on the property ready to rent.
Mr. Binegar, Cassie's father, loves the sea as do his sons. He is exuberant and loving.
Margaret Mary, Cassie's best friend, loves the eccentric Binegar household.
The Writer, actually Jason Thomas Moreau, but known best to Cassie as The Writer. He rents the first cottage on the Binegar property, helps Cassie see things more clearly, and marries Cassie's cousin, Coralinda.
Binnie, Coralinda's baby daughter, appears unable to talk, but when she does, her speech is crystal clear.
Coralinda, Cassie's cousin, is constantly covered with feathers.
Uncle Hat, Coralinda's father, speaks in numbers and rhymes and always wears a hat.
Plot: Cassie's family has moved and they are now living on the shore. Everyone else in the family loves the new life, but Cassie hates it because it's a change and she hates change. Cassie is embarrassed by her eccentric, messy family. Gran shows Cassie that life is change and that she must appreciate the change, not fight it.

Things to Talk About and Notice

□ Notice the title of each chapter. The titles are usually single words and don't tell you much about the chapter. Why did the author do that?
□ Discuss the characters' names, especially the Binegar name. Why would the author have used such an unusual last name? Most children would have made fun of it, yet it isn't a problem.
□ Talk about the poem by Brendan Galvin at the beginning of the book.
□ Talk about the article at the end of the book.
□ Discuss why the author doesn't really explain why Uncle Hat is the way he is.
□ Talk about the role the dollhouse and the dolls play in this book.

Things to Do

□ Compare Cassie's feeling about the sea at the beginning of the story to Sarah's feelings in *Sarah, Plain and Tall* (Harper, 1985).
□ Compare Cassie's feelings about the dollhouse to Fran Ellen's feelings in *The Bears' House* by Marilyn Sachs (Dutton, 1987).
□ Compare Cassie's eccentric family to the Bagthorpes in the Bagthorpe series by Helen Cresswell (Macmillan). Would anyone in Cassie's family have been comfortable in the Bagthorpe household? What about Margaret Mary?

Books
Written by Patricia MacLachlan
See page 234.

Dollhouses
See pages 11–13.

Eccentric Families
Bawden, Nina. *The Outside Child.* Lothrop, 1989. ✔
Bellairs, John. The Professor Childermass series. Dial. ✔
Cresswell, Helen. The Bagthorpe series. Macmillan. ✔
Pople, Maureen. *The Other Side of the Family.* Holt, 1986. ✔

Writers
See pages 31–33.

Catwings and Catwings Return

Catwings
by Ursula K. Le Guin. Orchard, 1988.

Catwings Return
by Ursula K. Le Guin. Orchard, 1989.

■■□□□□□□□□□□□

Setting: The slums and the countryside.
Characters: *Thelma, Roger, Harriet,* and *James,* the four flying kittens.
Mrs. Jane Tabby, their earthbound mother.
Hank and *Susan,* children who find and befriend the winged kittens.
Plot: Mrs. Jane Tabby can't explain why her kittens have wings, she only knows that they have a chance to escape the dangerous world of the slums and she unselfishly sends them off. However, their city skills don't help much in the country. In *Catwings* they almost starve after some fierce fights with the birds for territory. Although thye adapted to their new world, they miss their mother. In *Catwings Return,* two of them go back to the dangerous inner city to see how their mother is faring, only to discover that she has a new winged kitten. These are two short novels for beginning novel readers and listeners.

Things to Talk About and Notice
☐ Discuss how the author makes it believable that kittens could have wings.
☐ Talk about how the author maintains the cats' point of view throughout the book.
☐ Discuss the illustrations and whether they help or hinder the believability of the story.
☐ Where might your pets go if they could fly?

Books
Written by Ursula K. Le Guin
The Altered I. Ultramarine, 1978.
The Beginning Place. Harper, 1980.
Buffalo Gals and Other Animal Presences. Capra, 1987.
The Compass Rose. Harper, 1982.
The Farthest Shore. Macmillan, 1972.
Fire and Stone. Macmillan, 1989.
Rocannon's World. Ultramarine, 1977.
Solomon Leviathan's Nine Hundred Thirty-First Trip Around the World. Putnam, 1988.
Tehanu: The Last Book of the Earthsea. Atheneum, 1990.
The Tombs of Atuan. Macmillan, 1971.
Very Far Away From Anywhere Else. Macmillan, 1976.
The Visionary. McGraw, 1984.
A Visit from Dr. Katz. Atheneum, 1988.
Wild Oats and Fireweed. Harper, 1987.
The Wind's Twelve Quarters. Harper, 1975.
The Wizard of Earthsea. Houghton, 1968.

Winged Animals
Byars, Betsy. *The Winged Colt of Casa Mia.* Penguin, 1973. ✔
Ward, Lynd. *The Silver Pony.* Houghton, 1973. ✔

Cats
See pages 6–7.

Kindness
Andersen, Hans Christian. "The Ugly Duckling." Many versions.
Byars, Betsy. *The Pinballs.* Harper, 1977. ✔
Gabhart, Ann. *Discovery at Coyote Point.* Avon, 1989. ✔

Charlie Pippin

Charlie Pippin
by Candy Dawson Boyd. Macmillan, 1987.

■■■■■■■□□□□□□□

Theme: War is terrible and it sometimes takes years to resolve the feelings it produces, but we are not helpless to avoid future wars.
Setting: Berkeley, California.
Characters: *Charlie Pippin,* a young girl who is creative, unconventional, bright, and articulate. Her father's lack of affection toward her causes her great pain.
Mr. Pippin, Charlie's father. He's away a lot on business, but when he's home, he dominates the household. He is angry, and Charlie can't figure out why. A Vietnamese War hero, he believes the war was justified.
Mrs. Pippin, Charlie's mother. She manages to put herself between her husband's anger and Charlie but isn't able to help either.
Uncle Ben, Charlie's uncle who adores her. He too fought in Vietnam and thinks the war was unjustified. He has trouble accepting responsibility.
Mrs. Hayamoto, Charlie's teacher. She appears to be strict and uncompromising, but she's very supportive of Charlie once the Vietnam report is given.
Katie Rose, a new girl at school who becomes Charlie's friend.
Chris Saunders, the third member of the War and Peace team. He approaches the study of war statistically, but reports it emotionally.
Sienna, Charlie's selfish older sister.
Plot: Charlie's father seems to hate her. Nothing she does pleases him and he is often furious with her. Fortunately, she has the emotional support of her grandparents and her mother. Her relationship with her father who fought in Vietnam leads her to choose that war as her topic for a social studies report. Before she is finished, she knows a lot about the war, but it isn't until she makes an unauthorized trip to the Vietnam War Memorial in Washington that she and her father begin to understand each other.

Awards and Recommendations: IRA Children's Choice

Things to Talk About and Notice
- Talk about why Charlie's father is so angry with her.
- Discuss the ways others help Charlie and her father solve their problem.
- Talk about why Charlie went to Washington. Why did her uncle go with her? Do you think Charlie's father will ever go there? Why?
- Discuss the author's attitudes about war. What leads you to believe this?
- Talk about the setting of the book and whether it has anything to do with the plot. Why?

Things to Do
- Conduct a survey like Charlie's.
- Make some of the crafts Charlie and her grandmother make.
- Talk to people involved in the Peace Movement. Find out what you can do.

Books
Written by Candy Dawson Boyd
Breadsticks and Blessing Places. Macmillan, 1985.
Circle of Gold. Scholastic, 1948.
Forever Friends. Penguin, 1986.

Vietnamese War: Fiction
Clark, Ann Nolan. *To Stand Against the Wind.* Viking, 1978. ✔
Paterson, Katherine. *Park's Quest.* Lodestar, 1988. ✔

Vietnamese War: Nonfiction
Garland, Sherry. *Vietnam: Rebuilding a Nation.* Dillon, 1990.
Warren, James A. *Portrait of a Tragedy: America and the Vietnam War.* Lothrop, 1990.

Troubled Father/Child Relationships
Fritz, Jean. *Brady.* Coward, 1960. ✔
Smith, Robert Kimmel. *Bobby Baseball.* Delacorte, 1989. ✔

Charlotte's Web

Charlotte's Web
by E. B. White. Harper, 1952.

■■■■□□□□□□□□□□□

Setting: Zuckerman's barn.

Characters: *Charlotte,* a compassionate and literate spider.

Wilbur, an emotional, naive young pig destined for greatness.

Fern, a young girl so sensitive to the animals that she can understand their conversations until she falls in love with Henry.

Templeton, a greedy, self-centered rat who, when bribed, helps save Wilbur.

Plot: Charlotte saves the Zuckerman's pig, Wilbur, from slaughter by forming words in her web that hangs over the pig. Gullible townspeople fail to recognize the importance of the author. Charlotte prints one last word in the web and lays an egg mass before dying, leaving Wilbur distraught over the loss of his friend. When the eggs hatch, all but one of the baby spiders leave the barn.

Awards and Recommendations: Newbery Honor

Things to Talk About and Notice

☐ Talk about different types of friendships and how we determine who will be a friend and who won't.

☐ Discuss the ways in which the story characters are realistic and not realistic.

☐ In what ways did Wilbur and Fern become less naive?

☐ Discuss the reason you think the townspeople were gullible.

☐ Discuss other actions that might have saved Wilbur.

☐ Talk about people's fear of spiders. Is the fear based on fact?

☐ Talk about what might have happened if different farm animals had been involved in the story and why E. B. White chose the animals he did.

Things to Do

☐ Find out about other hoaxes.

☐ Trace the life cycles of some of the other animals used in the book.

☐ Examine livestock at a fair.

☐ Find out about county fairs.

☐ Make up advertising slogans that Charlotte might have used to describe Wilbur.

☐ Find out what the initials *E. B.* stand for. Why do you think Mr. White used his initials instead of his whole name? What other authors use their initials?

Books

Written by E. B. White
Stuart Little. Harper, 1945.
Trumpet of the Swan. Harper, 1970. ✔

Friendship
Burnford, Sheila. *The Incredible Journey.* Little, 1961. ✔
Brett, Jan. *First Dog.* Harcourt, 1988. ✔
Henry, Marguerite. *Justin Morgan Had a Horse.* Macmillan, 1954. ✔
McKnight, Eric. *Lassie, Come Home.* Many versions.

Animal Fantasy
Adams, Richard. *Watership Down.* Macmillan, 1974. ✔
Kipling, Rudyard. *The Jungle Book.* Many versions. ✔
———. *The Just So Stories.* Many versions. ✔
O'Brien, Robert. *Mrs. Frisby and the Rats of NIMH.* Macmillan, 1971. ✔
Peck, Robert Newton. *A Day No Pigs Would Die.* Knopf, 1972. ✔
Steig, William. *Abel's Island.* Farrar, 1976. ✔
Van Leeuwen, Jean. *The Great Rescue Operation.* Dial, 1982.
White, E. B. *Stuart Little.* Harper, 1945.
———. *Trumpet of the Swan.* Harper, 1970. ✔
Williams, Margery. *The Velveteen Rabbit.* Many versions. ✔

Advertising
Heide, Florence Parry. *Banana Blitz.* Holiday, 1983. ✔
MacLachlan, Patricia. *Sarah, Plain and Tall.* Harper, 1985. ✔

Come Sing, Jimmy Jo

Come Sing, Jimmy Jo
by Katherine Paterson. Lodestar, 1985.

■■■■■■■□□□□□□

Setting: Appalachia

Characters: *James (Jimmy Jo),* shy, sensitive, and musical. He loves his parents and grandmother but is torn by the conflicting roles he must play with them.

Grandma, a loving and wise woman who once sang with the family group. When her voice began to crack, Grandma was replaced by Jimmy Jo's mother.

Jerry Lee, Jimmy Jo's father. He is kind and realistic and knows what he must do to keep the group intact.

Olive (Keri Su), Jimmy Jo's mother. She is vain, self-centered, and jealous of her son's stardom. She goes overboard to please her fans and does not see her son's problems. She is also unscrupulous, robbing both her son and her husband of credit for a song.

Earl, Jimmy Jo's uncle. He's mean, jealous, and loves to complain. He likes flashier music than the group has been playing.

Eddie, the group's manager.

Grandpa, sings with the group and tries to maintain harmony within the family but is not strong enough.

Eleazer Jones, the leader of a tough gang. He befriends Jimmy Jo.

Will Short, a smart kid in the class who tutors James and is as friendless as James is.

Plot: Jimmy Jo's family has been singing country music for generations. Jimmy Jo is living with his grandmother while his parents and Uncle Earl are on the road. His mother is ambitious and has hired a manager who insists that Jimmy Jo join them as a star attraction. His mother becomes jealous of the acclaim Jimmy Jo receives and begins flirting with Uncle Earl and recording with him on her own. Jimmy Jo's role becomes a difficult one as the tensions in the group escalate.

Awards and Recommendations: American Library Association, IRA Children's Choice

Things to Talk About and Notice

☐ Discuss the envy that Olive experiences. In what ways is it like or different from the envy that Aunt Bea feels in *The Village by the Sea* by Paula Fox (Orchard, 1988)?

☐ Olive's mother died when Olive was little and it is believed her father beat her. Could that have anything to do with the way she is?

☐ Olive's anger concerns James. Talk about what causes it.

☐ Discuss Grandma's statement "Joy and pain show up in the same wrapper."

☐ Why do people refer to Jimmy Jo's voice as a gift?

☐ Talk about what Jimmy Jo means when he says, "He wasn't famous where it counted, just where it hurt."

☐ Discuss Jimmy Jo's statement to the man who claims to be his father: "I guess in a matter of speaking I am your son. But you ain't my daddy."

Things to Do

☐ The book refers to the Carter Family. Find out about them and listen to some of their music.

☐ Listen to other country music and decide what makes it "country."

☐ Listen to the song "Will the Circle Be Unbroken" that is referred to so frequently in the book.

Books

Written by Katherine Paterson
See page 237.

Music
See pages 41–43.

Dawn of Fear

Dawn of Fear
by Susan Cooper. Harcourt, 1970.

■■■■■■■■■■■■□□

Setting: A village twenty miles outside London.

Characters: *Derek,* a young boy with a keen sense of justice and right and wrong. He is unwilling to invade the White Road Gang's hideout in retaliation. He is squeamish about fighting and horrified to find the dead cat.

Geoffrey, less comfortable with himself and with others than Peter and Derek.

Peter, a very polite, loving boy who is a friend of Derek and Geoffrey and usually manages to make peace between the two during their frequent disagreements.

Tom, older than the other three. Tom is about to join the Merchant Marines.

Johnny, a ne'er-do-well and apparent draft dodger.

David, Johnny's younger brother. It is he who spits at Peter after the fighting, but he is also the one to return Peter's gun.

Plot: The three boys are so busy building a splendid hideout in an abandoned trench that they barely notice the war around them. What little they see of it, the nightly and sometimes daytime trips to the air raid shelters and the evidence of near-misses, seems exciting rather than ominous. When their hideout is maliciously destroyed by a nearby gang, they decide to ambush the gang with mudballs. Fighting soon breaks out among the boys, but their fight is quickly overshadowed by the more serious fight between Tom and Johnny.

Awards and Recommendations: American Library Association

Things to Talk About and Notice

□ Discuss Susan Cooper's decision to name the chapters by days of the week. What does she accomplish with this technique?

□ Discuss the foreshadowing technique that tells you something bad is about to happen during the time the boys are happily building their "camp."

□ Discuss Tom's feeling about Johnny Wiggs.

□ During the fight between Tom and Johnny, the author says, "almost as if the whole world had suddenly divided into two and the two halves were here flinging themselves one against the other." Discuss the silence and the feelings of the spectators during the fight. How did Derek feel after the fight?

□ When was the "Dawn of Fear"?

□ Why did Derek need to see the spot where Peter was killed?

□ Discuss Derek's parents' reaction to the deaths.

□ Why is Derek so horrified that Peter's gate is still there?

□ Discuss the reasons Derek buries the gun.

□ Tom quotes one of Winston Churchill's speeches. Find out who Winston Churchill was and what he did.

□ How close did the fighting get to the United States? Did people have bomb shelters here?

Things to Do

□ Compare this book to *Fireweed* by Jill Paton Walsh (Farrar, 1970). It takes place in the same time and involves children of approximately the same ages.

□ Ask someone who was alive during World War II about blackout curtains, air raid shelters, and anti-aircraft installations. Did we have these in the United States?

Books

Written by Susan Cooper
See page 207.

World War II
See pages 84–87.

Discovery at Coyote Point

> *Discovery at Coyote Point*
> by Ann Gabhart. Avon, 1989.
>
> ■■■■■■■■□□□□□□
>
> **Setting:** A rural area.
>
> **Characters:** *Ance Sanford,* ten years old, quiet, with a real ability to communicate with animals. He is anxious about being left with his grandparents who don't seem to want him. *Grandfather,* Ance's grandfather. He suffered a stroke and can no longer visit his beloved Coyote Point. Angry and hurt at the disappearance of his son, he has trouble communicating with Ance but not with animals. *Grandmother,* kind hearted and more talkative than her husband. She is also a worrier. *Carrie Kenton,* lives at the farm next to the Sanfords'. The Sanfords love her because she brings laughter and life to their existence. *Mr. Kenton,* Carrie's father. He hates coyotes and is sure they kill sheep. He is determined to wipe them out. He is also a trapper.
>
> **Plot:** Ance's father disappeared several years ago and opinions differ as to what happened to him. Ance's mother is sure her husband is dead; his grandmother is sure he's an amnesia victim and will come back some day. His grandfather is equally sure that he left on purpose and will never come back. Ance is living with his grandparents and exploring Coyote Point, the wild land where his father was last seen.

Things to Talk About and Notice

☐ Discuss the points at which Grandfather begins to understand Ance and when Ance begins to understand Grandfather.

☐ Discuss what you thought happened to Ance's father.

☐ Talk about the differences between Ance's mother and grandmother.

☐ Talk about the kinds of communication that are possible between humans and animals.

☐ Are there coyotes in your area? Were they ever in your area? If not, could they survive there? How would they change your community?

☐ Discuss whether wolves and coyotes should be reintroduced to areas where they are now extinct. Why?

☐ Discuss bounties on coyotes or other animals that are hazardous to livestock.

Things to Do

☐ Talk to a trapper about his/her job.

☐ Talk to an animal rights activist.

Books

Written by Ann Gabhart

The Gifting. Simon & Schuster, 1989.

A Kindred Spirit. Simon & Schuster, 1985.

Only in Sunshine. Avon, 1987.

Wish Come True. Avon, 1988.

Wild Animals

Baudouy, Michel-Aime. *Old One-Toe.* Harcourt, 1959.

Byars, Betsy. *The Midnight Fox.* Viking, 1968. ✔

Dunlop, Eileen. *Fox Farm.* Holt, 1979. ✔

Eckert, Allan W. *Incident at Hawk's Hill.* Little, 1971. ✔

George, Jean Craighead. *Julie of the Wolves.* Harper, 1972. ✔

———. *The Cry of the Crow.* Harper, 1980. ✔

McCutcheon, Elsie. *The Rat War.* Farrar, 1986. ✔

Morey, Walt. *Gentle Ben.* Dutton, 1965. ✔

North, Sterling. *Rascal.* Dutton, 1963. ✔

Nunes, Susan. *Coyote Dreams.* Macmillan, 1988.

Polseno, Jo. *This Hawk Belongs to Me.* McKay, 1977. ✔

Stranger, Joyce. *The Fox at Drummers' Darkness.* Farrar, 1977. ✔

Poetry

Lawrence, D. H. "Mountain Lion" from *Room for Me and a Mountain Lion: Poetry of Open Space* edited by Nancy Larrick. Evans, 1974.

The Double Life of Pocahontas

> ### The Double Life of Pocahontas
> by Jean Fritz. Putnam, 1983.
>
> ■■■■■■■■□□□□□
>
> **Summary:** This is another of Jean Fritz's longer biographies for children. As always, she brings the character to life without fictionalizing the history. We see Pocahontas as the young Native American princess who at first delights in her role as emissary between her people's world and that of the new settlers.
>
> **Awards and Recommendations:** American Library Association, Boston Globe/Horn Book, School Library Journal

Things to Talk About and Notice

- Discuss how Pocahontas saved John Smith's life twice. Did she really save him the first time or was this part of a ritual?
- Discuss Powhatan's feelings toward the settlers.
- Talk about the demands the London Company made on settlers and whether they were realistic.
- Talk about the original goals of the settlers and which were reached. List them.
- Compare Powhatan's feelings about guns to those of John Smith.
- Why did Pocahontas think John Smith was dead?
- Discuss how and why Pocahontas was betrayed by the Japizaws.
- Discuss King James' feelings about smoking.
- Why was Pocahontas sent to England?
- Discuss Tomocomo's feelings about England.
- How did Pocahontas feel about returning to Jamestown? Why?
- Talk about why John Smith didn't go to see his friend Pocahontas immediately. What did Pocahontas say to him? What would you have said?

Things to Do

- Make models of houses and forts such as the Native Americans and settlers used.
- Captain Smith mapped much of the territory. Make a map of a wilderness area or wooded area.
- Compare the Native Americans' view of the world to that of Europeans at that time.
- Compare John Smith and his relationship with the settlers to that of Miles Standish in Massachusetts a few years later.
- Pocahontas' name means "lively and frolicsome." What does your name mean?
- Make a chart showing what happened to each of the characters mentioned in the biography.

Books
Written by Jean Fritz
See page 217.

Pocahontas

D'Aulaire, Ingri and D'Aulaire, Edgar. *Pocahontas.* Doubleday, 1949.

Jassem, Kate. *Pocahontas, Girl of Jamestown.* Troll, 1979.

Richards, Dorothy. *Pocahontas, Child-Princess.* Childs World, 1978.

Santrey, Laurence. *Pocahontas.* Troll, 1985.

Wilkie, Katharine. *Pocahontas: Indian Princess.* Garrard, 1969.

The Elephant in the Dark

The Elephant in the Dark
by Carol Carrick. Clarion, 1988.

■■■■■■■■□□□□□

Setting: Cadbury, Massachusetts, in the early 1800's.

Characters: *Will,* a young boy who adores his mother and feels completely alone when she dies. His capacity for love is great and, when the elephant comes, Will sacrifices everything to be with it.

Toong, the first elephant in the United States.

Maddy, Will's beautiful and whimsical mother. She had been making a precarious living for them both by weaving baskets and gathering food. Now her illness has overtaken her.

Mr. and Mrs. Sanderson, village storekeepers. They offer Will a place to live, a job, and a kind of love or, at least, concern.

Plot: Will doesn't mind being an outcast at school and in the village while his whimsical and beautiful mother is alive. When she dies of consumption and Will has to leave the only home he's ever known, he feels completely alone and vulnerable. Even the kindness of Mr. and Mrs. Sanderson is not enough for Will. When the elephant, reportedly the first elephant in America, arrives, Will has something to love and something that appears to love or at least tolerate him.

Things to Talk About and Notice

☐ Discuss the villagers' reactions to the elephant.
☐ Discuss why Will was shunned by the community.
☐ Discuss why Will thought Miranda was his mother.
☐ Talk about what Ms. Carrick had to know to write this book.

Things to Do

☐ Compare Will and Toong to the boy and the gorilla in *The Stranger at Green Knowe* by Lucy Boston (Harcourt, 1961).
☐ Find out what parts, if any, of this book are true.

☐ Find out about early circus and stunt players in the United States.
☐ Find out about the kind of schools that existed in the early 1800s in the United States.

Books

Written by Carol Carrick

The Accident. Houghton, 1976.☑
Aladdin and the Magic Lamp. Houghton, 1989.
Beach Bird. Dial, 1978.
Ben and the Porcupine. Houghton, 1985.☑
Big Old Bones: A Dinosaur Tale. Clarion, 1989.
The Blue Lobster. Dial, 1975
The Climb. Houghton, 1980.☑
The Crocodiles Still Wait. Houghton, 1980.
Dark and Full of Secrets. Houghton, 1984.
The Dirt Road. Macmillan, 1970.
The Empty Squirrel. Greenwillow, 1981.
The Foundling. Houghton, 1977.
The Highest Balloon on the Common. Greenwillow, 1977.
Left Behind. Ticknor, 1988.☑
The Longest Float in the Parade. Greenwillow, 1982.
Lost in the Storm. Houghton, 1974.
Octopus. Houghton, 1978.
Old Mother Witch. Houghton, 1975.
Patrick's Dinosaurs. Houghton, 1983.☑
Paul's Christmas Birthday. Greenwillow, 1978.
Sand Tiger Shark. Houghton, 1976.
Sleep Out. Houghton, 1982.
Some Friend! Houghton, 1979.
Stay Away from Simon. Ticknor, 1985.
Two Coyotes. Houghton, 1982.
The Washout. Houghton, 1987.
What Happened to Patrick's Dinosaurs? Clarion, 1986.☑
What a Wimp! Houghton, 1983.

Relationships with a Wild Animal

Boston, Lucy. *The Stranger at Green Knowe.* Harcourt, 1961.
Byars, Betsy. *The Midnight Fox.* Viking, 1968. ✔

The Fairy Rebel

The Fairy Rebel
by Lynne Reid Banks. Doubleday, 1988.

■■■■■■■□□□□□□

Theme: There is magic hidden in each of us.
Setting: A country house just outside London.
Characters: *Tiki,* a fairy with a mind of her own. She spurns fancy gowns and prefers to wear jeans. She is stubborn, curious, and also very brave.
Wijic, loves Tiki and usually follows her lead, sometimes joining his magic with hers.
Jan, a young, lonely wife who badly wants a child. She believes in magic and has a strong sense of justice.
Charles, Jan's matter-of-fact physician husband. Eventually he is forced to believe in fairies and magic.
Bindi, the human child born to Jan and Charles with the help of Tiki. Tiki, however, made a mistake and Bindi has a tiny spot of blue hair on her head.
Fairy Queen, rules the fairies absolutely. They claim to love her, and she makes sure that they make the claim loudly each hour. She governs the wasps as well as the fairies and often uses them to accomplish her domination. She is also forgetful.
Plot: In the tradition of classic fairy tales, Tiki, a rather unconventional fairy, agrees to help a human couple, Jan and Charles, who want to have a baby. In so doing, Tiki incurs the wrath of the Fairy Queen. For a while, it looks as though all is safe. Tiki and her friend Wijic give Bindi a magic rose on each birthday until her seventh. On Bindi's seventh birthday, the Fairy Queen calls on her servants, the wasps, to bring down disaster on Tiki and Wijic and their all too human family.

Things to Talk About and Notice
☐ Discuss how the author makes us believe in Tiki.
☐ Talk about how the author uses flashback.
☐ What are the Fairy Queen's rules?

Things to Do
☐ Design clothes for Tiki and Wijic.
☐ Create one of the roses Tiki leaves for Bindi or design a new one for next year.
☐ Compare the Fairy Queen to the queens in *Alice's Adventures in Wonderland* by Lewis Carroll and *The Chronicles of Narnia* by C. S. Lewis.
☐ Compare the fairies' fear of humans to the Borrowers fear of humans in *The Borrowers* by Mary Norton (Harcourt, 1953).
☐ Compare Tiki to the fairy, Marvin, in *Out of the Bug Jar* by Kathleen Thomas (Dodd, 1981).

Books
Written by Lynn Reid Banks
I, Houdini. Doubleday, 1988.
Indian in the Cupboard. Doubleday, 1981. ✔
My Darling Villain. Harper, 1977.
Return of the Indian. Doubleday, 1986. ✔
The Secret of the Indian. Doubleday, 1988. ✔
The Writing on the Wall. Harper, 1982.

Fairies and Humans
Andersen, Hans Christian. *Thumbelina.* Many versions.
Barrie, James Matthew. *Peter Pan.* Many versions.
Baum, L. Frank. The Oz Books. Many versions.
Kendall, Carol. *The Gammage Cup.* Harcourt, 1986.
Lewis, C. S. *The Chronicles of Narnia.* Many versions. ✔
MacDonald, George. *The Light Princess.* Farrar, 1977.
Nesbit, Edith. "The Five Children and It." Many versions.
Norton, Mary. *The Borrowers.* Harcourt, 1953. ✔
Parrault, Charles. *Sleeping Beauty.* Many versions.
Thomas, Kathleen. *Out of the Bug Jar.* Dodd, 1981.

A Fine White Dust

A Fine White Dust
by Cynthia Rylant. Bradbury, 1986.

■■■■■■■■■■■■□□

Theme: There are many forms of religious feeling.

Setting: A small town in the rural South.

Characters: *Pete Cassidy,* an impressionable boy trying to come to grips with his religious beliefs and those of his family and friend.
Rufus, Pete's loyal, atheistic friend.
James W. Carson, a charismatic preacher who influences Pete.
Mrs. and Mrs. Cassidy, Pete's understanding and supportive parents.

Plot: Pete's parents are not particularly religious and go to church only on special occasions. His friend Rufus is an atheist, but Pete has strong religious beliefs. Pete's father suggests that he go to a revival, and there he is awed by the preacher, Jim Carson, and is "reborn" that night. Pete rejects Rufus and throws his energy into the world of Jim Carson who tells Pete he has the makings of a preacher and invites Pete to join him on the road. Rufus tries to dissuade Pete, but Pete will hear none of it. He packs a few mementos and waits at the gas station for Jim. Jim never shows up, but Rufus does. Later they find that Jim left with one of the women at the revival. Pete's relationships with his parents and Rufus are strengthened by the experience.

Awards and Recommendations: American Library Association, Newbery Honor Award, School Library Journal

Things to Talk About and Notice
□ Discuss why the author wrote this book from Pete's point of view.
□ Talk about character motivation in the story.
□ Discuss whether James Carson did any good.
□ Talk about why religion is important to people.
□ Discuss the appeal of preachers.
□ Discuss different styles of preaching.

Things to Do
□ Read Cynthia Rylant's autobiography, *But I'll Be Back Again.* What happened in her life that might have led her to writing this book?
□ Make a list of charismatic or persuasive people.
□ Find out about some famous preachers.

Books
Written by Cynthia Rylant
See page 245.

Religion

Blume, Judy. *Are You There, God? It's Me, Margaret.* Bradbury, 1970. ✔

Branscum, Robbie. *Spud Tackett and the Angel of Doom.* Viking, 1983. ✔

———. *Toby, Granny and George.* Doubleday, 1976. ✔

Byars, Betsy. *The Glory Girl.* Viking, 1983. ✔

Holland, Isabelle. *Abbie's God Book.* Westminster, 1982. ✔

Jones, Rebecca C. *The Believers.* Arcade, 1989.

Fireweed

Fireweed
by Jill Paton Walsh. Farrar, 1970.

■■■■■■■■■■■■■□

Theme: Wars change relationships.
Setting: London, 1940, during the Blitz.
Characters: *Bill,* a fifteen-year-old boy who was living with his father and aunt until his father is drafted. His aunt is not willing to keep him and sends him off to Wales. After running back to London, he finds Julie, also without a family, in a bomb shelter. He is more objective than Julie but eventually cares deeply for her.
Julie, Julia Vernon-Greene. She is younger than Bill and comes from a very sheltered, privileged life. Her emotions run closer to the surface than Bill's, yet she seems to have a clearer sense of responsibility.
Dickie, We're never sure what his real name is. He's a very young child whom Julie and Bill find and take in.
Mrs. Vernon-Greene, We don't meet her until after Julie is hospitalized. She is sympathetic to Bill but makes it clear there is little place for him in Julie's life.
Plot: Two children who were supposed to be evacuated from London during the Blitz pool their resources in order to survive there. Bill is older than Julie and comes from a less-privileged family. Their friendship deepens as the city is destroyed around them. Before their friendship is shattered, they set up housekeeping in the ruins.

Things to Talk About and Notice
☐ Notice the spirit of the people of London during this awful time.
☐ Discuss reasons for sending the children away from London and the results this decision must have had.
☐ Discuss why Hitler bombed London so ferociously.

Things to Do
☐ Read a nonfiction book about England during World War II.
☐ Talk to people who lived in England at that time.
☐ Find out what happened to the children who got to Canada and the U.S. from England at that time.
☐ Read newspaper accounts and photographs of the bombing of London.
☐ Find photographs of the landmarks the children talk about in the book.
☐ Find out what kinds of bombs were used.

Books
Written by Jill Paton Walsh
Babylon. Andre Deutsch, 1982.
Birdy and the Ghosties. Farrar, 1989.
A Chance Child. Avon, 1980.
Children of the Fox. Farrar, 1978.
The Emperor's Winding Sheet. Farrar, 1974.
Gaffer Samson's Luck. Farrar, 1980.
Goldengrove. Farrar, 1985.
The Green Book. Farrar, 1982. ✔
The Huffler. Farrar, 1975.
The Island Summer. Houghton, 1976.
Lost and Found. Andre Deutsch, 1985.
A Parcel of Patterns. Farrar, 1983.
Torch. Farrar, 1988.
Unleaving. Avon, 1986.

World War II
See pages 84–87.

Survival
See pages 74–76.

The Flunking of Joshua T. Bates

The Flunking of Joshua T. Bates
by Susan Shreve. Knopf, 1984.

■■☐☐☐☐☐☐☐☐☐☐☐☐

Theme: There are many ways to flunk.
Setting: Washington, D.C.
Characters: *Joshua Bates,* a good kid who wants very much to succeed in school and to keep his friends even though he's going through the worst year of his life.
Mrs. Goodwin, a middle-aged teacher who understands Joshua and is his friend.
Andrew Parker, Joshua's friend. He wants to remain Joshua's friend but is under pressure from his fourth-grade friends to desert him.
Amanda Bates, Joshua's big sister who seems to be good at everything.
Tommy Wilheim, a bully who teases Joshua about flunking.
Mrs. Bates, Joshua's mother who understands and loves him.
Plot: Joshua T. Bates is going to have to repeat third grade. He hates school. He can't read very well, but he's very good at baseball. When he tells his new teacher, Mrs. Goodwin, that this first day in third grade for the second time is the worst day of his life, she tells him it's her worst day too: she is getting a divorce. She tutors Josh and he finally makes fourth grade part way through the year, but not until they go through some pretty rough times.

Things to Talk About and Notice

☐ Discuss what life must have been like for Joshua last year.
☐ Discuss Mrs. Bates explanation of why Joshua is repeating third grade.
☐ Should Mrs. Bates have waited until the end of summer to tell Josh about his staying back? Why?
☐ Talk about Joshua's judgment of last year's teacher and whether it is fair.
☐ Discuss how it feels to fail.
☐ Talk about Mrs. Goodwin's tact in dealing with the situation. What doesn't she tell Joshua? Why?
☐ Discuss why Billy Nickel wasn't held back.
☐ Talk about Josh's fantasies of what should happen to Tommy.

☐ Talk about Andrew's feelings.
☐ Was Andrew really stung by a bee? Why did he say he was?
☐ Discuss Mrs. Goodwin's statement: "Today I feel a hundred years old, too old to teach school any longer—too fat, too wrinkled, too gray-haired."
☐ Why do Joshua's stomach aches disappear?
☐ Talk about feeling homesick.
☐ Discuss the way Mrs. Goodwin must feel when she promotes Joshua.

Books

Written by Susan Shreve
The Bad Dreams of a Good Girl. Knopf, 1982.
Family Secrets. Knopf, 1979.
How I Saved the World on Purpose. Holt, 1985.
Lily and the Runaway Baby. Random, 1987.
Lucy Forever and Miss Rosetree, Shrinks. Knopf, 1988.
The Masquerade. Knopf, 1980.
The Revolution of Mary Leary. Knopf, 1982.

School
Blume, Judy. *Tales of a Fourth Grade Nothing.* Dutton, 1972. ✔
Carrick, Carol. *What a Wimp!* Houghton, 1983.
Cazet, Denys. *Never Spit on Your Shoes.* Orchard, 1990.
Cleary, Beverly. *Dear Mr. Henshaw.* Morrow, 1983. ✔
DeClements, Barthe. *Nothing's Fair in Fifth Grade.* Viking, 1981.
Fitzgerald, John D. *The Great Brain at the Academy.* Dial, 1972.
Giff, Patricia Reilly. The Polk Street School Books.☑
Gilson, Jamie. *Thirteen Ways to Sink a Sub.* Lothrop, 1982.
Hurwtiz, Johanna. *Aldo Applesauce.* Morrow, 1979.
———. *Class Clown.* Morrow, 1987.
Keller, Charles. *School Daze.* Prentice, 1981.
Levy, Elizabeth. *Something Queer at the Haunted School.* Delacorte, 1982.
Oppenheim, Joanne. *Mrs. Peloki's Class Play.* Dodd, 1984.
Ruckman, Ivy. *What's an Average Kid Like Me Doing Way Up Here?* Delacorte, 1983.

Staying Back
Giff, Patricia Reilly. *The Beast in Ms. Rooney's Room.* Delacorte, 1986.☑
Roy, Ron. *Frankie Is Staying Back.* Houghton, 1981.

Fog Magic

Fog Magic.
by Julia Sauer. Viking, 1944.

■■■■□□□□□□□□□□

Setting: Nova Scotia, past and present.
Characters: *Greta Addington,* an eleven-year-old girl who moves between times.
Gertrude Addington, Greta's mother.
Walter Addington, Greta's father.
Old Man Himion, the first person Greta sees from the past.
Mrs. Trask, the woman who takes Greta to the Morrill's. She's gruff, but kind.
Retha Morrill, a girl about Greta's age from the past.
Laura Morrill, Retha's mother. She's seen people from "over the mountain" and knows that Greta can come only in the fog and must leave when the fog begins to lift.
Ardis Stanton, a woman from "down off the Islands" whose land is being taken away.
Father Amiraux, a priest from the "French shore."
Anthony, a legless man in Blue Cove who does not speak. He was found ashore after a strange ship pulled out.
Ann, a girl in Blue Cove falsely accused of theft who has been running away ever since.
Laleah Cornwall, wife of the ship captain. After he died of yellow fever, she forced the men to bring him home for burial.
Plot: Greta has always felt an affinity for the fog. When she discovers that she can walk through the fog and enter a village from the past, she knows why the fog is her special time. Time in Blue Cove is not the same as in Greta's world. The seasons are the same but the days are not. She finds that her father has also been able to visit the village and she dreads the time when she can't go back.

Like *Tom's Midnight Garden* by Philippa Pearce, this is a well-written time fantasy and the two should be compared. *Fog Magic,* however, is much easier to understand: the action is more direct and the writing simpler.

Awards and Recommendations: Newbery Honor

Things to Talk About and Notice

☐ Greta remembers a Bible verse that says, "Faith is the substance of things hoped for, the evidence of things not seen." Discuss what it means to her.
☐ Mrs. Morrill says, "Women who stay ashore have to learn the same lesson that men learn who go to sea . . . they have to learn to be content and at peace shut in by their horizon." Is that the theme for this book?
☐ Why do people in Blue Cove live so well and dress in silks?
☐ Discuss why days in Blue Cove are different than those in Little Valley.
☐ Discuss what you thought happened to Anthony.
☐ What did you think would happen to Ann?
☐ Talk about what Greta's father means when he says, "There's disappointment over the mountain, little girl." Was he right?
☐ In the Morrill household there's a "Loyalist rocker." Why is it called that?
☐ Discuss Greta's statement "Up to twelve [years old] it's been fun to look up. But after twelve the stairs turn. I can't see around the bend."
☐ Talk about the reaction the people of Blue Cove have to the strange ship in the harbor.
☐ How does Greta know that her father has been to Blue Cove too?
☐ Why can't Greta ask her father directly about what happened to the village of Blue Cove?
☐ Discuss why Mrs. Morrill wishes Greta "safe passage" on the night of her twelfth birthday.
☐ Talk about Greta's father's knife and her kitten.

Things to Do

☐ On a map locate the action of the story. Find as many of the places referred to as possible. Can you find what Greta's father calls "Old Fundy"?
☐ Read fog poetry and then go for a walk in the fog. Write fog poetry or descriptions.
☐ Look at fine silks and, if possible, a piece of ivory brocade and imagine how Ardis Stanton must have looked in it.

Books
Fog: Picture Books
McCloskey, Robert. *Time of Wonder.* Viking, 1957. ✔ ☑
Ryder, Joanne. *Fog in the Meadow.* Harper, 1979.
Tresselt, Alvin. *Hide and Seek Fog.* Lothrop, 1965.

Time Fantasies

Anderson, Margaret J. *The Druid's Gift.* Knopf, 1989.
——. *In the Keep of Time.* Knopf, 1977.
Cresswell, Helen. *A Game of Catch.* Macmillan, 1977. ✔
Duncan, Lois. *Locked in Time.* Little, 1985.
Farmer, Penelope. *Charlotte Sometimes.* Dell, 1987.
Hahn, Mary Downing. *The Doll in the Garden.* Clarion, 1989. ✔
L'Engle, Madeleine. *A Wrinkle in Time.* Dell, 1976.
Pearce, Philippa. *Tom's Midnight Garden.* Harper, 1984. ✔

Peck, Richard. *Voices After Midnight.* Delacorte, 1989. ✔
Weldrick, Valerie. *Time Sweep.* Lothrop, 1978.
Wells, H. G. *The Time Machine.* Many versions.
Westall, Robert. *The Wind Eye.* Greenwillow, 1977.

Poetry

Lawrence, D. H. "Things Men Have Made" from *Postcard Poems* edited by Paul B Janeczko. Bradbury, 1979.

From the Mixed-Up Files of Mrs. Basil E. Frankweiler

From the Mixed-Up Files of Mrs. Basil E. Frankweiler
by E. L. Konigsburg. Atheneum, 1967.

■■■■■■■□□□□□□□

Theme: Sometimes we must find answers just to satisfy our curiousity.
Setting: The Metropolitan Museum of Art and Mrs. Frankweiler's home.
Characters: *Claudia,* a bright, curious girl with a need to be noticed. She's a little pretentious, choosing to hide out in the museum.
Jamie, Claudia's brother, the moneybags of the excursion.
Mrs. Frankweiler, their grandfather's employer. She seems aloof, but she sees the humor in the situation and admires the children for their gumption.
Plot: Claudia feels unappreciated at home and decides to run away. Being a good planner but poor money manager, she allows her brother Jamie to join her. They hide in The Metropolitan Museum of Art where they get involved in a mystery: Did Michelangelo sculpt the small statue of an angel?

Awards and Recommendations: American Library Association, Newbery Medal, School Library Journal

Things to Talk About and Notice
☐ List the clues to the artist's identify.
☐ Talk about how the children avoided being caught.
☐ Who is telling the story?
☐ Tell the story from Mrs. Frankweiler's point of view.
☐ Talk about why Mrs. Frankweiler didn't reveal the answer to the mystery.
☐ Talk about public buildings where one could possibly hide out.

Things to Do
☐ Find out about Michelangelo.
☐ Visit an art museum.
☐ Find out how a museum researches the works of art it displays.
☐ Find out about the art mentioned in the book.
☐ Write to the Metropolitan for a brochure.
☐ Write to the Chamber of Commerce of New York City for information about the Metropolitan and other art museums.
☐ Make your own plan for hiding out in a public building or museum.
☐ Write a sequel to the story.

Books
Written by E. L. (Elaine) Konigsburg
See page 230.

Museums and Works of Art

Bjork, Christina. *Linnea in Monet's Garden.* Farrar, 1987.

Hutchins, Pat. *The Mona Lisa Mystery.* Greenwillow, 1981. ✔

Koch, Kenneth and Farrell, Kate. *Talking to the Sun.* Holt, 1985.

Marks, Claude. *Go In and Out the Window.* Holt, 1987.

Rudstrom, Lennart and Larsson, Carl. *Home.* Putnam, 1988.

Ventura, Piero. *Michelangelo's World.* Putnam, 1988.

Running Away from Home

Fleischman, Sid. *By the Great Horn Spoon.* Little, 1963. ✔

——. *Whipping Boy.* Greenwillow, 1986. ✔

Hermes, Patricia. *Who Will Take Care of Me?* Harcourt, 1983.

Holman, Felice. *Slake's Limbo.* Scribners, 1974. ✔

Thomas, Ruth. *The Runaways.* Lippincott, 1989.

Twain, Mark. *Huckleberry Finn.* Many versions.

——. *Tom Sawyer.* Many versions.

A Gathering of Days

A Gathering of Days:
A New England Girl's Journal 1830-1832
by Joan W. Blos. Scribners, 1979.

■■■■■■■■□□□□□□

Theme: We must learn to accept the realities of life.

Setting: A farm community in New Hampshire, mid-nineteenth century.

Characters: *Catherine Hall,* the journal's author. Catherine is a fourteen-year-old girl whose mother is dead. She is living with her father and younger sister. Catherine is determined to live her life as honestly as possible, even when such honesty puts her in jeopardy.

Cassie Shipman, Catherine's dearest friend who sometimes acts as Catherine's conscience but is as full of joy as Catherine is. It is Cassie who gets sick and dies in the second year of the journal.

Charles Hall, Catherine's father, who tries to provide guidance and love for his motherless children until he brings home a new wife.

Curtis, an escaped slave who never appears in the novel but is pivotal to the plot.

Ann Higham, Charles's second wife, mother of Daniel and stepmother to Catherine and Matty. Ann must make the difficult adjustment to farm life after living in Boston.

Plot: Told through a journal kept from 1830 to 1832, this is the story of a young girl's acceptance of life and death on a farm in New Hampshire. During these two years, Catherine befriends a runaway slave, risking the wrath of her family and community, and faces the death of her dearest friend.

Awards and Recommendations: American Library Association, Newbery Medal, School Library Journal

Things to Talk About and Notice

☐ Discuss Catherine's language style.

☐ Talk about the school's curriculum. For example, how is it different for boys and girls? What are the first four rules of arithmetic for girls?

☐ Discuss the roles of males and females in the household and village during this time.

☐ Talk about slavery. What were the views in your area during the time described in the book? How did they differ from Catherine's?

Things to Do

☐ Compare Charles Hall's trading trip to Boston with a similar trip taken in *Ox-Cart Man* by Donald Hall (Viking, 1979).

☐ Find the pattern of the Mariner's Compass that Catherine used for her quilt. Compare it to other quilts. Make one square of the pattern in cloth or paper.

☐ Find examples of the handwriting style used during the late 1800s to find out what Catherine's penmanship probably looked like. Try to write your own name that way. Use a quill pen and ink.

Books

Written by Joan Blos
Brothers of the Heart. Scribners, 1985.
Martin's Hats. Morrow, 1984.
Old Henry. Morrow, 1987. ✔

Journals
See pages 31–33.

Good Night, Mr. Tom

Good Night, Mr. Tom
by Michelle Magorian. Harper, 1982.

■■■■■■■■□□□□□□

Theme: We grow as we find love.
Setting: England, World War II.
Characters: *William Beech,* a frightened, half-starved child when he arrives at Tom's. Later, when he gains self-confidence, he is bright, extremely talented, sensitive, and loving.
Tom Oakley, the widowed older man to whom Will is brought for housing. He has shut himself off from the activities of the village since his wife and baby died. Will's presence forces him to reach out to others for help and to Will for love. Tom is a patient, understanding man whose love for Will surprises everyone including himself.
Zacharias Wrench, Will's best friend. He's brash, funny, and clever. His parents are show people and Zach is used to being among strangers. He understands Will better than anyone else.

Mrs. Beech, Will's mother, a religious fanatic. She whips him often and brutally and seems to hate him.

Plot: William Beech, an abused and terrified child, is evacuated from London into the English countryside where he is taken in by a gruff and lonely man, Tom Oakley. It takes as long for Tom to let go of his grief for his wife and child as it does for Will to feel strong and free. Both are beginning to feel real love for the first time when Will's mother forces him to return to London. Will is hopeful that the abuse is over and that things will be different between them, but her madness and abuse are worse than ever. By the time Tom finds him, Will's new baby sister is dead and Will is not far from it. Tom's determination to make Will well again forces him to kidnap Will. In spite of the child abuse and the casualties of war, this is not a mournful book but a celebration of love and life.

Awards and Recommendations: American Library Association, IRA Best Books for Children

Things to Talk About and Notice
☐ Notice the author's use of flashback while we learn about Mr. Tom's wife Rachel and the birth and death of his child.
☐ Notice the way the author puts us abruptly into the story with Tom's gruff reaction to the knock at his door.
☐ Talk about the accents in the book and in England. Why do people make fun of Carrie for her accent? Why can't they understand her or Mr. Tom?
☐ Discuss the steps Will takes in learning to love.
☐ Talk about why Mrs. Beech abuses her children.

Things to Do
☐ Compare this book to other books about the evacuees from London during World War II.

☐ Find out about the battle of Dunkirk, which is mentioned in the book.

Books
Written by Michelle Magorian
Back Home. Harper, 1984.

World War II
See pages 84–87.

Child Abuse
Branscum, Robbie. *Toby, Granny and George.* Doubleday, 1976. ✔
Byars, Betsy. *The Pinballs.* Harper, 1977. ✔
Orr, Rebecca. *Gunner's Run.* Harper, 1980. ✔
Roberts, Willo Davis. *Don't Hurt Laurie!* Atheneum, 1977. ✔

Goodbye, My Island

Goodbye, My Island
by Jean Rogers. Greenwillow, 1983.

Setting: An island ninety miles off the coast of Nome, Alaska.
Characters: *Esther,* a young Eskimo girl who loves the island and the life it represents.
Dixon, an off-island boy from another culture who has trouble adjusting to the Eskimo way of life but is determined to make it.

Plot: This is a first person account of Eskimo life on a small island 90 miles from Nome. Esther and her brother Roger love King Island and their family stays there during the winter when increasing numbers of families stay in Nome. The teacher's nephew, Dixon, comes from Wisconsin to spend the year on the island and tries to adapt to island ways. Because of the dwindling number of students, the Bureau of Indian Affairs decides to close the school. Without a school, the holdout families cannot stay on the island. This, then will be their last year and Dixon is in for some adjustment. For example, at the Christmas party there is Eskimo ice cream made of seal blubber and whipped fat and one-on-one contests between the men. The book also describes hunting for seals and other animals that are used for food and clothing, including all its attendant violence.

Things to Talk About and Notice
☐ Discuss hunting as a necessity rather than a sport.
☐ Discuss the food and customs of the island people.
☐ Notice the illustrations by Rie Munoz.

Things to Do
☐ Find out about other dying communities in Alaska.
☐ Find out about habitation on other islands.
☐ Find out about the effect of the Exxon oil spill on the people and environment of Alaska.
☐ Look at Eskimo art.
☐ Compare Esther's feelings about leaving her island to those of Karana in *Island of the Blue Dolphins* by Scott O'Dell.

Books
Written by Jean Rogers
Dinosaurs Are 568. Greenwillow, 1988.

King Island Christmas. Greenwillow, 1985. ✔ ☑
Runaway Mittens. Greenwillow, 1988. ✔ ☑
The Secret Moose. Greenwillow, 1985. ✔

Eskimo Culture
George, Jean C. *Julie of the Wolves.* Harper, 1972. ✔
———. *Water Sky.* Harper, 1987.
Houston, James. *Frozen Fire. Atheneum, 1977.* ✔
———. *Long Claws.* Atheneum, 1981.
Paulsen, Gary. *Dogsong.* Bradbury, 1985. ✔
Shemie, Bonnie. *Houses of Snow, Skin and Bones.* Tundra, 1989.

Islands
O'Dell, Scott. *Island of the Blue Dolphins.* Houghton, 1960. ✔
Paulsen, Gary. *The Island.* Orchard, 1988. ✔
Steig, William. *Abel's Island.* Farrar, 1976. ✔

Hatchet

Hatchet
by Gary Paulsen. Bradbury, 1987.

■■■■■■■■■□□□□□□

Setting: The wilds of northern Canada.
Characters: *Brian Robeson,* a confused, angry boy who becomes self-confident, thoughtful, and deeply appreciative of the beauty and challenge of the wilderness.
Plot: Brian's life is at a crisis point before his plane crashes: his mother and father are divorced. He is on his way to visit his father in northern Canada when the pilot of the tiny plane dies of a heart attack. He realizes that he might be beyond rescue with only a hatchet and no skills for survival.

Awards and Recommendations: American Library Association, Newbery Honor Award

Things to Talk About and Notice
☐ Talk about how finding the survival pack might have changed Brian and the story.

☐ Discuss how Brian's feelings might have been different if he had dropped his hatchet before or right after the crash.
☐ Which of the problems Brian faced would have been most difficult for you?
☐ Discuss Brian's chances for survival if the rescue hadn't come when it did.
☐ Discuss why the author told us about Brian's mother.
☐ Talk about whether this story would have been easier to write as a diary or journal.

Things to Do
☐ Build a fire the way Brian had to.
☐ Taste some of the foods Brian survived on.
☐ Find out what foods are available in the wilderness nearest you.
☐ Make a list of your own survival skills.

Books
Written by Gary Paulsen
See page 239.

Survival
See pages 74–76.

Hugh Pine

Hugh Pine
by Janwillem van de Wetering. Houghton, 1980.

■■■■□□□□□□□□□□

Setting: The town of Sorry, outside the town of Rotworth, which you will find if you go north and a little bit east.

Characters: *Hugh Pine,* a porcupine, disguised as a person by wearing a big floppy red hat and thick coat and walking erect.

Mr. McTosh, the postmaster who, unlike the other people in the story, sees right away that Hugh is a porcupine. Perhaps that's because he looks a little like a porcupine.

Plot: Hugh Pine finds a floppy red hat and decides to wear it so that cars won't run over him. That necessitates walking erect so that the hat won't fall off. Other porcupines, however, cannot learn that skill, so they select Hugh to be their liaison with people and to devise a way to stop porcupines from meeting untimely deaths by cars. The first solution is an enormous fenced-in place for the porcupines to live safely, but the porcupines soon feel caged.

Things to Talk About and Notice

☐ Notice how the animals talk about human things. When Hugh is talking about guns he says, "He might have pointed something at me, and he might have banged, like the people do sometimes when they are after deer or birds or jackrabbits."

☐ Notice the way Hugh describes himself.

☐ Talk about Hugh's difficulty communicating with Mr. McTosh and with the other porcupines.

☐ At what point did you realize that the first solution wasn't going to work?

☐ Notice how the author maintains as much reality as possible in this fantasy.

Things to Do

☐ Make a chart such as the following:

	Dress	Speech	Brains
Hugh Pine			
Other Porcupines			
Mr. McTosh			

Compare the characters according to the way they dress, their manner of speech, and their intelligence.

Books
Written by Janwillem van de Wetering
Hugh Pine and the Good Place. Houghton, 1986. ✔ ☑

Animal Fantasies
Bond, Michael. *Bear Called Paddington.* Houghton, 1961.
O'Brien, Robert. *Mrs. Frisby and the Rats of NIMH.* Atheneum, 1971. ✔
Steig, William. *Abel's Island.* Farrar, 1976. ✔
White, E. B. *Charlotte's Web.* Harper, 1952. ✔
———. *Trumpet of the Swan.* Harper, 1972. ✔

Poetry
Moore, Lilian. "Friend" from *I Like You, If You Like Me: Poems of Friendship* edited by Myra Cohn Livingston. Macmillan, 1987.

In the Year of the Boar and Jackie Robinson

In the Year of the Boar and Jackie Robinson
by Bette Bao Lord. Harper, 1984.

■■■■■■■■□□□□□□

Setting: Brooklyn, New York, 1947.
Characters: *Shirley Temple Wong,* alias Bandit Wong, Sixth Cousin.
Mr. and Mrs. Wong, Shirley's parents.
Señora Rodrigues, the Wong's landlady and music teacher.
Mrs. Rappaport, Shirley's teacher.
Plot: It is 1947, the Year of the Boar, Jackie Robinson's rookie year with the Brooklyn Dodgers, and Shirley Temple Wong's first year in America. During this year, Shirley Temple Wong becomes a ballplayer herself and a fan of the Dodgers.

Things to Talk About and Notice

□ Who is Shirley Temple? What does she have to do with the story?
□ Discuss why Jackie Robinson's being named Rookie of the Year was so important.
□ Discuss women's rights in China in 1947 and now.
□ Discuss the role of baseball in American life.
□ Notice how the author contrasts the two cultures.
□ Talk about problems that immigrants face in your community today.

Things to Do

□ Find out about Chinese names. Do they usually have meanings?
□ Find out why the Dodgers moved to Los Angeles.
□ Find the names for the years in China. In what year were you born?
□ Compare this book to *Thank You, Jackie Robinson* by Barbara Cohen (Lothrop, 1974). In which book does Jackie himself have a role?
□ Find out about Jackie Robinson's life.

Books
Baseball
See page 99.

Poetry
"Foreign Student" from *Crazy to Be Alive In Such a Strange World* edited by Nancy Larrick. Evans, 1977.

The Indian in the Cupboard Stories

Indian in the Cupboard
by Lynne Reid Banks. Doubleday, 1981.

Return of the Indian
by Lynne Reid Banks. Doubleday, 1986.

The Secret of the Indian
by Lynne Reid Banks. Doubleday, 1988.

■■■■■■■■□□□□□□□

Characters: *Omri,* a young boy with a strong sense of honor and responsibility.
Little Bear, a miniature, plastic Native American with a volatile temper.
Patrick, Omri's best friend. He is less thoughtful and more rash than Omri.
Boone, a miniature cowboy that Patrick insists on bringing to life. His lifestyle and Little Bear's are in direct conflict.

Plot: For his birthday, Omri is given an old, locked cupboard. He discovers that when a toy is placed in the cupboard and the cupboard is locked, the toy comes to life but remains small. First, he brings Little Bear to life. Little Bear is not all that happy to be transported from his normal existence. Initially, this is a game for Omri, but eventually the incredible responsibility of controlling and manipulating other lives becomes overwhelming. At the end of the first book, he resolves never to do it again and gives his mother the key to the cupboard. In the sequel, *The Return of the Indian,* Omri decides to check up on Little Bear only to find that Little Bear is dangerously involved in the French and Indian War. In the last book in the series, *The Secret of the Indian,* Omri vows again to put the figures away.

Things to Talk About and Notice
☐ How does Little Bear try to explain his life and culture to Omri?
☐ Talk about how Omri finds out about the Native American culture.
☐ Discuss how Omri finds things Little Bear needs.
☐ Talk about Omri's motives for bringing other toys to life.
☐ Discuss Omri's decision to keep the power of the cupboard secret.
☐ Discuss Patrick's bringing Boone to school. How did that change things?
☐ Talk about the conflict between cowboys and Native Americans.
☐ Discuss whether Native Americans like this book. Might they find anything in it that is stereotypical or demeaning?

Things to Do
☐ Find factual errors in the book. Would an Iroquois live in a teepee?
☐ Compare this book to *The Castle in the Attic* by Elizabeth Winthrop. How are they similar and what is the biggest difference?
☐ Find miniature toys and write stories about their "other lives."

Books
Written by Lynn Reid Banks
See page 114.

Toys That Come to Life
Adler, C. S. *Goodbye, Pink Pig.* Putnam, 1985. ✔
Cassedy, Sylvia. *Behind the Attic Wall.* Crowell, 1983. ✔
———. *Lucie Babbidge's House.* Crowell, 1989. ✔
Kennedy, Richard. *Amy's Eyes.* Harper, 1985. ✔
Sleator, William. *Among the Dolls.* Dutton, 1975. ✔
Williams, Margery. *The Velveteen Rabbit.* Many versions. ✔
Winthrop, Elizabeth. *The Castle in the Attic.* Holiday, 1985. ✔

Island of the Blue Dolphins

Island of the Blue Dolphins
by Scott O'Dell. Houghton, 1960.

■■■■■■■□□□□□□

Setting: An island off the coast of Santa Barbara, California, in the early 1800s.

Characters: *Karana,* a twelve-year-old native girl who has assumed a typical woman's role in the island culture. As the years go by, she breaks taboos with difficulty in order to survive. She becomes a self-sufficient, capable young woman who loves her island home. *Rontu,* the leader of the wild dog pack. Apparently, he was left behind by the Aleuts. He becomes Karana's only companion. *Rontu-Aru,* Rontu's son. *Ramo,* Karana's younger brother. *Chief Chowig,* Karana's gentle, wise father. *Tainor and Lurai,* two wild birds Karana tames. *Mon-a-nee/Won-a-nee,* a baby otter that Karana rescues.

Plot: Karana, the chief's daughter, lives with her father, brother, and older sister in a village on the Island of the Blue Dolphins. Aleuts, led by a Russian captain, come to hunt sea otters and betray the villagers, killing many of the men including Karana's father. The new chief decides to relocate the village on the far away mainland and so the island is evacuated. Karana's younger brother, Ramo, is left and Karana jumps overboard to be with him, convinced that the ship will return for them soon. Ramo is killed by wild dogs and Karana is left to survive there alone.

Awards and Recommendations: American Library Association, Newbery Medal

Things to Talk About and Notice
☐ Discuss the roles of women on the island.
☐ Talk about the secret names.
☐ Discuss the differences between Karana's and Ramo's personalities.
☐ Given what you know of her brother, talk about how Karana's life would have been different if he had survived.
☐ Notice the order in which Karana made her tools.
☐ What taboos does Karana break to survive? How does she feel about breaking them?
☐ Discuss what Karana kills and why she kills.
☐ Notice the number of wild dogs Karana kills and her matter-of-fact reaction to the killings.
☐ Discuss Karana's skills. Where and how did she learn them?
☐ What would have changed if the island had been located where less food was available or where the weather was more severe?
☐ Discuss Karana's changing feelings for Rontu, the leader of the wild dogs.
☐ Talk about what Rontu must have done to become leader of the pack.
☐ Why is Rontu so easily tamed?
☐ Discuss Rontu's decision to stay with Karana instead of rejoining the pack.
☐ Why does Karana not shoot the dogs who are attacking Rontu?
☐ Why did Black Cave frightened Karana so?
☐ Discuss Karana's contact with Tutok, the Aleut girl, and what Tutok must have felt. How did the two girls communicate?
☐ Discuss Tutok's gift for Karana. Notice the similarity of their words for *beautiful.* Why might this be?
☐ Talk about what it would be like for you in Karana's world and for her in yours.
☐ Discuss why Karana's people didn't come back for her? What might have happened if Karana had gone with them?

Things to Do
☐ Compare the tidal wave in this book to the one in *The Big Wave* by Pearl Buck (Harper, 1947).
☐ Make models of the house Karana built for herself and of her two other houses on the island.
☐ Karana measures things in leagues. Find out how long a league is. How many leagues wide is your town or the closest island?
☐ Find out about Aleuts. Where was their original home? Why did they come this far south?
☐ Find out about each of the animals, fish, and plants Karana talks about. Find pictures of them if possible. Write our names for them beside Karana's names. Why would some of the names be the same and others different?
☐ Find out about tidal waves and earthquakes. Do they often follow each other?
☐ Locate San Nicholas Island on a map. How many leagues from the mainland was Karana?

Books

Written by Scott O'Dell

Alexandra. Houghton, 1984.
The Amethyst Ring. Houghton, 1983.
The Black Pearl. Houghton, 1967.
Black Star, Bright Dawn. Houghton, 1988.
The Captive. Houghton, 1979.
Carlota. Houghton, 1977.
The Castle in the Sea. Houghton, 1983.
Child of Fire. Houghton, 1974.
The Cruise of the Arctic Star. Houghton, 1973.
The Dark Canoe. Houghton, 1968.
The Feathered Serpent. Houghton, 1981.
The Hawk That Dare Not Hunt by Day. Bob Jones, 1986.
Janey. Houghton, 1986.
Journey to Jericho. Houghton, 1968.

Kathleen, Please Come Home. Dell, 1980.
The King's Fifth. Houghton, 1966.
My Name Is Not Angelica. Houghton, 1989.
The Road to Damietta. Houghton, 1985.
Sarah Bishop. Houghton, 1980. ✔
The Serpent Never Sleeps. Fawcett, 1989.
Sing Down the Moon. Houghton, 1970. ✔
The Spanish Smile. Houghton, 1982.
Streams to the River, River to the Sea. Houghton, 1986. ✔
The 290. Houghton, 1976.
Zia. Dell, 1978. ✔

Islands
See page 123.

Survival
See pages 74–76.

Julie of the Wolves

Julie of the Wolves
by Jean Craighead George. Harper, 1972.

■■■■■■■■■■■■■□

Theme: It is important to acknowledge and accept one's heritage.
Setting: Alaskan Tundra.
Characters: *Julie (Miyax)*, a young teen in conflict with the life that was chosen for her. *Amaroq*, the lead wolf and Julie's friend. *Kapugin*, Julie's father, a traditional Eskimo.
Plot: Julie ran away from her new, and much older, husband and is attempting to get to a pen-pal's home in San Francisco. She becomes lost on the Alaskan Tundra without food or shelter. Knowing that she must become accepted by a wolf pack in order survive, she studies their behavior and gains acceptance. In the process, she turns toward the ways of the more traditional Eskimos.

Awards and Recommendations: American Library Association, Newbery Medal

Things to Talk About and Notice
- Discuss traditional values and customs and new values and customs.
- Talk about why different generations look at life and values differently.
- Discuss Julie's final decision.

Things to Do
- Find out about the Tundra.
- Do research about wolves.
- Find out about human and animal communication.
- Compare the wolves in this story to those in *The Wolves of Willoughby Chase* by Joan Aiken (Doubleday, 1963).
- Compare Julie to Karana in *Island of the Blue Dolphins* by Scott O'Dell (Houghton, 1960). Compare Julie's wolves to the wild dogs.
- Compare Julie's need to become one with the wolves with that of Wil's need to become one with the creatures on the island in Gary Paulsen's *The Island* (Orchard, 1988).
- Examine myths about wolves. Do they deserve their reputations?
- Find expressions about wolves. What do they mean?

Books
Written by Jean Craighead George
See page 220.

Survival in the Arctic
Houston, James. *Frozen Fire.* Atheneum, 1977. ✔
———. *Long Claws: An Arctic Adventure.* Atheneum, 1981.
Paulsen, Gary. *Dogsong.* Bradbury, 1985. ✔

Conflicting Cultures
See page 126.

Wolves
Blades, Ann. *Mary of Mile 18.* Tundra, 1971.
George, Jean Craighead. *The Wounded Wolf.* Harper, 1978. ✔

London, Jack. *White Fang.* Many versions.
Mowat, Farley. *Never Cry Wolf.* Little, 1963.
Murphy, Jim. *The Call of the Wolves.* Scholastic, 1989. ✔
Nolan, Dennis. *Wolf Child.* Macmillan, 1989.

Wild Animals Befriending Humans
Eckert, Allan W. *Incident at Hawk's Hill.* Little, 1971. ✔

Poetry
Larrick, Nancy, ed. *Room for Me and a Mountain Lion: Poetry of Open Space.* Evans, 1974.
 Abanaki Indian Song. "We Will Watch."
 Alaskan Eskimo Song. "Glorious It Is."
 "Eskimo Chant."
 Stafford, William. "In Fur."

The Jungle Book

The Jungle Book
by Rudyard Kipling. Many versions available.

■■■■■□□□□□□□□□□

Theme: There are laws in the jungle.
Setting: The jungle.
Characters: *Mowgli,* a young child raised by a wolf pack.
 Shere Khan, a lame tiger who is Mowgli's greatest enemy.
 Mother Wolf, the wolf who raises Mowgli.
 Akela, the noble wolf-pack leader.
 Bagheera, a panther who teaches and protects Mowgli as much as possible.
 Baloo, a bear and friend of Mowgli.
Plot: Mowgli is raised by Mother Wolf after a fire that killed his parents and, perhaps, injured Shere Khan. Bagheera purchases Mowgli for the price of one buffalo. Bagheera, Akela, and Baloo persuade the pack to allow Mowgli to stay. Later, Akela is overthrown and Mowgli is thrown out of the pack and forced to live with people. Mowgli and the loyal wolves trap Shere Khan and cause a buffalo stampede that kills him.

Things to Talk About and Notice
☐ Discuss the buffalo who changes Mowgli's life at least twice.
☐ Discuss Bagheera's advice to honor the buffalo.
☐ What are the laws of the jungle?
☐ Compare real animal societies to the animal societies portrayed in stories.
☐ Compare the wolf pack in this book to the one in *Julie of the Wolves* by Jean Craighead George (Harper, 1972).
☐ Discuss the behavior of the animals in the story. Are they true to their natures?
☐ Talk about Bagheera's knowledge of man and where he got it?
☐ Why do the animals fear Bagheera?
☐ Notice Mr. Kipling's use of the word *man* when he means "people." Do authors still do that?
☐ Compare Mowgli's life in the jungle to his life with people.
☐ What did Mr. Kipling apparently think about people and about animals?
☐ Discuss why Shere Khan hates Mowgli and why the villagers hate Shere Khan?
☐ Talk about why Shere Khan was trapped.
☐ Discuss the caste system of India.
☐ Notice examples of racism in the book.
☐ Why is being called a dog an insult?

Things to Do
☐ Find out about real people and people in other stories who were raised by wolves.

☐ Compare the jungle animals' society to animal societies in other books.

☐ Watch a video tape of "The Jungle Book" and compare it to the book.

☐ If Mowgli's family had been camping in the American Old West when the fire occurred, would Mowgli have been raised by coyotes? What animals would have taken the other roles?

Books
Written by Rudyard Kipling

Barrack-Room Ballads. Many versions.

Captains Courageous. Many versions.

The Elephant's Child. Many versions.☑

The Just So Stories. Many versions.✔

Kim. Many versions.

Many Inventions. Many versions.

The Second Jungle Book. Many versions.

The Seven Seas. Many versions.

The White Seal. Many versions.

Animal Societies
See page 108.

Justin Morgan Had a Horse

> *Justin Morgan Had a Horse*
> by Marguerite Henry. Rand, 1946.
>
> ■■■■■□□□□□□□□□
>
> **Setting:** Springfield, Massachusetts, and Randolph, Vermont.
>
> **Characters:** *Justin Morgan,* a schoolmaster and singing teacher who takes a colt to Vermont. *Joel Goss,* a boy who forms a bond with the colt and moves in and out of the animal's life. *Little Bub,* also known as "Figure" and finally as "the Justin Morgan Horse." A small colt who endures life as a draft horse, racer, military animal, carriage horse, riding horse, and the President's mount in a military parade at the end of the War of 1812. *Mr. Goss,* Joe's stubborn, harsh father. *Robert Evans,* a cruel man who enters the horse in pulling contests.
>
> **Plot:** Justin Morgan reluctantly accepts an undersized colt as payment for a debt. Little Bub grows up to be a highly versatile horse whose speed, strength, endurance, and personality are passed on to his descendants. This story of the founding father of the Morgan horse borders on a tall tale.
>
> **Awards and Recommendations:** Newbery Honor Award

Things to Talk About and Notice
☐ Notice Wesley Dennis' illustrations. How do they differ from those in other horse books?

☐ Decide which incidents in the story could be considered tall tales.

☐ Little Bub's heritage is uncertain. Some people believe he was part thoroughbred or a draft horse cross. What do you think?

Things to Do
☐ Watch the movie *Justin Morgan Had a Horse.*

☐ Find out about the origins of the Morgan horse. What liberties did Ms. Henry take with the facts?

☐ Write to the Morgan Horse Society in your state to find out more about the horse.

☐ Do research on other breeds of horses and compare them to the Morgan.

☐ Go to a horse show featuring several breeds of horses. Decide which kind you'd like to have.

☐ The Morgan horse had been used to "improve" and establish other breeds. Find out which ones.

☐ Find other novels about Morgan horses.

☐ Find out why Ms. Henry wrote so many books about horses.

Books

Written by Marguerite Henry
Album of Horses. Rand, 1951.
All About Horses. Random, 1962.
The Auction. Macmillan, 1987.
Battle of the Stallions. Macmillan, 1988.
Benjamin West and His Cat Grimalkin. Bobbs, 1947.
Birds at Home. Rand, 1942.
The Big Race. Macmillan, 1987.
Black Gold. Rand, 1957.
Born to Trot. Rand, 1950.
Brighty of the Grand Canyon. Rand, 1953.
The Capture. Macmillan, 1987.
Cinnabar, the One O'Clock Fox. Rand, 1956.
A Colt Is Born. Macmillan, 1988.
Five O'Clock Charlie. Rand, 1962.
Going Home. Macmillan, 1987.
An Innkeeper's Horse. Macmillan, 1988.
King of the Wind. Rand, 1948.
Misty of Chincoteague. Rand, 1947.
Mustang, Wild Spirit of the West. Rand, 1966.
Our First Pony. Macmillan, 1984.
A Pictorial Life Story of Misty. Rand, 1976.
The Rescue of Sham. Macmillan, 1988.
San Domingo: The Medicine Hat Stallion. Rand, 1972.
Sea Star: Orphan of the Chincoteague. Rand, 1949.

Sire of Champions. Macmillan, 1988.
The Storm. Macmillan, 1987.
Stormy: Misty's Foal. Rand, 1963.
The Sultan's Gift. Macmillan, 1988.
The Whirlpool. Macmillan, 1987.
White Stallion of Lipizza. Macmillan, 1979.

Horses: Fiction
Bauer, Marion Dane. *Touch the Moon.* Clarion, 1987.
Dryden, Pamela. *Riding Home.* Bantam, 1988.
Farley, Walter. *The Young Black Stallion.* Random, 1944.
Goble, Paul. *The Girl Who Loved Wild Horses.* Bradbury, 1978. ✔
Greene, Constance. *Beat the Turtle Drum.* Viking, 1976. ✔
Haas, Jesse. *Keeping Barney.* Greenwillow, 1982. ✔
———. *Working Trot.* Greenwillow, 1983.
Moeri, Louise. *A Horse for X.Y.Z.* Dutton, 1977.

Horses: Nonfiction
Patent, Dorothy. *Where the Wild Horses Roam.* Clarion, 1989.

Poetry
Cole, William. *The Poetry of Horses.* Scribners, 1979.
Hopkins, Lee Bennett. *My Mane Catches the Wind.* Harcourt, 1979.

Kneeknock Rise

Kneeknock Rise
by Natalie Babbitt. Farrar, 1970.

■■■■■■■■■■□□□□□

Theme: We sometimes enjoy our fears and fantasies and we don't want to lose them.

Setting: The village of Instep at the foot of the mysterious and frightening mountain, Kneeknock Rise.

Characters: *Egan,* a bright, rather brave boy who has come to Instep to visit relatives and to enjoy the fair.
Aunt Gertrude, a nervous, easily frightened and basically kind woman who faints a lot.
Uncle Anson, a wise clock maker.
Ada, Anson and Gertrude's obnoxious daughter. It's she who dares Egan to climb Kneeknock Rise.
Uncle Ott, a poet and dreamer who disappears, leaving his dog, Annabelle, behind. Egan discovers him on Kneeknock Rise.
Sweetheart, a vicious cat who is kept by Anson, Gertrude, and Ada because it is said that the Megrimum likes cats.

Plot: Egan visits relatives whose entire village is terrorized by the Megrimum that wails from the top of the mountain, Kneeknock Rise. A whole body of folklore has sprung up about the creature. Each year a fair is held so that people can come to be frightened. Egan climbs the mountain and discovers his missing relative and reunites him with his dog, Annabelle. They discover that the source of the noise is the steam from a hot spring, but the villagers don't want to know that.

Awards and Recommendations: Newbery Honor Award

Things to Talk About and Notice
☐ Notice the author's dedication of the book.
☐ Discuss the statement "Facts are the barren branches on which we hang the dear, obscuring foliage of our dreams." Then compare it to Anson's statement to Egan about whether or not the Megrimum is real, "I'll tell you what I think. I think it doesn't really matter. The only thing that matters is whether you want to believe he's there or not. And if your mind is made up, all the facts in the world won't make the slightest difference."
☐ Discuss how Ott's poetry is a foreshadowing of the plot.
☐ Notice the descriptive language, such as: the land is "as flat as if it had been knocked unconscious"; the Megrimum "moaned . . . like a huge and anguished something chained forever to its own great tragic disappointments."
☐ What are the elements of folk tales? Compare them to the elements of this story.

Things to Do
☐ Find folklore that has grown up around some phenomena or landmark in your area.
☐ Find similar stories in which a myth or legend is used to frighten the story characters.
☐ Discuss whether Egan should have exposed the truth to the villagers..

Books
Written and Illustrated by Natalie Babbitt
See page 182.

Unrealistic Fears
Baum, L. Frank. *The Wizard of Oz.* Many versions.
Cowley, Joy. *The Silent One.* Knopf, 1981.

The Legend of King Arthur

The Legend of King Arthur
Retold by Robin Lister. Doubleday, 1990.

■■■■■■■■■■■■■□

Setting: Ancient Britain.

Characters: *Merlin,* gifted with The Sight and a clever nature, he sometimes manipulates others but often is unable to avert their destinies. *King Arthur,* the central character of the legends. He is noble but human. He wants Britain to be peaceful but to stand for right. He's a tragic figure and a noble one, for he can't escape the results of his earlier deeds. *Morgan le Fay,* Arthur's half sister. She curses him at birth. *Guinevere,* Arthur's beloved wife. She loves Arthur, but their love is cursed by Morgan le Fay. For her crime of infidelity with Lancelot, she is sentenced to burn at the stake. *Mordred,* son by Morgause, Arthur's sister. Arthur adopts him as his heir to the throne. *Lancelot du lac,* son of King Ban. He is the strongest and bravest knight of the Round Table, but he is responsible for great unhappiness when he falls in love with Guinevere. *Elayne,* the daughter of Pelles. By Lancelot, she has a son, Galahad. *Bors,* another Knight of the Round Table. He sees more of the Grail than Lancelot. *Galahad,* the son of Lancelot and Elayne. He is the most perfect knight and finds the Grail. *Agravain,* a jealous knight who plots Lancelot's and Arthur's downfall with Mordred.

Plot: These traditional tales have been written in an easier to understand manner than many similar volumes, however, the text is not simplistic and the beauty and formality of the stories come through nicely. The illustrations illuminate and extend the text. This is the best version of the legend for young readers that we have seen. It concentrates on the story of Arthur, Guinevere, and Lancelot. The deeds of some of the other knights are included but are not as fully developed. From the point of view of Merlin, we watch Arthur from his birth through his triumphs and tragedies to his death.

Things to Talk About and Notice

☐ Notice the foreshadowing and flashbacks.
☐ Why is Arthur given two magic swords?
☐ Discuss Merlin's dilemma.
☐ Talk about why Merlin must leave King Arthur after he leads him to the Lady in the Lake and the sword Excalibur.
☐ Talk about the ways in which Merlin is like the scabbard for Excalibur.
☐ Where did the Round Table come from?
☐ Discuss the roles of women in the legend. Are they all helpless?
☐ What is the purpose of jousting. Were a lot of people needlessly hurt or killed?
☐ Discuss the quest for the Holy Grail and who started it.
☐ Discuss the Christian basis for the legend.
☐ Which knights see the Grail?
☐ Discuss the role of the hermits.
☐ Discuss Arthur's feelings during the battle against Lancelot. Why wasn't Arthur angry with Lancelot?
☐ Discuss Arthur and Guinevere's feelings for each other. In what ways did they change by the end of the story?
☐ Were any of the killings justified? Why?
☐ Discuss the fates of Arthur, Guinevere, Lancelot, and Merlin.

Things to Do

☐ Listen to a recording of the music from *Camelot.* Sing some of the songs.
☐ Compare the plot of the musical to the book you read. What was included? What was different? What was left out?
☐ What effects did chivalry have on history?
☐ Find out how much of the Arthurian legend is based on fact.
☐ Make a chart showing the names of all the Knights of the Round Table, their enemies, their qualities, and how they died.
☐ Compare *Young Merlin* by Robert San Souci (Doubleday, 1990) to this book. Which telling do you like best? Which illustrations? Why?
☐ Find out about Stonehenge and how people think it came to be. How does that compare with the story of Stonehenge in this book?

Books

Retold by Robin Lister
The Odyssey. Doubleday, 1988.

King Arthur and the Knights of the Round Table
Bulla, Clyde Robert. *The Sword in the Tree.* Crowell, 1956. ✔
Green, Roger L. *King Arthur and His Knights of the Round Table.* Penguin, 1974.
Gross, Gwen. *Knights of the Round Table.* Random, 1985.
Hastings, Selena. *Sir Gawain and the Green Knight.* Lothrop, 1981.
———. *Sir Gawain and the Loathly Lady.* Lothrop, 1985.
Hodges, Margaret. *Knight Prisoner: The Tale of Sir Thomas Mallory and His King Arthur.* Farrar, 1976.

Lang, Andrew. *King Arthur: Tales of the Round Table.* Schocken, 1968.
Lasker, Joe. *Tournament of Knights.* Crowell, 1986.
Pyle, Howard. *The Story of King Arthur and His Knights.* Many versions.
———. *The Story of Sir Lancelot and His Companions.* Scribners, 1985.
Riordan, James. *Tales of King Arthur.* Macmillan, 1982.
San Souci, Robert D. *Young Merlin.* Doubleday, 1990.
Scott, Dennis. *Sir Gawain and the Green Knight.* Anchorage, 1978.
Storr, Catherine. *The Sword in the Stone.* Raintree, 1985.
Winder, Blanche. *Stories of King Arthur.* Airmont.

The Lemming Condition

> *The Lemming Condition*
> by Alan Arkin. Harper, 1976.
>
> ■■■■■□□□□□□□□□□
>
> **Theme:** The loyalty of some species is unquestioned, regardless of the consequences.
> **Characters:** *Bubber,* a young lemming who is a misfit even before he questions mass suicide. *Crow,* Bubber's friend who alerts him to the dangers of jumping off the cliff into the sea. *Sarah,* Bubber's sister. She is impatient with Bubber's lack of enthusiasm for the journey. *The Old Lemming,* a misfit who gathers stones and loves their beauty. He thinks the suicide is silly, but then he thinks lemmings and chickens are born to be silly.
> **Plot:** The lemmings are preparing to jump off the cliffs into the sea. They call it "heading west." Bubber just can't get excited about it the way the others seem to. He might have accepted it but for his friend Crow who asks questions like "Can you swim?" Soon Bubber is asking the same questions.

Things to Talk About and Notice
□ Discuss whether this book is just about lemmings or whether there are implications for any society.
□ Talk about ways we exhibit lemminglike behavior.
□ Discuss the role of questioners in any society.
□ Talk about reasons it might be necessary for the lemmings to commit mass suicide.

Things to Do
□ Find out whether lemmings really commit suicide.
□ Find out whether any other species exhibit suicidal behavior.

Books
Written by Alan Arkin
The Clearing. Harper, 1986.
Tony's Hard Work Day. Harper, 1972.

Animal Societies
See page 108.

Conformity
Christopher, John. *The White Mountains.* Macmillan, 1967. ✔
L'Engle, Madeleine. *A Wrinkle in Time.* Farrar, 1962.

Lincoln: A Photobiography

Lincoln: A Photobiography
by Russell Freedman. Clarion, 1987.

■■■■■■■□□□□□□

Summary: This liberally illustrated biography of Abraham Lincoln covers his political and personal history from birth to death. It is not fictionalized at all, nor is it overly simplified.

Awards and Recommendations: American Library Association, Newbery Medal, School Library Journal

Things to Talk About and Notice
☐ Discuss how the author kept your interest.
☐ Other biographies have not received the Newbery Medal. Talk about why this one is so special.
☐ Discuss some of the quotes from Lincoln.

Things to Do
☐ Compare this biography of Lincoln to any other. Decide why each author might have decided to include some things and exclude others.
☐ Read a novel set in the same period and compare the information to the facts as you know them.

Books
Written by Russell Freedman
Animal Games. Holiday, 1976.
Animal Superstars. Prentice, 1984.
The Brains of Animals and Man. Holiday, 1972.
Buffalo Hunt. With Morriss, James. Holiday, 1988.
Can Bears Predict Earthquakes? Prentice, 1982.
Children of the Wild West. Clarion, 1983.
Cowboys of the Wild West. Clarion, 1985. ✔
Dinosaurs and Their Young. Holiday, 1983.
Farm Babies. Holiday, 1981.
The First Days of Life. Holiday, 1974.
Getting Born. Holiday, 1978.
Hanging On: How Animals Carry Their Young. Holiday, 1977.
How Birds Fly. Holiday, 1977.
Immigrant Kids. Dutton, 1980.
Indian Chiefs. Holiday, 1987. ✔
Killer Fish. Holiday, 1982.
Killer Snakes. Holiday, 1982.

Rattlesnakes. Holiday, 1984.
Scouting with Baden-Powell. Holiday, 1967.
Sharks. Holiday, 1985.
They Lived with the Dinosaurs. Holiday, 1980.
Two Thousand Years of Space Travel. Holiday, 1963.
When Winter Comes. Dutton, 1981.

Lincoln
Adler, David A. *A Picture Book of Abraham Lincoln.* Holiday, 1989.
Cary, Barbara. *Meet Abraham Lincoln.* Random, 1965.
Colver, Anne. *Abraham Lincoln.* Garrard, 1960.
D'Aulaire, Ingri and D'Aulaire, Edgar. *Abraham Lincoln.* Doubleday, 1957.
Hayman, Leroy. *The Death of Lincoln.* Scholastic, 1987.
McGovern, Ann. *If You Grew Up with Abraham Lincoln.* Scholastic, 1983.
Metzger, Larry. *Abraham Lincoln.* Watts, 1987.
Phelan, Mary. *Mr. Lincoln's Inaugural Journey.* Crowell, 1972.
Sandburg, Carl. *Abe Lincoln Grows Up.* Harcourt, 1975.
Stevenson, Augusta. *Abraham Lincoln: the Great Emancipator.* Aladdin, 1986.

The Civil War
Bailey, Ronald. *The Bloodiest Day.* Time-Life, 1984.
Burney, Eugenia. *Fort Sumter.* Childrens, 1975.
DeLeon, Thomas. *Four Years in Rebel Capitals.* Time-Life, 1983.
Fritz, Jean. *Stonewall.* Putnam, 1979.
Johnson, Neil. *The Battle of Gettysburg.* Four Winds, 1989.
Levenson, Dorothy. *The First Book of the Civil War.* Watts, 1977

Slavery
Hamilton, Virginia. *Anthony Burns: The Defeat and Triumph of a Fugitive Slave.* Knopf, 1988.
Warner, Lucille Schulberg. *From Slave to Abolitionist: The Life of William Wells Brown.* Dial, 1976.
Winter, Jeanette. *Follow the Drinking Gourd.* Knopf, 1988.

The Man Who Was Poe

The Man Who Was Poe
by Avi. Orchard, 1989.

■■■■■■■■■■■■■□

Setting: Providence, Rhode Island, 1848.

Characters: *Edmund Brimmer,* a determined, brave, and often confused boy who so desperately needs help that he will put up with Mr. Poe's often irrational behavior.

Edgar Allan Poe, half mad with drink, he often confuses real characters with those in his writing and from events in his past. He is convinced of his genius as a writer and as a detective. He is so driven that he is often as much of a villain as he is a hero in this book.

Mrs. Sarah Helen Whitman, a young widow who is half in love with Mr. Poe and whom he adores.

Mr. Rachett (Mr. Arnold), Edmund's villainous stepfather. He is part of Mrs. Whitman's social circle and is willing to go to any lengths to stay there.

Mr. Peterson, the young, fair-haired man who is Mr. Rachett's partner in crime and is willing to steal and kill.

Aunty, Edmund's missing aunt who has brought the children to America to find her lost sister, their mother.

Sis, Edmund's missing sister. Sis is also the name of Mr. Poe's deceased wife and he often confuses the two.

Plot: When Edmund's mother, aunt and, finally, his sister disappear, the young boy is without funds and resources to survive, let alone locate his missing relatives. A mysterious alcoholic writer, Edgar Allen Poe, masquerading as Auguste Dupin, the detective in several of Poe's stories, manages to solve the mystery, which involves a bank robbery, kidnapping, and murder, while trying to write it as a story. He is even willing to manipulate events to make a better story. The plot is convoluted and sometimes difficult to follow, but Avi manages to keep us intrigued. Avi includes a brief biography of Poe at the end of the tale.

Things to Do

☐ Read some of Edgar Allan Poe's short stories, particularly "The Cask of Amontillado," "The Gold Bug," or "The Telltale Heart," all obliquely referred to in this book.

☐ Plot the action of the story as a flow chart.

☐ Find and list clues in the story.

☐ Find out about the life of Edgar Allen Poe.

☐ Compare this mystery to those in the mystery theme on pages 44–47. Is this one harder or easier to understand? Why?

☐ List ways in which the time and place of this novel affect the plot.

Books

Written by Avi
See page 181.

Mysteries
See pages 44–47.

The Mermaid Summer

The Mermaid Summer
by Mollie Hunter. Harper, 1988.

■■■■■■■■■■■■□□

Setting: Northern Scotland.

Characters: *Anna,* a twelve-year-old girl who dares to bargain with the mermaid.

Jon, Anna's brother who becomes involved in thwarting the desires of the mermaid.

Eric Anderson, Anna and Jon's grandfather who speaks ill of the mermaid and must live in exile.

Sarah Anderson, Eric's wife who tries to cope with life after Eric leaves.

Robert Anderson, Anna and Jon's father.

Kristine Anderson, Anna and Jon's mother.

The Howdy, a strange woman who has the power of eolas, the skill of healing. She also can see into the future. It is she who helps the children fight the mermaid.

The mermaid, a vain, often angry creature of the sea.

Plot: The fishermen and shore people of Scotland know that the mermaid who haunts the Drongs, great pinnacles of rock that rise out of the sea, can cause strange things to happen, so they always speak well of her. Eric Anderson, however, is not so wise. He speaks ill of the mermaid and learns of his error when his boat smashes on the rocks, and he is forced to leave his home and family to look for other work or bring misfortune to the rest of the village. His granddaughter, Anna, never gives up hope that he will return. Years go by, and when Anna is twelve and Jon is thirteen, they match wits with the mermaid to save their grandfather.

Things to Talk About and Notice

☐ What gives Anna and Jon the strength to outwit the mermaid.

Things to Do

☐ Compare this mermaid to the one in "The Little Mermaid" by Hans Christian Andersen.

☐ Compare the villagers' feelings about mermaids in this story to the villagers' feelings about the Megrimum in *Kneeknock Rise* by Natalie Babbitt (Farrar, 1970). Which fears were better founded?

☐ Find out about Selkies, Davy Jones, Neptune, and other creatures of the sea.

☐ Create your own illustrated glossary of mythical sea creatures.

☐ Compare the Howdy to Alice Jardyne in *The Valley of Deer* by Eileen Dunlop (Holiday, 1989).

Books

Written by Mollie Hunter
See page 228.

Mermaids and Mythical Sea Creatures

Aiken, Joan. *The Kingdom Under the Sea.* Penguin, 1986.

Clymer, Susan. *The Glass Mermaid.* Scholastic, 1986.

———. *Seaward.* Macmillan, 1983. ✔

———. *The Selkie Girl.* Macmillan, 1986.

Hunter, Mollie. *A Stranger Came Ashore.* Harper, 1975. ✔

Jarrell, Randall. *The Animal Family.* Pantheon, 1965. ✔

Peck, Sylvia. *Seal Child.* Morrow, 1989.

Yolen, Jane. *The Faery Flag.* Watts, 1989.

———. *Neptune Rising.* Putnam, 1982.

The Sea
See pages 67–68.

Poetry

Aiken, Joan. "The Fisherman Writes a Letter to the Mermaid" from *The Skin Spinners.* Viking, 1976.

Morrison, Lillian. "Burning Bright" from *These Small Stones,* edited by Norma Farber and Myra Cohn Livingston. Harper, 1987.

Mostly Michael

Mostly Michael
by Robert Kimmel Smith. Delacorte, 1987.

■■■■■□□□□□□□□□

Theme: Cheating doesn't pay.
Setting: Suburbia.
Characters: *Michael Marder,* a basically honest eleven-year-old boy who does fairly well in school although he claims to hate it. During the course of this year, he learns to like reading and to appreciate his family.
Mindy Marder, Michael's younger sister who is potty trained and begins to adjust to being supplanted as the baby of the family.
Mr. Marder, Michael and Mindy's father who works very hard at his business as a realtor and tries, not always successfully, to make time for his family.
Mrs. Marder, The children's mother who has a traditional role. During the course of this year, she becomes pregnant and on Christmas, at the end of the diary, has a baby boy.
Jimmy, Michael's new friend. When the two enter a poster contest together and win, the friendship suffers but all is well eventually.
Carrie, Michael's girl friend for a very short while and then Jimmy's girl friend for about the same length of time. Carrie, Michael discovers, must have a boy friend at all times.
Steve, Michael's rival in the spelling bee and for just about every activity at school.
Grandma, one of the many bright spots in Michael's life. She's opinionated, lively, and loving.
Plot: Michael is a boy in contemporary suburbia whose is, at first, an unwilling diarist. Later he becomes an enthusiastic one. The reading level is fairly easy as novels go—probably well within reach of most fourth graders. There is no real climax to the story; it is, rather, a look at the minor and major concerns of a fairly normal child. A minor bout of cheating, off-again, on-again friendships, the beginning of puberty, a new sibling, his younger sister's potty training, and his loving family will provide many readers with a sense of comradeship.

Things to Talk About and Notice
☐ Talk about the lack of a climax to this story.
☐ Discuss the similarity between this fictional journal and most real journals.
☐ Discuss the traditional roles of Michael's mother and father.
☐ Which of the characters in this book is most like a person you know?

Things to Do
☐ Compare this journal to other fictional journals for realism and believability. Would the journalist have remembered so much dialogue and recorded it that way? Look in your own journals for examples of dialogue.
☐ Compare Mrs. Marder to mothers in other novels.
☐ Look in your own journal and find the entry that is most like one of Michael's.

Books
Written by Robert Kimmel Smith
See page 99.

Journals
See pages 31–33.

Mr. Popper's Penguins

Mr. Popper's Penguins
by Richard Atwater and Florence Atwater.
Little, 1938.

■■■■□□□□□□□□□□

Characters: *Mr. Popper,* a housepainter who is fascinated with penguins. He deals with Admiral Drake's unexpected gift with common sense and practicality.
Mrs. Popper, is more excitable than her husband and more distressed by the problems the penguins create.

Plot: Mr. Popper is fascinated with the Polar Explorations, especially with penguins. He has even written a letter to Admiral Drake who tells him during a radio broadcast from the South Pole that a surprise is coming. The surprise turns out to be a penguin and it changes the Popper's life. When the first penguin, Captain Cook, is languishing from loneliness, a female penguin is added and soon there are twelve. Although not wealthy, the Poppers support the penguins until the penguins, through their performing abilities, support the Poppers on a country-wide theater tour. Eventually, Admiral Drake himself appears with a plan to establish a penguin population at the Sorth Pole and takes the penguins and Mr. Popper to the South Pole.

Awards and Recommendations: Newbery Honor Award

Things to Talk About and Notice
□ Discuss the Popper family's acceptance of these unusual pets.
□ List the adjustments the Popper family had to make when the penguins arrived and decide how many of those adjustments you and your family would be willing to make.
□ Discuss how the story would have been different had Mr. Popper received a platypus.
□ Find evidence that this book was written a long time ago.

Things to Do
□ The book was first published in 1938. How much Polar exploration had been done by that time and by whom?
□ How should Antarctica be used? What do some nations want to do with it?
□ Make playbills and posters for the Popper Performing Penguins.
□ Some of the items Captain Cook finds in the house for his rookery are not common in our homes. Find out what the following things are and how they were used: hairpins, telephone slug, buttonhook, ink bottle cork, and darning egg.
□ Find out about the different kinds of penguins.

Books
Penguins
Bonner, Susan. *A Penguin Year.* Delacorte, 1978.
Dewey, Jennifer Owings. *Birds of Antarctica: The Adelie Penguin.* Little, 1989.
Stonehouse, Bernard. *Penguins.* McGraw, 1980.
Strange, Ian. *Penguin World.* Dodd, 1981.
Todd, Frank. *The Sea World Book of Penguins.* Harcourt, 1981.

Poetry
Stafford, William. "The View from Here" from *Room for Me and a Mountain Lion: Poetry of Open Space,* edited by Nancy Larrick. Evans, 1974.

Mrs. Frisby and the Rats of NIMH

Mrs. Frisby and the Rats of NIMH
by Robert C. O'Brien. Atheneum, 1971.

■■■■■□□□□□□□□□

Characters: *Mrs. Frisby,* a mouse whose home is threatened and who is befriended by the colony of rats.
Timothy, Mrs. Frisby's ill son.

Plot: The rats of NIMH (the National Institute of Mental Health) are an elite group of educated rats. They have escaped from a laboratory and plan to move into a preserve in order to set up their own culture. Mrs. Frisby, a mouse widow, seeks their help in order to save her family's winter home and her son, Timothy, who is too ill to be moved. While accepting the help of the rats, she herself is able to warn them about the plans of the government exterminators.

Awards and Recommendations: American Library Association, Boston Globe/Horn Book Honor Award, Newbery Medal

Things to Talk About and Notice
□ Notice the author's use of flashback.
□ Discuss the use of animals for research.

Things to Do
□ Make a map of the farm where Mrs. Frisby lives.
□ Make a model of Mrs. Frisby's house.
□ Design a model of the rats' agriculture society.
□ Read and record Nicodemus's flashback story.
□ Research the use of cyanide gas.
□ Find out about intelligence and learning research using rats.
□ Find out more about the National Institute of Mental Health.

□ Write descriptions of a day in the life of a laboratory rat from the rat's point of view and from the researcher's point of view.
□ Find and read the sequel completed by the author's daughter, Jane Conly, *Ratso and the Rats of NIMH* (Harper, 1986).
□ Watch the Walt Disney film "The Secret of NIMH." Decide what was changed and why.
□ Write epitaphs for the two rats who died.

Books
Written by Robert C. O'Brien
Report from Group Seventeen. Atheneum, 1972.
The Secret of NIMH. Scholastic, 1982.
The Silver Crown. Collier, 1988.
Z for Zachariah. Atheneum, 1975.

Intelligent Animals
Adams, Richard. *Watership Down.* Macmillan, 1974. ✔
Arkin, Alan. *The Lemming Condition.* Harper, 1976. ✔
King-Smith, Dick. *Babe, the Gallant Pig.* Crown, 1985. ✔
Le Guin, Ursula. *Catwings.* Orchard, 1988. ✔
———. *Catwings Return.* Orchard, 1989. ✔
Steig, William. *Abel's Island.* Farrar, 1976. ✔
van de Wetering, Janwillem. *Hugh Pine.* Houghton, 1980. ✔
White, E. B. *Charlotte's Web.* Harper, 1952. ✔
———. *Trumpet of the Swan.* Harper, 1972. ✔

The Night Watchmen

The Night Watchmen
by Helen Cresswell. Macmillan, 1970.

■■■■■■■□□□□□□□

Theme: People who live ordinary lives often envy those who don't.

Setting: The midlands of England

Characters: *Josh,* the friendliest and most trusting of the two tramps. He is a writer and his side of the tent is full of writing materials and books. When arriving in a town, he sends letters to all the important people requesting an interview, because he is, he says, writing a book about their town.

Caleb, the other tramp. He's a gourmet cook and his side of the tent is full of cooking implements, spices, and herbs. He's more cautious than Josh.

Henry Crane, a boy who is recently out of bed where he's been for almost a month. He is permitted to share some of Caleb's meals and admires the tramps' lifestyle.

Them, the people with green eyes who don't see well in the light, but can see very well at night. They are jealous of Caleb and Josh and want to get the Night Train.

Plot: Josh and Caleb come to town, dig a hole in a street, put up a sign that says "Danger, Men Working," put a tent next to it, and settle in, certain that no one questions people working on a hole in a street. They are "Do-as-you-pleasers." Their lives would be pleasant except for Them, the people so jealous of the life of Do-as-you-pleasers that their eyes have turned brilliant green. When discovered by Them, Josh and Caleb summon up the Night Train and go back There.

Things to Talk About and Notice

☐ Caleb gave Henry money to buy groceries. Where did he get it?

☐ Talk about what Caleb means when he says Josh's book won't get finished because there's too much in it.

☐ Caleb says they don't have surnames because "the minute you got a surname you're ticketed . . . They'd have your name filled in on forms and wrote on lines before you could say 'jackknife.' " Is that true?

☐ Discuss what the tramps mean by getting the ticking of a town.

☐ Notice what Josh writes in the children's books.

☐ Notice the author's technique of creating suspense through warnings Caleb gives Josh and that Josh gives Henry and by allowing the tramps to see just the back of one of Them.

☐ Discuss the advantages and disadvantages of being a Do-as-you-pleaser.

☐ Josh throws a twig into a stream and says, "That's us." What does he mean? Is that good or bad?

☐ Describe what you know about There.

☐ Josh and Caleb talk about signs they receive that everything is all right or that danger is near. List their signs.

☐ The tramps use sayings they appear to live by. Discuss what these sayings mean: "Give an inch and you'll lose a mile," "Don't drop into the glooms," "The cat's to be let out of the bag," "Waste not, want not."

Things to Do

☐ Make a dish Caleb makes or talks about.

☐ Hold an English tea.

☐ Draw posters of Josh and Caleb like the Green-Eyed People might circulate.

☐ Draw pictures of the Night Train.

Books

Written by Helen Cresswell
See page 209.

One-Eyed Cat

One-Eyed Cat
by Paula Fox. Bradbury, 1984.

■■■■■■■■□□□□□□

Theme: Guilt.

Setting: Tyler, New York, on the Hudson River in the 1930s.

Characters: *Ned Wallis,* a young boy whose life has changed drastically since his mother became ill.

Reverend James Wallis, Ned's father, a sincere minister who is torn between his work and his wife and gets little time for his son or for fun.

Mrs. Wallis, Ned's mother, a victim of rheumatoid arthritis. Her illness is such that some days she is overwhelmed by pain. She feels for her son and knows he is in pain himself.

Mr. Scully, an elderly neighbor with a survivor's instinct.

Plot: Ned Wallis lives in a large, quiet house with his clergyman father and his invalid mother. A rifle from his uncle Hilary changes him completely. His father and mother refuse to let him use the rifle and put it in the attic until they can decide what to do with it. Compelled to try it just once, Ned takes it and shoots at something in the night. Shortly thereafter, Ned sees a cat whose eye has been shot out. Mr. Scully, an elderly neighbor, befriends the cat and Ned's guilt causes him to become obsessed by the cat.

Awards and Recommendations: American Library Association, Newbery Honor Award

Things to Talk About and Notice

☐ Discuss the lines by Walt Whitman quoted at the beginning of the book.

☐ Discuss the relationship between Ned and his mother.

☐ Notice the changes in Ned throughout the book.

☐ Talk about kids and guns. What does the NRA think about it? What does your local police department think?

☐ Talk about Mrs. Wallace. Is she dealing with her illness realistically?

☐ Discuss the role of guilt in our lives.

Things to Do

☐ Compare *One-Eyed Cat* to *The Stone-Faced Boy* by the same author: the settings, the beloved relatives, the hidden feelings of both boys, the old people, the animals.

☐ Find out about rheumatoid arthritis. What can be done to help its victims?

Books

Written by Paula Fox
See pages 215–216.

Guilt

Bauer, Marion Dane. *On My Honor.* Clarion, 1986.

Bawden, Nina. *Carrie's War.* Lippincott, 1973. ✔

MacLachlan, Patricia. *Cassie Binegar.* Harper, 1982. ✔

Paterson, Katherine. *Bridge to Terabithia.* Crowell, 1977. ✔

Smith, Doris Buchanan. *The Taste of Blackberries.* Harper, 1973. ✔

Our Snowman Has Olive Eyes

Our Snowman Has Olive Eyes
by Charlotte Herman. Puffin, 1977.

■■■■■□□□□□□□□

Theme: Each of us has the need for understanding and privacy.

Characters: *Sheila,* a perceptive, creative ten-year-old girl.

Bubbie, Sheila's capable, intelligent, and stubborn eighty-year-old grandmother.

Muriel, Sheila's teenage sister. Muriel has a weight problem and is very difficult to live with; however, Sheila remembers when they had good times together.

Sheila's mother, Bubbie's daughter. She is determined to protect and coddle her mother even when she doesn't need it.

Sheila's father, a busy accountant who cares for his family but doesn't often get involved.

Plot: Sheila's parents have decided that Bubbie, her grandmother, is too old to live alone. Now she is to share Sheila's room. Though this is not ideal for Sheila, she adores her grandmother and they live together quite amicably. It's Sheila's mother who doesn't understand Bubbie's need to be useful and independent. And then there's Sheila's unhappy sister, Muriel, whose diary Sheila reads as often as possible.

Things to Talk About and Notice
□ Notice the way the family loves yet misunderstands each other.
□ Notice the subtle ways Bubbie tries to help Muriel.
□ Discuss how Bubbie's move changed her life and the lives of her family.
□ Talk about what life might be like for the family after Bubbie leaves.
□ Discuss the antique dealer's motives.
□ Talk about whether or not the antique dealer and Bubbie might have stayed friends if Sheila had not interfered.

Books
Written by Charlotte Herman
Millie Cooper, Take a Chance. Dutton, 1989.
Millie Cooper, 3B. Dutton, 1985. ✔
My Mother Didn't Kiss Me Goodnight. Dutton, 1980.

The Elderly
Byars, Betsy. *After the Goat Man.* Penguin, 1974. ✔
Clifford, Eth. *The Rocking Chair Rebellion.* Houghton, 1978. ✔
Ethridge, Kenneth. *Viola, Furgy, Bobbi and Me.* Holiday, 1989.
Gaeddert, Louann. *A Summer Like Turnips.* Holt, 1989.
Pople, Maureen. *The Other Side of the Family.* Holt, 1986. ✔

Poetry
Livingston, Myra Cohn. *Worlds I Know and Other Poems.* Macmillan, 1985.

The Outside Child

The Outside Child
by Nina Bawden. Lothrop, 1989.

■■■■■■■■■■□□□□□

Setting: Present-day London.

Characters: *Jane Tucker,* a bright, emotional, and determined girl. She loves her father and her aunts even when she is furious with them for withholding information.

Plato Jones, can outthink and outscheme almost everybody. He is embarrassed by his mother and is easily hurt.

Aunt Bill, overweight, brash with a loud laugh, a matter-of-fact and loving aunt. She is an artist who often uses her garden flowers as models.

Aunt Sophie, tiny and musical, she teaches piano to supplement her income, but her real pleasure is as a percussionist in a band.

Horatio Tucker, Jane's father, a seaman on a cruise ship. He is kind and loving toward Jane, but often absent. He is also so weak that he allows his new wife to banish Jane from his household.

Amy Tucker, Jane's stepmother. She's emotional, self-centered, afraid, and cruel.

Annabel, George, and Hugo Tucker, Jane's half-brothers and half-sister.

Plot: Jane has always known that hers is an unusual family. Her mother died soon after Jane was born, her father is at sea most of the time, and she lives with two eccentric but loveable aunts. She discovers that her father has another family: a wife and three children. Always intrigued by a mystery, she and her best friend and fellow misfit, Plato, set about to find her brothers and sister.

Awards and Recommendations: American Library Association

Things to Talk About and Notice
- ☐ Tell about the kind of hidden family you would like to discover.
- ☐ Decide which people in the book exhibited the most and the least mature behavior.
- ☐ Tell the story from Annabel's point of view.
- ☐ Do any of the excuses for keeping the secret make sense? When would you have told Jane? What would you have said?
- ☐ What is Plato's motivation?

Things to Do
- ☐ Compare Amy Tucker to Aunt Bea in *The Village by the Sea* by Paula Fox (Orchard, 1988). Are they equally cruel? Why?

Books
Written by Nina Bawden
See page 183.

The Phantom Tollbooth

The Phantom Tollbooth
by Norton Juster. Random, 1961.

■■■■■■■■■■□□□□□

Characters: *Milo,* a bored young man whose adventure expands his mind. He is a logical thinker in an illogical place.
Tock, a watchdog with a clock inside.
Plot: Milo has time on his hands and nothing to do until he drives through the Phantom Tollbooth and into The Lands Beyond where much of our language is literally true: the Land of Confusion can be reached only by jumping; a light meal consists of light bulbs. In the course of his travels, Milo learns a bit about life and a lot about language.

Things to Talk About and Notice
□ Notice all the puns in the book.
□ Discuss literal versus figurative language.

Things to Do
□ Find other puns and idioms. Illustrate them as they were meant and as they could be interpreted.
□ Find and tell jokes and riddles that rely on puns.
□ Make a map of the journey.
□ Look at the illustration of the pie eating contest in Wallace Tripp's *Granfa' Grig Had a Pig* (Little, 1976). Notice the names on the scoreboard—all puns. Make up more.

Books
Written by Norton Juster
As: A Surfeit of Similes. Morrow, 1989.
Otter Nonsense. Putnam, 1982.

Wordplay
Gwynne, Fred. *A Chocolate Moose for Dinner.* Prentice, 1987.☑
——. *The King Who Rained.* Prentice, 1987.☑
——. *Little Pigeon Toad.* Prentice, 1989.☑
——. *The Sixteen Hand Horse.* Prentice, 1987.☑
Parish, Peggy. The Amelia Bedelia Books.☑

The Pinballs

The Pinballs
by Betsy Byars. Harper, 1977.

■■■■■■■■■■□□□□□

Characters: *Carlie,* a tough young lady. She has been abused by stepfathers and is convinced that people are not to be trusted. The master of insult, she maintains her tough exterior.
Harvey, has two broken legs. He was run over by his alcoholic father after being abandoned by his mother. He is convinced that his father has kept his mother from communicating with him since she ran away to "find herself" in a commune.
Thomas J, found as a toddler by elderly sisters whose minimal love and care ended when both were hospitalized with broken hips. He is inarticulate and overly anxious to please.

Mrs. Mason, a housewife who tries to involve Carlie in stereotypical female roles. She also convinces Carlie that she can help the other two children and provides all of them with physical and emotional affection.
Mr. Mason, a special friend to Thomas J. He shares his childhood tragedies with Thomas J.
Jefferson and Thomas Benson, inseparable twins who see Thomas J as their last hope.
Plot: Carlie, Harvey, and Thomas J, three foster children, are taken in by the Masons. The Masons provide a supportive environment in which the children learn to care for each other and begin to experience love and trust.

Awards and Recommendations: American Library Association, IRA Children's Choice, School Library Journal

Things to Talk About and Notice

☐ Discuss how people learn to trust.
☐ In what ways do people show love?
☐ Talk about whether the children should return to their natural families.
☐ Discuss ways people grieve.
☐ Talk about the twins' inability to survive without each other.
☐ Discuss reasons for the behavior of Harvey's father.
☐ Discuss Mr. Mason's feelings at his mother's death.
☐ Talk about Thomas J's reactions to the illness and death of the twins.
☐ Discuss Mr. and Mrs. Mason's relationship.
☐ Talk about foster care. What used to happen to such children? Why do people want to become foster parents?
☐ Discuss child abuse and children's rights.

Things to Do

☐ Find out about foster care in your community: who's in charge? What are the child's rights?
☐ Make lists of successful people who were foster children or orphans.

☐ Make personal lists such as those Harvey makes.
☐ "The Pinballs" is a metaphor. Find other metaphors in book and movie titles.
☐ Find other metaphors to describe the characters.
☐ Write about taking control of one's life.

Books

Written by Betsy Byars
See page 197.

Child Abuse
See page 122.

Tough Characters
Greene, Constance. *Ask Anybody.* Viking, 1983. ✔
Sachs, Marilyn. *Veronica Ganz.* Doubleday, 1968.

Foster Children
Angell, Judie. *Tina Gogo.* Bradbury, 1978.
Bauer, Marion Dane. *Foster Child.* Clarion, 1976.
MacLachlan, Patricia. *Mama One, Mama Two.* Harper, 1982.
Paterson, Katherine. *The Great Gilly Hopkins.* Crowell, 1978. ✔

Popcorn Days and Buttermilk Nights

Popcorn Days and Buttermilk Nights
by Gary Paulsen. Lodestar, 1983.

Theme: Take pride in a job well done.
Setting: Norsten, Minnesota.
Characters: *Carly,* a fourteen-year-old boy who often erupted into senseless violence when living in the city.
Uncle David, a powerful man who calls himself a mechanic rather than a blacksmith. He loves making broken tools work again and forging steel.
Tinker, Carly's cousin who reaches out and teaches Carly the routines of the farm. He is full of mischief and determination.

Aunt Emily, David's wife. She understands her husband and Carly.
Nels Thompson, a lumberman from the old north woods.
Plot: A troubled boy is sent to stay with his uncle as an alternative to reform school. There he finds his anger disappearing as he becomes part of the rhythm of the farm and the blacksmith shop. Uncle David is not only a superb blacksmith, he is a dreamer. When his dream is of a circus for the children of the town, the whole town pitches in.

Things to Talk About and Notice
☐ Notice the descriptions of the horses.
☐ Notice when Nels Thompson lights the match. Find the same story in *Winter Room*.
☐ Talk about why the author tells us of Carly's past quickly, saving most of the story for what went on at the farm.
☐ Discuss the author's use of flashback in the following passage: "Tinker took me inside his world. That's why when I went crazy with rage and did what I did, it was so bad. It wasn't that I just did something bad, which I did, or that I really hurt him—I didn't."

Things to Do
☐ Compare David's dream of a circus to the dream of a baseball field in the movie *Field of Dreams*.
☐ Discuss other people who have the same pride in work that David showed.
☐ Write about someone who takes pride in his or her work.
☐ Describe something in your world as Gary Paulsen might describe it.

Books
Written by Gary Paulsen
See page 239.

Prairie Songs

Prairie Songs
by Pam Conrad. Harper, 1985.

■■■■■■■■■□□□□□

Setting: Nebraska Territory before the Civil War.

Characters: *Louisa Downing,* a young, plucky girl who loves the space and beauty of the prairie. She has taught herself to read from two magazines, the only reading material in her sod home.
Lester Downing, Louisa's painfully shy younger brother who speaks only within the family.
Clara Downing, Louisa and Lester's mother. She has lost a third child, Delilah, and she is lonely for the company of other women. She is a strong and loving woman.
J. T. Downing, Louisa's father. He loves the prairie, works hard, and is a kind and loving father and husband.
Dr. William Berryman, a young doctor who sets up a practice on the prairie. His work frequently takes him far from home, and he is not always patient with his wife's fears.
Emmeline Berryman, a beautiful and emotionally fragile pregnant woman. She is frightened and repulsed by life on the prairie.
Pru Whitfield, a neighbor. She is harsher than the other women, more pushy and less patient.
Carney Whitfield, Pru's husband, a kind and helpful man.
Paulie Whitfield, their son. He is mean, spiteful, and a great troublemaker.

Plot: Louisa loves the prairie and so does her father. Her mother has adjusted to it. When Dr. and Mrs. Berryman arrive, Mrs. Berryman faints at the sight of the sod hut she will live in. Louisa tries to help her see the beauty of the prairie, but Mrs. Berryman misses the city and its refinements. She has brought her books, however, and is going to teach the children to read and write. The prairie sparkles with wildflowers, but it takes three lives before the end of the book.

Awards and Recommendations: American Library Association, Boston Globe/Horn Book Honor Award, IRA Children's Book Award

Things to Talk About and Notice

☐ Notice the foreshadowing in the following passage: "Maybe she never should have left Mrs. Berryman that way, but there was no way she could have known that then."

☐ Discuss the characters' feelings about Native Americans. Were they typical?

☐ Talk about why the photographer was important and what he was trying to do.

☐ Discuss whether Mrs. Berryman would have had the same problems if they had lived in a different area. What if they had lived in a different time?

☐ Talk about whether the roles women played during that time made a difference in their ability to survive.

☐ What would you have taken if you were moving to the Nebraska Territory during that time?

☐ What do the books and the cradle symbolize?

Things to Do

☐ Compare Mrs. Berryman to Sarah in *Sarah, Plain and Tall* by Patricia MacLachlan and Ma in the Little House series by Laura Ingalls Wilder.

☐ What major changes have occurred in the medical field since those days?

Books

Written by Pam Conrad

Holding Me Here. Harper, 1986.

I Don't Live Here. Dutton, 1984.

My Daniel. Harper, 1989.

Seven Silly Circles. Harper, 1987.

Staying Nine. Harper, 1988.

Stonewords: A Ghost Story. Harper, 1990.

Taking the Ferry Home. Harper, 1988.

The Tub People. Harper, 1989.

What I Did for Roman. Harper, 1987.

Early Settlers on the Prairie

Brink, Carol Ryrie. *Caddie Woodlawn.* Macmillan, 1973. ✔

MacLachlan, Patricia. *Sarah, Plain and Tall.* Harper, 1985. ✔

Wilder, Laura Ingalls. The Little House series. Harper. ✔

Rabble Starkey

Rabble Starkey
by Lois Lowry. Houghton, 1987.

■■■■■■■■■■□□□□□

Theme: We have strength to handle problems.
Characters: *Rabble,* a twelve-year-old girl.
Sweet Hosanna (Sweet Ho), Rabble's mother, a strong, nurturing, very smart woman.
Veronica Bigelow, Rabble's best friend.
Gunther Bigelow, an ugly, dear child.
Mrs. Bigelow, Veronica's confused and ill mother.
Mr. Bigelow, Veronica's father who loves his family and wants to help his wife but needs a friend.
Plot: Rabble Starkey's real name is Parable Ann. Her father left when she was an infant and life has not been easy for her or for her mother. Now life is looking up as they move into the Bigelow household so that Sweet Ho can take care of Mrs. Bigelow who is mentally ill. When Mrs. Bigelow's illness reaches a crisis, Rabble and her mother must make some difficult decisions.

Awards and Recommendations: Boston Globe/Horn Book

Things to Talk About and Notice
□ Discuss the relationships among the characters and how they need each other.
□ Talk about why Sweet Ho is able to accept things as they are.
□ Discuss where Rabble's mother gets her strength.
□ Talk about what's wrong with Veronica's mother.
□ When were you first aware of what Mrs. Bigelow was going to do to Gunther?
□ What do you think will happen to each of the characters in the story?
□ Talk about what Veronica will be like as an adult. What about Rabble?
□ Discuss times when you've been uprooted or upset by family problems.

Things to Do
□ Make a family tree like the one Veronica and Rabble have to make.
□ Choose an unusual name, such as those in the book, and go by it for a day or period of time.
□ Read about some of the causes and treatments of mental illnesses.

Books
Written by Lois Lowry
See page 232.

Mental Illness
Adler, C. S. *The Shell Lady's Daughter.* Fawcett, 1984.
Bauer, Marion Dane. *Tangled Butterfly.* Houghton, 1980.
Moeri, Louise. *The Girl Who Lived on the Ferris Wheel.* Dutton, 1979.
Streatfeild, Noel. *Thursday's Child.* Dell, 1986.

Shades of Gray

Shades of Gray
by Carolyn Reeder. Macmillan, 1989.

■■■■■■■■■■□□□□□

Theme: We must have the courage to do what we think is right.

Setting: Virginia, following the Civil War.

Characters: *Will Page,* a twelve-year-old orphan whose parents had owned slaves and whose family fought bravely for the Confederacy. He is horrified at having to live with his aunt and uncle because he believes that their neutral stand during the War was caused by cowardice.

Uncle Jed, a quiet, gentle, and wise man. His family has suffered because of his refusal to aid the Confederate cause and he has been shunned by friends and family alike as a traitor and coward. His courage is only apparent to Will near the end of the story.

Meg Jones, Will's cousin and Jed's daughter. She is smart, hard-working, and very loving. She stands up to bullies, especially with Will's help. She longs to learn to read but the school was destroyed during the War and her mother lacks the time to teach her.

Aunt Ella, Jed's wife and Meg's mother. She's warm, outgoing, and forgiving.

Jim Woodley, a Yankee soldier whom the Jones's befriend after the War. It is Jim who causes Will to question whether all the right was on one side.

Dr. Martin, the doctor of Will's family and their friend.

Plot: Will Page feels strongly about the Civil War that has just ended. He has good reason—he lost his family for what he thought was a just cause. He goes to live with relatives whom he believes to be traitors. They had decided not to take sides during the Civil War and have suffered for their beliefs.

Awards and Recommendations: Scott O'Dell Award

Things to Talk About and Notice
☐ Discuss the way Will and Meg handle bullies.
☐ Talk about the way Uncle Jed handles the animosity from the townspeople.
☐ Discuss the roles of pacifists in society.
☐ Find out about other pacifists.
☐ Discuss several other unpopular stands and their affects on individuals and society.
☐ Notice the gradual change in Will's attitude.
☐ What are some signs of Will's growing admiration for the Joneses?
☐ Was Will's family's treatment of slaves typical or even common?

Things to Do
☐ Find out where your family was and whether or not they took sides during the Civil War.
☐ Find out about the Civil War battles closest to Winchester, Virginia.
☐ Watch all or part of the PBS series *The Civil War.*
☐ Sing some songs that were popular during and after the Civil War.

Books
The Civil War
Beatty, Patricia. *Charley Skedaddle.* Morrow, 1987.
———. *Turn Homeward, Hannalee.* Morrow, 1984.
De Angeli, Marguerite. *Thee Hannah.* Doubleday, 1989.
Fritz, Jean. *Brady.* Coward, 1960. ✔
Haugaard, Erik Christian. *Orphans of the Wind.* Houghton, 1966.
Hunt, Irene. *Across Five Aprils.* Follet, 1967.
Lunn, Janet. *The Root Cellar.* Scribners, 1983.
Meltzer, Milton. *Voices from the Civil War.* Crowell, 1989.
Perez, N. A. *The Slopes of War.* Houghton, 1984.

The Shrinking of Treehorn

The Shrinking of Treehorn
by Florence Parry Heide. Holiday, 1971.

■■■■□□□□□□□□□□□

Theme: Sometimes people refuse to understand each other.
Setting: Suburban home and school.
Characters: *Treehorn,* an earnest little boy who has a very perplexing problem.
Moshie, Treehorn's friend who thinks Treehorn is stupid to shrink.
Plot: Treehorn realizes he is shrinking when his sleeves hang down over his hands and he can't reach the top shelf in his closet any more. The problem is not so much that he is shrinking as that he can't get any of the adults in his world to help him solve the problem.

Awards and Recommendations: American Library Association

Things to Talk About and Notice
☐ Discuss times you haven't been able to get anyone to listen to you.
☐ Compare Treehorn's problem to Andrew's in the picture book *Nobody Listens to Andrew* by Elizabeth Guilfoile (Modern, 1957). Find other books that present the same or similar problem.
☐ What does the author say about people?

Things to Do
☐ Compare this problem to the one in *Jumanji* by Chris Van Allsburg (Houghton, 1981).
☐ Compare *Tales for the Perfect Child* by Florence Parry Heide to *The Shrinking of Treehorn*. Does she say some of the same things?
☐ Make a board game like the one Treehorn played.

Books
Written by Florence Parry Heide
Banana Blitz. Holiday, 1983. ✔
Banana Twist. Holiday, 1978. ✔
Benjamin Budge and Barnaby Ball. Scholastic, 1970.
Black Magic at Brillstone. With Heide, Roxanne. A. Whitman, 1981.
Body in the Brillstone Garage. With Heide, Roxanne. A. Whitman, 1980.
Brillstone Break-in. With Heide, Roxanne. A. Whitman, 1977.

By the Time You Count to Ten. Concordia, 1981.
Changes. Concordia, 1978..
The Day of Ahmed's Secret. With Heide, Judith Gilliland. Lothrop, 1990.
The Face at the Brillstone Window. With Heide, Roxanne. A. Whitman, 1979.
Fear at Brillstone. A. Whitman, 1978.
Growing Anyway Up. Harper, 1976.
I Love Everypeople. With Heide, Roxanne. Concordia, 1978.
Little One. Lion, 1970.
A Monster is Coming! A Monster is Coming! Watts, 1980.
The Mystery at Macadoo Zoo. With Van Clief, Sylvia. A. Whitman, 1973.
The Mystery at Southport Cinema. With Heide, Roxanne. A. Whitman, 1978.
The Mystery of the Bewitched Bookmobile. With Heide, Roxanne. A. Whitman, 1975.
The Mystery of the Forgotten Island. With Heide, Roxanne. Archway, 1983.
The Mystery of the Melting Snowman. With Heide, Roxanne. A. Whitman, 1974.
The Mystery of the Midnight Message. With Heide, Roxanne. A. Whitman, 1977.
The Mystery of the Missing Suitcase. With Heide, Roxanne. A. Whitman, 1972.
The Mystery of the Mummy's Mask. With Heide, Roxanne. A. Archway, 1982.
The Mystery of the Silver Tag. With Van Clief, Sylvia. A. Whitman, 1972.
The Mystery of the Vanishing Visitor. With Heide, Roxanne. A. Whitman, 1975.
The Mystery of the Whispering Voice. With Van Clief, Sylvia. A. Whitman, 1972.
The Mystery on Danger Road. With Heide, Roxanne. A. Whitman, 1983.
The Problem with Pulcifer. Harper, 1982.
Secret Dreamer. Harper, 1978.
Tales for the Perfect Child. Lothrop, 1985.
Time Bomb at Brillstone. With Heide, Roxanne. A. Whitman, 1982.
Time Flies! Holiday, 1984.
Treehorn's Treasure. Holiday, 1981.
Treehorn's Wish. Holiday, 1984.
The Wendy Puzzle. Holiday, 1982.
When the Sad One Comes to Stay. Harper, 1975.

The Sign of the Beaver

The Sign of the Beaver
by Elizabeth George Speare. Houghton, 1983.

■■■■■■■■■□□□□□

Theme: We should respect our cultures and those of others.
Setting: Maine woods, 1768.
Characters: *Matt Hallowell,* a brave, resourceful thirteen-year-old boy who is unaware of how little he knows about survival.
Attean, the chief's grandson. He is arrogant and disdainful of the white man and, therefore, of Matt. He is knowledgeable about survival and respectful of nature.
Saknis, chief of the Beaver tribe. He is wise and aware that the tribe cannot stop the coming of the white man and wants them to be as prepared as possible.
Plot: In 1768, Matt Hallowell and his father leave home to build a house in the Maine woods, leaving the rest of the family in Massachusetts. In early summer, when the cabin is finished, Mr. Hallowell leaves Matt with a rifle, a field of planted corn, and minimal skills for survival. After a fur-trapper steals the rifle and Matt is almost fatally injured, Saknis offers to help him learn to survive in return for teaching his grandson, Attean, how to read. Attean proves an unwilling pupil, at least at first, but gives Matt valuable survival techniques and at last a friendship develops.

Awards and Recommendations: American Library Association, Newbery Honor Award, School Library Journal, Scott O'Dell Award

Things to Talk About and Notice
☐ Discuss what the book *Robinson Crusoe* meant to Matt, to Attean, and to Saknis.
☐ Discuss the survival skills Matt developed. What survival skills would Attean need if he moved to Matt's Massachusetts world?

☐ Which of Matt's skills do the tribe admire?
☐ Matt talks about his snowshoes giving him freedom. What does he mean?
☐ Discuss the question of freedom: Who is more free, Matt or Attean? Would that change in a different environment?

Things to Do
☐ Compare Matt to Brian in *Hatchet* by Gary Paulsen (Bradbury, 1987).
☐ Make a dictionary of the Native American words in this book.
☐ Make a guide book for other settlers, using information from the book.
☐ Make an alphabet book, using the words Matt started with before he taught Attean to read: A is for arm, B is for bone, C is for candle, D is for door. Illustrate it.
☐ Make a chart showing the animals in the story and their effects on the plot.
☐ Use some of Matt's survival skills to cook or build a fire.
☐ Draw a map showing the action of the story and the trip Matt's father took.
☐ Create a catalog showing items from Matt's time.
☐ Build a model of Attean's village.

Books
Written by Elizabeth George Speare
The Bronze Bow. Houghton, 1961. ✔
Calico Captive. Houghton, 1957.
The Witch of Blackbird Pond. Houghton, 1958. ✔

Clash of Cultures
See page 125.

Survival
See pages 74–76.

The Sign of the Chrysanthemum

The Sign of the Chrysanthemum
by Katherine Paterson. Crowell, 1973.

■■■■■■■■□□□□□□

Theme: Our character develops as we struggle to solve problems.
Setting: Twelfth-century Japan.
Characters: *Muna (No Name),* an orphaned boy determined to find his father, a Samurai warrior with the tattoo of a chrysanthemum on his shoulder.
Tohanobei, a rogue ronin, whose negative influences cause many problems for Muna.
Fukuji, the swordmaker for the Samurai. He becomes Muna's benefactor and protector.
Okiho, a beautiful young girl, orphaned and sold into a life of service in a brothel.
Plot: This is the compelling adventure of a boy's attempt to discover his father's identity, and consquently, his own. The story is rich in details of feudal Japan, its culture, its harsh realities, and its customs. The plot weaves strands of conflict and drama with realistic, fast-paced action.

Things to Talk About and Notice
□ Discuss the remnants of the feudal Japanese culture in Japan today.
□ Discuss the Samurai code.
□ Notice the songs and poetry in the book.
□ Talk about the title of the book. Would you have named it differently?
□ Discuss the author's Japanese background.

Things to Do
□ Compare this story to *The Whipping Boy* by Sid Fleischman (Greenwillow, 1986).
□ Compare the feudalism in Japan to that in Europe.
□ Make a pronunciation guide for the Japanese names in the book.

Books
Written by Katherine Paterson
See page 237.

Japan
Paterson, Katherine. *The Master Puppeteer.* Crowell, 1976. ✔
———. *Of Nightingales That Weep.* Crowell, 1974. ✔
Say, Allen. *The Feast of Lanterns.* Harper, 1976.
———. *The Innkeeper's Apprentice.* Harper, 1979.

Slake's Limbo

Slake's Limbo
by Felice Holman. Scribners, 1974.

■■■■■■■■■□□□□□

Theme: People need beauty and sanctuary.
Setting: New York subway system.
Characters: *Artemis Slake,* an orphaned boy. The system has rejected him. He has known only cruelty and hatred. He is resourceful and has the soul of an artist.
Willie Joe Whinny, a motorman on the subway. Willie Joe wanted to be a sheepherder.
Waitress at the lunch counter, begins giving Slake more food than he ordered and, eventually, helps him get a job in exchange for food.

Cleaning woman, "the red-faced lady." She tells Slake about herself as she buys newspapers and gives him a warm jacket and jeans.
Joe, a boy Slake knew before he went into the cave. Joe was probably retarded and seldom spoke and was the closest thing Slake had to a friend. He was killed by a truck.
Man with the turban, another of Slake's many customers.
Plot: Artemis Slake, escaping some bullies, finds a cave in a subway tunnel outside Grand Central Station. The cave is his home and refuge for 121 days. During this time, Slake learns to survive, reaching out to some people and receiving unexpected kindness.

Awards and Recommendations: American Library Association

Things to Talk About and Notice

☐ Notice the bird symbolism that pervades the story: Slake's dream of swallowing the bird; the bird that flutters in his chest when he is afraid; the bird he sees when he leaves the hospital.

☐ Discuss the significance of Slake's spree in Central Park.

☐ Discuss the double meaning of the parallel plot title "On Another Track."

☐ Discuss the parallel story, "On Another Track."

☐ Discuss the meaning Slake gives to Willie Joe's life and the importance of Willie Joe's life to Slake.

☐ Why is the rat important to Slake?

☐ Discuss the significance of the blackout.

☐ If Slake does take to the rooftops next time, what will change for him. What new problems will he have? What parts of his subway life can he keep?

☐ Talk about people like Slake in your area.

☐ Find foreshadowing and discuss its significance: "The thing that happened when it finally happened, was so perfectly logical that it should not really be considered surprising." "So the day of the sweater—the end of the beginning."

☐ Discuss the author's choices and decision concerning what happens to Slake after the hospital.

Things to Do

☐ Find out about the subway nearest you. Could Slake hide out in it? Where else might he live?

☐ Find out about the third rail. Why does Slake compare it to a crocodile? Why is it dangerous?

☐ Empty the trash basket in your room. What would Slake find useable?

☐ Make a chart with two columns. In one column, list the kindnesses described in the story. In the other, list the cruelties.

☐ List the survival skills Slake exhibits at the beginning and the end of the story.

☐ Near the end of the book, Slake wonders for the first time, if there might not be other caves and other people hiding in them. Imagine what a meeting between one of them and Slake might be like. Write about it.

Books

Written by Felice Holman.

At the Top of My Voice and Other Poems. Scribners, 1970.

Blackmail Machine. Macmillan, 1968.

The Drac: French Tales of Dragons and Demons. With Valen, Nanine. Scribners, 1975.

The Murderer. Scribners, 1978.

Professor Diggins' Dragons. Collier, 1974.

The Songs in My Head and Other Poems. Scribners, 1985.

Terrible Jane. Scribners, 1987.

The Wild Children. Scribners, 1983.

Runaways

Cunningham, Julia. *Come to the Edge.* Avon, 1985.

Konigsburg, E. L. *From the Mixed-Up Files of Mrs. Basil E. Frankweiler.* Atheneum, 1967. ✔

McGraw, Eloise. *The Hideaway.* Macmillan, 1983.

Roth, David. *River Runaways.* Houghton, 1981.

Shreve, Susan. *The Revolution of Mary Leary.* Knopf, 1982.

Urban Survival

Lisle, Janet Taylor. *Afternoon of the Elves.* Orchard, 1989. ✔

Poetry

Aiken, Joan. "New York Sewers" from *The Skin Spinners.* Viking, 1976.

The Strange Night Writing of Jessamine Colter

The Strange Night Writing of Jessamine Colter by Cynthia C. deFelice. Macmillan, 1988.

■■■■■■☐☐☐☐☐☐☐

Characters: *Jessamine Colter,* a widow who lives alone outside of town. She is full of wonder at her strange power but gradually learns to accept it and use it wisely.
Jake, the restaurant owner who loves Jessie and wants to marry her.
Callie, a young girl Jessie befriends.

Plot: Jessamine Colter is a kind, wise widow who lives alone. She still talks things over with her dead husband, although she is quite aware that he's dead. She makes a living doing calligraphy for the villagers, including writing the weekly menus for Jake's restaurant. Jake would like very much to marry Jessie, but she likes her life the way it is. She has befriended a young girl, Callie, whose mother is an alcoholic. Suddenly, Jessie gets urges to write menu changes and announcements for events that have not yet been planned or have not yet occurred. She uses this power to see the future with the same wisdom with which she has always lived, even when she writes her death certificate.

Things to Talk About and Notice
☐ How did the author make you believe that Jessie's power was possible?
☐ What would you do with Jessamine's gift?

Things to Do
☐ Learn about calligraphy. Try it. Write invitations or announcements.
☐ Find out about Cassandra, the woman in Greek mythology who was doomed to see into the future and have no one believe her.
☐ The same author wrote *Weasel* about a totally evil man. Why would she write such vastly different books? What do you suppose she's like?
☐ Compare Jessie to Blossom Culp in *The Ghost Belonged to Me* by Richard Peck (Viking, 1975) and to Fiver in *Watership Down* by Richard Adams (Macmillan, 1974).

Books
Written by Cynthia C. deFelice
The Dancing Skeleton. Macmillan, 1989.
Weasel. Macmillan, 1990. ✔

Calligraphy
Baron, Nancy. *Getting Started in Calligraphy.* Sterling, 1979.
Korn, Ellen. *Teach Yourself Calligraphy.* Morrow, 1982.

Predicting the Future
Bawden, Nina. *Witch's Daughter.* Lippincott, 1966. ✔
Cresswell, Helen. *The Secret World of Polly Flint.* Macmillan, 1984. ✔
Dunlop, Eileen. *The Valley of Deer.* Holiday, 1989. ✔
Hunter, Mollie. *The Mermaid Summer.* Harper, 1988. ✔
Peck, Richard. *The Ghost Belonged to Me.* Viking, 1975. ✔

A Stranger Came Ashore

A Stranger Came Ashore
by Mollie Hunter. Harper, 1975.

■■■■■■■■■■□□□□

Setting: The village of Black Ness on the Shetland Islands off the northern coast of Britain.

Characters: *Finn Learson,* the stranger who is apparently shipwrecked and then taken into the Henderson family.

Da Henderson, the patriarch and storyteller of the family. He realizes too late who Finn Learson is.

Robbie Henderson, the youngest member of the family. He is the first to mistrust Finn, although he alternates between trust and distrust throughout the book.

Elspeth Henderson, Robbie's sister whom Finn is determined to marry. She has a quick temper and is torn between Finn and Nicoll.

Janet and Peter Henderson, Robbie and Elspeth's parents. They trust Finn and have no fears when he courts Elspeth.

Tam, the Hendersons' dog.

Nicoll Anderson, Elspeth's boyfriend who is jealous of Finn. He does not believe Robbie when he says that Finn is a selkie.

Yarl Corbie, the schoolmaster. Nicknamed Yarl because of his resemblance to a raven, he is said to have magical powers. He was once thwarted by a selkie when the selkie stole his bride.

Plot: Finn Learson is a handsome shipwrecked sailor who is taken in by the kindly Henderson family. There's a strangeness about him even from the first, however, and the dog, Tam, is the first to sense it. Gradually the stranger wins the respect of the entire village. When it becomes clear that he wants to marry Elspeth Henderson, Old Da and Robbie are determined to stop the marriage. When Da dies, Robbie alone is convinced that Finn is the Great Selkie come to lure Elspeth to his crystal kingdom under the sea.

Awards and Recommendations: American Library Association, Boston Globe/Horn Book Honor Award, School Library Journal

Things to Talk About and Notice

☐ Find the first clues that the sailor is a selkie. Who notices first?
☐ Notice what the schoolmaster later says about the stranger's unusual name.
☐ In what ways is the stranger seal-like?
☐ Discuss superstition in the story.
☐ Why do the last names of people on the islands seem more Scandinavian than British?
☐ Talk about the riddle.
☐ Notice the references to seals and selkies throughout the story.
☐ What would it be like to sleep in a bed such as the Hendersons use?
☐ When the stranger bursts into the cabin, he says, "I call myself Finn—Finn Learson." Why doesn't he say, "My name is Finn Learson"?
☐ How did Finn get the gold coin?
☐ Notice the language. Make a glossary of unusual words and expressions.
☐ Discuss how the selkies adapt to the climate and terrain of the islands.
☐ What is this statement a reference to: Robbie's "never thinking he was making the great mistake of his young life . . . ."
☐ Discuss the importance of the howling of the dog, the raven's landing on the roof of the Henderson's home, and the footprint in the ashes.
☐ Discuss Finn's statement "You will live to wed the man of your choice, and you will be rich when you wed. And what is more, you will be beautiful to the end of your days."
☐ Discuss the statement "The rest of the folk in Black Ness saw no harm in it at all—how could they, indeed, when they were all still of the opinion that any strangeness about Finn Learson was due to his being a foreigner?"
☐ What was Da referring to when he said "It has happened before"?
☐ Discuss Finn's relationship with Robbie.
☐ Discuss the funeral customs of the islanders.
☐ What was Finn's reaction to the Press Gang?
☐ What was Elspeth's reaction to Finn's tricking the Press Gang?
☐ Why is Robbie so often the only one able to see the truth?
☐ Discuss Robbie's isolation from the family.
☐ Talk about why Robbie needed to hold a seal.

☐ Why does Robbie decide that Finn is a selkie?

☐ Talk about when Finn knows Robbie is a threat to him.

☐ Discuss the conflict between religion and what the minister calls pagan superstition.

☐ What do you think the Merry Dancers are?

☐ Discuss the climax of the story.

☐ Describe the Shetland Islands using the information from this book.

☐ Compare selkies to mermaids.

Things to Do

☐ Find historical information about the Press Gang.

☐ The Henderson's house is carefully described.

☐ Build a model of it and pay special attention to the beds.

☐ Research Norse mythology for the names of the sea gods.

Books

Written by Mollie Hunter
See page 228.

Mermaids and Selkies
See page 137.

The Sea
See pages 67–68.

A Taste of Blackberries

A Taste of Blackberries
by Doris Buchanan Smith. Crowell, 1973.

■■■■☐☐☐☐☐☐☐☐☐☐☐

Characters: *Jamie,* a smart, imaginative, funny boy prone to exaggeration.
Narrator, Jamie's friend who lives next door.

Plot: The narrator tells us of his friendship with Jamie and how Jamie lived every minute to its fullest—even picking blackberries before they are ripe. When they are hired to pick Japanese beetles from Mrs. Houser's grapevine leaves, Jamie pokes a stick at a bee's hive and falls to the ground screaming and gasping. Convinced that it is just an act, the narrator does nothing and Jamie dies. He learns to accept the death when he picks the ripe blackberries.

Awards and Recommendations: American Library Association

Things to Talk About and Notice

☐ Discuss severe allergies and how people with allergies cope.

☐ Discuss grief and ways people express grief.

☐ Discuss the purposes of funerals and wakes. Do they help people or prolong the grief?

☐ Discuss the balance between risk and caution.

☐ Discuss dealing with guilt.

☐ Talk about the feelings of the one "left behind."

☐ What would you want people to do if you died?

☐ Discuss the part blackberries play in the story. Was the taste of blackberries ruined by Jamie's death?

Things to Do

☐ Talk to people who have experienced grief to find out what others can do to be helpful.

☐ Find ways to celebrate the life of one who died.

☐ Talk about appropriate memorials for people.

☐ Visit a graveyard and copy interesting epitaphs.

☐ Compare the narrator in this story to Joel Bates in *On My Honor* by Marion Bauer (Clarion, 1986).

☐ Compare this book to *The Tenth Good Thing About Barney* by Judith Viorst (Atheneum, 1971).

Books

Written by Doris Buchanan Smith
See page 247.

Death
See pages 101–102.

Thank You, Jackie Robinson

Thank You, Jackie Robinson
Barbara Cohen. Lothrop, 1974.

■■■■■■■□□□□□□□

Setting: Winterhill, New Jersey.

Characters: *Sam* a ten-year-old baseball fan.
Davy, the Black cook at the Inn who was an avid Dodger's fan.
Mrs. Green, Sam's widowed mother.
Henrietta, Davy's daughter.
Elliott, Henrietta's husband.
Rosy and Fran, Sam's younger sisters.
Sara, Sam's older sister.

Plot: Sam Green is such an avid Dodger's fan that he has memorized every single game they've played during his lifetime. When Sam discovers that the new cook at the inn loves the Dodgers as much as he does, a close friendship develops between them. Together they go to the games at Ebbets Field and to every other ballfield within a day's drive of New Jersey. Because Jackie Robinson was the first Black man in professional baseball, Davy admires him especially. When Davy becomes terminally ill, Sam overcomes his shyness enough to go to Ebbets Field, get Jackie Robinson's attention, and ask him to autograph a baseball for Davy.

Things to Talk About and Notice

☐ Talk about why Sam and Davy couldn't stop overnight on their drive to Pittsburgh.

☐ Discuss why Davy couldn't be buried in the cemetery that Sam's father could.

☐ What happened when Sam ate something that wasn't on his list?

☐ Discuss different burial customs.

Things to Do

☐ Find out about Preacher Roe, Roy Campanella, Jackie Robinson, Pee Wee Reese, and Gil Hodges, the men who talked to Sam. What was each player's baseball career like? What happened to Jackie Robinson?

☐ Read a biography of Jackie Robinson to find out how discrimination affected his life.

☐ From the information given in the book, figure out the batting order of the Brooklyn Dodgers. Check it out.

☐ Find out whether the Dodgers won the pennant the year Davy died.

☐ Look at baseball cards. Talk to collectors. Find out why some are more valuable than others.

☐ Find out whether baseball rules have changed since the time in which this story is set.

☐ Was racial discrimination legal during the time in which this story is set? Find out whether there were laws to protect African-Americans. Had the laws changed since Civil War days? Did they differ from state to state?

☐ Watch the movie *Field of Dreams*.

Books

Written by Barbara Cohen

Benny. Lothrop, 1977.
The Binding of Isaac. Lothrop, 1978.
Bitter Herbs and Honey. Lothrop, 1976.
Canterbury Tales. Lothrop, 1988.
The Carp in the Bathtub. Lothrop, 1972.
The Christmas Revolution. Lothrop, 1987.
Coasting. Lothrop, 1985.
The Demon Who Would Not Die. Atheneum, 1982.
Even Higher. Lothrop, 1987.
Fat Jack. Atheneum, 1980.
Gooseberries to Oranges. Lothrop, 1982.
Here Come the Purim Players. Lothrop, 1984.
I Am Joseph. Lothrop, 1980.
The Innkeeper's Daughter . Lothrop, 1979.
King of the Seventh Grade. Lothrop, 1982.
Lover's Games. Atheneum, 1983.
Molly's Pilgrim. Lothrop, 1983.
The Orphan Game. Lothrop, 1988.
People Like Us. Bantam, 1987.
Queen for a Day. Lothrop, 1981.
R My Name is Rosie. Lothrop, 1978.
Roses. Lothrop, 1984.
Seven Daughters and Seven Sons. With Lovejoy, Bahija. Atheneum, 1982.
Unicorns in the Rain. Collier, 1980.
Yussel's Prayer. Lothrop, 1981.

Baron, Nancy. *Tuesday's Child.* Atheneum, 1984.

Christopher, Matt. *The Year Mom Won the Pennant.* Little, 1986. ✔

Giff, Patricia Reilly. *Left-Handed Shortstop.* Delacorte, 1980. ☑

Kalb, Jonah. *The Goof That Won the Pennant.* Houghton, 1987.

Lord, Betty Bao. *In the Year of the Boar and Jackie Robinson.* Harper, 1984. ✔

Slote, Alfred. *Hang Tough, Paul Mather.* Harper, 1973. ✔

———. *Jake.* Lippincott, 1971. ✔

———. *The Trading Game.* Lippincott, 1990. ✔

Jackie Robinson

Adler, David A. *Jackie Robinson: He Was the First.* Holiday, 1989.

Epstein, Sam. *Jackie Robinson: Baseball's Gallant Fighter.* Garrard, 1974.

Frommer, Harvey. *Jackie Robinson.* Watts, 1984.

O'Connor, Jim. *Jackie Robinson and the Story of All-Black Baseball.* Random, 1989.

Poetry

Larrick, Nancy, ed. *Crazy to Be Alive In Such a Strange World.* Evans, 1977.

Cullen, Countee. "Incident"

Hughes, Langston. "Merry-Go-Round"

Tom's Midnight Garden

Tom's Midnight Garden
by Philippa Pearce. Harper, 1984.

■■■■■■■■■◘■■■□□

Setting: An old house in England.

Characters: *Tom Long,* a young boy who is lonely and unhappy in the old house until he discovers the garden.

Hatty Melbourne, the girl Tom meets in the garden. Hatty is an orphaned girl who is often teased by her cousins. She knows every plant in the garden.

Alan Kitson, Tom's well-meaning but distant, rigid, and unimaginative uncle.

Gwen Kitson, Alan's wife.

Mrs. Bartholomew, the lady who owns the house and lives in the attic.

Peter Long, Tom's brother and confidant.

Barty, the man Hatty falls in love with.

Abel, the gardener. He loves Hatty and is the only other one who can see Tom.

Plot: To avoid catching his brother's measles, Tom is sent to spend his vacation with a distant aunt and uncle in their flat in an old house. When the clock strikes thirteen, Tom discovers a beautiful garden in which time leaps forward and backward. Best of all, in the garden, he discovers Hatty. No one else except the gardener and Hatty can see Tom when he is in the garden and Hatty and Tom become great friends.

Things to Talk About and Notice

□ Find examples of foreshadowing, such as "He was looking only for Hatty, so he did not linger over this view, but later he had cause to remember it."

□ Notice how the clock dominates the story and its characters.

□ Discuss the first mention of Mrs. Bartholomew and her reactions to the clock.

□ Talk about the way Tom felt when confined to his bed every night.

□ Of what significance are the designs on the clock?

□ Talk about how Tom's feelings about the clock change during the story.

□ Notice the links Tom uses between times: the clock, the yew tree, the house itself.

□ Why do Tom's feet leave no prints in the garden?

□ Find clues to show that people are frightened by Mrs. Bartholomew.

□ Discuss why Tom and Hatty each think that the other is a ghost. Why is Tom visible only to Hatty and the gardener?

□ What might have happened if Tom had got inside the older house beyond the hall sooner?

□ Discuss how the story would have been different if Tom had been older when he visited the garden.

□ Discuss Hatty's aunt's statement: "Climbing trees, if you please! Has she no sense of what is fitting to her sex and to her age now?" Would girls today be judged so harshly?

□ Why does Abel change his mind about Tom?

□ What does "Time no longer" mean to Tom?

□ Discuss what "exchanged time for eternity" means.

Things to Do

□ List the things Tom tells Peter and compare what Peter knows to what Tom knows.

□ Use the descriptions of the main hall and garden to draw pictures or make models of them.

□ Summarize each visit to the garden in one sentence. Put them on a timeline of "real" time.

Books

Written by Philippa Pearce

The Battle of Bubble and Squeak. Andre Deutsch, 1979.

Emily's Own Elephant. Greenwillow, 1988 .

Lion at School and Other Stories. Greenwillow, 1986.

The Way to Sattin Shore. Greenwillow, 1984.

Who's Afraid? and Other Strange Stories. Greenwillow, 1987.

Time Fantasies

See page 119.

Gardens

Bosse, Malcolm. *The Seventy-Nine Squares.* Crowell, 1979.

Burnett, Frances. *The Secret Garden.* Many versions.

Van Allsburg, Chris. *The Garden of Abdul Gasazi.* Houghton, 1979. ✔ ☑

Wrightson, Patricia. *An Older Kind of Magic.* Harcourt, 1972.

Traitor: The Case of Benedict Arnold

Traitor: The Case of Benedict Arnold
by Jean Fritz. Putnam, 1981.

■■■■■■■☐☐☐☐☐☐☐☐

Setting: New York, during the Revolutionary War.

Characters: *Benedict Arnold,* showy, brave in battle, self-indulgent, and utterly convinced that whatever he did was right and should not be questioned.

Major Andre, handsome, talented, well-mannered British officer whose contacts with Arnold resulted in his being hung by the Patriots; however, most admired him.

Peggy Arnold, Arnold's second wife who is sympathetic to the British cause and as vain as her husband.

George Washington, initially an admirer of Benedict Arnold.

Summary: This is a biography of the man whose name has become synonymous with *traitor.* A longer book than some of those by the same author, it is intended for an older audience, probably at least sixth grade. Although Benedict Arnold's name is among the most widely known from the American Revolution, most of us aren't quite sure just what it is that he did, only that it was traitorous. Here is Benedict Arnold's flamboyant life from his boyhood in Norwich, Connecticut, to his death, not in battle as he had hoped, but in bed in London.

Things to Talk About and Notice
☐ Why did Benedict Arnold behave as he did?
☐ Discuss other people who justify behavior in the same way Arnold did.
☐ Why is Major Andre considered a hero even by the Americans when Benedict Arnold is not?
☐ What factors could have changed Benedict Arnold's story? Should he have been pardoned?
☐ Does revolution necessarily mean war? What are the options, if any?

Things to Do
☐ Make a chart of all the people mentioned in the book, listing which side they were on at the beginning and the end of the book, and adding as much information as possible from other sources.
☐ Use maps from that era to show location of the events in the story.
☐ Find other biographies of Benedict Arnold or Major Andre and decide whether Ms. Fritz was more kind or more harsh than other biographers.
☐ Write to West Point to find out about that point in the river then and now.
☐ Find information about spies and traitors in more recent times.

Books
Written by Jean Fritz
See page 217.

Revolutionary War
See pages 61–63.

Trouble at the Mines

Trouble at the Mines
by Doreen Rappaport. Crowell, 1987.

■■■■■■□□□□□□□□

Setting: Arnot, Pennsylvania, 1898.

Characters: *Rosie Wilson,* the daughter and niece of coal miners. Rosie's family life, like the others in Arnot, centers around the mine. *Mary Harris Jones (Mother Jones),* a real labor union organizer, Mother Jones devoted her life to helping coal miners improve working conditions until well into her nineties. She was charismatic and eloquent, as well as very brave. *Mary Wilson,* Rosie's cousin and best friend. *Louann Wilson,* Rosie's mother. She walks with Mother Jones and is a leader among the women for the strike. *Bryan Wilson,* Rosie's father. He's a leader among the other miners and is determined to hold to the strike. *Jack Wilson,* Rosie's uncle and her father's brother. Although he helps his brother declare the strike, he is unable to stick to the strike, becomes a scab, and goes back to work in the mines before the strike is over. *Sally Wilson,* Rosie's aunt, Jack's wife. She sides with her husband during the strike. *Henry and Willie Wilson,* Rosie's older brothers who work in the mines.

Plot: This is a fictionalized account of the coal miners' strike in Arnot and the part that Mother Jones played. It is told by Rosie Wilson, a young girl whose family suffers greatly because of the strike but comes out with jobs and lives intact.

Things to Talk About and Notice
☐ Notice the way Mother Jones organizes the women.
☐ Discuss the differences between what Mother Jones says to the women and to the men.
☐ Discuss the effect of the mine's collapse on the action of the story.
☐ Discuss the alternatives the miners had to striking.
☐ Talk about reasons for strikes in your community.
☐ Discuss reasons people cross picket lines or refuse to do so.
☐ Discuss Mother Jones' motivation.
☐ Talk about the idea of a "company town." Is your town a one-industry town? What effect does this have on your town?

Things to Do
☐ Find out about mining today. Is it safer? Why or why not?
☐ Locate a mine of any kind near your home. How safe is it? How well paid are the workers? Are they frequently laid off? Who owns the mine?
☐ Find out about other labor leaders.
☐ Ask your parents and friends what they think about unions.

Books
Written by Doreen Rappaport
The Boston Coffee Party. Harper, 1988.
But She's Still My Grandma. Human Science, 1982.
A Man Can Be . . . . With Kempler, Susan. Human Science, 1984.
The Night the Minute Hand Stopped. Kimbo, 1988.

Coal Mining
Hendershot, Judith. *In Coal Country.* Knopf, 1987.☑
White, Ruth. *Sweet Creek Holler.* Farrar, 1988.

Tuck Everlasting

Tuck Everlasting
by Natalie Babbitt. Farrar, 1975.

■■■■■■■■■■□□□□□

Setting: The village of Treegap.

Characters: *Winnie Foster,* an overprotected little girl whose family owns the woods where the spring is hidden and who becomes a friend of the Tucks.

Anson Tuck (Tuck), Tuck doesn't appear until well into the story, but he feels the tragedy of the family's existence more than the others and attempts to make Winnie understand why the life and death cycle are so important.

Mae Tuck, Tuck's wife. She's accepted their lot better than the others and goes about doing what has to be done and adjusting to things that can't be helped.

Jesse Tuck, frozen at seventeen. The first of the Tucks to come in contact with Winnie.

Miles Tuck, the older son, more settled and practical than Jesse. He was married with two children, but his wife left him when he didn't grow older.

The Man in the Yellow Suit, knows the secret. He extorts the woods from Winnie's family in exchange for taking the constable to where Winnie is being held. He plans to sell the water and to force Winnie to drink it.

Plot: The Tuck family inadvertently drinks from a spring that causes them to be immortal and unchanging. Winnie Foster stumbles onto their secret and becomes their friend. A man in a yellow suit has been following them. When he threatens to sell the water to the highest bidder and to force Winnie to drink it and thus remain a child forever, Mae kills him and is jailed for it. Winnie helps Mae escape and is given a vial of the water by Jesse who tells her to drink it when she is seventeen and then join them. She pours the water over a toad. Jesse finds Winnie's grave years later and knows she married and lived a long life.

Awards and Recommendations: American Library Association, IRA Children's Choice

Things to Talk About and Notice

- ☐ Examine the author's use of foreshadowing: Angus Tuck's dream in chapter one that they are all happy in heaven; the sinister man in the yellow suit; Tuck's forgotten shotgun in a corner of the room.
- ☐ Notice the author's use of symbolism: the wheel, the toad, the pond, the music box, the storm, and the gallows.
- ☐ Discuss the differences between Winnie's lifestyle and the Tucks' lifestyle, evident in their houses inside and out.
- ☐ Find examples of descriptive language.
- ☐ Natalie Babbit reveals the story conflict slowly. Find clues, such as when Tuck says "What in the world could possibly happen to me?" and Mae's three petticoats and old-fashioned dress.
- ☐ Find the examples of the wheel metaphor that pervades the book.
- ☐ The Tucks discuss the good and bad about their circumstances. Think of other good and bad things about it.
- ☐ Imagine that you had been taken by the Tucks the way Winnie was. What would your reaction have been? How would your family react? Why does Winnie react the way she does?
- ☐ If the man with the yellow suit had drunk from the spring while he was spying on the Tucks, how would the plot have changed?
- ☐ Discuss why Tuck was delighted to see Winnie.
- ☐ Talk about why Natalie Babbitt didn't have Mae shoot the man in the yellow suit. Why didn't we ever learn his name?
- ☐ Discuss whether Mae was right to kill the man in the yellow suit and whether violence and murder are ever justified?

Things to Do

- ☐ Find and compare music boxes. Try to find one similar to the one Mae loves.

Books

Written and Illustrated by Natalie Babbitt
See page 182.

Time Fantasies
See page 119.

The Valley of Deer

The Valley of Deer
by Eileen Dunlop. Holiday, 1989.

■■■■■■■■■■■■□□□

Theme: We must take charge of our destinies.

Setting: A village in the Valley of Deer, rural Scotland, 1954.

Characters: *Anne Farrar,* sensitive and so empathetic that she causes herself great misery over the ills of others. She is determined to convince others that she has seen visions of Alice Jardyne and must find out what happened to her centuries before.

Alice Jardyne, a young woman with a twisted spine and withered arm who lived in the same house in the seventeenth century. A healer who was once revered by the village, Alice is later accused of witchcraft, reviled, and ultimately murdered by those she helped.

Polly Jardine, a victim of polio, who resents her wheelchair-bound life. She is Anne's confidante and tries to convince her that these visions she has have a natural cause.

Jenny Farrar, Anne's older, practical sister.

Mr. and Mrs. Farrar, parents of Anne and Jenny. They are a dedicated team of archaeologists who love each other and their children but are often immersed in their work.

Plot: The Valley of Deer is doomed. It is about to be flooded by engineers and will soon lie at the bottom of a huge lake. Anne Farrar establishes a connection, real or imagined, with Alice Jardyne, a young woman accused of witchcraft centuries before. She also makes a more realistic connection with Polly. Anne's parents and Polly are convinced that Anne's visions are a result of an overactive imagination, but Anne is sure that they are caused by an amulet her archaeologist parents have uncovered. Both connections, although traumatic, help Anne come to terms with herself and the world around her.

Things to Talk About and Notice

☐ Find examples of foreshadowing in the book.

☐ Discuss Jenny's feelings throughout this story.

☐ Talk about what it would be like to have your town abandoned and flooded.

Things to Do

☐ Find out about witchcraft trials in America.

☐ Compare this story to *The Walking Stones* by Mollie Hunter (Harper, 1970).

☐ The author says that the witchcraft trials in Scotland were coming to an end about the time Alice was tried. When did they come to an end here?

Books

Written by Eileen Dunlop
Clementina. Holiday, 1987.
The House on the Hill. Holiday, 1987.
The Maze Stone. Putnam, 1983.

Witches and Witchcraft: Fiction
Curry, Jane. *The Great Flood Mystery.* Macmillan, 1985.
Jones, Diane. *Witch Week.* Greenwillow, 1982.
Konigsburg, E. L. *Jennifer, Hecate, Macbeth, William McKinley and Me, Elizabeth.* Macmillan, 1967. ✔
Naylor-Reynolds, Phyllis. *Witch Water.* Atheneum, 1977.
———. *Witch's Sister.* Dell, 1980.
Speare, Elizabeth George. *The Witch of Blackbird Pond.* Houghton, 1958. ✔
Starkey, Marion Lena. *The Tall Man from Boston.* Crown, 1975.

Witches and Witchcraft: Nonfiction
Auch, Mary. *The Witching of Ben Wagner.* Houghton, 1987.
Cohen, Daniel. *Curses, Hexes and Spells.* Harper, 1974.
Hahn, Mary D. *The Time of the Witch.* Houghton, 1982.
Jackson, Shirley. *Witchcraft of Salem Village.* Random, 1956.
Kent, Zachary. *The Story of the Salem Witch Trials.* Childrens, 1986.
O'Connell, Margaret. *The Magic Cauldron: Witchcraft for Good and Evil.* Phillips, 1975.
Starkey, Marion Lena. *The Visionary Girls: Witchcraft in Salem Village.* Little, 1973.

Predicting the Future
See page 155.

The Village by the Sea

The Village by the Sea
by Paula Fox. Orchard, 1988.

■■■■■■□□□□□□□

Setting: Long Island, New York.

Characters: *Emma,* the only child of loving parents. She is joyful and understanding and used to people's love.

Aunt Bea, has long frizzy gray hair and drinks copious amounts of tea and, perhaps, alcohol. The half-sister of Emma's father, she is consumed by envy and needs constant reinforcement and attention.

Uncle Crispin, Bea's husband. He is a music teacher and uses music to comfort himself.

Emma's father, is very ill and regrets having to send his daughter to stay with Bea and Crispin, but sees no other alternative.

Emma's mother, realizes that her time and attention must go to her husband as he goes through his heart surgery. She is sure Emma is strong enough to withstand Bea's wiles.

Alberta (Bertie), a tall, skinny girl who lives near Aunt Bea. She calls Bea "Lady Bonkers."

Plot: Emma's father is to undergo heart surgery, so Emma goes to stay with her Uncle Crispin and Aunt Bea. Uncle Crispin is kind and tries to help Emma, but Aunt Bea is thoughtless, at best, and heartless, at worst. She is consumed by envy and frightens Emma. When Emma and her new friend construct a tiny village from the debris and shells they find on the beach, Bea's envy becomes destructive.

Awards and Recommendations: American Library Association, Boston Globe/Horn Book Award, School Library Journal

Things to Talk About and Notice

☐ Talk about why Bea is so jealous and cruel.

☐ Emma's father says that the fear within him is almost separate from him. He tries to pity it and feels less afraid. Do you think that's possible? What do you do about fear?

☐ Discuss Emma's relationship with her father. She dares to ask him, "Are you afraid?"

☐ Talk about why Emma can't write in the diary as her father wished.

☐ Discuss the relationship between Crispin and Bea.

☐ Discuss what Bea writes in the diary and what that tells you about her.

☐ Crispin says he had a serious childhood and doesn't know what it is to play. How would you explain play to him?

☐ Emma is reading *The Secret Garden* by Frances Burnett. Do you think Mr. Craven is like Bea?

☐ Emma compares the table to the Mad Hatter's tea party and compares Bea to the dormouse. Does the comparison make sense?

☐ Discuss Crispin's reaction to the plastic deer that Emma found.

☐ Discuss Bea's attempts to be friends with Emma. Why don't they work?

☐ Look for similes in the book: Crispin says that English breakfasts start you into your day "like an overloaded donkey." Emma thinks Bea's hair stands up "like a milkweed in the wind."

☐ Discuss Emma's identification with her father, comparing his operation to her tonsillectomy.

☐ Why does Bea dig at her hands until they are raw?

☐ Talk about why Bea says that Bertie has a blazing talent when Bertie says she can't draw.

☐ Talk about why the girls build the village and why Bea destroys it. Is Bea mentally ill?

☐ Emma's mother sends Bea a bowl that Bea calls French Faience. Is there such a thing? What does it look like? Talk to an antique dealer or person who deals with fine dishes about faience.

Things to Do

☐ Find a copy of Monet's "Cliffs at Etretat" that Bea so loves. What do you think of it?

☐ Bea has a lot of strong beliefs. List them and then try to figure out which are based on fact.

Books

Written by Paula Fox
See Page 215.

Cruel People
Bawden, Nina. *Carrie's War.* Lippincott, 1973. ✔

Tiny Villages
Lisle, Janet Taylor. *Afternoon of the Elves.* Orchard, 1989. ✔

Paterson, Katherine. *Bridge to Terabithia.* Crowell, 1977. ✔

Wells, Rosemary. *Through the Hidden Door.* Dial, 1987.

The Voyage of The Frog

> *The Voyage of the Frog*
> by Gary Paulsen. Orchard, 1988.
>
> ■■■■■■■■■■□□□□
>
> **Setting:** The sailboat *The Frog* in the Pacific Ocean off the coast of California.
>
> **Characters:** *David Alspeth,* a fourteen-year-old boy who is mourning the death of his uncle. *Uncle Owen,* David's dead uncle who remains a powerful influence in David's life.
>
> **Plot:** David sets out on a small sailboat, *The Frog,* to spread the ashes of his favorite uncle, Owen, who taught him to be a competent sailor. David has water and food onboard, but he has not checked the weather. When a sudden violent storm comes up, David is hit by the boom and knocked unconscious. He comes to just in time to save the boat from sinking, but he has been blown far off course. He has to come to grips with himself and the sea in order to survive. When he is rescued, he decides not to desert *The Frog,* but to sail it home himself.
>
> **Awards and Recommendations:** School Library Journal

Things to Talk About and Notice

- ☐ Read just the first line in the book: "David Alspeth stopped at the locked gate, felt in his hands the weight of the small box which he could not stand to see yet, looked down on the sailboat, and tried not to cry." Predict what might happen next.
- ☐ Notice the flashback techniques the author uses to tell us about Uncle Owen.

- ☐ Discuss the author's decision to end the book, not when David gets home, but when David decides to stay with the boat.
- ☐ When David first wrote in the log book, he wrote, "I am hate." Then he erased it and wrote, "I am alone." Why do you think he changed it?
- ☐ At one point David feels a oneness with the boat. When and why did that occur?
- ☐ Notice the different ways David reacted to the two storms.
- ☐ When David realizes he is going to be alone and at sea for a long time, he sets up three rituals for each day: a water time, a food time, and a learning time. Discuss why he needed these rituals.

Things to Do

- ☐ Find out what kind of sailboat *The Frog* was.
- ☐ Trace David's journey on a classroom map.
- ☐ Make a chart of sailing terms and their meanings.
- ☐ Find out about each of the animals and phenomena David sees while on board: dolphins, phosphorescence, shark, killer whales, blue whales, and plankton.
- ☐ List some of the other perils of the sea David might have been exposed to.

Books

Written by Gary Paulsen
See page 239.

Storms
King, Clive. *The Night the Water Came.* Harper, 1982.

Survival
See pages 74–76.

Watership Down

> ### Watership Down
> by Richard Adams. Macmillan, 1974.
>
> ■■■■■■■■■■■■■□
>
> **Setting:** Rural England.
>
> **Characters:** *Fiver,* the runt of the litter whose psychic powers allow him to predict the impending doom of the home warren.
>
> *Hazel,* Fiver's sister and the leader of the group of rabbits who follow Fiver's warning and leave the warren.
>
> *Bigwig,* a member of the OWSLA, a military group that serves the Chief Rabbit, who joins the fleeing rabbits and whose military skill is called upon during the journey.
>
> *Silverweed,* members of the strange semi-domesticated warren who provide temporary shelter to Hazel and her group.
>
> *Captain Holly,* a member of the OWSLA of the home warren who tracks the group to Watership Down.
>
> *Kehaar,* a seagull the rabbits nurse back to health. He provides invaluable aid in helping the rabbits escape from Efrafa.
>
> *General Woundwort,* Chief of the OWSLA in Efrafa warren. An evil and violent rabbit in this highly structured, unpleasant warren.
>
> **Plot:** A small group of rabbits leave their warren to journey to a place where they can establish a new, safe warren. Along the way, they encounter many hardships from farm equipment, dogs, wild animals, and other rabbits.
>
> **Awards and Recommendations:** American Library Association

Things to Talk About and Notice

☐ Notice the rabbits' vocabulary. There's a Lapine glossary in the back of the book.

☐ Notice the hardships the rabbits endure on the journey: crossing the river, traveling in open fields, being threatened by people and animals.

☐ Discuss the differences among the four warrens.

☐ Discuss the personalities of the rabbits. What nonanimal characters in other books share similar character traits?

☐ Discuss the implications of the story, if any, for our own society.

☐ Do the names of the rabbits have any meaning?

☐ Why did Hazel need to set the farm rabbits free and raid the Efrafa warren?

☐ Discuss the dangers faced by wild animals where you live.

☐ Talk about the types of governments found in each of the warrens.

☐ How would the story have changed if the author had written about wolves instead of rabbits?

☐ Why do you think Richard Adams chose to write about rabbits?

Things to Do

☐ Map the rabbits' journey.

☐ Based on this journey, map another fictional journey for rabbits in your area to make.

☐ Watch the movie *Watership Down.* What is different from the book? Why were the changes made?

☐ Did this book accurately portray rabbits' behavior?

☐ Compare this story to *The Lemming Condition* by Alan Arkin (Harper, 1976).

☐ Find out about rabbit breeds.

Books

Written by Richard Adams

The Girl in the Swing. Knopf, 1980.

Maia. Knopf, 1985.

A Nature Diary. Viking, 1986.

Our Amazing Sun. Troll, 1983.

Our Wonderful Solar System. Troll, 1983.

Shardik. Avon, 1976.

Traveller. Knopf, 1988.

Animal Societies

See page 108.

Quests

See pages 59–60.

Rabbits

Howe, James and Howe, Deborah. *Bunnicula.* Atheneum, 1979. ✔

Lawson, Robert. *Rabbit Hill.* Viking, 1944.

Weasel

Weasel
by Cynthia deFelice. Macmillan, 1990.

■■■■■■■■■□□□□

Theme: Hatred drives out all other emotions.
Setting: Ohio, 1839.
Characters: *Nathan,* a twelve-year-old boy who tries to assume the role of a man in the wilderness. He is torn between his conscience and his need for revenge.
Ezra, an ex-Indian fighter whose family was killed by Weasel, who used to be his friend. He cannot speak because Weasel cut out his tongue, but he communicates his love and concern for the children and their father. In his own way, he is as imprisoned by his hatred for Weasel as Nathan is.
Weasel, an ex-Indian fighter who kills at will and without regard to consequences. He has no more Native Americans to kill and so he exercises his cruelty on the settlers.
Mr. Fowler, Nathan's father and Ezra's friend. He realizes that the hatred and need for revenge that Nathan feels for Weasel is harmful and that killing Weasel will not exorcise the guilt and grief Nathan and Ezra feel.
Molly Fowler, Nathan's sister. She has learned herbal medicine skills from her mother and proves herself to be a resourceful child. More practical than her brother, she copes with grief better than Nathan.
Plot: Nathan Fowler and his sister are alone in the cabin when Ezra arrives and wordlessly beckons them to follow him into the wilderness at night. Their mother is dead and their father left several days ago to hunt for food. With trepidation they follow and find their wounded father. Nathan is brought face-to-face with an evil killer, Weasel. Later, when Nathan has a chance and even a cause to kill Weasel, he does not and this decision returns to haunt him.

Things to Talk About and Notice
☐ Discuss reasons for Weasel's actions.
☐ Notice the spare, straight forward style of writing.
☐ Discuss why Nathan doesn't kill Weasel.
☐ Talk about why Nathan buries Weasel and the pig.
☐ The story tells about Daniel Boone's actions toward Native Americans. If this is true, why do we make a hero of him today?
☐ How would the story have changed if Weasel hadn't died?
☐ How would the story have changed if it had been set in modern times? Would justice have been done? How? Does that change the arguments for and against killing Weasel?
☐ Does the argument against killing Weasel apply to an argument against the death penalty in general? Is the death penalty justified?

Things to Do
☐ Find out about herbal medicine.
☐ Find out about real Indian fighters.
☐ Locate the action of the story on the map.
☐ Find out what other things were going on in the United States in 1839.
☐ Read about the "removal" of Native American tribes throughout our country.

Books
Written by Cynthia deFelice
See page 155.

Same Time Period
Blos, Joan. *A Gathering of Days: A New England Girl's Journal, 1830–1832. Scribners, 1979.* ✔

Shawnee Indians
Eckert, Allan W. *Blue Jacket: War Chief of the Shawnees.* Little, 1969.

The Whipping Boy

The Whipping Boy
by Sid Fleischman. Greenwillow, 1986.

■■■■■■■■■□□□□□□

Theme: Class struggles.

Characters: *Prince Brat (Horace),* a mischievous boy who refuses to learn to read or write.
Jemmy, the whipping boy for Horace.
Betsy, a girl who befriends Horace and Jemmy.
Petunia, Betsy's dancing bear.
Hold-Your-Nose-Billy, the villain, famous for eating garlic.
Cap'n Nips, a hot-potato man who befriends the boys.

Plot: Prince Horace doesn't have much to worry about when he is naughty at the palace because Jemmy, the whipping boy, is punished for Horace's misdeeds. However, he is as bored as Jemmy is miserable so the two escape. They are captured for ransom, but outwit the villains, eventually returning to the palace where life promises to be better.

Awards and Recommendations: American Library Association, Newbery Medal, School Library Journal

Things to Talk About and Notice
☐ Discuss lying for others and taking the blame.
☐ Do we still train animals to entertain as Petunia does? Is it humane?
☐ Discuss the expression "living by your wits."

Things to Do
☐ Compare this story to *The Prince and the Pauper* by Mark Twain.
☐ Find out about melodrama in general and decide whether this story is a melodrama.
☐ Compare Hold-Your-Nose-Billy to other villans. (See pages 77–78.)
☐ Find other rogues and ragamuffins in stories.
☐ List the funny names in the story.
☐ Make up last names for each of the characters based on their occupation, home, or character.
☐ Read "The Pied Piper of Hamlin" by Hans Christian Andersen.
☐ Find out about The Plague and other epidemics. Compare The Plague to the spread of AIDS today.

Books
Written by Sid Fleischman
See page 214.

The Wolves of Willoughby Chase

The Wolves of Willoughby Chase
by Joan Aiken. Doubleday, 1964.

■■■■■■■■■■■□□□□

Theme: Good will triumph over evil.
Setting: England.
Characters: *Bonnie Green,* the only beloved child of Sir Willoughby and Lady Green.
Sylvia Green, Bonnie's poor orphaned cousin who has been brought to Willoughby Chase as a companion for Bonnie.
Miss Slighcarp, a vicious distant cousin in charge of the mansion and the girls.
Simon, an orphaned gooseherd with artistic abilities and aspirations.
Plot: This Victorian melodrama tells of two cousins, Bonnie and Sylvia who, through the villainy of Miss Slighcarp become wards in an orphanage. With the help of Simon they escape from the orphanage, rescue an impoverished aunt, cause the arrest of Miss Slighcarp and her two accomplices, and regain control of the mansion just in time to greet Bonnie's parents who have not, after all, been lost at sea. Whew!

Things to Talk About and Notice
□ Find the amazing coincidences and unbelievable occurrences. Change one of them and find out what happens to the story.
□ Figure out why the book is called *The Wolves of Willoughby Chase.* Why are wolves such a threat at the beginning of the story and almost nonexistent by the end? Will they come again?
□ Look at the character's names. Does the author tell you anything about the characters through the names she gave them? Compare these to some of the names that Charles Dickens used.

Things to Do
□ Write the story for the TV show *Murder, She Wrote.*
□ Find out about wolves. Which of the behaviors they exhibit in the story are possible or probable?
□ Find out about orphanages and workhouses of that day. Were they all as bad as the one Mrs. Brisket ran?
□ Compare the wolves in this story to the wolves in *Julie of the Wolves* by Jean Craighead George (Harper, 1972).
□ Compare this story to the movie or play *Oliver.* Which of the songs would fit into this story?
□ Watch a silent movie melodrama.
□ Write and act out your own melodrama.

Books
Written by Joan Aiken
See page 175.

Orphans
Bronte, Charlotte. *Jane Eyre.* Many versions.
Burnett, Francis. *The Secret Garden.* Many versions.
Dickens, Charles. *Oliver Twist.* Many versions.
Edwards, Julie. *Mandy.* Harper, 1971.
Spyri, Johanna. *Heidi.* Many versions.
Warner, Gertrude. The Boxcar Children series. A. Whitman.

Wolves
See page 129.

Words by Heart

Words by Heart
by Ouida Sebestyen. Little, 1979.

■■■■■■■■□□□□□□

Theme: Racial prejudice controls people's fears, dreams, and lives.
Setting: Somewhere "Out West," 1910.
Characters: *Lena,* a young bright child who is proud of her abilities and is very competitive. She knows her pride and unthinking behavior cause her father to worry.
Papa, Lena's father. He loves his family and has a good deal of pride in his Black heritage.
Claudie, Lena's stepmother. She loves Lena, her father, and Lena's half-sisters. She is afraid of the prejudice and violence swirling around them and longs to return to the all-Black village.
Mrs. Chism, the wealthy and eccentric landowner for whom Lena's family and the Haney family work. She is selfish, demanding, greedy, and badly in need of love.
Winslow Starnes, until Lena came, he was the champion memorizer at school and everyone expects him to win the contest. He offers friendship to Lena until his father tries to teach him his own racial biases.
The Haneys, sharecroppers. They are less ambitious and poorer than Lena's family. When their livelihood is threatened, they react with violence and hatred.
Plot: Lena's family is the only Black family in this western town. Lena has not been aware of much racial prejudice; however, she had heard about it. When she wins the Bible verse contest at school, she and her whole family have to contend with prejudice.

Awards and Recommendations: American Library Association, IRA Children's Book Award, IRA Children's Choice, School Library Journal

Things to Talk About and Notice
□ Find similies in the story such as "The white faces looked like 'an orchard of pink-cheeked peaches.'" Lena was "different and comical looking, oozing like dark dough over the edges of her last year's Sunday dress."
□ Discuss Papa's wish that Lena "master" herself.

□ Discuss Lena's thought that Papa "stood at a distance seeing that everything was very small inside immense space, seeing that events were blinks of time in endless time, not important enough to hurt him or scare him."
□ Discuss Lena's thought that Bible words "seemed too large for her small mind."
□ Talk about Lena's dream of success: "She had a house with twenty windows, and a lap robe for her buggy with a hunting scene woven in it, and pet ducks for her children." Compare it to your own dream.
□ Talk about the bow-tie prize for the Bible contest.
□ Discuss Lena's wish that she could "see past the outside of things to the true, lasting part at the center that was good and exactly as it should be."
□ Discuss sharecropping versus renting and working the land.
□ Notice the train symbolism in the story.
□ Discuss the part religion plays in the town people's lives.
□ What does the title mean?
□ What are Mrs. Chism's needs and fears?
□ Discuss the teacher's ideas about inferior and superior races and Lena's and Winslow's reactions.
□ What price did Papa pay to get Lena the books?
□ Discuss Papa's death and why Lena refuses to tell who killed him.

Things to Do
□ Listen to ragtime music. Does it make you feel the way it made Lena feel? Why might she have felt differently?
□ Read the poems quoted in the book.
□ Memorize and recite a poem as Lena might have.

Books
Written by Ouida Sebestyen
Far from Home. Little, 1980.
The Girl in the Box. Little, 1988.
IOU's. Little, 1982.
On Fire. Atlantic, 1985.

Racial Violence and Prejudice
Armstrong, William H. *Sounder.* Harper, 1969. ✔
Cohen, Barbara. *Thank You, Jackie Robinson.* Lothrop, 1974. ✔
Taylor, Mildred. *Gold Cadillac.* Dial, 1987.
———. *Roll of Thunder, Hear My Cry.* Dial, 1976. ✔

Authors and Illustrators

Introduction

☐ Fortunately, the field of children's literature is burgeoning with fine writers, each having a unique style. Here are some of our favorite authors and illustrators with a few facts about their lives. When an author's work appears to have a common subject, technique, or characterization, we've pointed that out. We read as many of these people's works as possible and summarized those we could locate. In general, we provided as much information for author study as we could cram in.

☐ As adult readers, most of us latch on to an author we like and wait anxiously for the next volume. Children, especially those from literature-poor environments, are often unaware that if you love one book by an author, you are apt to like others by the same author. Author studies are also a way for children to discover what authors know and feel and a way to watch while a theme and subject are approached and developed throughout an author's life.

☐ Author biographies also serve to point out that people, not machines, write books and that the children can choose writing as a career.

☐ Whenever possible, we've listed addresses for contacting authors and have indicated, when we know it to be true, that an author will answer letters and visit schools for presentations. Publishers of children's books usually have publicists to work with schools and to help you contact the author through letters, telephone calls, and visits. They will often provide posters, biographies, and photographs.

Joan Aiken

Author
Living
Answers letters
Mailing address
    The Hermitage
    East Street
    Petworth
    West Sussex GU 28 OAB, England

Biography

Joan Aiken's mother was Canadian and her father was the American poet Conrad Aiken. She was born in Sussex, England, where the Aikens lived because they liked the British system of education. Ms. Aiken's first writing was published when she was a teenager. She married Ronald Brown and had two children. Her husband died in 1955. Ms. Aiken then edited a British magazine until her novel writing began to take most of her time. Her first novel was *The Kingdom and the Cave* (published in England), but she didn't become famous until *The Wolves of Willoughby Chase* was published in 1962. Later she wrote a series of Gothic children's novels set in the early 19th century. Ms. Aiken has written over fifty books for young people, including several collections of short stories.

About Joan Aiken's Work

☐ Notice the impossibilities in her work; these make her stories fantasies.
☐ Notice the time in which many of her fantasies are set: the early nineteenth century.
☐ You will find a similarity between Joan Aiken's work and novels by Charles Dickens, particularly *Oliver Twist.*
☐ Look for the humor in her novels, short stories, and poems.
☐ Watch for extraordinarily intelligent animals.

Books by Joan Aiken

Arabel and Mortimer. Doubleday, 1981.
Black Hearts in Battersea. Dell, 1987.
Bridle the Wind. Delacorte, 1983.
Dido and Pa. Delacorte, 1986.
The Faithless Lollybird. Doubleday, 1977.
The Far Forests. Viking, 1977.
The Kingdom Under the Sea. Penguin, 1986.

The Last Slice of Rainbow and Other Stories. Harper, 1988.
Midnight Is a Place. Viking, 1974.
The Moon's Revenge. Knopf, 1987.
Mortimer Says Nothing. Harper, 1987.
Mortimer's Cross. Harper, 1984.
Night Birds on Nantucket. Dell, 1981.
Past Eight O'Clock. Viking, 1987.
The Shadow Guest. Delacorte, 1980.
The Skin Spinners. Viking, 1976.
The Stolen Lake. Delacorte, 1981.
The Teeth of the Gale. Harper, 1988.
A Touch of Chill. Delacorte, 1979.
Up the Chimney Down. Harper, 1985.
A Whisper in the Night. Delacorte, 1984.
The Wolves of Willoughby Chase. Doubleday, 1962.

Book Awards and Recommendations
American Library Association: *The Skin Spinners*
IRA Children's Choice: *Midnight Is a Place, The Moon's Revenge*

Summaries of Selected Titles
Arabel and Mortimer

■■■■■■□□□□□□□□

Mortimer, the irrepressible raven, is at it again. This time he succeeds in undoing a cruise ship, a zoo, and an archaeological dig.

Black Hearts in Battersea

■■■□□□□□□□□□□□□

Fifteen-year-old Simon goes to London to study painting, but Dr. Field, who invited him there, has disappeared. Dr. Field's landlords, the Twites, seem to be plotting against the Duke and Duchess of Battersea and King James. Simon wants to prove his ideas, but it seems that he might need the help of Dido Twite.

Bridle the Wind

■■■■■■■■■■■■□□

Pursued by an evil abbot from the monastery, Felix is befriended by Juan, the Gypsies, and bandits of the Pyrenees.

175

Midnight Is a Place

In this melodrama, Lucas Bell and Anna-Marie Murgatroyd suffer great travail when their only refuge is burned to the ground. Not only have they lost their home, but the only person who offers them any solace at all is Mr. Oakapple, and he has been very badly hurt in the fire.

Mortimer Says Nothing

Here are four short stories about Mortimer, Arabel's talking raven, in which he outwits cousin Annie, loses his wasp collection, drinks martinis, and tricks a telephone trickster.

The Shadow Guest

After his mother and brother disappear, Cosmos goes to live with his cousin. Once in his cousin's home, however, Cosmos has strange visions and supernatural events occur.

The Stolen Lake

This sequel to *Nightbirds on Nantucket* finds Dido near Brazil where, apparently, the ancient Britons landed after the Saxons invaded England. While trying to understand their archaic language, Dido and her friends fight off carniverous birds, avoid man-eating fish, and cope with a queen who is waiting for Pendragon.

The Wolves of Willoughby Chase

See page 170.

Lloyd Alexander

Author
Living
Does telephone interviews
Contact:
    Children's Book Marketing
    E. P. Dutton
    2 Park Avenue
    New York, NY, 10016
    212-725-1818

Biography

Lloyd Alexander decided to become an author when he was fifteen, but he had no idea how to go about becoming one. He had always loved to read and was, and still is, fascinated by words. He was very interested in mythology, especially the King Arthur stories. His parents were poor and could not afford to send him to college so he went to work as a messenger in a Philadelphia bank. When he had saved enough money, he went to college but left at the end of one term because they didn't teach him enough about writing.

Mr. Alexander joined the Army during World War II and was assigned to military intelligence. He was sent to Wales to finish his training, where he fell in love with the country and spent time exploring it before he was sent to Paris. In Paris, he fell in love with and married Janine, a French woman.

The Alexanders moved to Philadelphia, and he began to write novels, but publishers rejected his work for seven years. During this time, he worked as a cartoonist, advertising writer, layout artist, and editor of a magazine. His first published work was for adults, but he soon began writing for young people. He enjoys this because he says, "In books for young people, I was able to express my own deepest feelings far more than I ever could when writing for adults."

Mr. Alexander loves music, especially Mozart, and claims to be the world's worst violinist. He also loves cats, and many of his cats appear in his books.

About Lloyd Alexander's Work

☐ Lloyd Alexander had planned only to adapt Welsh mythology for young readers. Instead he found himself involved in the characters and actions of his Prydain cycle.

☐ Mr. Alexander uses many elements of folk literature in his stories: the inexhaustible knapsack of food, the sword, and the cauldron. The books are about good versus evil, but the evil is the evil within oneself, not just external evil.

Books by Lloyd Alexander

The Beggar Queen. Dutton, 1984.
Black Cauldron. Holt, 1965.
The Book of Three. Holt, 1964.
The Castle of Llyr. Holt, 1966.
The Cat Who Wished to Be a Man. Dutton, 1973.
The Drakenburg Adventure. Dutton, 1988.
The El Dorado Adventure. Dutton, 1987.
The First Two Lives of Lukas-Kasha. Dutton, 1978.
The Four Donkeys. Holt, 1968.
The Foundling. Dell, 1982.
The High King. Holt, 1968.
The Illyrian Adventure. Dutton, 1986.
The Jedera Adventure. Dutton, 1989.
The Kestrel. Dutton, 1982.
Marvelous Misadventures of Sebastian. Dutton, 1970.
The Philadelphia Adventure. Dutton, 1990.
Taran Wanderer. Holt, 1967.
Time Cat. Avon, 1982.
The Town Cats and Other Tales. Dutton, 1977.
Westmark. Dutton, 1981.
The Wizard in the Tree. Dutton, 1975.

Book Awards and Recommendations
American Library Association: *The Book of Three, The Black Cauldron, The Castle of Llyr, The High King, The Four Donkeys, The Cat Who Wished to Be a Man, The Foundling, The Westmark Trilogy*
Boston Globe/Horn Book Honor Award: *The Cat Who Wished to Be a Man*
Newbery Medal: *The High King*
Newbery Honor Award: *The Black Cauldron*
School Library Journal: *Westmark*

Summaries of Selected Titles
The Book of Three

■■■■■■■■■■□□□□

This is the first Prydain Cycle book. Here Taran, the pig keeper, fights with Prince Gwydion against the evil threatening the kingdom. The foundations for the rest of the cycle are laid in this book.

The Cat Who Wished to Be a Man

■■■■■■■■□□□□□□

Lionel the cat overcomes his master's objections and becomes a man only to learn that humans are strange characters indeed.

The First Two Lives of Lukas-Kasha

■■■■■■■■□□□□□□

Lukas-Kasha comes out of the sea and is declared king. This incurs the wrath of the evil vizier who had himself in mind for the job.

The High King

■■■■■■■■■■□□□□

This is the last book in the Prydain Cycle. Taran goes home after an unsuccessful search to prove that he is of noble blood—something he must prove if he is to be allowed to marry Eilonwy. He learns that Arawn, the evil lord capable of assuming any shape, tricked Gwydion into battle by pretending to be Taran and has captured the magic sword. After regaining his sword, Taran is offered eternal life but refuses so he can continue the fight against evil. This fulfills a prophecy and Taran is made High King and marries Eilonwy.

The Illyrian Adventure

■■■■■■■■■■□□□□

Vesper Holly is a resourceful and determined sixteen-year-old who drags her guardian, Brinnie, behind her as she finds a treasure, thwarts a murder conspiracy, and manages a peace conference between two bitter enemies.

The Kestrel

■■■■■■■■■■□□□□

In this sequel to *Westmark*, the king has died and his minister is plotting with the Regians to invade Westmark. Mickle, now Queen Augusta, takes command. Theo, now known as the bloodthirsty guerilla general Kestrel, and his revolutionary band join forces with the queen.

Marvelous Misadventures of Sebastian

■■■■■■□□□□□□□□

Sebastian the fiddler is involved with a cruel usurper of the throne.

The Town Cats and Other Tales

■■■■■■■■□□□□□□

See page 7.

Westmark

■■■■■■■■□□□□□□

Theo is a printer's devil and when the police break into the shop, kill his master, and destroy the press, Theo becomes a fugitive. He is taken in by revolutionaries and becomes involved in their plot to overthrow the monarchy.

The Wizard in the Tree

■■■■■■■□□□□□□□

A bungling wizard manages to save Mallory and her fellow villagers from the cruel squire.

Mitsumasa Anno

Author/Illustrator
Living
Answers letters
Mailing address
   4-5-5 Midoricho
   Koganei Shi
   Tokyo, 184, Japan

Biography

Mitsumasa Anno was born in and still lives in Tokyo, Japan. He loved math as a child because it helped him see the world more clearly. When he grew up, he was an elementary school teacher for ten years. He loves drawing so much that each day he does some drawing or sketching. He has learned that the more elaborately and freely he works, the closer he comes to mathematics. Mr. Anno didn't visit America until he was grown. He had thousands of images about the United States, but they were all mixed up in his head. When he wrote the book *Anno's USA,* he mixed the images just as they were in his head.

About Mitsumasa Anno's Work

☐ Anno's work is full of optical illusions, mathematics, and puzzles. He usually works with soft colors and precise lines. Solve the puzzles.
☐ Make photocopies of the back covers of the books. Display the books by the front covers and try to match the backs to the fronts.
☐ Plot the locations in his books on a world map.

Books by Mitsumasa Anno

Written and Illustrated by Mitsumasa Anno

All in a Day. Putnam, 1986.
Anno's Aesop. Orchard, 1989.
Anno's Alphabet. Harper, 1975.
Anno's Animals. Putnam, 1979.
Anno's Britain. Putnam, 1982.
Anno's Counting Book. Harper, 1977.
Anno's Counting House. Putnam, 1982.
Anno's Faces Putnam, 1989.
Anno's Flea Market. Putnam, 1984.
Anno's Hat Tricks. Philomel, 1985.
Anno's Italy. Putnam, 1984.
Anno's Journey. Putnam, 1978.
Anno's Magical ABC. Philomel, 1981.
Anno's Masks. Philomel, 1990.

Anno's Math Games. Putnam, 1987.
Anno's Math Games II. Putnam, 1989.
Anno's Medieval World. Putnam, 1980.
Anno's Mysterious Multiplying Jar. Putnam, 1983.
Anno's Peekaboo. Putnam, 1988.
Anno's Sundial. Putnam, 1987.
Anno's USA. Putnam, 1983.
Dr. Anno's Magical Midnight Circus. Weatherhill, 1972.
In Shadowland. Orchard, 1988.
The King's Flower. Putnam, 1979.
Topsy-Turvies: Pictures to Stretch the Imagination. Weatherhill, 1970.
The Unique World of Mitsumasa Anno. Putnam, 1980.
Upside-Downers: More Pictures to Stretch the Imagination. Weatherhill, 1971.

Illustrated by Mitsumasa Anno

Anno's Hat Tricks. Nozaki, Akihiro. Putnam, 1985.
Socrates and the Three Little Pigs. Mori, Tuyosi. Putnam, 1986.

Book Awards and Recommendations

American Library Association: *Anno's Alphabet, Anno's Journey, The King's Flower, Anno's Medieval World, Anno's Magical ABC, Anno's Counting House, Anno's Mysterious Multiplying Jar*
Boston Globe/Horn Book Award: *Anno's Alphabet, Anno's Journey*
Boston Globe/Horn Book Honor Award: *Anno's Counting House*
Hans Christian Andersen Award
IRA Children's Choice: *The King's Flower*

Summaries of Selected Titles

Anno's Alphabet

Letters apparently made of wood are optical illusions. Each object whose name begins with the target letter is an impossibility. The filigreed borders contain creatures whose names begin with that letter.

Anno's Britain
Anno's Italy
Anno's Journey
Anno's USA

In each of these sophisticated wordless books, a traveler goes through the countryside surrounded by vignettes of that country's culture and history.

Anno's Aesop

When his son asks him to read Aesop's Fables to him, Mr. Fox is in a dilemma: He doesn't read very well. However, he has a creative mind and the pictures give him many clues. True, the stories he comes up with bear little resemblance to the work of Aesop, but they might be even better. This is a little more difficult than many picture books; however, using the book with children can lead them to the creative interpretation of other picture books.

Anno's Counting Book

A village is built with sets of numbers as the seasons change. Numbers, numerals, sets, one-to-one correspondence cover each page.

Anno's Counting House

Children living in a house on one side of the street move, one at a time, across the street to another house, taking something with them each time.

Anno's Flea Market

See page 37.

Anno's Mysterious Multiplying Jar

We start with a beautiful jar. Inside the jar there are an ocean and an island. On the island are two countries. In each country are three mountains, and so on. The question? How many objects in all? (3,628,800) A book for older children.

Dr. Anno's Magical Midnight Circus

This is a most unusual circus full of optical illusions and absurdities.

Topsy-Turvies: Pictures to Stretch the Imagination
Upside-Downers: More Pictures to Stretch the Imagination

Verbal and visual illusions and rhymes.

Avi

Author
Living
Answers letters
Mailing address
    Macmillan Children's Book Group
    866 Third Avenue
    New York, NY 10022

Biography
Avi and his twin sister were born in New York City. Although Avi has dysgraphia, a writing dysfunction, he was determined to be a writer. Avi rewrites and rewrites until he gets what he likes. He spent fourteen years writing *Bright Shadow*. Avi is a librarian and the father of two sons. He likes backpacking and playing the recorder. He lives in New Jersey. By the way, his sister gave him the name Avi.

Books by Avi
Bright Shadow. Bradbury, 1985.
Captain Grey. Pantheon, 1977.
Devil's Race. Lippincott, 1984.
Emily Upham's Revenge. Pantheon, 1978.
Encounter at Easton. Pantheon, 1980.
The Fighting Ground. Lippincott, 1984.
The History of Helpless Harry. Pantheon, 1980.
Man from the Sky. Knopf, 1981.
The Man Who Was Poe. Orchard, 1989.
Night Journeys. Pantheon, 1979.
No More Magic. Pantheon, 1975.
A Place Called Ugly. Pantheon, 1981.
Romeo and Juliet: Together and Alive at Last. Orchard, 1987.
Shadrach's Crossing. Pantheon, 1983.
Snail Tail. Pantheon, 1972.
Sometimes I Think I Hear My Name. Pantheon, 1982.
S.O.R. Losers. Bradbury, 1984.
Something Upstairs: A Tale of Ghosts. Orchard, 1988.
Who Stole the Wizard of Oz? Knopf, 1981.
Wolf Rider. Bradbury, 1986.

Book Awards and Recommendations
American Library Association: *The Fighting Ground, Wolf Rider, Romeo and Juliet*
IRA Children's Choice: *Man from the Sky, Romeo and Juliet*
Scott O'Dell Award: *The Fighting Ground*

Summaries of Selected Titles
Emily Upham's Revenge

■■■■■■■■■■□□□□□

In this spoof of a nineteenth-century melodrama, Emily, a seven-year-old girl, is sent to live with her wealthy aunt and uncle in Massachusetts, only to become involved in a suspicious bank robbery.

Encounter at Easton

■■■■■■■■■■□□□□□

This is a sequel to *Night Journeys*. Through the testimony of witnesses in a 1768 hearing, we hear about the indenture, Elizabeth's illness from an infected arm wound, experiences in the cave of Old Mad Moll, and Elizabeth's death.

The Fighting Ground

■■■■■■■■■□□□□□□

See page 61.

Night Journeys

■■■■■■■■■■□□□□□

Peter York, an orphan, is taken in by Quaker Everett Shinn. When Peter and Everett find two escaped servants, Everett won't turn them in.

Romeo and Juliet: Together and Alive at Last

■■■■■■■■■■■■■□□

In this sequel to *S.O.R. Losers,* a class production of "Romeo and Juliet" sets Ed Sitrow to scheming again. He decides to help his friend Saltz in his pursuit of romance by casting him as Romeo.

S.O.R. Losers

■■■■■■■■■■■■□□

The eighth-grade soccer team may have its good points but not on the soccer field. Here's the biggest bunch of athletic bunglers you'll ever find.

Who Stole the Wizard of Oz?

■■■■■□□□□□□□□□□

See page 45.

Natalie Babbitt

Author/Illustrator
Living

Biography

Natalie Babbitt grew up in Ohio where her mother, an artist, made sure Natalie's artistic interests were encouraged. Natalie majored in art in college, intending to become an illustrator. She married Samuel Fisher Babbitt, an educator, and had three children: Christopher, Tom, and Lucy. Her first novel was *Search for Delicious.* Her picture book *The Something* grew out of her own fear of the dark. She gets lots of mail about *Tuck Everlasting,* usually about whether Winnie made the right choice at the end of the story. Ms. Babbitt is now a grandmother and lives in Providence, Rhode Island.

Books by Natalie Babbitt

Written and Illustrated by Natalie Babbitt
The Devil's Storybook. Farrar, 1974.
The Devil's Other Storybook. Farrar, 1987.
The Eyes of the Amaryllis. Farrar, 1977.
Goody Hall. Farrar, 1971.
Herbert Rowbarge. Farrar, 1982.
Kneeknock Rise. Farrar, 1970.
Nellie, A Cat on Her Own. Farrar, 1989.
Phoebe's Revolt. Farrar, 1977.
The Search for Delicious. Farrar, 1969.
The Something. Farrar, 1970.
Tuck Everlasting. Farrar, 1975.

Illustrated by Natalie Babbitt.
Worth, Valerie. *Curlicues.* Farrar, 1980.
———. *Small Poems.* Farrar, 1972.
———. *More Small Poems.* Farrar, 1976.
———. *Still More Small Poems.* Farrar, 1978.
———. *Small Poems Again.* Farrar, 1985.
———. *All the Small Poems.* Farrar, 1987.

Book Awards and Recommendations
American Library Association: *Tuck Everlasting*
IRA Children's Choice: *The Devil's Storybook, Tuck Everlasting*
Newbery Honor Award: *Kneeknock Rise*

Summaries of Selected Titles

The Devil's Other Storybook

■■■■■■■□□□□□□□

Here are ten stories about the Devil, who is usually shown as tricky and mischievous rather than evil. In several of these stories, he is outwitted.

The Eyes of the Amaryllis

■■■■□□□□□□□□□□

In the late nineteenth century, Geneva is searching for a sign that her husband and his crew on the Amaryllis are alive. Her granddaughter, Jenny, joins her in the search and, as she does so, Jenny becomes convinced that she is invincible.

Goody Hall

■■■■■■■■■■■□□□

It appears to be a tame job for Hercules Feltwright: being a tutor to the master of Goody Hall, Willet Goody. On the contrary, Willet is convinced that his father is not dead, and solving the mystery leads Hercules through some weird experiences.

Kneeknock Rise

■■■■■■■■□□□□□□

See page 132.

The Search for Delicious

■■■■□□□□□□□□□□

See page 59.

The Something

■□□□□□□□□□□□□□

A monster child has nightmares and his mother encourages him to make a model of the thing that has been so scary. He models a human girl.

Tuck Everlasting

■■■■■■■■■□□□□□

See page 163.

Nina Bawden

> Author
> Living

Biography
Nina Bawden was born in London in 1925, and she still lives there. She is a reviewer for the *Daily Telegraph,* is a Fellow in the Royal Society of Literature, and was a Justice of the Peace for several years. She writes for both children and adults.

About Nina Bawden's Work
☐ Nina Bawden has said, "I write about emotions, motives, the difficulties of being honest with oneself, the gulf between what people say and what they really mean." Can you find examples of each of these themes in her books?

☐ Look for times when Ms. Bawden surprises us: When good guys interfere, it sometimes brings disaster, not a happy ending. When people act out their fantasies, they often get in too deep.

Books by Nina Bawden
Carrie's War. Lippincott, 1973.
The Finding. Lothrop, 1985.
A Handful of Thieves. Lippincott, 1967.
Henry. Lothrop, 1988.
The House of Secrets. LIppincott, 1964.
Kept in the Dark. Lothrop, 1982.
The Outside Child. Lothrop, 1989.
The Peppermint Pig. Lippincott, 1975.
Princess Alice. Andre Deutsch, 1985.
Rebel on a Rock. Lippincott, 1978.
The Robbers. Lothrop, 1978.
The Runaway Summer. Lippincott, 1969.
Squib. Lippincott, 1971.
Three on the Run. Lippincott, 1965.
The Witch's Daughter. Lippincott, 1966.
The White Horse Gang. Lippincott, 1966.

Book Awards and Recommendations
American Library Association: *The Outside Child, Henry, Kept in the Dark, The Robbers, Carrie's War, Squib*
School Library Journal: *Carrie's War, The Robbers*

Summaries of Selected Titles
Carrie's War

See page 104.

The Finding

See page 38.

Kept in the Dark

The children are sent to live with their undemonstrative and distant grandparents while their mother copes with their father's nervous breakdown. As if that isn't enough, David, Grandpa's illegitimate son, arrives and terrorizes them all. When David digs an asparagus bed of coffin proportions, the situation becomes desperate in this suspense story.

The Outside Child

See page 144.

The Peppermint Pig

Accused of theft, Poll's father leaves England for America, and Poll and her brothers and sister are left with their mother in England. Mother buys them a peppermint pig to divert their questions.

Rebel on a Rock

This is the sequel to *Carrie's War.* Children intervene in a political coup in a Mediterranean country and create disaster.

The Robbers

■■■■■■■■■□□□□□

Philip goes to live with his father and gets in trouble with the police because of his intense loyalty to a friend.

The Runaway Summer

■■■■■■■■■□□□□□

Mary is sure that her parents don't want her and she cherishes that feeling. She ignores the caring offered by her aunt and grandfather with whom she lives. When she discovers Krishna Patel, a Kenyan boy, she is determined to save him from the authorities.

Squib

■■■■■■■■□□□□□□

Kate Pollack encounters an abused boy and discovers that the realities of life can be more frightening than the make-believe situation she has dreamed up for him.

The Witch's Daughter

■■■■■■■□□□□□□□

Perdita, a lonely orphan, is rejected by others when she claims to be able to see into the future. Eventually, she realizes that her powers are not witchcraft, but a special and useful talent.

Byrd Baylor

Author
Living
Visits schools
Does interviews
Answers letters
Mailing address:
> Macmillan Children's Book Group
> 866 Third Avenue
> New York, NY 10022
> 212-702-9052

Biography

Byrd Baylor loves the southwestern desert and says she feels at home there. Most of her books were inspired by the area, its people, and its wildlife. After she found bits of ancient Indian pottery in the desert, she wrote *When Clay Sings.* After she went hunting for fossils, she wrote her book about it. Her father had told her tales about the town where he grew up, so she wrote about that in *The Best Town in the World.* She thinks of her books as her own private love song to her own part of the world.

About Byrd Baylor's Work

☐ Byrd Baylor lives in the southwestern United States and most of her books call attention to that region and its Indian heritage. Her prose suggests a certain philosophy: that the spirit, and not material things, is necessary for personal growth.

☐ Her collaboration with Peter Parnall is particularly apt. His dramatic lines illuminate the world of the desert and seem to echo its simplicity.

Books by Byrd Baylor

And It Is Still That Way. Scribners, 1976.
Amigo. Aladdin, 1963.
Before You Came This Way. Dutton, 1969.
The Best Town in the World. Scribners, 1983.
Coyote Cry. Lothrop, 1972.
The Desert Is Theirs. Scribners, 1975.
Desert Voices. Scribners, 1981.
Everybody Needs a Rock. Scribners, 1974.
A God on Every Mountain Top. Scribners, 1981.
Guess Who My Favorite Person Is. Aladdin, 1977.

Hawk, I'm Your Brother. Scribners, 1976.
If You Are a Hunter of Fossils. Scribners, 1980.
I'm In Charge of Celebrations. Scribners, 1986.
Moon Song. Scribners, 1982.
The Other Way to Listen. Scribners, 1978.
Plink! Plink! Plink! Houghton, 1972.
Sometimes I Dance Mountains. Scribners, 1973.
The Way to Start a Day. Scribners, 1978.
We Walk in Sandy Places. Scribners, 1976.
When Clay Sings. Scribners, 1972.
Your Own Best Secret Place. Scribners, 1979.

Book Awards and Recommendations

American Library Association: *Desert Voices, The Way to Start a Day, Hawk, I'm Your Brother, The Desert Is Theirs, When Clay Sings, Everybody Needs a Rock*

Boston Globe/Horn Book Honor Award: *The Desert Is Theirs, The Way to Start a Day, When Clay Sings*

Caldecott Honor Award: *The Way to Start a Day, Hawk, I'm Your Brother, The Desert is Theirs, When Clay Sings*

IRA Children's Choice: *Guess Who My Favorite Person Is, The Desert Is Theirs, The Way to Start a Day*

Summaries of Selected Titles

Amigo

> Francisco is a lonely boy who wants a dog. When his father says they are too poor for a dog, Francisco's mother suggests something small and wild as a pet: a prairie dog. Francisco has wonderful plans for its training and care and even names it Amigo before he finds it.

The Best Town in the World

This town in the Texas hill country was called the Canyon, as were all the ranches and farms around it. The narrator's father has told him all about it. The best cooks, dogs, chickens, and everything else were to be found there. The summer lasted longest there, and the people were the smartest, in spite of their unconventional spelling.

Coyote Cry

Antonio never forgets that the coyote is his enemy. Grandfather makes excuses for the coyote and claims he is their neighbor. As they tend the sheep in the hills, the man and boy are always alert to the sounds of the coyote so they can protect the summer lambs. Blanca, the yellow collie, cannot help because of her four new pups. When a female coyote steals one of Blanca's pups, Antonio vows to get the thief. Finding the pup leads Antonio to an understanding of the coyote's song.

The Desert Is Theirs

This is an introduction to many of the creatures who live in the desert. There is an ecological message here about each species adaptation to the climate. The desert people chose a place where life would be hard. There the Papago tribe shared the land with the coyote, spider, lizard, buzzard, gopher, badger, deer, dove, rat, and hawk. There is a feeling that all are brothers and desert creatures together.

Desert Voices

Each desert animal tells its story in prose that is very nearly poetry. Thus, the animals of the desert are brought into focus and, viewing them all while we listen to their thoughts, we are given a look at the total desert environment.

Everybody Needs a Rock

Of course, they do! Here are ten carefully explained rules for choosing the absolutely perfect rock for you. It must have exactly the right feel, color, texture, and size. The specifications will make you smile, but they should also cause you to look a little closer at even the rocks in your driveway. You might even want to list ten ways for choosing a shell, a leaf, or a friend.

Guess Who My Favorite Person Is

Here is a game of choosing favorites. By making choices, the friends force the reader into thinking about specific things that bring joy. In the book, the friends are a man and a child, but they could be any two people who play the game of favorites and become friends during an afternoon together.

Hawk, I'm Your Brother

Rudy wants to fly with the hawks. He knows the hawks intimately and steals a young one from its aerie. He tries in vain to tame the hawk who only screams at him. Finally, he realizes that he must let the hawk go so it can fly with the other young hawks. On his release, the hawk cries to Rudy who, in his mind, is also flying.

If You Are a Hunter of Fossils

Millions of years have passed since the desert was covered by an ocean, but the fossils tell its story. Hunters search a Kansas wheatfield or a grey ledge in Utah. Everywhere hunters read the rocks and uncover mysteries.

The Other Way to Listen

Most people never hear corn singing and wildflower seeds bursting. But if you listen to a sky full of stars, you can hear it. You have to know how to listen, of course. An old man shares his secrets with a child. First, get to know one thing well, but it's best to start with something very small.

The Way to Start a Day

The way to start a day is to greet the sun with a blessing, chant, or song. Others have done it from the beginning of time, from cavemen to the present day. The natives of North America greeted the Great Spirit. Over the Ganges River, the people of India greet the sun also. If you have a ceremony of your own with which to begin the day, "you'll be one more person in one more place, at one more time in the world."

When Clay Sings

Native American children in the desert uncover pieces of pottery created by their ancestors that celebrate the life of the desert. Their elders teach them to regard these with respect, and the children learn to listen to the song the pottery sings.

John Bellairs

Author
Living
Visits schools
Does interviews
Contact:
    Children's Book Marketing
    E. P. Dutton
    2 Park Avenue
    New York, NY, 10016
    212-725-1818

Biography

Mr. Bellairs loves spooky things like haunted houses and cemeteries so it's no wonder his stories are frequently scary. He puts characters in his stories that are based on people in his own life. He also sets his stories in towns like the ones he has lived in: Hoosac is Winona, Minnesota, and Dutton Heights is Haverhill, Massachusetts, where he has lived for the last seventeen years. He grew up in Michigan and frequently visits there.

Books by John Bellairs

The Chessmen of Doom. Dial, 1989.
The Curse of the Blue Figurine. Dial, 1983.
The Dark Secret of Weatherend. Dial, 1984.
Eyes of the Killer Robot. Dial, 1986.
The Figure in the Shadows. Dial, 1975.
The House with a Clock in Its Walls. Dial, 1973.
The Lamp from the Warlock's Tomb. Dial, 1988.
The Letter, the Witch, and the Ring. Dial, 1976.
The Mummy, the Will, and the Crypt. Dial, 1983.
The Revenge of the Wizard's Ghost. Dial, 1985.
The Spell of the Sorcerer's Skull. Dial, 1984.
The Treasure of Alpheus Winterborn. Dial, 1978.
The Trolley to Yesterday. Dial, 1989.

Book Awards and Recommendations

IRA Children's Choice: *The Figure in the Shadows,
    The Letter, the Witch, and the Ring*
School Library Journal: *The Mummy, the Will, and
    the Crypt*

Summaries of Selected Titles
The Chessmen of Doom

■■■■■■■■□□□□□□□

When his brother Peregrine dies, Professor Roderick Childermass receives a strange riddle with his huge inheritance and the requirement that the professor must spend the summer on Peregrine's estate. The Professor and his young friends Johnny and Fergie find a madman who is determined to destroy the world.

The Curse of the Blue Figurine

■■■■■■■■□□□□□□□

Johnny's father is in the Korean War and his mother is dead so he lives with his grandparents and is intrigued by their eccentric neighbor Professor Childermass. It is the professor who tells Johnny of the mysterious disappearance of Father Remigius Baart, the priest at the church in 1880. Later Johnny is chased into the basement of that church and finds a mysterious statue and a note in a hollowed out missal. The note warns that the items must never be removed from the church, but Johnny inadvertently removes them and then is cursed with nightmares and frightening occurrences culminating in a confrontation with the professor and the evil sorcerer.

The Dark Secret of Weatherend

■■■■■■■■□□□□□□

This is the sequel to *The Treasure of Alpheus Winterborn.* The son of the late J. K. Borkman wants to destroy the world. It is Miss Eels, the librarian, who picks the lock on the carriage house and removes a precious box, thus releasing all the terrors that J. K.'s son can unleash.

The Lamp from the Warlock's Tomb

■■■■■■■■■■□□□□

The lamp that Miss Eels insists on buying seems innocent enough. When Anthony Monday borrows it for his science project and lights it, however, terrible forces are set loose.

The Mummy, the Will, and the Crypt

■■■■■■■■□□□□□□

In this sequel to *The Curse of the Blue Figurine,* Professor Childermas tells Johnny about H. Blagwell Glomus's missing will. The cereal tycoon also left three mysterious clues to the whereabouts of the will. Johnny finds the Glomus estate near the Boy Scout camp in New Hampshire, but the estate is fiercely guarded by the grandson and the weird Mrs. Woodley.

Judy Blume

Author
Living
Visits schools
Answers letters
Mailing address:
    Orchard Books
    387 Park Avenue South
    New York, NY 10016

Biography

Judy Blume loves tap dancing and still takes lessons five days a week. She lives in New York City in a penthouse seventeen stories up overlooking the Hudson River. She has another home in Santa Fe, New Mexico, where she says the view is so beautiful that she often has to face the wall to get any writing done. Because she gets over two thousand letters a month from children, she also has an office with a full-time secretary. Ms. Blume has been married and divorced twice. She has two grown children, Randy and Larry and a calico cat named Channelle.

About Judy Blume's Work

☐ Ms. Blume often writes from her experiences. Margaret, she says, is herself in sixth grade and Sally J. Freedman is her most autobiographical work. Her son Larry was the inspiration for *Fudge;* however, she read in a newspaper about a toddler who swallowed a turtle.

Books by Judy Blume

Are You There, God? It's Me, Margaret. Bradbury, 1970.
¿Estás Ahí, Díos? Soy Yo, Margaret. Bradbury, 1983.
Blubber. Bradbury, 1974.
La Ballena. Bradbury, 1974.
Deenie. Bradbury, 1973.
Forever. Bradbury, 1975.
Freckle Juice. Four Winds, 1971.
Iggie's House. Bradbury, 1970.
It's Not the End of the World. Bradbury, 1972.
The Judy Blume Diary. Dell, 1982.

Just as Long As We're Together. Orchard, 1987.
The One in the Middle is a Green Kangaroo. Bradbury, 1981.
Otherwise Known As Sheila the Great. Dutton, 1972.
The Pain and the Great One. Bradbury, 1984.
Starring Sally J. Friedman As Herself. Bradbury, 1977.
Superfudge. Dutton, 1980.
Tales of a Fourth Grade Nothing. Dutton, 1972.
Tiger Eyes. Bradbury, 1981.
Then Again, Maybe I Won't. Bradbury, 1971.

Book Awards and Recommendations

American Library Association: *Forever, Tiger Eyes*
IRA Children's Choice: *Blubber, Superfudge, The Pain and the Great One, Just as Long as We're Together, Are You There God? It's Me, Margaret*

Summaries of Selected Titles

Are You There, God? It's Me, Margaret
¿Estás Ahí, Díos? Soy Yo, Margaret

■■■■■■■■■□□□□□□

Margaret is confused about religion and now that's she's moved from New York to New Jersey, she doesn't know whether to be Jewish, like her father, or Christian, like her mother. She has a very personal relationship with God, however, and consults him about everything from growing up to prayer.

Blubber
La Ballena

■■■■■■■■□□□□□□

Linda is an overweight fifth grader who is constantly being teased by the other students who nickname her "Blubber." Eventually, a few people manage to turn the whole class against her.

Deenie

■■■■■■■■■■□□□□

Deenie has scoliosis, a curvature of the spine, and is forced to wear a Milwaukee brace for four years, until she is 17. This cuts short her aspiring modeling career and drastically alters her self-concept. She experiences some of the prejudice against the handicapped and learns that her life can and will go on.

Freckle Juice

■■□□□□□□□□□□□□

See page 24.

It's Not the End of the World

■■■■■■■■■■□□□□□

Karen Newman is sure that she can prevent her parents impending divorce. When her parents do meet, things go from bad to worse and Karen is forced to see that her parents have grown apart.

Otherwise Known As Sheila the Great

■■■■■■■■■■□□□□□

Sheila is afraid of so many things that she can hardly keep track of them all. When her parents insist that she go with them to their summer home, Sheila is forced to face most of her fears.

Starring Sally J. Friedman As Herself

■■■■■■■■□□□□□□

Because of her brother's poor health, Sally and her family must move to Florida for the winter. Sally's excited but also worried about school, friends, and living without her father who stayed in New Jersey. These worries don't kill her active imagination and she goes on creating fabulous stories with herself as the center of attention.

Superfudge

■■■■■□□□□□□□□□

See page 24.

Tales of a Fourth Grade Nothing

■■■■■□□□□□□□□□

See page 24.

Then Again, Maybe I Won't

■■■■■■■■■■■□□□□

Tony's bothered by the family's new home in suburbia. He liked the city apartment better. He's also bothered by his parents' attempt to keep up with the Joneses, with the shoplifting on the part of his new "friend," and with his own emerging sexual maturity.

Robbie Branscum

Author
Living

Biography

Robbie Branscum was born on June 17, 1937, near Big Flat, Arkansas. Her parents were farmers and her father died when she was four. She and her four brothers and sisters went to live with their grandparents way, way, way back in the hills of Arkansas, the setting for many of her books. Their home had no inside water or electricity. They took baths together in a big tub, using water warmed by the sun. The inside of their house was papered with newspapers for warmth and Robbie claims to have read every word in every paper, even standing on her head sometimes to read it all. Ms. Branscum went to a one-room school and when she was in eighth grade, she discovered a library. She got married when she was fifteen, had a daughter, Deborah, and is now divorced.

Books by Robbie Branscum

The Adventures of Johnny May. Harper, 1984.
Cameo Rose. Harper, 1989.
Cheater and Flitter Dick. Viking, 1983.
For Love of Jody. Lothrop, 1980.
The Girl. Harper, 1986.
Johnny May Grows Up. Harper, 1987.
Me and Jim Luke. Avon, 1975.
The Murder of Hound Dog Bates. Viking, 1982.
The Saving of P. S. Doubleday, 1977.
Spud Tackett and the Angel of Doom. Viking, 1983.
Three Buckets of Daylight. Lothrop, 1978.
The Three Wars of Billy Joe Treat. Doubleday, 1975.
To the Tune of a Hickory Stick. Doubleday, 1978.
Toby Alone. Doubleday, 1978.
Toby and Johnny Joe. Doubleday, 1978.
Toby, Granny and George. Doubleday, 1977.
The Ugliest Boy. Lothrop, 1978.

Book Awards and Recommendations

American Library Association: *The Girl*
IRA Children's Choice: *The Saving of P.S., Johnny May Grows Up*
Edgar Allen Poe Award: *The Murder of Hound Dog Bates*

Summaries of Selected Titles

The Adventures of Johnny May

Eleven-year-old Johnny May has many responsibilities in rural Arkansas: she must keep her grandparents fed and cared for in spite of overwhelming poverty. She even wants to provide Christmas for them. As if that isn't enough, she's witnessed a murder.

For Love of Jody

Frankie has ambivalent feelings toward Jody, her retarded younger sister. Pa wants to send Jody away, but Frankie covers up her deeds and Ma will hear none of it.

Johnny May Grows Up

Johnny May is now thirteen and ambitious for more than the farm. Her good friend, Aron McCoy, is now in high school and, she realizes, is growing away from her. Her attempts to grow up fast and become worldly lead her into some very embarrassing situations.

The Murder of Hound Dog Bates

See page 45.

The Saving of P. S.

Priscilla Sue, otherwise known as P. S., discovers that her preacher father is courting a city woman with two daughters. Determined to kill the romance, P. S. tries many tactics, but her father announces that the marriage will take place and it does. There's nothing left for P. S. to do but run away, so she does.

Spud Tackett and the Angel of Doom

■■■■■□□□□□□□□□

A hypnotic preacher is convincing everyone to sell their Arkansas farms and follow him. Grandma will have none of it, but Spud and his cousin Leroy are about to follow after learning that Leroy's father has been killed in World War II. Grandma joins ranks with a mean moonshiner to debunk the preacher.

To the Tune of a Hickory Stick

■■■■■■■□□□□□□□

Nell and JD live with their Uncle Jock and his family because their father is dead and their mother is off working. She sends money for their support, but Uncle Jock is a cruel and tyrannical man and the children suffer needlessly. When he almost kills JD, the children set off on their own, hiding out in the schoolhouse that is closed for the winter. Before they are snowed in, their senile grandfather and his dog arrive and so does wonderful Mr. Davis, the school teacher. After that, things start looking up.

Toby, Granny and George

■■■■■■□□□□□□□□

Toby remembers no other home but this one with Granny, and she doesn't know who her real parents are. While she searches carefully among church members and other villagers for any resemblance to her, life in this part of Arkansas goes on. The church, meanwhile, is torn apart after an accidental drowning for which some people blame the preacher. Others side with the preacher against Deacon Treat who leads the opposition. When Deacon Treat is murdered, the suspicion against Preacher Davis deepens.

Clyde Robert Bulla

Author
Living

Biography

Clyde Bulla grew up in King City, Missouri where he attended a one-room school. One day the teacher asked the children what they would buy if they had a hundred dollars. Clyde said, "A table," because he wanted to be a writer and he knew writers needed tables on which to work. His first book was *The Donkey Cart* and he has written over fifty other children's books. He now lives in Los Angeles, but he travels extensively.

Books by Clyde Robert Bulla

Almost a Hero. Dutton, 1981.
The Beast of Lor. Crowell, 1977 .
Benito. Crowell, 1961.
The Cardboard Crown. Crowell, 1984.
The Chalkbox Kid. Random, 1987.
Charlie's Horse. Crowell, 1983.
Conquista! With Syson, Michael Crowell, 1978.
Dandelion Hill. Dutton, 1982.
Daniel's Duck. Harper, 1979.
Dexter. Crowell, 1973.
The Donkey Cart. Crowell, 1946.
Down the Mississippi. Crowell, 1954.
Eagle Feather. Crowell, 1953.
The Ghost of Windy Hill. Crowell, 1968.
Ghost Town Treasure. Crowell, 1957.
Indian Hill. Crowell, 1963.
John Billington, Friend of Squanto. Crowell, 1956.
Johnny Hong of Chinatown. Crowell, 1952.
Keep Running, Allen! Crowell, 1978.
Last Look. Crowell, 1979.
Lincoln's Birthday. Crowell, 1966.
A Lion to Guard Us. Crowell, 1981.
Marco Moonlight. Crowell, 1976.
Mike's Apple Tree. Crowell, 1968.
The Moon Singer. Crowell, 1969.
My Friend the Monster. Crowell, 1980.
New Boy in Dublin. Crowell, 1969.
Old Charlie. Crowell, 1957.
Open the Door and See All the People. Crowell, 1972.
Pirate's Promise. Crowell, 1958.
Pocahontas and the Strangers. Crowell, 1971.

Poor Boy, Rich Boy. Harper, 1982.
The Poppy Seeds. Crowell, 1955.
A Ranch for Danny. Crowell, 1951.
Riding the Pony Express. Crowell, 1948.
St. Valentine's Day. Crowell, 1965.
The Secret Valley. Crowell, 1949.
Shoeshine Girl. Crowell, 1975.
Singing Sam. Random, 1989.
Song of St. Francis. Crowell, 1952.
Squanto, Friend of the White Men. Crowell, 1954.
Star of Wild Horse Canyon. Crowell, 1953.
The Stubborn Old Woman. Crowell, 1980.
The Sugar Pear Tree. Crowell, 1961.
Surprise for a Cowboy. Crowell, 1950.
The Sword in the Tree. Crowell, 1956.
Three-Dollar Mule. Crowell, 1960.
A Tree Is to Plant. Crowell, 1960.
The Valentine Cat. Crowell, 1959.
Viking Adventure. Crowell, 1963.
Washington's Birthday. Crowell, 1967.
What Makes a Shadow? Crowell, 1962.
White Bird. Crowell, 1966.
White Sails to China. Crowell 1955.
The Wish at the Top. Crowell, 1974.

Book Awards and Recommendations

American Library Association: *Daniel's Duck*
IRA Children's Choice: *The Wish at the Top, Charlie's Horse*

Summaries of Selected Titles

The Beast of Lor

■■■■■□□□□□□□□□

Lud's guardian is accused of witchcraft and Lud runs from the village. He meets Edric who tells him all about Lor, his home. Edric dies and Lud sets out to get to Lor with a jewel Edric has given him. On the way, Lud learns that Britain has been invaded by the Romans and meets an elephant escaping from the battle. Together Lud and his elephant help Cass rid his village of the tyrants who have taken over. The jewel turns out to be a symbol of royalty.

The Cardboard Crown

Olivia is a strange friend for Adam. She insists that she is a princess and Adam's father thinks she's ridiculous. His aunt calls her a troublemaker, but Olivia is the answer to Adam's loneliness.

Dexter

Dexter is a horse and is the initial reason for the friendship between Dave and Alex. Dexter is hurt and left for dead. When Dave finds him, he is so skittish that no one can approach him. Dave nurses Dexter back to health in spite of seemingly overwhelming obstacles.

The Ghost of Windy Hill

Jamie's family does not believe in ghosts and they move into a house reported to be haunted to prove that it's not. However, Jamie and his sister Lorna find stranger things going on outside the house than in.

A Lion to Guard Us

Three motherless children set sail for Jamestown to find their father who went ahead to the new land the previous year. The ship is wrecked near Bermuda and the children save only the lion's head doorknocker from their home in England.

Shoeshine Girl

Sarah Ida is not pleased that she must spend the summer at Aunt Claudia's. She knows that it's because her parents can't cope with her and that many consider her spoiled. Aunt Claudia refuses to give Sarah Ida the allowance she feels she needs in order to be independent, so Sarah becomes a shoeshine girl. To her surprise Aunt Claudia thinks that's fine.

The Sword in the Tree

See page 35.

Robert Burch

Author
Living
Visits schools
Answers letters
Mailing address:
    Children's Marketing
    Viking Penguin
    40 West 23rd Street
    New York, NY 10010
    212-337-5417

Biography
Mr. Burch has lived in Tokyo, New York, and London, but his real home is in Fayette County, Georgia. He grew up in rural Georgia with seven other children during the Great Depression. He began writing when he was thirty and wrote for more than four years before he had a story published. He has two dogs and raises Japanese carp that are about two feet long.

Books by Robert Burch
Christmas with Ida Early. Viking, 1983.
D.J.'s Worst Enemy. Viking, 1965.
Doodle and the Go-Cart. Viking, 1972.
A Funny Place to Live. Viking, 1962.
The Hunting Trip. Viking, 1971.
Hut School and the Wartime Home-Front Heroes. Viking, 1974.
Ida Early Comes Over the Mountain. Viking, 1983.
Joey's Cat. Viking, 1969.
The Jolly Witch. Viking, 1975.
King Kong and Other Poets. Viking, 1986.
Queenie Peavy. Viking, 1966.
Refroe's Christmas. Viking, 1968.
Simon and the Game of Chance. Viking, 1970.
Skinny. Viking, 1964.
The Traveling Bird. McDowell, 1959.
Two That Were Tough. Viking, 1976.
Tyler, Wilkin, and Skee. Viking, 1963.
The Whitman Kick. Dutton, 1977.
Wilkin's Ghost. Viking, 1978.

Book Awards and Recommendations
American Library Association: *Queenie Peavy, Ida Early Comes Over the Mountain*
Boston Globe/Horn Book Honor Award: *Ida Early Comes Over the Mountain*
IRA Children's Choice: *Hut School and the Wartime Home-Front Heroes*
School Library Journal: *Ida Early Comes Over the Mountain*

Summaries of Selected Titles
Christmas with Ida Early

■■■■■■□□□□□□□

This sequel to *Ida Early Comes Over the Mountain* finds Ida still with the Sutton family where she has been their housekeeper and friend. Randall tells us about Ida's effect on the Christmas pageant.

Ida Early Comes Over the Mountain

■■■■■■■□□□□□□

Ida comes over the mountain to help the motherless Sutton family and life will never be the same for them. This eccentric, tall-tale telling, strong female has plans and they include fun.

King Kong and Other Poets

■■■■■■■□□□□□□□□

Marilyn, the new girl in school, is almost unnotice-able until she wins the city poetry contest. Then she dresses strangely and says that she lives in Garden Hills, an elegant resort. Is it true?

Queenie Peavy

■■■■■■■□□□□□□□□

Queenie loves her father even though he's been in jail for a long time. Her mother has to work hard to help Queenie come to grips with reality. It isn't until her father's release that the glamorous picture she has painted changes.

Wilkin's Ghost

■■■■■■■□□□□□□□□

Under the hanging tree, Wilkin finds Alex, a runaway boy. Alex becomes his friend, luring Wilkin into more and more dangerous activities. It's while they're about to hop a freight to see the world that Wilkin discovers the truth about Alex.

Betsy Byars

Author
Living
Visits schools
Answers letters
Mailing address:
Children's Marketing
Viking Penguin
40 West 23rd Street
New York, NY 10010
212-337-5417

Biography

Betsy Byars was brought up in a cotton mill community in rural North Carolina. She began writing magazine articles to keep herself busy while her husband was in engineering school. As her family grew and the children learned to read, she began to write books for them. It takes about a year for her to write a book but she's never bored. Her favorite book is *Midnight Fox,* which was inspired by a fox she saw in the woods. Her own dog, Sport, was the model for the dog in *Trouble River.* When she was young, she had big feet and she used that for her character in *Summer of the Swans.* Ms. Byars now lives in Charleston, South Carolina, where she was active in setting up a home for battered wives. She has four grown children and five grandchildren. She and her husband are very interested in gliding and antique airplanes.

About Betsy Byars' Work

☐ Ms. Byars' books usually concern a child whose life is dominated by a private fear or uncertainty.

Books by Betsy Byars

After the Goat Man. Viking, 1974.
The Animal, the Vegetable, and John D. Jones. Delacorte, 1982.
Beans on the Roof. Delacorte, 1988.
Bingo Brown and the Language of Love. Viking, 1989.
Bingo Brown, Gypsy Lover. Viking, 1990.

The Blossoms and the Green Phantom. Delacorte, 1987.
The Blossoms Meet the Vulture Lady. Delacorte, 1986.
A Blossom Promise. Delacorte, 1987.
The Burning Questions of Bingo Brown. Viking, 1988.
The Cartoonist. Viking, 1978.
The Computer Nut. Viking, 1984.
Clementine. Houghton, 1962.
Cracker Jackson. Viking, 1985.
The Cybil War. Viking, 1981.
The Dancing Camel. Viking, 1965.
The 18th Emergency. Viking, 1973.
The Glory Girl. Viking, 1983.
Go and Hush the Baby. Puffin, 1982.
The Golly Sisters Go West. Harper, 1986.
Goodbye, Chicken Little. Harper, 1979.
The Groober. Harper, 1967.
The House of Wings. Viking, 1972.
The Lace Snail. Viking, 1975.
The Midnight Fox. Viking, 1968.
The Night Swimmers. Delacorte, 1980.
The Not-Just-Anybody Family. Delacorte, 1986.
Rama, the Gypsy Cat. Avon, 1981.
The Summer of the Swans. Viking, 1970.
Trouble River. Viking, 1969.
The TV Kid. Viking, 1976.
The Two-Thousand-Pound Goldfish. Harper, 1982.
The Winged Colt of Casa Mia. Viking, 1973.

Book Awards and Recommendations

American Library Association: *Trouble River, The House of Wings, After the Goat Man, The Pinballs, The Cybil War, The Two-Thousand-Pound Goldfish, Cracker Jackson*

Boston Globe/Horn Book Honor Award: *The Night Swimmers*

IRA Children's Choice: *The Pinballs, Good-Bye, Chicken Little, The Night Swimmers, Cracker Jackson*

Newbery Medal: *The Summer of the Swans*

School Library Journal: *Trouble River, After the Goat Man, The Cartoonist, The Night Swimmers, The Cybil War, The Animal, the Vegetable, and John D. Jones, Cracker Jackson, The Burning Questions of Bingo Brown*

Summaries of Selected Titles

After the Goat Man

■■■■■■□□□□□□□□

Figgy's grandfather, the Goatman, has barricaded himself in his cabin and vows to stop the wrecking crew determined to put in a superhighway. Ada, Figgy, and Harold first attempt to change his mind, but end up joining ranks with him.

The Animal, the Vegetable and John D. Jones

■■■■■■■■■□□□□□

When Clara and Deanie's father decides to share their island retreat with Delores and her son John D., all three kids hate it. The hostility escalates throughout the vacation. John D., who disdains them all, refers to the two girls as The Animal and The Vegetable. It isn't until Clara is in very real danger that there is any change in feelings.

Bingo Brown, Gypsy Lover

■■■■■■■■■■□□□□

Bingo loves Melissa who spoils everything by buying Bingo a Christmas present. Now Bingo must get her something. This dilemma comes on top of the one his parents have already presented—a baby brother.

A Blossom Promise

■■■■■■■□□□□□□□

The Blossom saga continues and we find Maggie with her mother on the rodeo circuit as a member of the Wrangler Riders. The others are involved in their own adventures: Vern and Michael are about to float down a flooded creek and Junior is planning an overnight with Mad Mary in the cave.

The Blossoms and the Green Phantom

■■■■■■■□□□□□□□

This time Junior is determined to invent something that works. He creates a green phantom. When it too fails to operate, Junior is stranded on a mean neighbor's chicken coop. The family bands together to help Junior make his creation work.

The Blossoms Meet the Vulture Lady

■■■■■■■■□□□□□□

Caught in his own coyote trap, Junior Blossom is rescued by Mad Mary who eats road kills and takes Junior to her cave. Meanwhile, the Blossom family, which has been searching frantically for him, is lead to the cave by Mud, their dog.

The Cartoonist

■■■■■■■□□□□□□□

Alfie's life is miserable: his mother is harsh and insensitive and his teachers and friends often misunderstand him. It's no wonder he retreats into the imaginary world of the cartoons he draws. Ultimately, he must reconcile his imaginary world with the real one, but only with great difficulty.

Cracker Jackson

■■■■■■■■■■□□□□

Cracker lives with his mother in a city apartment and has almost adjusted to the single parent household. His father calls him every week at exactly the same time and Cracker finds his father somewhat boring. When Cracker discovers that Alma, a long time friend, is being abused by her husband, he tries to rescue her. It isn't until the adults in his life, his father and his mother, enter the picture and until Alma and her baby are hospitalized, that he succeeds in getting Alma to a shelter for battered wives.

The Cybil War

Simon is despondent. He is in love with Cybil, a girl who smiled at him and crossed her eyes in second grade. Now he must go on a date with a girl he can't stand. He also has to play the role of a jar of peanut butter in the school nutrition play.

The 18th Emergency

See page 24.

The Glory Girl

The Glory family are gospel singers. The oldest daughter is the lead singer and is called The Glory Girl. She hates everything about her life. Eventually, she realizes that her family is right for her.

Goodbye, Chicken Little

Jimmie Little calls himself Chicken because of his fears, most of which developed after his father was killed in a mine accident. When his mother blames him for his Uncle Pete's death, life becomes unbearable. His mother and her family's resiliency is boundless, however, and they are soon as involved in celebrating Pete's life as they were in mourning his death.

The House of Wings

Sammy is temporarily abandoned by his parents and is left with his grandfather whom he loathes. A wounded crane mends their relationship while they mend its broken wing.

The Midnight Fox

Tommy is left with his Aunt Millie on her farm while his parents bicycle through Europe. A black fox becomes Tommy's focus and he learns to understand her through careful observation. When the animal is in danger, Tommy saves it.

The Night Swimmers

Retta has been responsible for her younger brothers and sisters since their mother was killed in a plane crash and their father went on with his career as a country singer. She decides they are going to do all the things rich kids do, but they'll do them at night. This means sneaking into a rich neighbor's pool for a midnight swim. When two of the brothers become friends with another boy, Retta is jealous. When her dogged pursuit of them almost results in Roy's drowning in the pool, Retta is shocked into looking at herself realistically.

The Not-Just-Anybody Family

This is the first book about the Blossom family. Maggie, Vera, and Junior Blossom are staying with their grandfather, Pap, while their father rides in the rodeo. Junior is in the hospital with two broken legs, Pap is in the city jail for disturbing the peace, and Maggie and Vera must get them out.

The Pinballs

See page 145.

The Summer of the Swans

We live through two summer days in the life of fourteen-year-old Sara Godfrey. Annoyed by the persistent demands of her retarded brother, she reacts with impatience. Then he gets lost while trying to find the swans.

Trouble River

■■■■■■■□□□□□□□

Dewey Martin and his grandmother go down Trouble River on a raft to escape hostile Native Americans.

The TV Kid

■■■■■■■■□□□□□□

Lennie loves TV and doesn't care that he scores so low on the school tests. In his fantasy life, he is a contest winner. Life with his mother in the sleazy motel doesn't offer much so he breaks into summer cottages for excitement. He gets more than he bargains for when he is bitten by a rattlesnake.

The Two-Thousand-Pound Goldfish

■■■■■■■■■□□□□□

Warren's mother is a fugitive, wanted by the FBI since she joined a revolutionary movement in the 1960's. Warren and his sister Weezie are living with their grandmother. Warren dreams of being reunited with his mother, but Weezie has realized that their mother's commitment to causes doesn't extend to her children. Meanwhile, Warren delights in horror movies, and inventing plots for new ones. His current plot concerns a two-thousand-pound goldfish loose in the sewers of New York. When the grandmother dies and his mother doesn't show up, even Warren has to admit that Weezie is right and regretfully lets go of all his fantasies, including the goldfish.

The Winged Colt of Casa Mia

■■■■■■■□□□□□□□

A boy lives with his father, a former rodeo star who had to quit because of an injury. The winged colt is born on the ranch his father owns. Together they take care of the colt.

Beverly Cleary

Author

Living

Answers letters

Mailing address:
> Children's Marketing
> William Morrow and Co., Inc.
> 105 Madison Avenue
> New York, NY 10016

Biography

Beverly Cleary and her husband live in northern California with a carefully tended garden in the backyard. She loves to sew and keep house, which she does very neatly. Beverly Cleary is very shy and hates being interviewed and photographed. She does her writing in a small room in the house.

Books by Beverly Cleary

Beezus and Ramona. Morrow, 1955.
Dear Mr. Henshaw. Morrow, 1983.
Ellen Tebbits. Morrow, 1951.
Emily's Runaway Imagination. Morrow, 1961.
Fifteen. Morrow, 1956.
A Girl from Yamhill. Morrow, 1988.
The Growing-Up Feet. Morrow, 1987.
Henry and Beezus. Morrow, 1952.
Henry and Ribsy. Morrow, 1954.
Henry and the Clubhouse. Morrow, 1962.
Henry and the Paper Route. Morrow, 1957.
Henry Huggins. Morrow, 1950.
Janet's Thingamajigs. Morrow, 1987.
Jean and Johnny. Morrow, 1959.
The Luckiest Girl. Morrow, 1958.
Lucky Chuck. Morrow, 1984.
Mitch and Amy. Morrow, 1967.
The Mouse and the Motorcycle. Morrow, 1965.
Otis Spofford. Morrow, 1953.
Ralph S. Mouse. Morrow, 1982.
Ramona and Her Father. Morrow, 1977.
Ramona and Her Mother. Morrow, 1979.
Ramona Forever. Morrow, 1984.
Ramona Quimby, Age 8. Morrow, 1981.
Ramona the Brave. Morrow, 1975.
Ramona the Pest. Morrow, 1968.
The Real Hole. Morrow, 1986.
Ribsy. Morrow, 1964.
Runaway Ralph. Morrow, 1970.
Sister of the Bride. Morrow, 1963.
Socks. Morrow, 1973.
Two Dog Biscuits. Morrow, 1986.

Book Awards and Recommendations

American Library Association: *Henry Huggins, The Mouse and the Motorcycle, Ramona and Her Father, Ramona and Her Mother, Ramona Quimby, Age Eight, Dear Mr. Henshaw, Ramona Forever, A Girl from Yamhill*

Boston Globe/Horn Book Honor Award: *Ramona and Her Father*

IRA Children's Choice: *Ramona the Brave, Ramona and Her Father, Ramona and Her Mother, Ramona Forever*

Newbery Medal: *Dear Mr. Henshaw*

Newbery Honor Award: *Ramona and Her Father, Ramona Quimby, Age Eight*

School Library Journal: *Ramona and Her Father, Ramona and Her Mother, Ramona Quimby, Age Eight, Ralph S. Mouse, Dear Mr. Henshaw, Ramona Forever*

Summaries of Selected Titles

Beezus and Ramona

■■■■■■□□□□□□□□

Ramona, age four, is as strong willed as you'd expect. Her well-behaved sister Beezus tries to be a model for Ramona, but Ramona is irrepressible.

Dear Mr. Henshaw

■■■■■■■■■□□□□□□

See page 31.

Ellen Tebbits

■■■■■□□□□□□□□□

Ellen is like many other eight-year-olds: she takes ballet, wears braces, likes friends, but she also wears woolen underwear. When she finds someone else with the same problem, there's bound to be a bond.

Henry Huggins

■■■■■□□□□□□□□□

Henry loves to surprise his mom and he usually does, although not always the way he plans.

Mitch and Amy

■■■■■□□□□□□□□□

The twins are in fourth grade where Mitch is the victim of a bully and has developed reading problems while Amy has a hard time with math.

The Mouse and the Motorcycle

■■■□□□□□□□□□□□

Ralph, a mouse, learns to ride a toy motorcycle and careens along the corridors of the hotel where his friend, Keith, lives.

Otis Spofford

■■■■■■□□□□□□□□

Otis is always in trouble, and he has plenty of time for trouble when he is left on his own by his busy mother. When a trick he plays on Ellen Tebbits backfires, Otis gets his comeuppance.

Ralph S. Mouse

■■■■□□□□□□□□□□

Still in California and still addicted to his motorcycle, Ralph's nighttime cycle excursions have caused envy among the rest of the rodent population at

the inn; so Ralph talks his friend Ryan into taking him off to live at his school. There, Ralph inspires a mouse project. Later, his beloved motorcycle is destroyed in a fight between Ryan and Brad and he is given a new and exciting sports car.

Ramona and Her Father

■■■■■□□□□□□□□□

After Ramona's father loses his job, her mother goes to work full time, and the family suffers from increasing shortages. Forced to eat pumpkin for most of their meals, the family tries to cope. Ramona becomes involved in a campaign to get her father to stop smoking. Her father's new job comes a few days before Christmas and Ramona can join the others in a joyful Christmas pageant.

Ramona and Her Mother

■■■■■□□□□□□□□□

Father's working in the supermarket, but he hates it. Ramona is having trouble finding a role for herself. She feels replaced and angry when a guest remarks that a little girl is a second Ramona. When her mother states that she couldn't get along without Beezus, Ramona's older sister, Ramona really comes to a boil.

Ramona Forever

■■■■■□□□□□□□□□

Ramona resents going to the babysitter after school and so Beezus volunteers to babysit at home. Even this has its disadvantages, however. The two often quarrel. They soon become involved in naming a baby due in July and in their aunt's wedding.

Ramona Quimby, Age 8

■■■■■□□□□□□□□□

Third grade for Ramona promises to be a busy year. Her mother is working and her father has returned to college. Helping her big sister Beezus make dinner isn't easy, neither is getting along with her teacher, whom Ramona overhears calling her a nuisance.

Vera and Bill Cleaver

Authors
Vera Cleaver is living.
Bill Cleaver died August 20, 1981.

Biography

Vera was born in Virgil, South Dakota and Bill was born in Seattle, Washington. When they were children, they each thought of themselves as writers. Vera began writing stories when she was six and continued throughout her childhood. Bill studied graphic arts and thought about becoming a children's book illustrator. They were married in 1945 and wrote magazine stories together. Bill took a job with the Air Force in Japan and Vera joined him there. Later, they lived in France, and when they returned to the United States, they moved into a cabin in Boone, North Carolina, where they settled down to become professional writers. Their first novel was *Ellen Grae.* They wrote books together until Bill's death. Vera still lives in Winter Haven, Florida where she continues to write novels.

Books by Vera and Bill Cleaver

Belle Pruitt. Lippincott, 1988.
Delpha Green and Company. Lippincott, 1972.
Dust of the Earth. Lippincott, 1975.
Ellen Grae. Lippincott, 1967.
Grover. Lippincott, 1970.
Hazel Rye. Lippincott, 1983.
I Would Rather Be a Turnip. Lippincott, 1971.
The Kissammee Kid. Lothrop, 1981.
Lady Ellen Grae. Lippincott, 1968.
A Little Destiny. Lothrop, 1979.
Me Too. Lippincott, 1973.
The Mimosa Tree. Lippincott, 1970.
The Mock Revolt. Lippincott, 1971.
Moon Lake Angel. Lothrop, 1987.
Queen of Hearts. Lippincott, 1978.
Sweetly Sings the Donkey. Lippincott, 1985.
Sugar Blue. Lothrop, 1984.
Trial Valley. Lippincott, 1977.
Where the Lilies Bloom. Lippincott, 1969.
The Whys and Wherefores of Littabelle Lee. Atheneum, 1973.

Book Awards and Recommendations

American Library Association: *Where the Lilies Bloom, Me Too, Queen of Hearts, Hazel Rye*

Boston Globe/Horn Book Honor Award: *Where the Lilies Bloom*
IRA Children's Choice: *Trial Valley*
School Library Journal: *Ellen Grae, Grover, Queen of Hearts, Trial Valley*

Summaries of Selected Titles

Belle Pruitt

When her baby dies, Belle's mother retreats in her grief. At Belle's suggestion, Aunt George comes to live with them until Mrs. Pruitt can take over again. Unfortunately, Aunt George likes being in charge and Belle is the only one who sees that she is keeping Mrs. Pruitt dependent. Belle sees renewal of life in growing things and finally gets her mother to see it too. Together they plant a garden and a tree while Mrs. Pruitt faces life again.

Delpha Green and Company

Delpha, the daughter of a preacher, tries to get along by thinking that everything will turn out all right. Her Pollyanna attitude soon fails her, however, and she is forced to confront real life.

Dust of the Earth

Jenny Drawn inherits her estranged father's house and land in South Dakota and moves her family there. The story is told by Fern, Jenny's daughter, who says, "The word love was not spoken in our house." Fern grows up there, learning to be a sheep rancher while coping with tornadoes, wolves, and an influenza epidemic. Eventually, the family begins to care for each other.

Ellen Grae

The small town of Thicket, Florida, is populated by eccentric and stagnant people. Ellen's mother and father are getting a divorce and Ellen is living with the McGruders. She tells tall tales, but her real life becomes more horrible than her tales.

Grover

■■■■■■■■■□□□□□

This is a sequel to *Ellen Grae.* Grover's life is happy. He likes to go fishing and have fun with his friends, but then his mother, dying of cancer, shoots herself. His father can't handle the grief and rejects Grover and his help.

Hazel Rye

■■■■■■■■■■□□□□

Hazel's success in school is less than adequate, but neither she nor her family seem to mind very much. Millard, her father who is subject to great although nonviolent rages, deeds a few acres of neglected orange grove to Hazel after one of his rages. When a family comes to live in the grove and starts caring for it, Hazel becomes interested in developing her own land.

The Mimosa Tree

■■■■■■■■□□□□□□

Forced off the farm, Marvella Profitt goes to Chicago with her blind father and younger brothers and sisters. Help from the government has not arrived so Marvella and her brother steal pocketbooks in an attempt to survive. They finally decide that they cannot live this way.

Moon Lake Angel

■■■■■■■■■■□□□□

Kitty Dale has been with the Fords for two years. There are other girls there whose parents can't or won't care for them. Kitty hates her mother for her weakness and barely remembers her father. Now the Fords are closing down and Kitty sets off for her father only to find he has married again and has a new family. Having no alternative, she heads for her mother. Her mother is getting married again and has no time for Kitty. Aunt Petal, a kindly neighbor, takes Kitty in while her mother is gone and the two become fast friends. When Kitty's mother and new husband return, Kitty plans her revenge.

Queen of Hearts

■■■■■■■■■□□□□□

When independent, feisty Granny has a stroke and returns from the hospital as a hostile old woman, Wilma Lincoln becomes her grandmother's unwilling housekeeper. Wilma must fight the willful domination of Granny and she does so, becoming tougher and more mature.

Sugar Blue

■■■■■■■■□□□□□□

Amy Blue is withdrawn and hostile, feeling shut out by her parents who are caught up in the management of a restaurant under the watchful eyes of their own tyrannical parents. Amy must share a room with her four-year-old niece Ella. Ella is everything Amy refuses to be: warm, exuberant, curious, and loving. She also adores Amy and calls her Sugar Blue.

Trial Valley

■■■■■■■■□□□□□□

In this sequel to *Where the Lilies Bloom,* Mary Call Luther and her brother and sister continue to find and sell medicinal herbs to Mr. Connell, who sells them to laboratories. The younger two are rebelling against Mary Call's insistence that they learn to read. Mary Call has conflicting feelings about them and about her role in life. When five-year-old Jack comes into their lives, Mary Call's life becomes even more difficult.

Where the Lilies Bloom

■■■■■■■■□□□□□□

Mary Call and her family try to make a living collecting medicinal plants in the mountains of North Carolina after their father dies.

Eth Clifford

| Author |
| Living |

Biography

When Eth Clifford was young, she wanted to be an actress, a dancer, a singer, a lawyer, and a princess. She didn't think about becoming a writer until she submitted a story to a magazine and they published it. From then on she was hooked. Ms. Clifford was born in New York City but grew up in New Jersey, New York, and Philadelphia. For a while, she lived in the country and went to a one-room schoolhouse. She has been married for forty-seven years to a man who is a "prince of a fellow." He calls her his "green pea princess," so she became a princess after all.

Books by Eth Clifford

The Dastardly Murder of Dirty Pete. Houghton, 1981.
Harvey's Horrible Snake Disaster. Houghton 1984.
Harvey's Marvelous Monkey Mystery. Houghton, 1987.
Help! I'm a Prisoner in the Library. Houghton, 1979.
I Hate Your Guts, Ben Brooster. Houghton, 1989.
I Never Wanted to Be Famous. Houghton, 1986.
Just Tell Me When We're Dead! Houghton, 1983.
The Killer Swan. Houghton, 1980.
The Man Who Sang in the Dark. Houghton, 1987.
The Remembering Box. Houghton, 1985.
The Rocking Chair Rebellion. Houghton, 1978.
Scared Silly. Houghton, 1988.
The Strange Reincarnation of Hendrik Verloom. Houghton, 1982.
The Wild One. Houghton, 1974.

Summaries of Selected Titles

The Dastardly Murder of Dirty Pete

■■■■□□□□□□□□□□

See page 45.

Harvey's Marvelous Monkey Mystery

■■■■□□□□□□□□□□

This is the sequel to *Harvey's Horrible Snake Disaster.* There are no snakes, just a monkey and a sinister stranger who lurks in the bushes.

Help! I'm a Prisoner in the Library

■■■■□□□□□□□□□□

During a blizzard, Mary Rose and Jo-Beth leave the car shortly after their father goes for gas. They find shelter and get locked inside an unusual library. It turns out the moaning that scares them half to death is an injured librarian and together they work out a solution to her problem.

I Hate Your Guts, Ben Brooster

■■■■□□□□□□□□□□

See page 45.

The Man Who Sang in the Dark

■■■■■■■■■□□□□□

During the Depression, Leah's father dies and she, her mother, and younger brother Daniel move to a tiny two-room apartment over a store. Eventually, the elderly couple that own the store and Gideon, the blind singer who lives in the room below them, become part of an extended family. Still they have a hard time making it and when a wealthy couple wants to adopt Daniel, the mother permits it.

The Remembering Box

■■■■■■■□□□□□□□

The relationship between a boy and his grandmother grows stronger on each Sabbath until the boy is strong enough to accept her death.

The Rocking Chair Rebellion

■■■■■■■■■□□□□□

After Opie becomes a volunteer at the Maple Ridge Home for the Aged, some of the residents decide to become more independent and purchase a house together. Opie and the residents need her lawyer father's help.

James L. and Christopher Collier

Authors
Living

Biography

These two brothers refer to themselves as Jamie and Kit. They collaborate on historical novels, usually set in the period of the American Revolution. Kit does the historical research and sees these books as teaching tools. Jamie does the actual writing and tries to make them exciting by developing the characterization and the plot. Everything that happens to the characters in their books actually did happen to someone. When Kit is doing the research, he looks for the details Jamie will need to make the action believable and accurate. He finds out what kinds of plates the people used and what clothes and colors they wore. To find this information, he goes to museums often. Then he lays out the episodes, creating a family, a locale, and the events. He sends this outline to Jamie in New York. Jamie writes the first draft of the story and sends it back to Kit to check for historical accuracy before he writes the final draft. This process usually takes months.

Both brothers are musicans. Jamie plays the trombone and works as a jazz musician three or four times a week. Kit plays the trumpet but hasn't played professionally for years. He teaches history at the University of Connecticut.

Books by James L. and Christopher Collier
Written by James L. Collier
Give Dad My Best. Four Winds, 1976.
It's Murder at St. Basket's. Grosset, 1972.
Louis Armstrong: An American Success Story. Macmillan, 1985.
Outside Looking In. Macmillan, 1987.
Planet Out of the Past. Macmillan, 1983.
Rich and Famous. Four Winds, 1975.
Rock Star. Four Winds, 1970.
The Teddy Bear Habit. Norton, 1967.
When the Stars Begin to Fall. Delacorte, 1986.
Why Does Everybody Think I'm Nutty? Grosset, 1971.
The Winchesters. Macmillan, 1988.

Written by James L. and Christopher Collier.
The Bloody Country. Four Winds, 1976.
My Brother Sam is Dead. Four Winds, 1974.

Jump Ship to Freedom. Delacorte, 1981.
War Comes to Willy Freeman. Delacorte, 1983.
Who Is Carrie? Delacorte, 1983.
The Winter Hero. Four Winds, 1978.

Book Awards and Recommendations
American Library Association: *My Brother Sam is Dead*
Newbery Honor Award: *My Brother Sam is Dead*

Summaries of Selected Titles
The Bloody Country

See page 57.

Jump Ship to Freedom

See page 39.

My Brother Sam Is Dead

See page 62.

War Comes to Willy Freeman

This novel takes place before *Jump Ship to Freedom* and centers around Daniel's cousin Willy who tells the story of what happened during the last two years of the Revolutionary War. Willy's father was killed and her mother disappeared. She makes her way to Fraunces Tavern in New York where, her uncle had told her, she might get help.

Who Is Carrie?

Still in the same time frame as *War Comes to Willy Freeman* and *Jump Ship to Freedom*, we meet Carrie, a kitchen slave in Samuel Fraunces Tavern. When Daniel Arabus arrives with notes with which to buy his mother's freedom, it is to Carrie that he comes for help. In helping Daniel, Carrie finds out about herself.

Susan Cooper

Author
Living
Visits schools
Answers letters
Mailing address:
　　Macmillan Children's Book Group
　　866 Third Avenue
　　New York, NY 10022

Biography

As a child, Susan Cooper lived in rural England. When she was ten, she wrote three puppet plays, a weekly newspaper, and a small book. When she grew up, she became a newspaper reporter, but she began writing books at the same time. Some of her books are for adults and others are for children. Ms. Cooper also writes screen plays for television. She collaborated with Hume Cronyn to write the play *Foxfire*, which ran for seven months on Broadway.

Ms. Cooper married a widower with three teenage children and now lives in Cambridge, Massachusetts. She has two other children, Jonathan and Kate, living at home.

About Susan Cooper's Work

☐ Susan Cooper often writes fantasies that concern the triumph of good over evil. Some critics say that she describes landscape and weather better than she creates characters. Do you agree? Why?

Books by Susan Cooper

The Dark Is Rising. Atheneum, 1973.
The Dawn of Fear. Harcourt, 1970.
Greenwitch. Atheneum, 1974.
The Grey King. Atheneum, 1975.
Jethro and the Jumbie. Atheneum, 1979.
Over Sea, Under Stone. Harcourt, 1966.
Seaward. Macmillan, 1983.
The Selkie Girl. Macmillan, 1986.
The Silver Cow. Macmillan, 1983.
Silver on the Tree. Macmillan, 1977.

Book Awards and Recommendations

American Library Association: *The Silver Cow, The Dark Is Rising, The Grey King*
Boston Globe/Horn Book Award: *The Dark Is Rising*
IRA Children's Choice: *Greenwitch*
Newbery Medal: *The Grey King*
Newbery Honor Award: *The Dark Is Rising*

Summaries of Selected Titles

The Dark Is Rising

Will Stanton, now eleven years old, learns that he is the last of the Old Ones and must find the Signs of the Light that will defeat the Dark. The Twelve Days of Christmas this year will be very different for Will.

Dawn of Fear

See page 110.

Greenwitch

The Grail was stolen and Simon, Jane, and Barnaby along with Uncle Merry and Will Stanton go to Cornwall to get it back. Because of Jane's unselfish wish, the Greenwitch gives her the map and key from the bottom of the sea.

The Grey King

■■■■■■■■■■■■■□

Will Stanton is sent to Wales to recover from an illness. There he meets King Arthur's son, Bran, who was sent forward in time to escape the evil that surrounds him.

Over Sea, Under Stone

■■■■■■■■■■□□□□

Simon, Jane, and Barnaby go to Cornall on vacation and discover a chalice, believed to be the Grail, but lose the map and key to its inscription.

Seaward

■■■■■■■■■□□□□□

Cally and West are hunting for their parents. Suspecting that Cally's ancestors may have been seals, they head for the sea.

Silver on the Tree

■■■■■■■■□□□□□□

Will Stanton, and King Arthur's son, Bran, join the forces of light to triumph over the evil at last.

Helen Cresswell

| Author |
| Living |

Biography

Helen Cresswell is a prolific children's writer from Nottinghamshire, England. She is married and has two daughters. Many of her books were originally written for television. Although her works are characterized by the fantastic, they are also humorous and touched by reality.

Books by Helen Cresswell

Absolute Zero. Macmillan, 1978.
Awful Jack. Hodder and Stoughton, 1977.
Bagthorpes Abroad. Macmillan, 1984.
Bagthorpes Haunted. Macmillan, 1985.
Bagthorpes Liberated. Macmillan, 1990.
Bagthorpes Unlimited. Macmillan, 1978.
Bagthorpes vs the World. Macmillan, 1979.
The Barge Children. Hodder and Stoughton, 1968.
The Beachcombers. Macmillan, 1972.
The Beetle Hunt. Longman, 1973.
Bluebirds over Pit Row. Benn, 1972.
The Bird Fancier. Benn, 1971.
The Bower Birds. Benn, 1973.
Butterfly Chase. Kestrel, 1975.
A Day on Big O. Follett, 1968.
Dear Shrink. Macmillan, 1982.
Donkey Days. Benn, 1977.
Dragon Ride. Kestrel, 1987.
Ellie and the Hagwitch. Hardy, 1984.
The Flyaway Kite. Kestrel, 1979.
A Game of Catch. Macmillan, 1977.
A Gift from Winklesea. Brockhampton, 1969.
Greedy Alice. Andre Deutsch, 1986.
Hokey Pokey Did It! Ladybird, 1989.
A House for Jones. Benn, 1969.
Jane's Policeman. Benn, 1972.
Jumbo Afloat. Brockhampton, 1966.
Jumbo and the Big Dig. Brockhampton, 1968.
Jumbo Back to Nature. Brockhampton, 1965.
Jumbo Spencer. Lippincott, 1966.
Lizzie Dripping. BBC, 1974.
Lizzie Dripping Again. BBC, 1974.
Lizzie Dripping and the Little Angel. BBC, 1974.
Lizzie Dripping by the Sea. BBC, 1974.
The Long Day. Benn, 1972.

Moondial. Macmillan, 1987.
More Lizzie Dripping. BBC, 1974.
My Aunt Polly by the Sea. Wheaton, 1980.
The Night Watchmen. Macmillan, 1970.
The Outlanders. Faber, 1970.
Ordinary Jack. Macmillan, 1977.
Petticoat Smuggler. Macmillan, 1985.
The Piemakers. Lippincott, 1968.
Pietro and the Mule. Merrill, 1965.
Rainbow Pavement. Benn, 1970.
Roof Fall! Benn, 1972.
Rosie and the Boredom Eater. Heinemann, 1989.
The Sea Piper. Oliver and Boyd, 1968.
The Secret World of Polly Flint. Macmillan, 1984.
Short Back and Sides. Benn, 1972.
The Signposters. Faber, 1968.
Sonya-by-the-Shore. Dent, 1960.
A Tide for the Captain. Oliver and Boyd, 1967.
Time Out. Macmillan, 1990.
Trouble. Dutton, 1988.
Two Hoots. Crown, 1978.
Up the Pier. Macmillan, 1972.
The Weather Cat. Benn, 1971.
Where the Wind Blows. Funk & Wagnalls, 1968.
Whodunnit? Cape, 1986.
The White Sea Horse. Lippincott, 1965.
The Winter of the Birds. Macmillan, 1976.

Book Awards and Recommendations

American Library Association: *Up the Pier, The Winter of the Birds, Absolute Zero, Bagthorpes Unlimited, The Secret World of Polly Flint, Ordinary Jack*
IRA Children's Choice: *Bagthorpes Unlimited, Absolute Zero*

Summaries of Selected Titles

Absolute Zero

■■■■■■■□□□□□□□

The Bagthorpe's competitive spirit is at an all-time high when Uncle Parker enters a slogan contest. Nearly everyone is in on the act, except Grandpa and Jack. Most of their efforts are disastrous for the rest of the family. Father removes all the labels from the cans, which creates some strange meals in the Bagthorpe family. Eventually, they're all on TV as "The Happiest Family in England."

Bagthorpes Unlimited

■■■■■■■■□□□□□□

It's the *Guinness Book of World Records* that intrigues the zany Bagthorpes this time. First, of course, they must get Bible-quoting Aunt Penelope to cut her visit short. Their methods include putting maggots and other disgusting things into Grandma's reunion dinner. Then it's on to the feat that will include them in the Book of Records: constructing the world's longest daisy chain.

Bagthorpes vs the World

■■■■■■■■□□□□□□

The Bagthorpes' four-year-old cousin Daisy loves funerals, so the Bagthorpes decide to take advantage of this to drive out Great-Aunt Lucy and her Pekingese. When Daisy runs out of dead animals, they bring her chops from the freezer.

Dear Shrink

■■■■■■■■■□□□□□□

In his diary, Oliver regales us with the adventures he and his siblings have while left in London by their parents who are off to the Amazon. When the woman who was supposed to care for them dies, the children are separated and sent to different foster homes.

A Game of Catch

While visiting a castle, Kate and Hugh become involved with two children from a painting.

The Night Watchmen

■■■■■■■■□□□□□□

See page 141.

Ordinary Jack

■■■■■■■■□□□□□□

Eleven-year-old Jack Bagthorpe feels outdone and outshone by the other members of the Bagthorpe family. All of them are gifted and successful, but Jack thinks that he is just ordinary. Then Uncle Parker devises a plan to turn Jack into a prophet and it works.

The Secret World of Polly Flint

See page 21.

The Winter of the Birds

In his attempt to become a hero, the narrator discovers that he already is one.

Roald Dahl

Author
Died in November, 1990.

Biography
Roald Dahl was born in Wales of Norwegian parents. His father died when Roald was three. He was sent to boarding school when he was seven, and his boarding school experiences are detailed in his book *Boy: Tales of Childhood*. Mr. Dahl said the chapter "Lucky Break" from his book *The Wonderful Story of Henry Sugar* describes an event that really happened to him. He liked to write when he was young, but his teachers didn't like his writing very much until Mrs. O'Connor was his teacher when he was nine. She taught him to love literature. During World War II, he flew for the Royal Air Force and was shot down in the Libyan Desert. He was then sent to Washington D.C. to work. There he wrote *The Gremlins* about little creatures who sabotage planes.

When Mr. Dahl had children of his own, he told them stories that he later wrote down. He called himself a man of metal because his severe arthritis necessitated the replacement of several of his real joints with metal ones. He did most of his writing in a tiny brick hut up in the apple orchard about two hundred yards from his main house. The hut, he said, was not cleaned or swept for as long as he could remember, although the main house was spotless. He wrote in long hand because he couldn't type.

Books by Roald Dahl
The BFG. Farrar, 1982.
Boy: Tales of Childhood. Farrar, 1986.
Charlie and the Chocolate Factory. Knopf, 1964.
Charlie and the Great Glass Elevator. Knopf, 1972.
Danny, the Champion of the World. Knopf, 1975.
Dirty Beasts. Farrar, 1984.
The Enormous Crocodile. Knopf, 1978.
Ezio Trot. Viking, 1990.
Fantastic Mr. Fox. Knopf, 1978.
The Giraffe and the Pelly and Me. Farrar, 1985.
Going Solo. Farrar, 1986.
The Gremlins. Random, 1943.
James and the Giant Peach. Knopf, 1961.
The Magic Finger. Harper, 1966.
Matilda. Viking, 1988.
Revolting Rhymes. Knopf, 1983.
The Twits. Knopf, 1981.

The Witches. Farrar, 1983.
The Wonderful Story of Henry Sugar. Knopf, 1977.

Book Awards and Recommendations
American Library Association: *The Witches, Boy: Tales of Childhood*
IRA Children's Choice: *Danny, the Champion of the World*

Summaries of Selected Titles
The BFG

■■■■□□□□□□□□□□

Sophie, an orphan, awakes at midnight while being snatched from her bed by a giant. She's carried off past the last page in the atlas. However, the giant is a friendly one (hence, the BFG: Big, Friend Giant) and is in charge of dispensing dreams. The other giants are people-eaters. Sophie and the BFG devise a scheme, which involves the Queen, to protect the world from those giants.

Charlie and the Chocolate Factory

■■■■■■■□□□□□□□

Willy Wonka, owner of the world's most famous chocolate factory, wants a successor. He sets up a contest that has six winning children, one of whom he hopes will do. The winners visit the chocolate factory where they must follow his rules. One by one they are eliminated, in ways suited to their individual weaknesses and temptations, until only Charlie Bucket remains.

Danny, the Champion of the World

■■■■■■■□□□□□□□

Nine-year-old Danny's father is a poacher. When Danny discovers this, he determines to become the best poacher, a feat that involves running afoul of the disagreeable Mr. Hazell. The plot revolves around the boy's relationship with his father and whether or not crime is ever justified.

Fantastic Mr. Fox

■■■■■■□□□□□□□□

These are the attempts of a fox to maintain his family, which he does by stealing from three disgusting farmers. The farmers join forces to thwart and kill the fox, but to no avail. Mr Fox, through perseverance and ingenuity, prevails for his own family and for all the animal families.

James and the Giant Peach

■■■■■■■□□□□□□□

James, an orphan, escapes from his dastardly aunts through magic that transforms a peach into a giant home peopled by formerly tiny creatures that are now enormous. These creatures reflect a gamut of human strengths and weaknesses. Together they pilot the peach through many perils until they land at the top of the Empire State Building.

The Magic Finger

■■■■□□□□□□□□□□

This is an anti-hunting statement. A girl has the power to change anything she points her finger at. She changes a family of cruel hunters into the ducks they normally hunt.

Roald Dahl's Revolting Rhymes

■■■■■■■□□□□□□□

These are rewrites of common fairy tales in mocking, irreverent, and sometimes shocking rhymes.

The Twits

■■■■□□□□□□□□□□

Mr. and Mrs. Twit play all kinds of tricks on each other. They are in turn tricked by escaping monkeys who save themselves and the birds the Twits have been preying on.

The Witches

■■■■■■■□□□□□□□

We know how to spot witches: they wear wigs to cover their baldness and have itchy scalps. When Roald Dahl spies delegates to the Royal Society for the Prevention of Cruelty to Children scratching their heads, he knows, and we know, there are witches about. When they unveil their Formula 86 Delayed Action Mouse-Maker, they find him hiding behind a screen and make him drink it. However, he has not lost his voice or his resourcefulness, and he and his witch-hating grandmother outwit the witches.

Paula Danziger

Author
Living
Visits schools
Answers letters
Mailing address:
 Publicist
 Dell/Delacorte Books for Young Readers
 666 Fifth Avenue
 New York, NY 10103

Biography

Paula Danziger was born August 18, 1944, in Washington, D.C. Now she has two homes: one in New York City and a country home in Woodstock, New York. She says she has wanted to be a writer since she was six. Instead, she became a teacher. Two car accidents, one caused by a drunken driver, caused her to stop teaching for a while. Then she took courses in graduate school and started writing. She wrote for the kids she remembered teaching. She resumed her teaching career for a while, but now she's a full-time writer. She likes the writer's life: few alarm clocks, lots of flexibility, and lots of travel.

Books by Paula Danziger

Can You Sue Your Parents for Malpractice? Delacorte, 1979.
The Cat Ate My Gymsuit. Delacorte, 1974.
The Divorce Express. Delacorte, 1982.
Everyone Else's Parents Said Yes. Delacorte, 1989.
It's an Aardvark-Eat-Turtle World. Delacorte, 1985.
Make Like a Tree and Leave. Delacorte, 1990.
The Pistachio Prescription. Delacorte, 1978.
Remember Me to Harold Square. Delacorte, 1987.
There's a Bat in Bunk Five. Delacorte, 1980.
This Place Has No Atmosphere. Delacorte, 1986.

Book Awards and Recommendations

IRA Children's Choice: *The Pistachio Prescription, Can You Sue Your Parents for Malpractice? There's a Bat in Bunk Five*

Summaries of Selected Titles

The Cat Ate My Gymsuit

Thirteen-year-old Marcy thinks she hasn't got much going for her. She says she's "a blimp with an impending case of acne," but when her favorite teacher is fired, Marcy is the leader of a revolt.

The Divorce Express

The express goes between Phoebe's mother's home in New York City, where she goes weekends and her artist father's home in Woodstock. This is a fairly realistic look at the two-home child.

Everyone Else's Parents Said Yes

See page 25.

It's an Aardvark-Eat-Turtle World

In this sequel to *The Divorce Express,* Rosie's mother and Phoebe's father get married and the two friends become sisters. The dog, Aardvark, eats a new pet turtle, which seems an apt analogy of the attempts of the two girls to cope with each other and their new family situation.

Sid Fleischman

Author
Living

Biography
Albert Sidney Fleischman was born in Brooklyn, New York. His first career was as a magician in vaudeville and night clubs. After World War II, he became a journalist in San Diego before turning to writing novels for adults and children.

Books by Sid Fleischman
The Bloodhound Gang in the Case of the Secret Message. Random, 1981.
The Bloodhound Gang in the Case of the 264-Pound Burglar. Random, 1982.
The Bloodhound Gang's Secret Code Book. Random, 1983.
By the Great Horn Spoon. Little, 1953.
The Case of the Cackling Ghost. Random, 1981.
The Case of the Flying Clock. Random 1981.
The Case of Princess Tomorrow. Random, 1981.
Chancy and the Grand Rascal. Little, 1966.
The Ghost in the Noonday Sun. Little, 1965.
The Ghost on Saturday Night. Little, 1963.
The Hey Hey Man. Little, 1979.
Humbug Mountain. Little, 1978.
Jingo Django. Little, 1987.
Kat's Secret Riddle Book. Avon, 1978.
McBroom and the Beanstalk. Little, 1978.
McBroom and the Big Wind. Little, 1982.
McBroom and the Great Race. Little, 1980.
McBroom Tells a Lie. Little, 1976.
McBroom Tells the Truth. Little, 1981.
McBroom the Rainmaker. Little, 1982.
McBroom's Almanac. Little, 1984.
McBroom's Ear. Little, 1982.
McBroom's Ghost. Little, 1981.
McBroom's Zoo. Little, 1981.
Me and the Man on the Moon-Eyed Horse. Little, 1977.
The Midnight Horse. Greenwillow, 1990.
Mr. Mysterious and Company. Little, 1962.
Mr. Mysterious's Secrets of Magic. Little, 1975.
The Scarebird. Greenwillow, 1988.

Book Awards and Recommendations
American Library Association: The Whipping Boy
IRA Children's Choice: The Ghost on Saturday Night, Mr. Mysterious's Secrets of Magic, McBroom Tells a Lie
Newbery Medal: The Whipping Boy
School Library Journal: The Whipping Boy

Summaries of Selected Titles
By the Great Horn Spoon

■■■■■□□□□□□□□□

See page 60.

The Ghost in the Noonday Sun

■■■■■□□□□□□□□□

See page 78.

Humbug Mountain

■■■■■□□□□□□□□□

See page 80.

McBroom Tells a Lie

■■■■■□□□□□□□□□

See page 80.

The Scarebird

■■□□□□□□□□□□□□

See page 14.

The Whipping Boy

■■■■■■■■□□□□□□

See page 169.

Paula Fox

Author
Living
Visits schools
Does interviews
Answers letters
Mailing address:
   Orchard Books
   387 Park Avenue South
   New York, NY 10016

Biography

Paula Fox was born in New York City in 1923. She lived in Cuba for two years and went to a one-room school there. Her parents moved around a lot and she seldom stayed in any place for more than a year. When she grew up, she taught school and especially liked teaching fifth graders. Perhaps that's why she often writes stories for children of that age. She has two sons, and when they were ten and twelve years old, she began to write stories for publication.

About Paula Fox's Work

☐ Ms. Fox's books often deal with children facing very real problems, but she does not try to offer solutions to the problems as some of the novelists seem to. Many of her main characters are in some way isolated, go through extraordinary experiences, and then reach out for people. She develops characters and often lets them triumph through the choices they make. Many of those characters take a journey. There is often confusion in her books and much is left unresolved.

Books by Paula Fox

Blowfish Live in the Sea. Bradbury, 1970.
How Many Miles to Babylon? Bradbury, 1967.
The King's Falcon. Bradbury, 1969.
A Likely Place. Macmillan, 1967.
Lily and the Lost Boy. Orchard, 1987.
The Little Swineherd and Other Tales. Bradbury, 1968.
Maurice's Room. Aladdin, 1966.
The Moonlight Man. Bradbury, 1984.
One-Eyed Cat. Bradbury, 1984.

A Place Apart. Farrar, 1980.
Portrait of Ivan. Bradbury, 1969.
The Slave Dancer. Bradbury, 1968.
The Stone-Faced Boy. Bradbury, 1968.
The Village by the Sea. Orchard, 1988.

Book Awards and Recommendations

American Library Association: *The Stone-Faced Boy, Portrait of Ivan, The Slave Dancer, One-Eyed Cat, The Moonlight Man, The Village by the Sea, How Many Miles to Babylon?*
Boston Globe/Horn Book Award: *The Village by the Sea*
Newbery Medal: *The Slave Dancer*
Newbery Honor Award: *One-Eyed Cat*
School Library Journal: *The Slave Dancer, A Place Apart, The Moonlight Man, The Village by the Sea*

Summaries of Selected Titles
Blowfish Live in the Sea

■■■■■■■■■■■■■■□

This book is best suited to older children. Ben Felix has felt defeated for years. He doesn't care for his stepfather and his own father has meant nothing to him since he was six. On almost every available surface he writes, "Blowfish live in the sea." Later we find that his father sent him a blowfish that he claimed to have found on the Amazon River. Ben's anger is resolved by confronting his father.

How Many Miles to Babylon?

■■■■■■■■■□□□□□

James Douglas, "Little Bits," becomes involved in the dognapping scheme of some bigger boys. His father has deserted the family and his mother is in the hospital. He is living with three aging aunts in one room. When fully pressed, he returns the dog he was forced to kidnap even though it means facing the terrors of the city.

A Likely Place

■■■■■■■□□□□□□□

Too many people care for Lewis and hover over him. Then he is turned over to the care of Miss Fitchlow, an Auntie Mame-type who practices yoga and allows him greater freedom than he has ever had before.

Maurice's Room

■■■■□□□□□□□□□□

A boy in New York City has everything possible in his apartment bedroom. He is constantly building more shelves and storage space. He is heart-broken to hear that the family is moving to the country and that he must get rid of all his collections. The book ends as Maurice discovers, on the country property, an abandoned barn.

One-Eyed Cat

■■■■■■■■■□□□□□

See page 142.

A Place Apart

■■■■■■□□□□□□□□

Victoria Finch moves from Boston to a small New England town after the death of her father and finds that she cannot make it without help.

Portrait of Ivan

■■■■■■■□□□□□□□

This story explores many ways of perceiving reality. Ivan's father is a businessman who deals in facts and depends on photographs for recall. Geneva is attempting to record the world in her book *The Book of Things, Volume One*. Matt, the artist, tells her that the more ways you draw a thing, the more understanding of it you will have.

The Slave Dancer

■■■■■■■□□□□□□□

This book deals with men who transported and sold the slaves. Jesse is a young white street entertainer who plays the fife. He is on board a slave ship, Moonlight, and is almost as much a captive as the slaves are. It is his job to exercise the slaves by playing for their forced dancing.

The Stone-Faced Boy

■■■■■■■□□□□□□□

Gus Oliver is called Stone Face by his family and classmates because he seldom shows what he is thinking, but he is afraid of many things, one of which is the dark. He is faced with the choice of going out into the dark to search for his sister's lost dog or lying to his sister, the person he most cares about.

Jean Fritz

Author
Living
Answers letters
Mailing address
G. P. Putnam's Sons
200 Madison Avenue
New York, NY 10016

Biography

Jean Fritz and her husband, Michael, have two children. Ms. Fritz was the only child of missionary parents and was born in China. She first came to the United States when she was 13. She loves China and returned there for a visit not too long ago. In her home are many Chinese works of art.

About Jean Fritz's Work

☐ Jean Fritz is known primarily for her short, fascinating biographies of historical figures. As you will notice by looking at the list of books she has published, she also writes fantasies and realistic fiction. All of her books are marked by her understanding of human nature and her gentle sense of humor. Among her many honors is the Laura Ingalls Wilder Award for her "substantial contribution to children's literature."

Books by Jean Fritz

And Then What Happened, Paul Revere? Coward, 1973.
The Animals of Dr. Schweitzer. Coward, 1958.
Back to Early Cape Cod. National Park Service, 1979.
Brady. Coward, 1960.
Brendan the Navigator. Coward, 1979.
Bunny Hopwell's First Spring. Wonder, 1954.
The Cabin Faced West. Coward, 1958.
Can't You Make Them Behave, King George? Coward, 1982.
Champion Dog, Prince Tom. With Clute, Tom. Coward, 1958.
China Homecoming. Putnam, 1985.
China's Long March. Putnam, 1988.
December Is for Christmas. (As Ann Scott) Wonder, 1961.
The Double Life of Pocahontas. Putnam, 1983.
Early Thunder. Coward, 1967.

Fish Head. Coward, 1954.
George Washington's Breakfast. Coward, 1969.
The Good Giants and the Bad Pukwudgies. Putnam, 1982.
The Great Little Madison. Putnam, 1989.
Growing Up. Rand, 1956.
Help Mr. Willy Nilly. Treasure, 1954.
Homesick: My Own Story. Putnam, 1982.
How to Read to a Rabbit. Coward, 1959.
Hurrah for Jonathan! A. Whitman, 1955.
I, Adam. Coward, 1963.
The Late Spring. Coward, 1957.
Magic to Burn. Coward, 1964.
Make Way for Sam Houston. Putnam, 1986.
The Man Who Loved Books. Putnam, 1981.
121 Pudding Street. Coward, 1955.
The Secret Diary of Jeb and Abigail: Growing Up in America 1776-1783. Coward, 1969.
Shh! We're Writing the Constitution. Putnam, 1987.
Stonewall. Putnam, 1979.
Tap, Tap, Lion—One, Two, Three. Coward, 1962.
Traitor: The Case of Benedict Arnold. Putnam, 1981.
What's the Big Idea, Ben Franklin? Coward, 1976.
Where Do You Think You're Going, Christopher Columbus? Putnam, 1980.
Where Was Patrick Henry on the 29th of May? Putnam, 1975.
Who's That Stepping on Plymouth Rock? Putnam, 1975.
Why Don't You Get a Horse, Sam Adams? Coward, 1974.
Will You Sign Here, John Hancock? Coward, 1976.

Book Awards and Recommendations

American Library Association: *I, Adam, Where Do You Think You're Going, Christopher Columbus? The Good Giants and the Bad Pukwudgies, Homesick: My Own Story, Make Way for Sam Houston, The Great Little Madison, And Then What Happened, Paul Revere? Stonewall, Traitor: The Case of Benedict Arnold, The Double Life of Pocahontas, Why Don't You Get a Horse, Sam Adams?*
Boston Globe/Horn Book Award: *The Double Life of Pocahontas*
Boston Globe/Horn Book Honor Award: *And Then What Happened, Paul Revere? Will You Sign Here, John Hancock? Stonewall, Homesick: My Own Story*

IRA Children's Choice: *What's the Big Idea, Ben Franklin? Will You Sign Here, John Hancock? Can't You Make Them Behave, King George?*
Newbery Honor Award: *Homesick: My Own Story*
School Library Journal: *Where Do You Think You're Going, Christopher Columbus? Homesick: My Own Story, Make Way for Sam Houston, The Great Little Madison, Traitor: The Case of Benedict Arnold, The Double Life of Pocahontas, Brendan the Navigator, China Homecoming, Early Thunder, Where Was Patrick Henry on the 29th of May? Why Don't You Get a Horse, Sam Adams? Will You Sign Here, John Hancock?*

Summaries of Selected Titles
And Then What Happened, Paul Revere?

■■■□□□□□□□□□□□

See page 61.

Brady

■■■■■■■■□□□□□□

See pages 78 and 100.

Brendan the Navigator

■■■■■□□□□□□□□□

The European who may have been here nine hundred years before Columbus is depicted here in Fritz's usual witty style.

The Cabin Faced West

■■■■■■■■□□□□□□

Ten-year-old Ann Hamilton lives with her family in colonial western Pennsylvania. Her father built the cabin facing west because he wants the family to look to the future not to the past. Life as the only little girl in that pioneer area is not what Ann wants. She resents the lack of books, windows, and other niceties. Then George Washington comes to dinner. This story is based on the true experiences of the author's great-geat-grandmother.

Can't You Make Them Behave, King George?

■■■□□□□□□□□□□□

See page 61.

The Double Life of Pocahontas

■■■■■■■■□□□□□□

See pages 54 and 112.

Early Thunder

■■■■■■■■□□□□□□

See page 62.

George Washington's Breakfast

■■■■□□□□□□□□□□

A boy with a great deal of curiosity and very indulgent parents determines to find out exactly what George Washington had for breakfast. The search leads him and us through a good deal of information about the first president. George, the hero of our story, is served the meal at last, but then queries, "I wonder what George Washington had for lunch?"

The Great Little Madison

■■■■■■■■□□□□□□

This is a delightful account of the modest and diminutive president who played a big part in our history from pre-Revolutionary times through the battle over slavery.

Homesick: My Own Story

■■■■■■■■□□□□□□

Jean Fritz tells her story from the early days in Hankow, China, describing the busy Yangtze River as her backyard, to her school days in a British school, to her goodbye to the only country she had known.

The Man Who Loved Books

The story of the Irish saint Columba who lived in the sixth century is told as if it were being sung by an Irish bard.

Shh! We're Writing the Constitution

See page 63.

Traitor: The Case of Benedict Arnold

See page 62 and 161.

What's the Big Idea, Ben Franklin?

Franklin's long and varied life is described in this brief but humorous biography from his birth in Boston to his death in Philadelphia with all the inventing, writing, and diplomacy along the way.

Why Don't You Get a Horse, Sam Adams?

Sam Adams was a rabble rouser who hated the King of England and refused to ride a horse. He dressed shabbily and walked all over Boston with Queue, his dog, to get people to join the fight for independence. He led the list of the King's most wanted men.

Will You Sign Here, John Hancock?

This is one of Fritz's brief biographies. The privileged life of John Hancock was marred by his great need to be noticed and liked by everybody. He dressed in the most flamboyant manner and threw large parties, but he wanted to be elected to office and have power. Sam Adams became his friend and helped him win his election as Selectman of Boston, involving him in revolutionary activities. Eventually, John Hancock was on King George's list of dangerous Americans. His illustrious career is told with humor and insight.

Jean Craighead George

| Author/Illustrator |
| Living |

Biography

Jean George was born in Washington, D.C. Her family were all naturalists and her life has always focused on writing and nature. She was a member of the White House press corps for *The Washington Post,* and she's written over forty books, some of which she also illustrated. She likes hiking, canoeing, and making sourdough pancakes. Ms. George has three children and grandchildren. Over the years she has kept over 170 pets, not including dogs and cats. She lives in Chappaqua, New York.

Ms. George began writing *Julie of the Wolves* during a summer she spent studying wolves in Barrow, Alaska. There she saw a small girl walking on the tundra. Later she saw a magnificent alpha wolf pack leader in Mt. McKinley National Park. She put the two images together for *Julie of the Wolves.*

Books by Jean Craighead George

All upon a Sidewalk. Crowell, 1974.
All upon a Stone. Crowell, 1971.
The American Walk Book. Dutton, 1977.
Beastly Inventions. McKay, 1970.
Bubo the Great Horned Owl. With George, John. Dutton, 1954.
Coyote in Manhattan. Crowell, 1968.
The Cry of the Crow. Harper, 1980.
Dipper of Copper Creek. Dutton, 1956.
Going to the Sun. Harper, 1976.
The Grizzly Bear with the Golden Ears. Harper, 1982.
Gull Number Seven-Three-Seven. Harper, 1964.
Hold Zero. Crowell, 1966.
The Hole in the Tree. Dutton, 1957.
Hook a Fish, Catch a Mountain. Dutton, 1975.
How to Talk to Your Animals. Harcourt, 1986.
How to Talk to Your Cat. Warner, 1986.
How to Talk to Your Dog. Warner, 1986.
Journey Inward. Dutton, 1982.
Masked Prowler. With George, John. Dutton, 1950.
Meph, the Pet Skunk. With George, John. Dutton, 1952.
The Moon of the Fox Pups. Crowell, 1968.
My Side of the Mountain. Dutton, 1959.
On the Far Side of the Mountain. Harper, 1990.

One Day in the Alpine Tundra. Harper, 1984.
One Day in the Desert. Harper, 1983.
One Day in the Prairie. Harper, 1986.
One Day in the Tropical Forest. Harper, 1990.
One Day in the Woods. Harper, 1988.
Red Robin Fly Up! Reader's Digest, 1963.
River Rats, Inc. Dutton, 1979.
Shark Beneath the Reef. Harper, 1989.
Snow Tracks. Dutton, 1958.
The Summer of the Falcon. Harper, 1962.
The Talking Earth. Harper, 1983.
The Thirteen Moons. Crowell, 1967-1969.
Vison, the Mink. With George, John. Dutton, 1949.
Vulpes the Red Fox. With George, John. Dutton, 1948.
Water Sky. Harper, 1987.
The Wentletrap Trap. Dutton, 1977.
Who Really Killed Cock Robin? Dutton, 1971.
The Wild, Wild Cookbook. Harper, 1982.
The Wounded Wolf. Harper, 1978.

Book Awards and Recommendations

American Library Association: *Gull Number Seven-Three-Seven, All upon a Stone, Julie of the Wolves*
IRA Children's Choice: *All upon a Sidewalk, The Wounded Wolf*
Newbery Medal: *Julie of the Wolves*
Newbery Honor Award: *My Side of the Mountain*

Summaries of Selected Titles

Julie of the Wolves

■■■■■■■■■■■□

See pages 60 and 128.

My Side of the Mountain

■■■■■■□□□□□□

See page 74.

The Summer of the Falcon

■■■■■■■■□□□□

In *My Side of the Mountain* we learned a lot about falconry. Now Ms. George concentrates on this magnificent creature. June is given a falcon that offers her escape and then strength to cope with the reality of her own growing up.

The Talking Earth

■■■■■■■■■□□□□□

See page 74.

Who Really Killed Cock Robin?

■■■■■■■■■□□□□□

When the mayor of Saddleboro finds his beloved robin killed by some unidentified pollution, he and the townspeople are alarmed. Two children decide to investigate, and as they learn, we are given the opportunity to absorb a great deal of ecological information.

The Wounded Wolf

■■■■■■■■■□□□□□

Roko the wolf is crippled and separated from his pack on the Arctic ridge. Surrounded by predators, Roko's life is saved by Kiglo, the leader of the wolf pack.

Jamie Gilson

| Author |
| Living |

Biography

Jamie Gilson reads a lot. When she was young, her favorite books were *Caddie Woodlawn, The Wonderful Wizard of Oz,* and *Homer Price.* Her father was a flour miller and they moved a lot, to Beardstown, Illinois, Boonville, Missouri, Pittsfield, Illinois, and Independence, Missouri. She wore out library cards because she used them so much. She wanted to be an actress and studied speech and drama at Northwestern University. Ms. Gilson taught speech and English in a junior high. She then directed and wrote for radio and for Encyclopedia Britannica Films. It wasn't until she married and had children that she decided to write for children. Because her own children liked funny books, she decided to write funny books. *Harvey, the Beer Can King* was inspired by a boy who lived on their street and had collected 1,000 beer cans. Ms. Gilson gets most of her ideas for books from watching and talking to the kids in her town. She usually writes stories with a classroom and/or small town setting.

Books by Jamie Gilson

Can't Catch Me, I'm the Gingerbead Man. Lothrop, 1981.
Do Bananas Chew Gum? Lothrop, 1980.
Double Dog Dare. Lothrop, 1988.
4B Goes Wild. Lothrop, 1983.
Harvey, the Beer Can King. Lothrop, 1978.
Hello, My Name is Scrambled Eggs. Lothrop, 1985.
Hobie Hanson, You're Weird. Lothrop, 1987.
Thirteen Ways to Sink a Sub. Lothrop, 1982.

Summaries of Selected Titles

Do Bananas Chew Gum?

■■■■■■□□□□□□□

Sam Mott thinks he's dumb. He can only read and write at the second grade level and he's in sixth grade. It isn't until he decides to cooperate with people who claim they can help him that any progress is made.

Double Dog Dare

■■■■■■□□□□□□□

Hobie Hanson goes to a school that has a program for talented and gifted students. When Hobie's best friend Nick is chosen for the program, the friendship undergoes a terrible strain.

4B Goes Wild

■■■■■■□□□□□□□

It's Hobie Hanson again. This time he's telling of a time his fourth grade class went camping for three days in the country.

Hello, My Name Is Scrambled Eggs

■■■■■■□□□□□□□

Harvey's home is opened to a Vietnamese family their church is sponsoring. Harvey decides to make Tuan, the twelve-year-old, his project for Americanization.

Hobie Hanson, You're Weird

■■■■■■□□□□□□□

In the third book in the Hobie series, Hobie is facing a dull summer without his friend, Nick, who's off to computer camp. Molly is around, however, and she's got her own brand of weird.

Paul Goble

Author/Illustrator
Living
Visits schools
Answers letters
Mailing address:
Macmillan Children's Book Group
866 Third Avenue
New York, NY 10022
212-702-9063

Biography

Although his books are about Native Americans, Paul Goble is not one. While he was living in England, he visited America and attended dances and ceremonies of the Native Americans. He was disappointed to see many young people who were not particularly interested in their own culture. He wanted them to feel proud of their heritage and to help the older people of the tribes remember their past and share it with the children. His illustrations are stylized and often contain repeating shapes and patterns. Paul Goble now lives in the Black Hills of South Dakota with his wife, Janet, and their son, Robert.

Books by Paul Goble

Beyond the Ridge. Bradbury, 1989.
Buffalo Woman. Bradbury, 1984.
Death of the Iron Horse. Bradbury, 1987.
Dream Wolf. (Originally *The Friendly Wolf.*) Bradbury, 1990.
The Gift of the Sacred Dog. Bradbury, 1980.
The Girl Who Loved Wild Horses. Bradbury, 1978.
The Great Race of the Birds and Animals. Bradbury, 1985.
Her Seven Brothers. Bradbury, 1988.
Iktomi and the Berries. Orchard, 1989.
Iktomi and the Boulder. Orchard, 1988.
Lone Bull's Horse Raid. Bradbury, 1973.
Star Boy. Bradbury, 1983.

Book Awards and Recommendations
American Library Association: *The Girl Who Loved Wild Horses, Buffalo Woman, Iktomi and the Boulder*
Caldecott Medal: *The Girl Who Loved Wild Horses*
IRA Children's Choice: *The Girl Who Loved Wild Horses, Star Boy, Her Seven Brothers*

School Library Journal: *Buffalo Woman, Her Seven Brothers, Iktomi and the Boulder*

Summaries of Selected Titles
Buffalo Woman

See page 53.

Dream Wolf

Two Native American children wander off and are lead home by a friendly wolf.

The Girl Who Loved Wild Horses

A Native American girl communicates with horses. During a storm, the girl and the horses are driven far from the tribe. The next day, a beautiful stallion, the leader of the wild horses, asks her to live with the horses.

The Great Race of the Birds and Animals

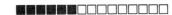

The Creator wants to help people escape from the tyranny of the buffalo, so he stages a race among the animals. The animals side with the buffalo because they have four legs and the birds side with the people because they have two. The magpie sits on a buffalo's back. One by one the animals drop out until only a young man and the buffalo with the magpie on its back are left. When the young man falls far behind, the magpie flies on to win the race for the two-legged ones.

Iktomi and the Berries

Iktomi is the trickster of Plains Indian folklore; however, he is often called by different names. He may be related to Anansi of African folklore. This story is told with room for participation by the audience as the Native American storytellers might have told it.

Virginia Hamilton

Author
Living

Biography

Virginia Hamilton was born and raised on a small farm in Yellow Springs, Ohio. Yellow Springs was a station on the Underground Railroad. Her mother was the daughter of a runaway slave. Virginia comes from a family of storytellers, and their stories influenced her writing. Ms. Hamilton is married to poet Arnold Adoff and has two children.

Books by Virginia Hamilton

Anthony Burns: The Defeat and Triumph of a Fugitive Slave. Knopf, 1988.
Arilla Sun Down. Greenwillow, 1976.
The Bells of Christmas. Harcourt, 1990.
The Dark Way: Stories from the Spirit World. Harcourt, 1990.
Dustland. Greenwillow, 1980.
The Gathering. Greenwillow, 1981.
The House of Dies Drear. Macmillan, 1969.
In the Beginning: Creation Stories from Around the World. Harcourt, 1988.
Jahdu. Greenwillow, 1980.
Junius Over Far. Harper, 1985.
Justice and Her Brothers. Greenwillow, 1978.
A Little Love. Philomel, 1984.
The Magical Adventures of Pretty Pearl. Harper, 1983.
M.C. Higgins, The Great. Macmillan, 1975.
The Mystery of Drear House. Greenwillow, 1987.
Paul Robeson: The Life and Times of a Free Black Man. Harper, 1974.
The People Could Fly: American Black Folk Tales. Knopf, 1985.
The Planet of Junior Brown. Macmillan, 1971.
Sweet Whispers, Brother Rush. Philomel, 1982.
Time-Ago Lost: More Tales of Jahdu. Macmillan, 1973.
The Time-Ago Tales of Jahdu. Macmillan, 1969.
W.E.B. Du Bois: A Biography. Crowell, 1972.
A White Romance. Philomel, 1987.
Willie Bea and the Time the Martians Landed. Greenwillow, 1983.
Zeely. Macmillan, 1967.

Book Awards and Recommendations

American Library Association: *The House of Dies Drear, The Planet of Junior Brown, Arilla Sun Down, Anthony Burns, The Gathering, Sweet Whispers, Brother Rush, The Magical Adventures of Pretty Pearl, Willie Bea and the Time the Martians Landed, The People Could Fly*
Boston Globe/Horn Book Award: *M.C. Higgins, The Great, Sweet Whispers, Brother Rush, Anthony Burns*
Coretta Scott King Award: *Sweet Whispers, Brother Rush, The People Could Fly*
Newbery Medal: *M.C. Higgins, The Great*
Newbery Honor Award: *The Planet of Junior Brown, Sweet Whispers, Brother Rush, In the Beginning*
School Library Journal: *Sweet Whispers, Brother Rush, The People Could Fly, Anthony Burns*

Summaries of Selected Titles

Arilla Sun Down

■■■■■■■■■■■□□□

See page 53.

Dustland

■■■■■■■□□□□□□

This is the sequel to *Justice and Her Brothers*. All four children possess extraordinary mental powers and are propelled into the future to the bleak futuristic reality called Dustland.

The House of Dies Drear

■■■■■■■■□□□□□

When thirteen-year-old Thomas Small moves into the old house in Ohio, which is reputed to be haunted by the slaves who were once housed there, he discovers as much about himself as he does about the secrets held in the house.

Junius Over Far

His grandfather is Junius's entire heritage, so when his grandfather returns to the dangers in the Caribbean, Junius feels he must follow in spite of the loneliness, shyness, and self-delusion that combine to make the task more difficult.

Justice and Her Brothers

■■■■■■■■□□□□□□□

Eleven-year-old Justice is left with only her twin brothers for company this summer. Levi tries to protect Justice, but his twin is more dominant and is antagonistic toward Justice. Because they are able to communicate telepathically, Justice has a hard time indeed.

M.C. Higgins, the Great

■■■■■■■■■□□□□□□

M.C. Higgins dreams of saving his family home from the damage of an Ohio strip-mining slag heap but must use both folklore and superstition to achieve his aims.

The Magical Adventures of Pretty Pearl

■■■■■■■■■□□□□□□

A half-god, half-human African child travels to the United States where she lives among free blacks who have created their own separate world.

The Mystery of Drear House

■■■■■■■■□□□□□□□

Thomas Small and his family are living in the Drear house, once part of the Underground Railroad, with all its secret rooms and passages and even an awesome treasure.

The People Could Fly

■■■■□□□□□□□□□□□

See page 19.

The Planet of Junior Brown

■■■■■■■■■□□□□□□

Buddy Clark is a leader among the homeless children he runs with in New York and takes on the task of protecting his emotionally disturbed friend, Junior Brown, who has been playing hooky from school all year.

Willie Bea and the Time the Martians Landed

■■■■■■■■■□□□□□□

Here is the effect on one black family living in Ohio in 1938 of Orson Welles' famous broadcast of "The War of the Worlds."

Zeely

■■■■■■■■□□□□□□□

Zeely Taylor is a magnificent, stately, and tall Black woman and Geeder thinks she looks like a magazine picture of a Watusi queen. Getting to know her takes some doing for this eleven-year-old girl, but when she does, she finds Zeely is less and more than she appears.

James Howe

Author
Living
Visits schools
Answers letters
Mailing address:
Children's Marketing
Macmillan Publishing
866 3rd Avenue
New York, NY 10022
212-702-9063

Biography

James Howe, a tall and very friendly man, loves puns. When he was little, he wanted to be an actor. He tried acting when he left college and decided he liked to eat better than he liked to act. After working for the welfare department in New York City for a while, he went to work in a literary office. He took a course on writing plays and then wrote *Bunnicula*. He lives with his wife, Betsy Imershein, in a quiet neighborhood in Hastings-on-Hudson, a few miles north of New York City. To write his books, he uses a word processor in a studio lined with books and pictures and rabbits made of cloth and pottery. He carries notebooks with him all the time so that he can quickly jot down any ideas. His acting experience helps him with dialogue in his books.

Books by James Howe

Annie Joins the Circus. Random, 1982.
Babes in Toyland. Harcourt, 1986.
Bunnicula: A Rabbit Tale of Mystery. With Howe, Deborah. Athenuem, 1979.
Carol Burnett: The Sound of Laughter. Viking, 1987.
The Case of the Missing Mother. Random, 1983.
The Celery Stalks at Midnight. Atheneum, 1983.
The Day the Teacher Went Bananas. Dutton, 1984.
Dew Drop Dead. Atheneum, 1990.
Eat Your Poison, Dear. Atheneum, 1986.
The Fright Before Christmas. Morrow, 1988.
The Hospital Book. Crown, 1981.
How the Ewoks Saved the Trees. Random, 1984.
Howliday Inn. Atheneum, 1982.

I Wish I Were a Butterfly. Harcourt, 1987.
A Love Not for Baby Piggy. Marvel, 1986.
Morgan's Zoo. Atheneum, 1984.
Mister Tinker in Oz. Random, 1985.
The Muppet Guide to Magnificent Manners. Random, 1984.
A Night Without Stars. Atheneum, 1983.
Nighty-Nightmare. Atheneum, 1987.
Pinky and Rex. Atheneum, 1990.
Pinky and Rex Get Married. Atheneum, 1990.
Scared Silly. Morrow, 1980.
The Secret Garden (retelling). Random, 1987.
Stage Fright. Atheneum, 1986.
Teddy Bear's Scrapbook. With Howe, Deborah. Atheneum, 1980.
There's a Monster Under My Bed. Atheneum, 1986.
What Eric Knew. Atheneum, 1985.
When You Go to Kindergarten. Knopf, 1986.

Book Awards and Recommendations

American Library Association: *Bunnicula, The Hospital Book*
Boston Globe/Horn Book Honor Award: *The Hospital Book*
IRA Children's Choice: *Bunnicula, Nighty-Nightmare, What Eric Knew*
School Library Journal: *The Hospital Book*

Summaries of Selected Titles

Bunnicula

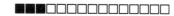

See page 25.

The Celery Stalks at Midnight

Chester the Cat discovers that Bunnicula the vampire rabbit has vanished from his cage. Everybody knows that victims of vampires turn into vampires, so Harold and Chester must save the neighborhood vegetables from becoming zombies.

Dew Drop Dead

David, Carrie, and Sebastian discover a dead body that disappears before the police arrive, and that's just the beginning of this entertaining mystery.

Howliday Inn

The family leaves Chester and Harold in a kennel. Bunnicula has been seen in the area and suddenly animals disappear and strange howls are heard at night. Again, Chester and Harold must act.

A Night Without Stars

Maria finds the people who are preparing her for open-heart surgery something less than helpful: her parents simply soothing and the medical personnel impressed with their own knowledge but not very good at transmitting it to Maria. It is Donald, a badly burned fellow patient whom the other children call Monster Man, who helps her through the night before her operation, the night without stars. After the surgery, Donald shares his poetry with her but turns surly again when Maria prepares to leave.

Mollie Hunter

Author
Living

Biography

Mollie Hunter was born in East Lothian of a Scottish mother and an Irish father. She lives in Scotland near Inverness with her husband Michael. She loves to write, garden, and tell stories to her grandchildren. She also likes music, theater, exercise, dogs, traveling, and coming home. She has been in a movie and has published several one-act plays. She says she never wanted to be anything but a writer.

Books by Mollie Hunter

Cat, Herself. Harper, 1986.
Escape from Loch Leven. Canongate, 1987.
The Ferlie. Funk & Wagnalls, 1986.
A Furl of Fairy Wind. Harper, 1977.
The Ghosts of Glencoe. Funk & Wagnalls, 1969.
The Haunted Mountain. Harper, 1972.
Hi, Johnny. Evans, 1963.
Hold On to Love. Harper, 1984.
The Kelpie's Pearls. Harper, 1976.
The Knight of the Golden Plain. Harper, 1983.
The Lothian Run. Funk & Wagnalls, 1970.
The Mermaid Summer. Harper, 1988.
A Pistol in Greenyards. Funk & Wagnalls, 1968.
The Smartest Man in Ireland. Funk & Wagnalls, 1965.
A Sound of Chariots. Harper, 1972.
The Spanish Letters. Funk & Wagnalls, 1967.
A Stranger Came Ashore. Harper, 1975.
The Stronghold. Harper, 1974.
The Third Eye. Harper, 1979.
The 13th Member. Harper, 1970.
The Three-Day Enchantment. Harper, 1985.
Thomas and the Warlock. Funk & Wagnalls, 1968.
The Walking Stones. Harper, 1970.
The Wicked One. Harper, 1977.
You Never Knew Her as I Did! Harper, 1981.

Book Awards and Recommendations

American Library Association: *The Haunted Mountain, A Sound of Chariots, A Stranger Came Ashore, The Wicked One, Cat, Herself*
Boston Globe/Horn Book Honor Award: *A Stranger Came Ashore*
IRA Children's Choice: *A Sound of Chariots*
School Library Journal: *A Stranger Came Ashore*

Summaries of Selected Titles

A Furl of Fairy Wind

The book contains four stories: the first is about a Scottish brownie; the second is about a boy entering the fairy world; the third is about the relationship between a peddler and a fairy woman; and the fourth has a furl of fairy wind bringing a smile to the lips of a girl who had forgotten how to smile.

The Knight of the Golden Plain

Here is a tongue-in-cheek, virtuous-knight-and-damsel-in-distress story in which the brave knight must slay dragons, rout witches, rescue the lovely Dorabella, and defeat the evil demon Arriman.

The Mermaid Summer

See pages 68 and 137.

A Sound of Chariots

Bridie McShane's only solace after the death of her father seems to be her writing. Putting thoughts into poetry helps, but Bridie must also face the fact of her own mortality.

A Stranger Came Ashore

See pages 68 and 156.

The Three-Day Enchantment

In this sequel to *The Knight of the Golden Plain* a boy's daydream transforms him into Sir Dauntless, the fearless knight.

The Walking Stones

■■■■■■■□□□□□□□

The Bodach is said to have special powers but tells Donald that "Magic is something that happens when everything is right to happen." Surely it should happen now that the peaceful valley is about to be flooded by the engineers. This fantasy mixes ecology and magic with great mystery.

The Wicked One

■■■■■■■■■■■□□□

The monster Grollican takes pleasure in tormenting people, especially Colin Grant, a hard-working man with a fierce temper. Grollican marks Colin by rubbing a hole in his hat. Colin's son Ian, who has a crooked shoulder, feels sorry for the monster who, it is said, is too ugly to show himself. Colin and his family, except for the twins, flee to America, only to be greeted at the dock by Grollican.

E.L. Konigsburg

Author/Illustrator
Living
Visits schools
Answers letters
Mailing address:
Macmillan Children's Book Group
866 Third Avenue
New York, NY 10022
212-702-9063

Biography

Elaine Konigsburg was born in New York City and wanted to be a chemist for a long time. Then she taught biology and science. It wasn't until her children were in school that she began to write. She was inspired to write *From the Mixed-Up Files of Mrs. Basil E. Frankweiler* when she read an article about the purchase of an unknown sculpture by the Metropolitan Museum of Art. Shortly after that, her own family had a picnic during which the children complained that everything wasn't perfect, and she began to wonder how they would ever adjust to roughing it. She thought that if they ever ran away from home the Metropolitan was the only place they'd consider good enough for a hideout.

She lives in Ponte Vedra Beach, Florida, and has three children: Paul, Laurie, and Ross whom she uses for illustrations in her books. Laurie was Claudia and Ross was Jamie in *The Mixed-Up Files,* and Paul was Benjamin in *(George)*. Her husband's name is David and he is a psychologist.

Books by E.L. Konigsburg

About the B'Nai Bagels. Atheneum, 1969.
Altogether, One at a Time. Atheneum, 1971.
The Dragon in the Ghetto Caper. Dell, 1985.
Father's Arcane Daughter. Atheneum, 1976.
From the Mixed-Up Files of Mrs. Basil E. Frankweiler. Atheneum, 1967.
(George). Atheneum, 1970.
Jennifer, Hecate, Macbeth, William McKinley, and Me, Elizabeth. Atheneum, 1967.

Journey to an 800 Number. Atheneum, 1982.
A Proud Taste for Scarlet and Miniver. Atheneum, 1973.
Samuel Todd's Book of Great Colors. Atheneum, 1990.
The Second Mrs. Giaconda. Aladdin, 1975.
Throwing Shadows. Atheneum, 1979.
Up from Jericho Tel. Atheneum, 1986.

Book Awards and Recommendations

American Library Association: *From the Mixed-Up Files of Mrs. Basil E. Frankweiler, About the B'Nai Bagels, Father's Arcane Daughter, Journey to an 800 Number, Jennifer, Hecate, Macbeth, William McKinley, and Me, Elizabeth, A Proud Taste for Scarlet and Miniver, Throwing Shadows, Up from Jericho Tel*
IRA Children's Choice: *Father's Arcane Daughter, Journey to an 800 Number*
Newbery Medal: *From the Mixed-Up Files of Mrs. Basil E. Frankweiler*
Newbery Honor Award: *Jennifer, Hecate, Macbeth, William McKinley, and Me, Elizabeth*
School Library Journal: *From the Mixed-Up Files of Mrs. Basil E. Frankweiler*

Summaries of Selected Titles

About the B'Nai Bagels

A Jewish Little League team is the focus of this book in which twelve-year-old Mark Stezer faces the problems that can result when your mother is the coach.

Altogether, One at a Time

■■■■■■■□□□□□□

Here are thoughtful short stories about young children in moments of change.

From the Mixed-Up Files of Mrs. Basil E. Frankweiler

■■■■■■■□□□□□□

See pages 15 and 119.

Jennifer, Hecate, Macbeth, William McKinley, and Me, Elizabeth

■■■■□□□□□□□□□

Two girls, one black and one white, convince themselves, and a few others, that they are witches.

Journey to an 800 Number

■■■■■■■□□□□□□

Maximillian's mother is marrying an old rich man, so Max stays with his father while she's on her honeymoon. This is not the style to which Maximillian has been accustomed. His father lives in a mobile home and sells camel rides at carnivals. The carnival people manage to adapt to Max and even let him in on some of the joy of their lives.

Throwing Shadows

■■■■■■■■□□□□□

These five short stories explore the world of five young people and their relationships with others.

Lois Lowry

Author
Living
Answers letters
Mailing address:
     Children's Book Marketing
     Houghton Mifflin Company
     2 Park Street
     Boston, MA 02198

Biography

Lois Lowry lives in an apartment on Beacon Hill in Boston, Massachusetts. She worked for several years as a freelance journalist, writer, and photographer. Her first book was *A Summer to Die*. Since then she has written about twenty books. She is divorced and has four children.

Books by Lois Lowry

All About Sam. Houghton, 1988.
Anastasia Again! Houghton, 1981.
Anastasia, Ask Your Analyst. Houghton, 1984.
Anastasia at Your Service. Houghton, 1982.
Anastasia Has the Answers. Houghton, 1986.
Anastasia Krupnik. Houghton, 1979.
Anastasia on Her Own. Houghton, 1985.
Anastasia's Chosen Career. Houghton, 1987.
Autumn Street. Houghton, 1980.
Find a Stranger, Say Goodbye. Houghton, 1978.
Number the Stars. Houghton, 1989.
The One Hundredth Thing About Caroline! Houghton, 1983.
Rabble Starkey. Houghton, 1987.
A Summer to Die. Houghton, 1977.
Switcharound. Houghton, 1975.
Taking Care of Terrific. Houghton, 1983.
Us and Uncle Fraud. Houghton, 1974.
Your Move, J.P.! Houghton, 1990.

Book Awards and Recommendations

American Library Association: *A Summer to Die, Anastasia Krupnik, Autumn Street, Anastasia Again! The One Hundredth Thing About Caroline*

Boston Globe/Horn Book Award: *Rabble Starkey*
IRA Children's Choice: *A Summer to Die, Anastasia Krupn*
Newbery Medal: *Number the Stars*
School Library Journal: *Autumn Street*

Summaries of Selected Titles

Anastasia Again!

A move to the suburbs is not what twelve-year-old Anastasia wants. She likes life in Cambridge and has some very stereotypical ideas about suburban life. Once ensconced in her new room in a delightful Victorian house in the suburbs, however, Anastasia continues her writing career and takes up the cause of the elderly, trying to get the withdrawn lady next door to enter life again.

Anastasia, Ask Your Analyst

Anastasia has reached the age when her parents' faults are apparent. She decides that psychiatry is her only recourse but has to settle for a plaster bust of Sigmund Freud and a volume of his writings. In her journal she keeps track of her progress in psychoanalysis and her science project about gerbils.

Anastasia Krupnik

Anastasia's parents have announced that she will soon have a brother or sister. Bright, and blessed with equally bright and perceptive parents, Anastasia is a list keeper and a poet. When her teacher doesn't appreciate her poems, she visits her father's college class where she shines. When the new baby arrives, Anastasia is ready with a vindictive name for him, but at the last minute she relents and names him after his grandfather.

Anastasia On Her Own

Before Anastasia's mother leaves on a business trip, she makes careful plans for the household in her absence. Then Sam gets chicken pox, Anastasia's father's old girlfriend shows up, and Anastasia's household skills deteriorate rapidly.

Autumn Street

See page 56.

Number the Stars

See page 85.

Rabble Starkey

See page 149.

A Summer to Die

Life seems almost idyllic for Meg and her family after they move to the country so her father can write a book. Then her older sister Molly becomes ill. As the summer progresses, Molly gets weaker. Meg and her family face Molly's death, while participating in the birth of a neighbor's child.

Taking Care of Terrific

Enid Crowley, who prefers the pseudonym Cynthia, takes care of four-year-old Joshua, who prefers the pseudonym Tom Terrific. Their daily walks to Boston's Public Garden yield some strange and fascinating friendships among the street people. Eventually they organize a demonstration of twenty-four bag ladies.

Us and Uncle Fraud

Uncle Claude, their mother's younger brother, comes to visit, and father is less than thrilled. Even their mother, who loves him, tells Claude to stop telling the children such outlandish tales. Shortly after he leaves, silver is missing from a nearby mansion he and the children visited. A flood nearly kills Tom, the oldest brother, but also results in the discovery of the man who really stole the silver and the recognition that Claude did leave them a valuable gift of love and a sense of family.

Your Move, J. P.!

J. P. Tate is in love with Angela, the beautiful new seventh grader from England. To win her attention, he lies. Unfortunately, one lie leads to another and soon he's claiming to be the victim of a rare and incurable disease. Angela's father is a doctor and she's sure he can cure J. P.

Patricia MacLachlan

Author
Living

Biography

Patricia MacLachlan grew up in Cheyenne, Wyoming, in a home where everybody read a lot, to themselves and to each other. She also loved music and still does. She went to the University of Connecticut where she married Robert MacLachlan, a psychologist and, after her three children were born, she began to write informational articles about adoption and foster parents. One of her early books, *Mama One, Mama Two,* came from this experience.

Before she began writing children's books, she read them—sometimes thirty to forty books a week. She says she is like Cassie in *Cassie Binegar* because she spent hours as a child hiding and eavesdropping. Aunt Elda and Uncle Wrisby in *Arthur, For the Very First Time* are based on her parents. *Sarah, Plain and Tall* was inspired by her family's history and by a trip she took with her husband and children to the prairie where she was born. She has two homes: one in Leeds, Massachusetts, and the other on Cape Cod.

Books by Patricia MacLachlan

Arthur, For the Very First Time. Harper, 1980.
Cassie Binegar. Harper, 1982.
The Facts and Fictions of Minna Pratt. Harper, 1988.
Mama One, Mama Two. Harper, 1982.
Moon, Stars, Frogs and Friends. Pantheon, 1980.
Sarah, Plain and Tall. Harper, 1985.
Seven Kisses in a Row. Harper, 1983.
The Sick Day. Pantheon, 1979.
Through Grandpa's Eyes. Harper, 1980.
Tomorrow's Wizard. Harper, 1982.
Unclaimed Treasures. Harper, 1984.

Book Awards and Recommendations

American Library Association: *Arthur, For the Very First Time, Unclaimed Treasures, Sarah, Plain and Tall, The Facts and Fictions of Minna Pratt*
Boston Globe/Horn Book Honor Award: *Unclaimed Treasures*
IRA Children's Choice: *Sarah, Plain and Tall*
Newbery Medal: *Sarah, Plain and Tall*
School Library Journal: *Sarah, Plain and Tall*
Scott O'Dell Award: *Sarah, Plain and Tall*

Summaries of Selected Titles
Arthur For the Very First Time

■■■■■□□□□□□□□

See pages 32 and 94.

Cassie Binegar

■■■■□□□□□□□□□

See pages 12 and 105.

The Facts and Fictions of Minna Pratt

■■■■■■■□□□□□□

See page 43.

Sarah, Plain and Tall

■■■■■□□□□□□□□

See page 83.

Seven Kisses in a Row

■■■■■■□□□□□□□

Emma's parents leave her with Aunt Evelyn and Uncle Elliot while they go to a conference, and she is not happy about it. For one thing, her aunt and uncle don't know anything about children, and they refuse to adhere to her customs. Furthermore, they have strange rules about everything. Things become pretty tense by the time Emma discovers that they are expecting a baby and, obviously, she has to teach them all she knows.

Through Grandpa's Eyes

■■■■■□□□□□□□□

Grandpa has much to teach John about the world around him even though Grandpa is blind. The two are kindred spirits and enjoy life together.

Tomorrow's Wizard

■■■■■■□□□□□□□

Here are six short stories with the same characters—a wizard, his apprentice, and a horse—trying to fill the wishes of humans who inhabit the villages.

Walter Dean Myers

Author
Living
Visits schools
Answers letters
Mailing address:
    Viking Penguin
    40 West 23rd Street
    New York, NY 10010
    212-337-5417

Biography

Growing up poor and Black in the care of foster parents was not the tragic experience it might have been for Walter Dean Myers. His foster parents loved him and he felt loved and secure. His foster father could not read or write, but his foster mother had taught herself to read and she read to Walter often. School was harder for him. He had a severe speech problem that made him angry and frustrated and the butt of classroom jokes. One teacher encouraged him to write and he began writing poetry with words that were easy for him to pronounce so that he could read it aloud in class. Even with that success, he hated school and dropped out when he was in high school to enter the Army.

After his discharge he worked in a factory, in a mail room, and unloaded trucks at the post office. He finally realized he needed an education in order to get anywhere so he finished high school and some college. All that time, he was writing. He says he wanted to be somebody but didn't think of himself as a writer, even though some of his poetry had been published. He entered a contest for minority writers of picture books, submitting his first book *Where Does the Day Go?* He won the contest and became an editor for a publishing company. When he was laid off, he went back to writing. Since then he has written over thirty books, mostly novels. He is married and has three children and three grandchildren.

Books by Walter Dean Myers

Adventure in Granada. Viking, 1985.
Ambush in the Amazon. Penguin, 1986.
The Black Pearl and the Ghost. Viking, 1980.
Brainstorm. Watts, 1977.
Crystal. Viking, 1987.
The Dancers. Parents', 1972.
The Dragon Takes a Wife. Merrill, 1972.
Duel in the Desert. Viking, 1986.
Fallen Angels. Scholastic, 1988.
Fast Sam, Cool Clyde, and Stuff. Viking, 1975.
Fly, Jimmy, Fly! Putnam, 1974.
The Golden Serpent. Viking, 1980.
The Hidden Shrine. Viking, 1986.
Hoops. Delacorte, 1981.
It Ain't All for Nothin'. Viking, 1978.
The Legend of Tarik. Viking, 1981.
Me, Mop, and the Moondance Kid. Delacorte, 1988.
Mojo and the Russians. Viking, 1977.
The Mouse Rap. Harper, 1990.
Motown and Didi: A Love Story. Viking, 1984.
Mr. Monkey and the Gotcha Bird. Delacorte, 1984.
The Nicholas Factor. Viking, 1983.
The Outside Shot. Delacorte, 1984.
Scorpions. Harper, 1988.
Shadow of the Red Moon. Harper, 1987.
Tales of a Dead King. Morrow, 1983.
Victory for Jamie. Scholastic, 1977.
Where Does the Day Go? Parents', 1969.
Won't Know Till I Get There. Viking, 1982.
The Young Landlords. Viking, 1979.

Book Awards and Recommendations

American Library Association: *Fast Sam, Cool Clyde, and Stuff, It Ain't All for Nothin', The Young Landlords, Fallen Angels, Scorpions*

Coretta Scott King Award: *The Young Landlords, Motown and Didi, Fallen Angels*

IRA Children's Choice: *Fast Sam, Cool Clyde, and Stuff*

Newbery Honor Award: *Scorpions*

School Library Journal: *Fallen Angels*

Summaries of Selected Titles

Fast Sam, Cool Clyde, and Stuff

■■■■■■■■■■□□□□

Stuff, now a mature eighteen, recalls his thirteenth year, hanging around on 116th Street and being part of a wonderful threesome, which came face to face with a dope ring.

Me, Mop, and the Moondance Kid

■■■■■■■□□□□□□□

The Moondance Kid is Billy, younger brother of eleven-year-old T. J. They've been living with their adoptive parents for several months now and things seem to be going well. Their concern is for Mop, their friend, who has not yet been adopted and who is in danger of being sent to a distant orphanage. Mop has a plan, however, involving a Little League team and its coach who just may be in the market for a little girl.

Mojo and the Russians

■■■■■■□□□□□□□□

See page 56.

The Mouse Rap

■■■■■■■■■■■□□□

See page 39.

The Scorpions

■■■■■■■■■■■□□□

Gang pressure is the predominant force in this book in which Jamal Hicks is forced to take the place of his gang leader brother who is in prison for armed robbery. Before his term as leader is over, Jamal has learned a lot about loyalty, danger, and guns.

The Young Landlords

■■■■■■■■■■□□□□

Paul Williams and his friends have an unusual opportunity when they become landlords of a run down building in an undesirable neighborhood. Convinced that they can do it right, the group finds that simple solutions are not so simple and that it's easier to dream up solutions than to realize them.

Katherine Paterson

| Author |
| Living |

Biography

Katherine Paterson was born in China where her parents were missionaries. Chinese was her first language, but she has since forgotten most of it. She came to the United States for the first time when she was five-years-old but only stayed for one year. In China, she lived in a Chinese house while her father traveled the countryside taking food and medicine to people. After she grew up, she lived in Japan for four years, returning to America in 1962. Ms. Paterson studied to become a minister in order to return to Japan but she never did. She has four children. Her husband does stained glass work.

Books by Katherine Paterson

Angels and Other Strangers. Crowell, 1979.
Come Sing, Jimmy Jo. Lodestar, 1985.
The Great Gilly Hopkins. Crowell, 1978.
Jacob Have I Loved. Crowell, 1980.
The Master Puppeteer. Crowell, 1976.
Of Nightingales That Weep. Crowell, 1974.
The Sign of the Chrysanthemum. Crowell, 1973.
Park's Quest. Lodestar, 1988.
Rebels of the Heavenly Kingdom. Lodestar, 1983.

Book Awards and Recommendations

American Library Association: *The Master Puppeteer, The Great Gilly Hopkins, Jacob Have I Loved, Come Sing, Jimmy Jo, Bridge to Terabithia, Of Nightingales That Weep*
IRA Children's Choice: *Come Sing, Jimmy Jo, Park's Quest*
Newbery Medal: *Bridge to Terabithia, Jacob Have I Loved*
Newbery Honor Award: *The Great Gilly Hopkins*
School Library Journal: *Bridge to Terabithia, Jacob Have I Loved, Come Sing, Jimmy Jo*

Summaries of Selected Titles

Angels and Other Strangers

■■■■■■■□□□□□□□

Each of the characters in these stories is touched by the Christmas miracle.

Bridge to Terabithia

■■■■■■■■□□□□□□

See page 101.

Come Sing, Jimmy Jo

■■■■■■■■■■□□□□

See pages 43 and 109.

The Great Gilly Hopkins

■■■■■■■■■■□□□□

Gilly is the latest foster child to arrive at the Trotters' home. Intelligent but bratty, Gilly is convinced that her natural mother, Courtney Rutherford Hopkins, will take her back and so she contrives to keep others at a distance. She is not as successful at school in doing this. Her new teacher, Miss Harris, is cool and not easily ruffled or taken in by Gilly's schemes. Gilly steals from a blind man Mr. Randolph and from Mrs. Trotter, hoping to use the money to escape to San Francisco. Caught and returned to the Trotters, Gilly begins to return the love. After she is "rescued" by her maternal grandmother, Gilly longs to return to the Trotters but she can't and doesn't.

Jacob Have I Loved

■■■■■■■■■■■■■□

Everyone loves Caroline, Louise's selfish younger sister. Isolated on a tiny Chesapeake Bay island, Louisa feels that Caroline has robbed her of friends, her mother, and her dreams. Louise learns the ways of the island but soon realizes that she must find her own identity.

The Master Puppeteer

■■■■■■■■■■■□□□

See page 39.

Of Nightingales That Weep

■■■■■■■■■■■■■■□

A famous Samurai warrior's daughter, Takiko, is taken into the court of the boy emperor, Antoku, as his musician and personal servant. War rages around them as Takiko learns to accept her grotesque stepfather, the luxury of the court, and the love of a young man.

Park's Quest

■■■■■■■■■■■□□□□

See page 87.

The Sign of the Chrysanthemum

■■■■■■■■■■■■■■□

See page 153.

Gary Paulsen

Author
Living
Visits schools
Answers letters
Mailing address:
    Macmillan Children's Book Group
    866 Third Avenue
    New York, NY 10022
    212-702-9063

Biography

Gary Paulsen lives on a farm in an isolated area south of Bemidji, Minnesota, with his wife Ruth, who is a painter, and his son Jim. Ruth paints in a studio they made out of a hog barn. Gary Paulsen has participated three times in the Iditarod race, a 1,049 mile dogsled race from Anchorage to Nome, Alaska. He's been attacked by moose and dragged by his dogs. He's fallen through ice and believed he was dying. His book *Dogsong* came from some of those experiences. He had a pack of 37 dogs, all but one of which he sold. He kept Cookie, the lead dog, as a pet.

He once had a real problem with alcoholism and he even tried to commit suicide. Then, fifteen years ago, he quit drinking and began writing children's books. His favorite work is *Sentries.*

About Gary Paulsen's Work

- ☐ Some of Mr. Paulsen's books center around one character, who is self-indulgant and without apparent ability, isolated in an alien environment and forced to develop new attitudes and skills in order to survive. Most of his characters come to a self-awareness through nature.
- ☐ His characters seem to use survival as a rite of passage and, having survived, seem able to take on a "manly" role in society.
- ☐ There is often an older character with an obvious weakness whom the lead character must depend on. That older character lives up to expectations.
- ☐ Mr. Paulsen says that his characters "aren't faced with easy, answerable questions, but some find inner peace." He has the ability to propel a plot with little or no dialogue.

Books by Gary Paulsen

The Boy Who Owned the School. Orchard, 1990.
The C.B. Radio Caper. Raintree, 1977.
The Crossing. Orchard, 1987.
The Curse of the Cobra. Raintree, 1977.
Dancing Carl. Bradbury, 1983.
Dogsong. Bradbury, 1985.
Downhill, Hotdogging, and Cross-Country. Raintree, 1979.
Facing off, Checking, and Goaltending. Raintree, 1979.
Forehanding and Backhanding. Raintree, 1978.
Going Very Fast in a Circle. Raintree, 1979.
The Golden Stick. Raintree, 1977.
The Green Recruit. Independence, 1978.
Hatchet. Bradbury, 1987.
Hitting, Pitching, and Running. Raintree, 1976.
Hope and a Hatchet. Nelson, 1978.
The Island. Orchard, 1988.
Launching, Floating High, and Landing. Raintree, 1979.
Martin Luther King, The Man Who Climbed the Mountain. Raintree, 1976.
Mr. Tucket. Funk & Wagnalls, 1969.
The Night the White Deer Died. Nelson, 1978.
Popcorn Days and Buttermilk Nights. Lodestar, 1983.
Pummeling, Falling, and Getting Up. Raintree, 1979.
Riding, Roping, and Bulldogging. Raintree, 1977.
Running, Jumping, and Throwing. Raintree, 1978.
Sentries. Bradbury, 1986.
The Spitball Gang. Elsevier, 1980.
Tackling, Running, and Kicking. Raintree, 1977.
Tiltawhirl John. Nelson, 1977.
Track, Enduro, and Motocross. Raintree, 1979.
Tracker. Bradbury, 1983.
The Voyage of the Frog. Orchard, 1988.
The Winter Room. Orchard, 1989.
Winterkill. Nelson, 1977.

Book Awards and Recommendations

American Library Association: *Dancing Carl, Tracker, Dogsong, The Crossing, Hatchet, The Island*
Newbery Honor Award: *Dogsong, Hatchet, The Winter Room*
School Library Journal: *Dogsong*

Summaries of Selected Titles

The Crossing

■■■■■■■■□□□□□□

Manny's tough and he has to be. Mere survival in this town near the Mexican border takes every skill he can muster and crossing the border seems his only hope. To do so, however, he must team up with a weird American soldier.

Hatchet

■■■■■■■□□□□□□□

See pages 75 and 123.

The Island

■■■■■■■■■■■■□□

See page 32.

Popcorn Days and Buttermilk Nights

■■■■■■■□□□□□□□

See page 146.

The Voyage of the Frog

■■■■■■■■■■□□□□

See pages 60 and 166.

The Winter Room

■■■■■■■□□□□□□□

This book is different than most of Paulsen's other work. It is the story of an extended family on a farm in the north country. Eldon describes his life on the farm through the year, letting you feel the seasons and the rhythms of the farm. The killing of the farm animals for food is also described in all its harshness. The family's hard day's work often ends with a story from Uncle David. David's stories are sometimes terrible and sometimes funny, but the story about the great woodsman who could light a match with his axe is the last straw for Wayne. Wayne calls David a liar, and David doesn't tell stories again until he proves the truth of the tale.

Robert Newton Peck

Author
Living

Biography
Robert Newton Peck grew up in Vermont in a home where the Bible was the main reading material. He has been a farmer, soldier, football player, lumberjack, paper mill worker, hog butcher, and advertising executive. He writes songs and television commercials. Mr. Peck married a librarian, Dorrie, in 1958. Fred Rogers was his best man. He has two children whom he hopes will grow up to have "a tough gut and a gentle heart."

About Robert Newton Peck's Work
☐ Mr. Peck's work is often hilarious. His characters, particularly Soup, are believable and yet they dare to do what most of us only dream of doing.

Books by Robert Newton Peck
Arly. Walker, 1989.
Banjo. Knopf, 1982.
Basket Case. Doubleday, 1979.
Bee Tree and Other Stuff. Walker, 1975.
Clunie. Knopf, 1979.
A Day No Pigs Would Die. Knopf, 1972.
Dukes. Pineapple, 1984.
Hallapoosa. Walker, 1988.
Hamilton. Little, 1976.
Hang for Treason. Doubleday, 1976.
The Horse Hunters. Random, 1988.
Hub. Knopf, 1979.
I Am the King of Kazoo. Knopf, 1976.
Jo Silver. Pineapple, 1985.
Justice Lion. Little, 1981.
Kirk's Law. Doubleday, 1981.
Last Sunday. Doubleday, 1977.
Millie's Boy. Knopf, 1973.
Mr. Little. Doubleday, 1979.
My Vermont. Peck, 1987.
My Vermont II. Peck, 1988.
Patooie. Knopf, 1977.
Rabbits and Redcoats. Walker, 1976.
The Seminole Seed. Pineapple, 1983.
Soup. Knopf, 1974.
Soup and Me. Knopf, 1975.
Soup for President. Knopf, 1978.
Soup in the Saddle. Knopf, 1983.
Soup on Fire. Delacorte, 1987.
Soup on Ice. Knopf, 1985.
Soup on Wheels. Knopf, 1981.
Soup's Drum. Knopf, 1980.
Soup's Hoop. Delacorte, 1989.
Soup's Uncle. Delacorte, 1988.
Spanish Hoff. Knopf, 1985.
Trig. Little, 1977.
Trig Goes Ape. Little, 1980.
Trig or Treat. Little, 1982.
Trig Sees Red. Little, 1978.
Wild Cat. Holiday, 1975.

Book Awards and Recommendations
American Library Association: *A Day No Pigs Would Die*
School Library Journal: *A Day No Pigs Would Die*

Summaries of Selected Titles
A Day No Pigs Would Die

■■■■■■■■■■■☐☐☐

While accepting the love and responsibility for a pig, Rob comes to terms with his Shaker father and learns to accept the reality and the beauty of life on the Vermont farm. An extremely sensitive book, it also contains harsh violence.

Soup

■■■■☐☐☐☐☐☐☐☐☐☐

See page 26.

Soup's Drum

■■■■■☐☐☐☐☐☐☐☐☐

Soup has met Juliet, the new girl at school, and it's love at first sight. Then Soup's old enemy, Janice Riker, sees "Soup Loves J. R" carved on a tree. Soup and Rob have to cope with Janice while finding a way to star in the Fourth of July parade.

Soup's Hoop

Soup and Rob are determined to see their basketball team, the Groundhogs, beat their arch-rivals, the Pratt Falls Wombats. Their triumph depends on key player, Piffle Shootensinker, who can't play without music from the Spitzentootle and without being able to see his dog. Soup's got a scheme and it involves a revenge on Janice Riker as well as the winning of the game.

Trig

This is the story of a determined, pigtailed, bespectacled young lady, unhappy with her treatment by two neighborhood boys. In spite of their actions, Trig tries to find a way to be friends.

Willo Davis Roberts

Author
Living
Visits schools
Answers letters
Mailing address:
    Macmillan Children's Book Group
    866 Third Avenue
    New York, NY 10022
    212-702-9063

Biography

Willo Davis Roberts lives in Washington with her husband David, who is also a writer, and an Airedale named Susie. Their grown children also write. They have two grandsons and four granddaughters. She was born in Michigan and has been writing since she was nine. Ms. Roberts has published over seventy books, many of which are for adults. Besides writing, she likes to take long walks along the Stillaguamish River near her home, read, knit and play the organ. The couple has a motor home with a built in office so that they can travel and work at the same time. She writes with a word processor. She wrote her first book for children, *The View from the Cherry Tree,* while her own family was going through the turmoil of her daughter's big formal wedding. Although nobody witnessed a murder, most of the other events in the story really happened.

Books by Willo Davis Roberts

Baby-Sitting is a Dangerous Job. Atheneum, 1985.
Caroline. Scholastic, 1984.
Don't Hurt Laurie! Atheneum, 1977.
Eddie and the Fairy Godpuppy. Atheneum, 1984.
The Girl with the Silver Eyes. Atheneum, 1980.
The Magic Book. Atheneum, 1986.
Megan's Island. Atheneum, 1988.
The Minden Curse. Atheneum, 1978.
More Minden Curses. Atheneum, 1980
The Nightmare. Atheneum, 1989.
No Monsters in the Closet. Atheneum, 1983.
The Pet-Sitting Peril. Atheneum, 1983.
Sugar Isn't Everything. Atheneum, 1987.
To Grandmother's House We Go. Atheneum, 1990.
The View from the Cherry Tree. Atheneum, 1975.
What Could Go Wrong? Atheneum, 1989.

Summaries of Selected Titles

Don't Hurt Laurie!

■■■■■■■■■□□□□□□

Laurie is being abused by her mother and she's sure that no one will believe her.

The Girl with the Silver Eyes

■■■■■■■■■□□□□□□

Blessed or cursed with the power to move things with her mind, the girl with the silver eyes, Katie, has just moved in with her divorced mother after the death of her grandmother. When she overhears that she is being blamed for her grandmother's fatal fall, Katie runs away. She knows that her mother was part of a drug experiment when her mother was pregnant with her, so Katie tracks down the other three children whose mothers were in the experiment.

The Magic Book

■■■■■■□□□□□□□□□

Alex finds an ancient book of spells at a used book sale, or maybe it finds him. In it he finds a spell that seems to be the answer to his problem of what to do about Norm Winthrop who has been bullying Alex for years.

More Minden Curses

■■■■■■■■□□□□□□

In this sequel to *The Minden Curse,* Danny is still doomed to turning up wherever funny things happen. He and Clarissa, known as C.B., set out to discover who or what is making it appear that Rosie and Anna are too infirm to remain in their mansion where it is thought their father hid lots of money.

The Pet-Sitting Peril

■■■■■■■□□□□□□□

Mike takes care of the assorted cats and dogs that belong to the tenants in his apartment building that is subject to mysterious happenings such as a suspicious fire and disappearing hall lights.

To Grandmother's House We Go

■■■■■■■■□□□□□□

The children have never met their grandmother. They know that she gave her daughters away when they were children and that both of them hate her for it. Now, with their father dead and their mother seriously ill, their distant grandmother seems to be the children's only hope of staying together. They find her surrounded by mystery.

The View from the Cherry Tree

See page 47.

What Could Go Wrong?

■■■■■■■■□□□□□□

See page 40.

Cynthia Rylant

Author
Living
Answers letters
Mailing address:
    Orchard Books
    387 Park Avenue South
    New York, NY 10016

Biography

Cynthia Rylant grew up in a small town in West Virginia and she didn't read many books because there was no library or bookstore around. Instead, she read comic books, those she bought and those she traded. It wasn't until she got to college that she really began to read. She didn't write much when as a child either, except a story in which she imagined meeting the Beatles, her favorite music group.

When she was four, her parents divorced and her mother took her to stay in the Ozarks with her grandparents for four years. *When I Was Young in the Mountains* is about that time. So are *Night in the Country, This Year's Garden* and *The Relatives Came.* Ms. Rylant missed her parents a lot at that time, but felt very safe with her grandparents.

A Blue-Eyed Daisy is also based on a time in her real life and the poems in *Waiting to Waltz* are about her from eight- to fourteen-years-old. She thinks the best writing is the kind that is most personal.

Books by Cynthia Rylant

All I See. Orchard, 1988.
Birthday Presents. Orchard, 1987.
A Blue-Eyed Daisy. Bradbury, 1985.
But I'll Be Back Again. Orchard, 1989.
Children of Christmas: Stories for the Season. Orchard, 1987.
A Couple of Kooks and Other Stories About Love. Orchard, 1990.
Every Living Thing. Bradbury, 1985.

A Fine White Dust. Bradbury, 1986.
Henry and Midge. Bradbury, 1987.
Henry and Mudge and the Happy Cat. Bradbury, 1990.
Henry and Mudge Get the Cold Shivers. Bradbury, 1989.
Henry and Mudge in Puddle Trouble. Bradbury, 1987.
Henry and Mudge in the Green Time. Bradbury, 1987.
Henry and Mudge in the Sparkle Days. Bradbury, 1988.
Henry and Mudge Under the Yellow Moon. Bradbury, 1987.
Henry and Mudge. Bradbury, 1987.
A Kindness. Orchard, 1988.
Miss Maggie. Dutton, 1983.
Mr. Griggs' Work. Orchard, 1989.
Night in the Country. Bradbury, 1986.
The Relatives Came. Bradbury, 1985.
This Year's Garden. Bradbury, 1984.
Waiting to Waltz. Bradbury, 1984.
When I Was Young in the Mountains. Dutton, 1982.

Book Awards and Recommendations
American Library Association: *When I Was Young in the Mountains, Waiting to Waltz, A Blue-Eyed Daisy, The Relatives Came, A Fine White Dust, A Kindness*
Caldecott Honor Award: *When I Was Young in the Mountains, The Relatives Came*
IRA Children's Choice: *A Blue-Eyed Daisy, Birthday Presents, All I See, Henry and Mudge in the Sparkle Days*
Newbery Honor Award: *A Fine White Dust*
School Library Journal: *Waiting to Waltz, Every Living Thing, A Fine White Dust, Night in the Country, Children of Christmas, A Kindness*

Summaries of Selected Titles

All I See

An artist with his cat come to the lake each day. On the shore, he sets up his easel and paints. After painting for a while, he and the cat lie down in a canoe on the lake and watch the sky. A child watches this behavior day after day and sneaks down to look at what the artist has painted. Each time the artist has painted whales. Eventually, the artist and the child paint together.

Birthday Presents

A child's parents remember her first six birthdays and the thing that comes through most clearly in this funny, realistic, and heart-warming book is the love she and her parents share.

A Blue-Eyed Daisy

Ellie is the youngest of five sisters and this, her twelfth year of life, is full of her love. Seven people live in a tiny house in the mountains and life isn't easy. Ellie worries about the holes in her teeth and her father's drinking since his accident in the mine, but the hope shines through for Ellie and for the others.

But I'll Be Back Again

This is Cynthia Rylant's own story of growing up in the age of the Beatles. Photographs from her own album illustrate the book and we gain some insight into Ms. Rylant's artistry.

Children of Christmas

See page 15.

Every Living Thing

These are twelve short stories about that moment when life changes forever.

A Fine White Dust

See page 115.

Miss Maggie

See page 15.

The Relatives Came

They came, all right, by the carful—full of luggage, gifts, and skads of love. The house is full now, too—full of relatives and love.

When I Was Young in the Mountains

Growing up in the coal mining region is shown from a child's point of view. It doesn't seem so grim through her eyes.

Waiting to Waltz

Here is a collection of short, pithy poems about the humor and pathos of a young girl growing up in the small town of Beaver, West Virginia.

Doris Buchanan Smith

Author
Living
Visits schools
Answers letters
Mailing address:
Viking Penguin
40 West 23rd Street
New York, NY 10010

Biography
Doris Buchanan Smith spends half of each year in a cabin in the North Carolina mountains. For the rest of the year she lives near the coast of Georgia where she has a small yard, a large house, and two great liveoak trees. She says the hardest part of being a writer is sitting down and writing. She celebrates the uniqueness of each individual in her writing and knows her characters from the inside out. Ms. Smith has five grown children and many foster children, but now she lives alone with her cat, Zephyr.

Books by Doris Buchanan Smith
The Country Life of J.B. Rabbit. Grossett, 1983.
Dreams and Drummers. Harper, 1978.
The First Hard Times. Viking, 1983.
Karate Dancer. Putnam, 1987.
Kelly's Creek. Harper, 1975.
Kick a Stone Home. Harper, 1974.
Last Was Lloyd. Viking, 1981.
Laura Upside-Down. Viking, 1984.
Moonshadow of Cherry Mountain. Four Winds, 1982.
Return to Bitter Creek. Viking, 1986.
Salted Lemons. Four Winds, 1980.
A Taste of Blackberries. Crowell, 1973.
Tough Chauncey. Penguin, 1986.
The Travels of J. B. Rabbit. Grossett, 1982.
Up and Over. Morrow, 1976.
Voyages. Viking, 1989.

Book Awards and Recommendations
American Library Association: *A Taste of Blackberries, The First Hard Times, Return to Bitter Creek*
Boston Globe/Horn Book Honor Award: *Tough Chauncey*
School Library Journal: *Last was Lloyd, Return to Bitter Creek*

Summaries of Selected Titles
The First Hard Times

In this sequel to *Last Was Lloyd,* Ancil's father is declared "missing in action," and it seems things can't get any worse. Then her mother remarries.

Kelly's Creek

Kelly has learning disabilities. His parents don't understand and refuse to let him go to his place of solace, a marsh, until his school work improves.

Last Was Lloyd

Lloyd is fat, overprotected by his mother, and the kids don't like him.

Moonshadow of Cherry Mountain

See page 9.

Return to Bitter Creek

Lacey wants to fit in with her grandparents and other relatives, but her grandmother doesn't approve of the family's living arrangements. When tragedy strikes, Lacey's behavior has to change.

Salted Lemons

See page 86.

A Taste of Blackberries

See page 157.

Voyages

See page 60.

Chris Van Allsburg

Biography

Chris Van Allsburg was born on June 18, 1949, in Grand Rapids, Michigan. He loved stamp collecting as a child until he became very sick one day and dreamed he was in a stamp. After he got well, he gave away his stamp collection. He hated board games when he was a child and wished they were more real. Perhaps that's why he wrote *Jumanji.*

About Chris Van Allsburg's Work

☐ Mr. Van Allsburg's work has a surreal quality that mystifies even as it intrigues. His perspective is often unique and dramatic with a sculptured quality. Sometimes, in *Jumanji* for instance, his perspective lets us be in two places at once. This manipulation of space creates impossible worlds.

☐ He seems more comfortable drawing objects than people and his human characters often seem skewed or strangely flattened.

☐ His landscapes seem frozen in time and he plays with light and shadow in his illustrations.

☐ Mr. Van Allsburg's plots are often bizarre and he seldom lets us assume it was just a dream.

Books by Chris Van Allsburg

Written and Illustrated by Chris Van Allsburg
Ben's Dream. Houghton, 1982.
The Garden of Abdul Gasazi. Houghton, 1979.
Jumanji. Houghton, 1981.
The Mysteries of Harris Burdick. Houghton, 1984.
The Polar Express. Houghton, 1985.
The Stranger. Houghton, 1986.

Two Bad Ants. Houghton, 1988.
The Wreck of the Zephyr. Houghton, 1983.
The Z Was Zapped. Houghton, 1987.

Illustrated by Chris Van Allsburg
Swan Lake. Helprin, Mark. Houghton, 1989.

Book Awards and Recommendations
American Library Association: *The Garden of Abdul Gasazi, Jumanji, The Wreck of the Zephyr, The Mysteries of Harris Burdick, The Polar Express, The Stranger, The Z Was Zapped*
Boston Globe/Horn Book Award: *The Garden of Abdul Gasazi, Jumanji*
Caldecott Medal: *Jumanji, The Polar Express*
Caldecott Honor Award: *The Garden of Abdul Gasazi*
IRA Children's Choice: *Two Bad Ants*

Summaries of Selected Titles
Ben's Dream

    Ben comes home to an empty house and falls asleep over his book. He awakes to find himself and his house afloat, drifting slowly by submerged monuments and landmarks.

Garden of Abdul Gasazi

    See page 15.

Jumanji

    An innocent-looking jungle gameboard turns out to be more real than is comfortable for the two children playing the game.

The Mysteries of Harris Burdick

See page 44.

Polar Express

A boy who still believes in Santa Claus is picked up by a strange train that appears where there are no tracks. The train is loaded with other children and is bound for the North Pole. Once there the children meet Santa and the boy is given the special first gift of Christmas, a silver bell from the sleigh, which he promptly loses. On Christmas morning the sleigh bell is under his Christmas tree with a note from Santa.

The Stranger

See page 15.

Two Bad Ants

A troop of ants is off in search of very special crystals that the scouts have discovered. A host of adventures await two of them who elect to remain with the crystals. We're aware that the crystals are sugar and that the ants are in the kitchen of a house. Everything is seen through the perspective of the ants. Van Allsburg's art style is different here than in any of his other books.

The Wreck of the Zephyr

The narrator finds a wrecked sailboat high on the cliffs outside a village. An old man tells a haunting tale of an overly ambitious boy determined to be the greatest sailor of them all. When he is taught to sail above the waves, even that is not enough. He must sail higher.

The Z Was Zapped

This is an alphabet book that stretches the vocabulary and the imagination. Each letter appears on a stage and is removed or destroyed by an action beginning with that letter. The picture appears alone on the page with the answer on the reverse to give you a chance to come up with your own possibilities before going to Mr. Van Allsburg's.

Cynthia Voigt

Author

Living

Visits schools

Answers letters

Mailing address:
    Macmillan Children's Book Group
    866 Third Avenue
    New York, NY 10022
    212-702-9063

Biography

Cynthia Voigt was born in Boston, Massachusetts, on February 25, 1942. She went to Smith College and now lives in Annapolis, Maryland, with her husband, two children, and a dog. Their daughter Jessica is in college. Their son Peter is in grade school. Ms. Voigt teaches at The Key School in Annapolis, Maryland. Ms. Voigt met her husband when they were teaching at the same school. They live in the city during the year and in the country during the summer.

Ms. Voigt wrote *Homecoming* after she saw a bunch of kids quietly waiting in a station wagon in a supermarket parking lot. She began to wonder what would happen if the person they were waiting for never came back.

Books by Cynthia Voigt

Building Blocks. Macmillan, 1984.
The Callender Papers. Macmillan, 1973.
Come a Stranger. Macmillan, 1986.
Dicey's Song. Atheneum, 1982.
Homecoming. Macmillan, 1981.
Izzy Willy Nilly. Macmillan, 1986.
Jackaroo. Macmillan, 1985.
On Fortune's Wheel. Atheneum, 1990.
The Runner. Macmillan, 1985.
Seventeen Against the Dealer. Atheneum, 1989.
A Solitary Blue. Macmillan, 1983.
Sons from Afar. Macmillan, 1987.
Stories about Rosie. Macmillan, 1986.
Tell Me If the Lovers Are Losers. Macmillan, 1982.
Tree by Leaf. Atheneum, 1988.

Book Awards and Recommendations

American Library Association: *Dicey's Song, A Solitary Blue*

Boston Globe/Horn Book Honor Award: *Dicey's Song, A Solitary Blue*

Edgar Allen Poe Award: *The Callender Papers*

Newbery Medal: *Dicey's Song*

Newbery Honor Award: *A Solitary Blue*

School Library Journal: *Building Blocks, Come a Stranger, Seventeen Against the Dealer*

Summaries of Selected Titles

Building Blocks

■■■■■■□□□□□□□□

Brian, who doesn't have much respect for his father, goes through a transformation in which he becomes a ten-year-old friend of his ten-year-old father.

The Callender Papers

■■■■■■■■■□□□□□

Jean, an orphan in nineteenth-century Massachusetts, is sorting the papers of an artist when he becomes intrigued by the death of the artist's wife and the disappearance of his child.

Come a Stranger

■■■■■■■■□□□□□□

Mina Smiths, a minor character in *Dicey's Song,* is the center of this story about a young black girl growing up. Mina loves ballet and attends a special ballet camp on a scholarship. The following year, however, she is not accepted because they say she has become too awkward. She wonders whether it's because she is black.

Dicey's Song

■■■■■■■■□□□□□□

In *Homecoming* Dicey led her brothers and sister from Connecticut where their mother abandoned them to Eastern Maryland where their reclusive grandmother lives. Now that mere survival is assured, Dicey and her grandmother must combine efforts to make a family.

Homecoming

■■■■■■■■□□□□□□

See page 76.

Izzy Willy Nilly

■■■■■■■■□□□□□

Fifteen-year-old Izzy loses her leg in an automobile accident and has to face not only her loss but also the way her family and friends deal with her.

Tree by Leaf

■■■■■■■□□□□□□□

Clothilde has discovered that the land and cottage in which the family lives belong to her. Her mother wants to sell it. Her father, disfigured by a wound from World War I, has become a recluse and lives nearby. In desperation, Clothilde asks "the Voice" to help her solve her problems.

Jane Yolen

Author
Living

Biography

Jane Yolen was born in New York City and now lives in Hatfield, Massachusetts, in a big, old house built at the turn of the century. Her mother made up crossword puzzles, which might explain Jane's love for words. Her father was a writer and a champion kite flyer. Ms. Yolen writes in a studio on the third floor of her house every morning until about noon. She writes using a typewriter and then edits in longhand. The next day, she re-edits her work. Her husband, David Stemple, teaches computer science at the University of Massachusetts. They have three children who are now grown up.

Ms. Yolen loves to sing. She composes songs and sings them to her own piano or guitar accompaniment. She is active in many organizations including those that work for peace. She runs a monthly writers' workshop for people who are trying to become children's authors.

Books by Jane Yolen

The Acorn Quest. Harper, 1981.
All in the Woodland Early. Philomel, 1983.
Baby Bear's Bedtime Book. Harcourt, 1990.
Best Witches. Putnam, 1989.
The Boy Who Spoke Chimp. Knopf, 1981.
Children of the Wolf. Viking, 1984.
Commander Toad and the Big Black Hole. Coward, 1983.
Commander Toad and the Planet of the Grapes. Coward, 1982.
Commander Toad in Space. Coward, 1980.
Dove Isabeau. Harcourt, 1989.
Dragon's Blood. Dell, 1984.
Dream Weaver. Philomel, 1989.
Elphabet. Little, 1990.
The Emperor and the Kite. Philomel, 1988.
The Faery Flag. Orchard, 1989.
The Giant's Farm. Clarion, 1977.
The Gift of Sarah Barker. Viking, 1981.
The Girl Who Cried Flowers. Crowell, 1974.
The Girl Who Loved the Wind. Crowell, 1972.
Heart's Blood. Delacorte, 1984.
The Hundredth Dove. Harper, 1977.

Invitation to the Butterfly Ball. Putnam, 1983.
Lullaby Songbook. Harcourt, 1986.
The Magic Three of Solatia. Crowell, 1974.
Mice on Ice. Dutton, 1980.
Milkweed Days. Crowell, 1976.
Neptune Rising. Putnam, 1982.
No Bath Tonight. Harper, 1978.
Owl Moon. Philomel, 1987.
Rainbow Rider. Harper, 1974.
The Robot and Rebecca the Missing Owser. Knopf, 1981.
The Seeing Stick. Crowell, 1977.
Shirlick Holmes and the Case of the Wandering Wardrobe. Coward, 1981.
Simple Gift. Viking, 1976.
The Simple Prince. Parents, 1978.
Sleeping Ugly. Putnam, 1981.
The Stone Silenus. Philomel, 1984.
Touch Magic. Philomel, 1981.
The Transfigured Hart. Harper, 1975.
Uncle Lemon's Spring. Dutton, 1977.

Book Awards and Recommendations

American Library Association: The Girl Who Cried Flowers
Caldecott Medal: Owl Moon
Caldecott Honor Award: The Emperor and the Kite
IRA Children's Choice: The Transfigured Hart, Mice on Ice, The Robot and Rebecca the Missing Owser

Summaries of Selected Titles
Picture Books
Best Witches

Here is a funny collection of poems about witches, including a recipe for Witch Pizza.

The Emperor and the Kite

A Chinese emperor's youngest daughter frees her father from prison with the aid of a kite.

Owl Moon

A parent and child walk through the woods on a winter's night in the hope that they will be able to see an owl.

The Seeing Stick

The seemingly helpless blind daughter of the Emperor of China learns to "see" through the efforts and wisdom of a poor old man.

Novels

Children of the Wolf

■■■■■■■□□□□□□□

Mohandas, a young orphan boy of India, is given the task of civilizing two feral girls who have been raised by wolves. That's difficult enough, but Mohandas must also fight the superstition and fear of the villagers and that's even harder.

Sleeping Ugly

■■■■■■■□□□□□□□

Nasty, albeit beautiful, Princess Miserella foolishly insults a fairy who has taken her to the home of a real plain Jane. The fairy gives the three wishes to Jane, rather than Miserella, for a twist on "Sleeping Beauty."

Special Pages

Introduction

☐ No matter how carefully one packs, some things just don't fit into the suitcase, and some things we think are really important just didn't fit into Themes, Books at a Glance, and Authors and Illustrators. That's why we have Special Pages. Call them miscellany, potpourri, or salmagundi.

☐ Here we have special listings of books on such delicate subjects as divorce and death, which should be noticed and read and could serve as themes in many classrooms. Be careful with such books. They probably aren't the best things for a child currently going through such a trauma; but wouldn't it be nice if a child going through a divorce had previously read a book in which some very believable characters were doing something similar? The moment a child's dog dies is not the moment to approach him/her with a book about the same topic. But if he/she had already read such a book, the memory might lessen some of the guilt and isolation. Also, after the tragedy has faded, a child might be ready to read such a book and talk about it.

☐ You'll also find a time line of children's novels because we feel strongly that history is often best understood through stories rather than cold facts. There's a section of regional books in which books from each state are listed. Children in other parts of the country might seem so remote as to be unreal; it would be nice to see that they have the same problems and the same emotions. Also, the children will pick up a great deal of incidental information about climate, economy, topography, and history through these stories.

☐ We focused on authors in this section by listing some of their books according to such literary techniques as flashback, foreshadowing, exaggeration, and cliff-hanging.

☐ There are first paragraphs of some books that will give readers a chance to see how authors "grab" the reader from the beginning.

☐ There's also information about arranging author or illustrator visits and ways to make these visits more successful.

☐ The poetry section gives you background information on poets and their work and some suggestions for using poetry books in your classroom.

☐ We've included a list of resource books for you to help you bring books and kids together.

☐ You will also find our Literary Pursuit games about children's books.

Books About Divorce

Novels

Abercrombe, Barbara. *Cat-Man's Daughter.* Harper, 1981.

■■■■■■■■■■□□□

Kate's father is a TV star living in Beverly Hills. She spends a good deal of time shuttling between her mother in New York and her father in California. Kate knows her parents are using her as a weapon in their own war. It's her grandmother who understands and kidnaps Kate to force her parents to consider Kate's best interests.

Cleaver, Vera and Cleaver, Bill. *Ellen Grae.* Lippincott, 1967.

■■■■■■■■□□□□□□

See page 203.

Danziger, Paula. *The Divorce Express.* Delacorte, 1974.

■■■■■■■■□□□□□□

See page 213.

Klein, Norma. *Taking Sides.* Avon, 1974.

■■■■■■■■□□□□□□

Twelve-year-old Nell and five-year-old Hugo feel that they are forced to take sides in their parents divorce. Nell has chosen her father; therefore, she is delighted when her father is awarded custody of the children. Hugo, however, cannot adjust to the situation. Then their father has a heart attack.

Moore, Emily. *Something to Count On.* Dutton, 1980.

■■■■■■■■□□□□□□

Coming to terms with what her father really is like is difficult for Lorraine and her younger brother Jason. The children are constantly in trouble at school until Lorraine gets an understanding teacher.

Park, Barbara. *Don't Make Me Smile.* Knopf, 1981.

■■■■■■■■■□□□□□

Charlie is upset about his parents' divorce. Running away shows them how angry he is. The passage of time and a psychologist help Charlie survive this difficult period.

Pfeffer, Susan. *Dear Dad, Love Laurie.* Scholastic, 1989.

■■■■■■■■■□□□□□

See page 32.

Nonfiction

Krementz, Jill. *How It Feels When Parents Divorce.* Knopf, 1984.

Here are interviews with children who tell their very real stories.

LeShan, Eda. *What's Going to Happen to Me? When Parents Separate or Divorce.* Four Winds, 1978.

After addressing the concerns of a child whose parents are divorcing, Ms. LeShan deals with children's feelings and rights.

Rofes, Eric. *The Kids' Book of Divorce.* Stephen Green, 1981.

Children interview experts on the why's and wherefore's of divorce.

Poetry

Whitman, Ruth. "Listening to Grownups Quarreling" from *A New Treasury of Children's Poetry,* edited by Joanna Cole. Doubleday, 1984.

Widerberg, Sid. "Divorce" from *Crazy to Be Alive In Such a Strange World,* edited by Nancy Larrick. Evans, 1977.

Books About Death

Novels

Bunting, Eve. *The Happy Funeral.* Harper, 1982.

■■■□□□□□□□□□□□

Laura's mothers says that Grandfather's funeral will be happy, but Laura is certain that there is no such thing. However, the Chinese-American leave-taking does prove to have its happy side. Each funeral custom is designed to help Grandfather have a happy afterlife.

Coerr, Eleanor. *Sadako and the Thousand Paper Cranes.* Dell, 1986.

■■■■□□□□□□□□□□

See page 85.

Greene, Constance. *Beat the Turtle Drum.* Viking, 1976.

■■■■■■■■□□□□□□

Kate is a dreamer and budding poet. Her sister Joss is obsessed with horses and spends her days figuring out ways to get one. A week after Joss gets a horse, she falls from an apple tree and is killed. Kate spends the rest of the summer coping with her death.

Jukes, Mavis. *Blackberries in the Dark.* Knopf, 1985.

■■■■■■□□□□□□□□

Eating blackberries after dark was a tradition Austin and his grandfather shared. Now Grandfather is dead and Austin's summer visit to the farm is sad. Austin and his grandmother establish a connection and share their grief.

Mann, Peggy. *There Are Two Kinds of Terrible.* Avon, 1979.

■■■■■■■■■□□□□□

The first kind of terrible is a bicycle accident that leaves Robbie with a metal plate in his arm. The second kind is Robbie's mother dying of cancer.

Marino, Jan. *Eighty-Eight Steps to September.* Little, 1989.

■■■■■■□□□□□□□□

Amy refuses to deal with her brother Robbie's leukemia even though her parents try to prepare her for his coming death.

Steele, Mary Q. *The Life (and Death) of Sarah Elizabeth Harwood.* Greenwillow, 1980.

■■■■■■■■□□□□□□

Obsessed with death and convinced that hers is imminent, Sarah decides to get hers over with. It's Gram, an adopted grandmother in a nursing home, who takes the time and has the understanding to talk to Sarah frankly, although lightly, about death.

Nonfiction

Anders, Rebecca. *A Look at Death.* Lerner, 1978.

This book deals with how and why people die and ways survivors handle the loss.

Hyde, Margaret and Hyde, Lawrence. *Meeting Death.* Walker, 1989.

Here is a thorough exploration of the topic from ancient superstitions to modern customs, including a chapter on grief and mourning.

Krementz, Jill. *How It Feels When a Parent Dies.* Knopf, 1981.

The book is a series of interviews with children who have lost a parent.

LeShan, Eda. *Learning to Say Goodbye.* Macmillan, 1976.

There is no right or wrong way to feel about death. This book is intended to help children deal with the conflicting feelings of survivors.

Pringle, Laurence. *Death Is Natural.* Four Winds, 1977.

The death of a rabbit leads to a discussion of death as a natural occurrence.

Rofes, Eric. *The Kids' Book about Death and Dying.* Little, 1985.

With help from teachers and advisors, children researched death and the customs and beliefs surrounding death.

Books About Wild Animals

Novels

Byars, Betsy. *The Midnight Fox.* Viking, 1975.

■■■■■■■■□□□□□□

See page 199.

Dunlop, Eileen. *Fox Farm.* Holt, 1979.

■■■■■■■■■□□□□□

Adam, a foster child in the Scottish lowlands, is placed in a warm, understanding family. Unfortunately, because he has been so hurt, he cannot respond in kind. It isn't until he finds a starving fox cub that Adam can show any love.

Eckert, Allan W. *Incident at Hawk's Hill.* Little, 1971.

■■■■■■■■■□□□□□

Ben's special ability to communicate with wild animals helps him survive when a badger befriends him on the Manitoba prairies.

George, Jean Craighead. *The Cry of the Crow.* Harper, 1980.

■■■■■■■■■□□□□□

In this novel set in Florida, Mandy learns to decipher crow talk.

———. *Julie of the Wolves.* Harper, 1972.

■■■■■■■■■■■■■□

See pages 60 and 128.

McCutcheon, Elsie. *The Rat War.* Farrar, 1986.

■■■■■■■□□□□□□□

Nicholas strikes up a friendship with a rat and decides to save him from the rat catcher.

Morey, Walt. *Gentle Ben.* Dutton, 1965.

■■■■■■■■□□□□□□

Mark, a lonely boy in an Alaskan village, makes friends with a wild bear. Together they have an exciting series of adventures.

North, Sterling. *Rascal.* Avon, 1976.

■■■■■■■□□□□□□□

Here are the amusing adventures of a racoon who finds his way into everything.

Polseno, Jo. *This Hawk Belongs to Me.* McKay, 1977.

■■■■■■■□□□□□□□

See page 56.

Stranger, Joyce. *The Fox at Drummers' Darkness.* Farrar, 1977.

■■■■■■■□□□□□□□

The only human to befriend the red fox is Johnny Toosmall who is just as much a loner as the fox. The fox is driven by starvation into raiding farms and, eventually, to the chemical factory in the city.

Nonfiction

Clark, Margaret Goff. *The Vanishing Manatee.* Cobblehill, 1990.

These gentle creatures, perhaps the mermaids of legend, might be protected by law, but they face many dangers from careless people.

Dewey, Jennifer Owings. *Birds of Antarctica: The Adelie Penguin.* Little, 1989.
———. *Birds of Antarctica: The Wandering Albatross.* Little, 1989.

In these stunningly beautiful books, Ms. Dewey takes us through the lifecyles of two amazing Antarctic creatures.

Dingerkus, Guido. *The Shark Watchers' Guide.* Messner, 1985.

Shark-expert Guido Dingerkus established the shark tank at the New York Aquarium. This book describes sharks' lifestyles and natural habitats.

Gardner, Robert. *The Whale Watchers' Guide.* Messner, 1984.

Mr. Gardner describes a whale watch and supplies tips for identifying whales by the ways they dive and surface. He also provides information and background on many kinds of whales.

Miller, Susanne Santoro. *Whales and Sharks and Other Creatures of the Deep.* Messner, 1982.

This tour of the ocean takes us from the shore to the Trenches, 6,000 feet down.

Norsgaard, E. Jaediker. *Nature's Great Balancing Act.* Cobblehill, 1990.

Watch a backyard allowed to grow wild and you'll see how animals and plants depend on each other for survival.

Petty, Kate. The Baby Animals series. Watts, 1990.

Full-color photographs and illustrations of chimpanzees, elephants, kangaroos, and lions fill these books for younger readers. The text covers habitat, diet, and parental care.

Poetry

Lawrence, D. H. "Mountain Lion" from *Room for Me and a Mountain Lion: Poetry of Open Space,* edited by Nancy Larrick. Evans, 1974.

Regional Books

Alabama

Ellison, Lucile Watkins. *The Tie That Binds.* Scribners, 1981.

■■■■■■■■■□□□□□□

Here is family life on a farm in Alabama during the 1920's. Each chapter is a memory written in affecting prose.

Gibbons, Faye. *King Shoes and Clown Pockets.* Morrow, 1989.

■■■■■■■■■□□□□□□

When Raymond Brock, alias King Shoes, moves into a trailer park, nothing has changed but his address. His parents still seem to have no time for him and his siblings think he's a pest. Bruce Manis, known as Clown Pockets, becomes Raymond's friend.

Alaska

George, Jean Craighead. *Julie of the Wolves.* Harper, 1972.

■■■■■■■■■■■■■■□

See pages 60 and 128.

Rogers, Jean. *The Secret Moose.* Greenwillow, 1985.

■■■■■■■■■□□□□□□

When Gerald finds a wounded moose not far from his home near Fairbanks, he is not at all sure he can protect it, let alone help it survive.

Arizona

Baker, Betty. *The Spirit Is Willing.* Macmillan, 1974.

■■■■■■■■■■■□□□□

See page 80.

Arkansas

Branscum, Robbie. *Spud Tackett and the Angel of Doom.* Viking, 1983.

■■■■■■■■■□□□□□□

See page 192.

Greene, Bette. *Philip Hall Likes Me I Reckon Maybe.* Dial, 1974.

■■■■■■■□□□□□□□□

Beth has a crush on Philip Hall who is adept at avoiding her except when she does his farm work for him.

California

O'Dell, Scott. *Zia.* Houghton, 1976.

■■■■■■■■■■□□□□□

This sequel to *Island of the Blue Dolphins* concerns the dilemma of Karana's children, Zia and Mando, as they leave the Island of the Blue Dolphins and try to cope with life in the mission at Santa Barbara.

Yep, Lawrence. *Child of the Owl.* Harper, 1977.

■■■■■■■■■■■■■□□

Casey Young has spent the years since the death of her mother with her father Barney. Eventually, Casey is taken to her maternal grandmother, Ah Paw, who lives in San Francisco's Chinatown. There Casey learns about her Chinese heritage and attends the Chinese school. When a thief steals Ah Paw's antique owl charm and injures her, it is Casey who finds that the thief was her father and she retrieves the charm.

Colorado

Hobbs, Will. *Bearstone.* Atheneum, 1989.

■■■■■■■■■□□□□□□

A boy named Cloyd in search of himself and a home finds both in the Colorado mountains.

Connecticut

Speare, Elizabeth George. *The Witch of Blackbird Pond.* Houghton, 1958.

Set in 1687, this is a story of witch hunting, ignorance, and prejudice. Kit Tyler moves to Connecticut from Barbados to live with her relatives. There she is accused of and tried for witchcraft.

Delaware

Harely, Ruth. *Henry Hudson.* Troll, 1979.

Henry Hudson explores the area of the New World now known as Delaware and New York.

Florida

Cleaver, Vera and Cleaver, Bill. *The Kissammee Kid.* Lothrop, 1981.

Evelyn Chestnut loves her family, particularly her brother-in-law Camfield, a cowhand on the Kissammee Prairie in Florida. On a surprise visit, Evelyn discovers that Cam is probably a cattle rustler.

George, Jean Craighead. *The Talking Earth.* Harper, 1983.

See page 74.

Georgia

Sargent, Sarah. *Seeds of Change.* Bradbury, 1989.

Rachel's father has big plans. He's going to change the swamp into a recreation area and make a fortune. The ecology of the swamp, however, is something too perfect to be tampered with.

Smith, Doris Buchanan. *Salted Lemons.* Four Winds, 1980.

See page 86.

Hawaii

Slepian, Jan. *The Broccoli Tapes.* Philomel, 1989.

The family is sent to Hawaii for five months and, although it sounds wonderful, both Sam and Sara have trouble adjusting. A wild cat named Broccoli is the means through which they adjust and learn to love. The tale is told through tapes that Sara sends to her teacher and class back home.

Idaho

Gleiter, Jan and Thompson, Kathleen. *Sacajawea.* Raintree, 1987.

This is the story of Sacajawea, the interpreter for the Lewis and Clark expedition.

Illinois

Cleaver, Vera and Cleaver, Bill. *The Mimosa Tree.* Lippincott, 1970.

See page 204.

Herman, Charlotte. *Millie Cooper, 3B.* Puffin, 1985.

Millie attends school in Chicago where her third-grade classmates are typical. She craves a new invention to help her with her homework: a Reynolds Rocket Ballpoint Pen. With this fantastic new invention she could do unblemished spelling tests and an essay on why she is special. Through her normal everyday activities, Millie finds out she really is special.

Indiana

Bell, W. Bruce. *A Little Dab of Color.* Lothrop, 1980.

Life on an Indiana farm in 1915 peps up considerably when Grammaw joins the family. Though still wearing black for her twenty-year widowhood, Grammaw proceeds to scatter color as she takes over household chores and rearing the two boys.

Goodwin, Marie D. *Where the Towers Pierce the Sky.* Four Winds, 1989.

■■■■■■■■■□□□□□□

There seems to have been a mix-up: In 1429, Jacques is sent into the future to spy on Joan of Arc, where the towers of Notre Dame pierce the sky. Instead, he lands at Notre Dame University in South Bend, Indiana, in Lizzie's world of the 1980s.

Iowa
Thomas, Jane. *The Princess in the Pigpen.* Clarion, 1989.

■■■■■□□□□□□□□□□

When Elizabeth is suddenly transported from her bed in seventeenth-century England to a pigpen in modern day Iowa, she is shocked, but then so is the family who finds her there.

Kansas
Barger, Gary W. *What Happened to Mr. Forster.* Clarion, 1981.

■■■■■■■■■■□□□□□

The sixth-grade teacher at this school in Kansas City is a man, the first in 1958. He gets the kids involved in the legends of King Arthur, and they put on a successful play, but Mr. Forster is fired.

Ruby, Lois. *Pig-Out Inn.* Houghton, 1987.

■■■■■■■■□□□□□□□

Dovi's mother has them on the move again, this time to Kansas to a truckstop she plans to run. When one of the regular customers leaves his son Tag behind, Dovi has a new family member to cope with and worry about.

Kentucky
Lyon, George Ella. *Borrowed Children.* Orchard, 1988.

■■■■■■■■■□□□□□□

Because Amanda's mother is ill after the baby's birth, Amanda quits school to care for the family.

Life seems pretty bad until she goes to her grandparents' home and sees her aunt's unhappy life.

Louisiana
Callen, Larry. *Pinch.* Little, 1976.

■■■■■■■□□□□□□□□

See page 38.

Maine
Greene, Constance. *Ask Anybody.* Viking, 1983.

■■■■■■■■□□□□□□□

Schuyler Sweet comes from a fairly stable, normal family in a small village in Maine. When flamboyant, daring Nell Foster and her family move in, Schuyler is alternately attracted and repulsed by the girl's behavior and beliefs.

Speare, Elizabeth George. *The Sign of the Beaver.* Houghton, 1983.

■■■■■■■■■■□□□□□

See page 152.

Maryland
Voigt, Cynthia. *Dicey's Song.* Atheneum, 1982.

■■■■■■■■■□□□□□□

See page 251.

Massachusetts
Lowry, Lois. *Taking Care of Terrific.* Houghton, 1983

■■■■■■■■□□□□□□□

See page 233.

Michigan
Robertson, Keith. *In Search of a Sandhill Crane.* Viking, 1973.

■■■■■■■■□□□□□□□

Link promised his uncle to take a picture of a sandhill crane while enduring two weeks on Michigan's Upper Peninsula. At first totally uninterested in the wilderness around him, Link gradually learns to appreciate its beauty.

Minnesota

Paulsen, Gary. *Popcorn Days and Buttermilk Nights.* Lodestar, 1983.

■■■■■■■□□□□□□□

See page 146.

———. *The Winter Room.* Orchard, 1989.

■■■■■■■■■□□□□

See page 240.

Hassler, Jon. *Four Miles to Pinecone.* Warne, 1977.

■■■■■■■■■□□□□□

Tom works in a grocery store in St. Paul and is horrified when his friend, Mouse Brown, robs the store and wounds the owner. Tom leaves the city to work in the country, but discovers crime there as well and decides to turn Mouse in to the police.

Mississippi

Taylor, Mildred D. *Roll of Thunder, Hear My Cry.* Dial, 1976.

■■■■■■■■■■□□□□

A black child, Cassie Logan, lives with her family in Mississippi during the Depression surrounded by white neighbors who despise them. The Night Riders bring fear and violence but Cassie and her brothers retain their pride and integrity.

Missouri

Peck, Richard. *The Ghost Belonged to Me.* Viking, 1975.

■■■■■■■■■■□□□□

See page 22.

Potter, Marian. *Blatherskite.* Morrow, 1980.

■■■■■■■■□□□□□□

Maureen, the blatherskite, is full of adventure, even getting on the passenger train for St. Louis without tickets or money. Her fast talking saves her there and through more perilous adventures.

Montana

Lasky, Kathryn. *The Bone Wars.* Morrow, 1988.

■■■■■■■■□□□□□□

In the Badlands of Montana, there is a fiece battle between palentologists. Into this battle come two orphans determined to thwart the scientists.

Nebraska

Talbot, Charlene. *An Orphan for Nebraska.* Atheneum, 1979.

■■■■■■■□□□□□□□

See page 58.

Conrad, Pam. *Prairie Songs.* Harper, 1985.

■■■■■■■■■□□□□□

See page 147.

Nevada

Gleiter, Jan and Thompson, Kathleen. *Kit Carson.* Raintree, 1987.

■■■■■□□□□□□□□□

Here are stories and legends of Kit Carson told with a lively text and full-color illustrations.

New Hampshire

Blos, Joan. *A Gathering of Days.* Macmillan, 1979.

■■■■■■■□□□□□□□

See page 120.

Butterworth, Oliver. *The Enormous Egg.* Little, 1956.

■■■■■□□□□□□□□□

When Nate Twitchell's hen lays an outsized egg, Freedom, New Hampshire, will never be the same. Out comes a live dinosaur!

New Jersey

Cohen, Barbara. *Thank You, Jackie Robinson.* Lothrop, 1988.

■■■■■■■□□□□□□□

See page 158.

Robertson, Keith. *Henry Reed's Baby-Sitting Service.* Viking, 1966.

■■■■■□□□□□□□□

All of the books about Henry Reed, an enterprising young man, take place in suburban New Jersey.

New Mexico
Schaefer, Jack. *Old Ramon.* Houghton, 1973.

■■■■■□□□□□□□□

Old Ramon is to teach the boy how to herd sheep. As they move the flock to the mountains with their two dogs, the boy learns the ways of the sheep and the ways of himself.

New York
Clements, Bruce. *Anywhere Else But Here.* Farrar, 1981.

■■■■■■■■□□□□□

See page 93.

Konigsburg, E.L. *From the Mixed-Up Files of Mrs. Basil E. Frankweiler.* Macmillan, 1976.

■■■■■■□□□□□□□

See page 119.

Edmonds, Walter. *The Matchlock Gun.* Putnam, 1971.

■■■■■■■□□□□□□

This books tells about the troubles between the settlers and Indians in early upstate New York.

North Carolina
Hooks, William. *Circle of Fire.* Atheneum, 1982.

■■■■■■■■■□□□□□

In 1936, almost everyone feels the effects of the Ku Klux Klan and its activities. Three young people befriend a tinker boy. When Harrison is convinced that his father is a member of the Klan, he must make a difficult decision when he learns that the Klan is about to raid the tinker camp.

Smith, Doris Buchanan. *Return to Bitter Creek.* Viking, 1986.

■■■■■■■□□□□□□

See page 247.

North Dakota
Lawlor, Laurie. *Addie's Dakota Winter.* A. Whitman, 1989.

■■■■■■■□□□□□□

Life in a prairie sod house has its hardships, but Addie develops a friendship and has fun as well.

Ohio
Cameron, Eleanor. *To the Green Mountains.* Dutton, 1975.

■■■■■■■■■□□□□□

Kath, grows up during World War I in Columbus, Ohio, where her mother runs a hotel. Life in the hotel reaches a climax when her mother befriends the Black couple who work for her.

Gondosch, Linda. *The Best Bet Gazette.* Lodestar, 1989.

■■■■■■■□□□□□□

In this story set in Cleveland, Ohio, in 1954, the children's plans for a newspaper are tossed aside as one of their babysitting charges becomes a victim of polio.

Oklahoma
Bauer, Marion Dane. *Shelter from the Wind.* Clarion, 1976.

■■■■■■■□□□□□□

This book is set in the Oklahoma panhandle. There, Stacy, feeling left out because of her father's remarriage and new baby, runs away to an isolated area where she finds an old woman who takes her in.

Wallace, Bill. *Danger in Quicksand Swamp.* Holiday, 1989.

■■■■■■■■■□□□□□□

In their sleepy town in southeastern Oklahoma, Ben and Jake find a treasure map, and they're sure they're in for an exciting adventure. They don't know how exciting, however. Soon they face the dangers of the swamp, some voracious alligators and an unknown vicious killer.

Oregon
Lewis, Claudia. *Long Ago in Oregon.* Harper, 1987.

■■■■■■■■■■□□□□□

These poems tell of the events of the time from the point of view of one family in Oregon.

McGraw, Eloise Jarvis. *The Money Room.* Atheneum, 1981.

■■■■■■■□□□□□□□

See page 39.

Pennsylvania
Collier, James L. and Collier, Christopher. *The Bloody Country.* Macmillan, 1985.

■■■■■■■■■■■■■■□

See page 57.

Rappaport, Doreen. *Trouble at the Mines.* Crowell, 1987.

■■■■■■□□□□□□□□□

See page 162.

Rhode Island
Avi. *The Man Who Was Poe.* Orchard, 1989.

■■■■■■■■■■■■■□

See page 136.

Avi. *Something Upstairs.* Orchard, 1988.

■■■■■□□□□□□□□□□

In their new home in Providence, Kenny finds the ghost of a slave boy who needs his help. Kenny must return to the 1800's to prevent a murder.

South Carolina
Tate, Eleanora. *The Secret of Gumbo Grove.* Watts, 1987.

■■■■■■■■□□□□□□

The town on the South Carolina coast is ashamed of its history, and it's up to Raisin Stackhouse to get the Black community to value its heritage.

South Dakota
Cleaver, Vera and Cleaver, Bill. *Dust of the Earth.* Lippincott, 1975.

■■■■■■■■■■■■□□

See page 203.

Turner, Ann Warren. *Grasshopper Summer.* Macmillan, 1989.

■■■■■■■■□□□□□□

Moving from Kentucky to southern Dakota territory in 1874 means coping with harsh conditions made worse with a plague of locusts.

Tennessee
Steele, William O. *The Lone Hunt.* Harcourt, 1976.

■■■■■■■■■■□□□□□

Yance Caywood is allowed to participate in the hunt for the first buffalo seen in Tennessee for thirty years. One by one other hunters drop off, but Vance continues, determined to succeed.

Texas
Nelson, Theresa. *Devil Storm.* Orchard, 1987.

■■■■■■■■□□□□□□

See page 72.

Utah
Fitzgerald, John D. *The Great Brain*. Dell, 1972.

■■■■■■□□□□□□□□

This is the first of a funny series of books about the Great Brain and his brother, two boys growing up in Utah.

Vermont
Haas, Jesse. *Keeping Barney*. Greenwillow, 1982.

■■■■■■■□□□□□□□

Sarah wants a horse and now there seems little reason to deny her since the family has moved to a small Vermont farm. Then Barney comes into Sarah's life.

Kinsey-Warnock, Natalie. *The Canada Geese Quilt*. Dutton, 1989.

■■■■■■□□□□□□□□

Life in rural Vermont in 1940 takes a turn for the worse for Ariel when her grandmother suffers a stroke and her mother announces the coming of a new sibling.

Peck, Robert Newton. *Soup*. Knopf, 1974.

■■■■□□□□□□□□□□

See page 26.

Wallace-Brodeur, Ruth. *The Kenton Year*. Atheneum, 1980.

■■■■■■■■□□□□□□

After the death of her father, Mandy and her mother rent a cottage in rural Vermont where the people, the climate, and the general atmosphere heal the grieving pair.

Virginia
Reeder, Carolyn. *Shades of Gray*. Macmillan, 1989.

■■■■■■■■■□□□□□

See page 150.

Washington
Beatty, Patricia. *Sarah and Me and the Lady from the Sea.*. Morrow, 1989.

■■■■■■□□□□□□□□

See page 67.

Washington, D. C.
Brady, Esther Wood. *The Toad on Capitol Hill*. Crown, 1978.

■■■■■■□□□□□□□□

When her father remarries, Dorsy's freedom is curtailed. She wishes on a white toad that her new family would disappear. When the British army arrives, Dorsy finds that she needs her family.

Shreve, Susan. *The Flunking of Joshua T. Bates*. Scholastic, 1984.

■■□□□□□□□□□□□□

See page 117.

West Virginia
Rylant, Cynthia. *A Blue-Eyed Daisy*. Bradbury, 1985.

■■■■■■■□□□□□□□

See page 246.

Wisconsin
Brink, Carol Ryrie. *Caddie Woodlawn*. Macmillan, 1973.

■■■■■■■■□□□□□□

See page 57.

Paulsen, Gary. *The Island*. Orchard, 1988.

■■■■■■■■■■■■□□

See page 32.

Wyoming
Collier, James L. and Collier, Christopher. *The Bloody Country*. Four Winds, 1976.

■■■■■■■■■■■■■□

See page 57.

Book Series

The Bagthorpes by Helen Cresswell
Absolute Zero. Macmillan, 1978.
Ordinary Jack. Macmillan, 1977.
Bagthorpes Unlimited. Macmillan, 1978.
Bagthorpes vs the World. Macmillan, 1979.
Bagthorpes Abroad. Macmillan, 1984.
Bagthorpes Haunted. Macmillan, 1985.
Bagthorpes Liberated. Macmillan, 1990.

■■■■■■■□□□□□□□□

This zany family and their relatives, the Parkers, get into laugh-aloud trouble as they try to be more than they are or at least what they are not. The Bagthorpes are the epitome of eccentricity. See page 209.

The Borrowers by Mary Norton
The Borrowers. Harcourt, 1953.
The Borrowers Afield. Harcourt, 1955.
The Borrowers Afloat. Harcourt, 1959.
The Borrowers Aloft. Harcourt, 1961.
The Borrowers Avenged. Harcourt, 1982.

■■■■■■□□□□□□□□□

These stories of a family of tiny people who live around us and survive by "borrowing" the things we think we've lost was inspired by Mary Norton's own nearsightedness as a child, which led her to look closely at the plants and creatures around her and to imagine that there were tiny people there as well. She forgot about that fantasy until the Great Depression of the 1930s when it seemed to her that the victims were much like the tiny people she had imagined.

The world of Pod, Homily, and Arriety Clock (their front door is in the grandfather clock) is completely dependent upon the "human beans" they live near but fear greatly. There used to be more Borrowers, but they have been driven away by the cat or other horrors. The Borrowers are convinced that the human beans exist just for them, but they must not be seen by them and with good reason, for each time a Borrower is "seen" disaster results.

Encyclopedia Brown by Donald J. Sobol
Encyclopedia Brown: Boy Detective. Lodestar, 1963.
Encyclopedia Brown and the Case of the Secret Pitch. Lodestar, 1965.

Encyclopedia Brown Finds the Clues. Lodestar, 1966.
Encyclopedia Brown Gets His Man. Lodestar, 1967.
Encyclopedia Brown Solves Them All. Lodestar, 1968.
Encyclopedia Brown Saves the Day. Lodestar, 1970.
Encyclopedia Brown Tracks Them Down. Lodestar, 1971.
Encyclopedia Brown Shows the Way. Lodestar, 1972.
Encyclopedia Brown Keeps the Peace. Lodestar, 1973.
Encyclopedia Brown Takes the Case. Lodestar, 1973.
Encyclopedia Brown Lends a Hand. Lodestar, 1974.
Encyclopedia Brown and the Case of the Dead Eagles. Lodestar, 1975.
Encyclopedia Brown and the Case of the Midnight Visitor. Lodestar, 1977.
Encyclopedia Brown's Record Book of Weird and Wonderful Facts. Delacorte, 1979.
Encyclopedia Brown's Second Record Book of Weird and Wonderful Facts. Delacorte, 1981.
Encyclopedia Brown Carries On. Four Winds, 1980.
Encyclopedia Brown Sets the Pace. Four Winds, 1982.
Encyclopedia Brown's Book of Wacky Crimes. Lodestar, 1982.
Encyclopedia Brown Takes the Cake. Four Winds, 1983.
Encyclopedia Brown and the Case of the Exploding Plumbing. Scholastic, 1984.
Encyclopedia Brown's Book of Wacky Spies. Morrow, 1984.
Encyclopedia Brown's Book of Wacky Sports. Morrow, 1984.
Encyclopedia Brown's Book of Wacky Animals. Morrow, 1985.
Encyclopedia Brown's Third Record Book of Weird and Wonderful Facts. Morrow, 1985.
Encyclopedia Brown and the Case of the Mysterious Handprints. Morrow, 1985.
Encyclopedia Brown's Book of Wacky Cars. Morrow, 1987.
Encyclopedia Brown and the Case of the Treasure Hunt. Morrow, 1988.

■■■■□□□□□□□□□□□

It's the son of the chief of police, ten-year-old "Encyclopedia" Brown who solves most of the mysteries in this series. Each book in the series contains ten mysteries with solutions printed in the back of the book. The stories are simple but require careful reading. They're perfect for the meticulous reader.

The Little House by Laura Ingalls Wilder
Little House in the Big Woods. Harper, 1932.
Farmer Boy. Harper, 1933.
Little House on the Prairie. Harper, 1935.
On the Banks of Plum Creek. Harper, 1937.
By the Shores of Silver Lake. Harper, 1939.
The Long Winter. Harper, 1940.
Little Town on the Prairie. Harper, 1941.
These Happy Golden Years. Harper, 1943.
The First Four Years. Harper, 1971.

■■■■■■■□□□□□□□

The narrative in these books is simple and straight-forward, the product of an older woman's memories of her childhood on the Great Plains. Mrs. Wilder began writing these stories when she was in her sixties. The books cover the day to day experiences of the Ingalls family and their love for each other.

The Moffats by Eleanor Estes
The Moffats. Harcourt, 1941.
The Middle Moffat. Harcourt, 1942.
Rufus M. Harcourt, 1943.
The Moffat Museum. Harcourt, 1983.
Ginger Pye. Harcourt, 1951.
Pinky Pye. Harcourt, 1958.

■■■■□□□□□□□□□□

Although only four of the books are directly about the Moffat family, the Pye family are relatives of the Moffats. The stories, set in the 1910s, are about a family that holds together in spite of poverty and bad times. The books are humorous celebrations of the individuality of each family member.

The Chronicles of Narnia by C.S. Lewis
The Lion, The Witch, and the Wardrobe. Macmillan, 1950.
Prince Caspian: The Return to Narnia. Macmillan, 1951.
The Voyage of the "Dawn Treader." Macmillan, 1952.
The Silver Chair. Macmillan, 1953.
The Horse and His Boy. Macmillan, 1954.
The Magician's Nephew. Macmillan, 1955.
The Last Battle. Macmillan, 1956.

■■■■■■■■□□□□□□

These adventure books can also be taken as religious allegories. In the series, children enter and return from Narnia, a land where the forces of evil and good are in conflict. Good is represented by Aslan, a gentle, enormous lion who can only be seen by those who believe in him. Many of the creatures of Narnia are aligned with him, as are the children who enter and fulfill the prophesies there. The forces of evil are aligned with the White Queen. In each book, some of the children from the preceding book return to Narnia while others are too old to go back.

Poetry Books

Sources of Poetry

Adoff, Arnold. *Celebrations: a New Anthology of Black Poetry.* Follett, 1977.
Two hundred forty poems by eighty-five African-American authors.

Brewton, Sara. *Of Quarks, Quasars and Other Quirks.* Crowell, 1977.
Poems about science.

Cole, Joanna, ed. *A New Treasury of Children's Poetry.* Doubleday, 1984.
A sizeable collection of familiar and unfamiliar poetry for children.

Cosman, Anna. *How to Read and Write Poetry.* Watts, 1979.
Although this book has several poems, it's really just what the title says.

Fleming, Alice. *America Is Not All Traffic Lights: Poems of the Midwest.* Little, 1976.

Holman, Felice. *The Song in My Head.* Scribner, 1985.
These poems are, for the most part, playful. The nature poems are particularly well done.

Hopkins, Lee Bennett, ed. *Pass the Poetry, Please.* Harper, 1972.
Here are poems by many poets with some background material about the poet and the rhyme.

Hughes, Langston. *The Dream Keeper.* Knopf, 1986.
Fifty-nine poems of the Black experience, most within the grasp of intermediate-level children.

Janeczko, Paul B. *The Place My Words Are Looking For: What Poets Say About and Through Their Work.* Bradbury, 1990.
The subtitle says it all: the poems and the background behind them are all here.

————. *Postcard Poems: A Collection of Poetry for Sharing.* Bradbury, 1979.
Short poems by poets who share their visions.

Kennedy, X.J. *Fresh Brats.* Macmillan, 1990.
Short, snappy poems with an irreverent twist about subjects like vampires and dinosaurs.

————. *The Forgetful Wishing Well.* Atheneum, 1985.
Many verse forms describe growing up and other subjects, real and fanciful. There are fresh images in this delightful collection.

————. *Knock at a Star.* Little, 1983.
Short contemporary poems.

Kuskin, Karla. *Dogs and Dragon, Trees and Dreams.* Harper, 1980.
Poems with notes by the poet about the source of their inspiration.

Larrick, Nancy, ed. *Crazy to be Alive In Such a Strange World: Poems about People.* Evans, 1977.
These poems celebrate people with all their eccentricities, illustrated with black-and-white photos.

————. *Room for Me and a Mountain Lion: Poems of Open Space.* Evans, 1974.
As the title suggests, these are poems to celebrate the out-of-doors.

Livingston, Myra Cohn. *4-Way Stop and Other Poems.* Atheneum, 1976.

————. *Worlds I Know and Other Poems.* Atheneum, 1985.
A poet's view of the special feelings of childhood.

————. *I Like You, If You Like Me: Poems of Friendship.* Macmillan, 1987.
Poems from around the world by a variety of poets on the subject of friendship.

McCord, David. *One at a Time.* Little, 1986.
A collection of his children's poetry until 1986.

Merriam, Eve. *Fresh Paint.* Macmillan, 1986.
Short poems provide new looks at common things.

————. *Rainbow Writing.* Atheneum, 1976.
Thirty-nine poems on a variety of subjects.

Morrison, Lillian, ed. *Overheard in a Bubble Chamber and Other Science Poems.* Lothrop, 1981.
Thirty-eight poems about science.

————. *Rhythm Road: Poems to Move To.* Lothrop, 1988.
Poems by many poets with strong rhythms or about things that move.

Moss, Jeff. *The Butterfly Jar.* Bantam, 1989.
Short and usually funny poems by one of the original creators of Sesame Street.

Parker, Elinor. *Echoes of the Sea.* Scribner, 1977.
Ten groupings of poems about the sea and the creatures in it.

Plotz, Helen, ed. *The Gift Outright: America to Her Poets.* Greenwillow, 1977.
Poems about America by eighty-eight poets.

Prelutsky, Jack. *The Headless Horseman Rides To-night: More Poems to Trouble Your Sleep.* Greenwillow, 1980.
Really gruesome poems illustrated by Arnold Lobel.

———. *Nightmares: Poems to Trouble Your Sleep.* Greenwillow, 1976.
Another picture book of scary poems illustrated by Arnold Lobel.

Silverstein, Shel. *A Light in the Attic.* Harper, 1981.
———. *Where the Sidewalk Ends.* Harper, 1974.
What can you say about these outrageous and wonderful books except that they opened the world of poetry to many, many children.

Thurman, Judith. *Flashlight and Other Poems.* Atheneum, 1976.
Simple poems that look at things with a new slant.

Turner, Ann. *Street Talk.* Houghton, 1986.
Poems that catch the rhythm of the city.

Viorst, Judith. *If I Were in Charge of the World and Other Worries.* Atheneum, 1981.
Here are the poet's thoughts from a child's point of view, as well as some delightful poetic turn-arounds of fairy tales.

Worth, Valerie. *All the Small Poems.* Farrar, 1987.
Ms. Worth's poems are non-rhyming, careful looks at familiar things.

Poets and Their Rhymes

Myra Cohn Livingston

☐ In addition to being a poet, Myra Cohn Livingston is a talented musician who plays the French horn. She and her husband, an accountant, live in a villa with beautiful gardens on the side of one of the Santa Monica mountains in California. She collects rare books, including over 10,000 volumes of poetry. She thinks writing poetry is difficult and she tries to put a poem away for a while after she has written it. She takes it out later and works on it again. She has three children: Joshua, Jonas, and Jennie. Ms. Livingston often writes on contemporary topics. Her poems are often short and are more apt to be about people and their feelings than about nature.

Books of Poetry Written for Young People by Myra Cohn Livingston
Birthday Poems. Holdiay, 1989.
Celebrations. Holiday, 1985.
Christmas Poems. Holiday, 1984.
A Circle of Seasons. Holiday, 1982.
Come Away. Macmillan, 1974.
A Crazy Flight and Other Poems. Harcourt, 1969.
Earth Songs. Holiday, 1986.
4-Way Stop and Other Poems. Atheneum, 1976.
Higgledy-Piggledy. Macmillan, 1986.
I Like You, If You Like Me. Atheneum, 1987.
A Lolligag of Limericks. Atheneum, 1978.
The Malibu and Other Poems. Atheneum, 1974.
Monkey Puzzle and Other Poems. Atheneum, 1984.
The Moon and a Star and Other Poems. Harcourt, 1965.
My Head Is Read and Other Riddle Rhymes. Holiday, 1990.
No Way of Knowing. Atheneum, 1980.
O Sliver of Liver, Together with Other Triolets, Cingquains, Haiku, Verses, and a Dash of Poems. Atheneum, 1979.
Old Mrs. Twindlytart and Other Rhymes. Harcourt, 1967.
Remembering and Other Poems. Holiday, 1989.
Sea Songs. Holiday, 1986.
Sky Songs. Holiday, 1984.
A Song I Sang to You. Harcourt, 1984.
Space Songs. Holiday, 1988.
The Way Things Are. Atheneum, 1974.
There Was a Place and Other Poems. McElderry, 1988.
Up in the Air. Holiday, 1989.
Whispers and Other Poems. Harcourt, 1958.
Wide Awake and Other Poems. Harcourt, 1959.
Worlds I Know and Other Poems. Atheneum, 1985.

David McCord

☐ David McCord was born on November 15, 1897. He grew up in Oregon but now lives at the Harvard Club in Boston. He loves to fish, smoke cigars, and paint with watercolors. One of his teachers once told him, "Never let a day go by without looking on three beautiful things," and he says that's not difficult. He also loves to read and often does so with a pencil in his hand. He underlines things he likes or writes notes in the margins of the book. Mr. McCord's work is rhythmic and usually rhymes. He often writes about nature but is also intrigued by words themselves and many of his poems play with words and their meanings. In one poem he says that a human's first word must have been *wonder* and, in many of the poems, he wonders about things in nature. He once wrote that "No poet worth his salt has ever been able to write the kinds of poems he wanted to write without a basic knowledge of meter, rhythm, rhyme and the established verse forms." Mr. McCord writes poetry for young people and adults.

Books of Poetry Written for Young People by David McCord
All Day Long. Little, 1966.
All Small. Little, 1986.
Away and Ago. Little, 1974.
Everytime I Climb a Tree. Little, 1967.
Far and Few. Little, 1952.
For Me to Say. Little, 1970.
Mr. Bidery's Spidery Garden. Harrap, 1972.
Pen, Paper and Poem. Little, 1974.
One at a Time. Little, 1977.
Speak Up. Little, 1980.
The Star in the Pail. Little, 1975.
Take Sky. Little, 1962.

Eve Merriam
☐ Ms. Merriam looks at common sights with a poet's eye. Her poems are usually short and straight to the point. Eve Merriam writes plays as well as poetry and fiction for adults and children. She was born in Philadelphia, Pennsylvania, but she now lives in Greenwich Village in New York. She loves the noise and excitement there. She has two grown sons, one of whom did the artwork for *The Birthday Cow.* She likes to work with the playfulness of language. She says poetry is a fresh look at something familiar.

Books of Poetry Written for Young People by Eve Merriam
The Birthday Cow. Knopf, 1978.
Blackberry Ink. Morrow, 1985.
A Book of Wishes for You. Gibson, 1985.
Catch a Little Rhyme. Atheneum, 1966.
Chortles: New and Selected Wordplay Poems. Morrow, 1989.

Don't Think about a White Bear. Putnam 1965.
Finding a Poem. Atheneum, 1970.
Fresh Paint. Macmillan, 1986.
Funny Town. Crowell, 1963.
Halloween ABC. Macmillan, 1987.
I Am a Man: Ode to Martin Luther King, Jr. Doubleday, 1971.
If Only I Could Tell You: Poems for Young Lovers and Dreamers. Knopf, 1983.
Independent Voices. Atheneum, 1968.
It Doesn't Always Have to Rhyme. Atheneum, 1964.
Jamboree: Rhymes for All Times. Dell, 1984.
Poem for a Pickle: Funnybone Verses. Greenwillow, 1989.
Out Loud. Atheneum, 1973.
Rainbow Writing. Atheneum, 1976.
A Sky Full of Poems. Dell, 1986.
There is No Rhyme for Silver. Atheneum, 1962.
A Word or Two With You: New Rhymes for Young Readers. Atheneum, 1981.
You Be Good and I'll Be Night: Jump-on-the-Bed Poems. Morrow, 1988.

Jack Prelutsky
☐ Jack Prelutsky's poems are often funny and are seldom about nature. His poems are frequently short, usually rhyme, and are often about food, monsters, and ridiculous people. He has been a cab driver, a photographer, a furniture mover, a potter, a folksinger, and an actor. He wanted to be an opera singer, but he decided that others did that better. He spends a great deal of time traveling and visiting schools. He thinks that poetry is one way we tell each other what's going on in our hearts and minds.

Books of Poetry Written for Young People by Jack Prelutsky
The Baby Uggs Are Hatching. Greenwillow, 1982.
Beneath a Blue Umbrella. Greenwillow, 1990.
Circus. Macmillan, 1974.
A Gopher in the Garden and Other Animal Poems. Macmillan, 1967.
The Headless Horseman Rides Tonight. Greenwillow, 1980.
It's Christmas. Greenwillow, 1981.
It's Halloween. Greenwillow, 1977.
It's Snowing! It's Snowing! Greenwillow, 1984.
It's Thanksgiving. Greenwillow, 1982.

It's Valentine's Day. Greenwillow, 1983.
Kermit's Garden of Verses. Random, 1982.
Lazy Bird and Other Verses. Macmillan, 1969.
My Parents Think I'm Sleeping. Greenwillow, 1985.
The New Kid on the Block. Greenwillow, 1984.
Nightmares: Poems to Trouble Your Sleep. Greenwillow, 1976.
The Pack Rat's Day and Other Poems. Macmillan, 1974.
The Queen of Eene. Greenwillow, 1978.
Rainy, Rainy Saturday. Greenwillow, 1980.
Ride a Purple Pelican. Greenwillow, 1986.
Rolling Harvey Down the Hill. Greenwillow, 1980.
The Sheriff of Rottenshot. Greenwillow, 1982.
The Snopp on the Sidewalk and Other Poems. Greenwillow, 1977.
Something Big Has Been Here. Greenwillow, 1990.
The Terrible Tiger. Macmillan, 1969.
Three Saxon Nobles and Other Verses. Macmillan, 1969.
Toucans Two and Other Poems. Macmillan, 1970.
Tyrannosaurus Was a Beast. Greenwillow, 1988.
What I Did Last Summer. Greenwillow, 1984.
Zoo Doings. Greenwillow, 1983.

Valerie Worth

□ Ms. Worth's free-verse poems have a delicate nature. Often she seems to observe common acts in slow motion. She looks at small things with a slanted view and gets inside them somehow to make us look closer. Ms. Worth began writing fiction and verse for adults, and "adult techniques" are part of her poetry for young people. She is married and has three children.

Books of Poetry Written for Young People by Valerie Worth

All the Small Poems. Farrar, 1987.
Gypsy Gold. Farrar, 1983.
More Small Poems. Farrar, 1976.
Small Poems. Farrar, 1972.
Small Poems Again. Farrar, 1985.
Still More Small Poems. Farrar, 1978.

Using Poetry

□ Poetry belongs in your classroom, of course. It belongs there every day, not just in a special three-week poetry unit. You need to know poems that you can spout off the top of your head when the moment arises. Your own anthology of favorites that you've culled from the masters is almost a necessity. You need books of poems by your favorite poets and specific subject anthologies.

□ Unless children have had many positive experiences with poetry before this, introduce the book yourself in a special way. Pick two or three selections that especially delight you and that are on subjects for which the children will have some affinity. After the kids get settled in the morning, and before the business of the day, read one or more poems aloud. Don't push the kids for reactions; if they happen, take them. In most cases, it's best to close the book and leave it in a prominent spot on your desk with book marks or slips of paper to show the pages you've just shared. Of course, the children can borrow it and go on from there. Do the same thing at least once a day, and preferably three or four times a day, for the next week or so.

□ Carolyn Bauer, who's written some fine books about getting children and literature together, recommends using a picketer's sign on which you've printed "POETRY BREAK" in large colorful letters. Whenever the spirit moves, pick up the sign and yell "Poetry Break!" Put down the sign, pick up the book, and read a poem. She advocates doing the same to other classrooms in the school as you pass by. Sometimes wear a costume or carry a prop appropriate to the poem. Other times it's just you, the poem, and the sign. After a few experiences, let the children take over the role of Poetry Breaker. Make sure, of course, that they have read the poem aloud enough times to do it fluidly and make sure the poem is a short one.

□ After a week or so, you and the children may be ready to explore the book more systematically—of course, systematically is a relative term. You don't want to start with page one and plod through. You'll hate the book, the kids, and the poems by page 50 if you do that. What you might like to do, however, is gather a small group of children around the book and make up some "found" poems. Form a poetry chain by reading one line and letting a child find a line in another poem that begins with the last word of your line. You can hunt through the book together, reading poems that convey the same mood on different subjects. Try matching the mood lines or poems to the mood in prints of famous paintings. How about looking for poems in which color is accented?

☐ Try some of these bulletin board ideas: a playground with each piece of equipment bearing an appropriate poem such as "The Base Stealer" and Stevenson's "My Swing." Mother Goose's "Seesaw Margery Daw" surely belongs there. A construction site could start with "The Steam Shovel." A circus, a farm, an ocean, and a forest are other possible locales for poetry displays.

☐ Have the children find a poem about the earth or ground such as "Mud" and print it so that it forms the ground of the bulletin board. Poems about trees such as "Birch Trees" or "Trees" form the trunk of the tree. Up in the branches go such poems as "To a Squirrel at Kyle-Na-No" and "The McIntosh Apple," "Up in the Pine," and "I Heard a Bird Sing." If you're feeling whimsical, put "wearing of the Green" up there. If you expand the picture, you have room for poems about the sky, the moon, the stars, the wind and clouds, and things along the ground as well. City poems could be displayed in a similar way.

☐ Those of us on the lookout for whole language activities should be pleased to find such chantables as "On the Ning Nang Nong " full of great sound words. Still on the whole language trail are pattern poems such as "Solomon Grundy" for days of the week and "The Adventures of Isabel" and "Click-beetle," each with one often-repeated word. Whole language people need literature with phrases and words that can be played with and changed. Try "Rhyme," "Misnomer," and "Eletelephony."

☐ By this time the children should be fans of poetry, and perhaps a few authors in particular. It's probably time to find out about poets. Read the information on the dust jackets of the books and then send the children to the library for more facts. Surround the author's picture on the bulletin board with the facts the children have uncovered. Lace the bulletin board with lines or verses of the poems the children particularly like.

☐ Poetry and music are natural partners. Maybe it's time for a musical extravaganza starring your favorite poetry enthusiasts. Construct a backdrop and staging for a city street. Find an instrumental rendition of "New York, New York." At various points, stop the music and have the children recite Lois Lenski's "Sing a Song of People" and "City, City" as crowds of people carrying packages and bundles criss-cross the stage. Then have the spotlight fall on individuals dressed and equipped to render "Sing a Song of Subways," "The People," "Sidewalk Racer," "Pigeons," "City Lights," "The Riveter," "Barbershop," "Stickball," or "J's the Jumping Jay Walker." If you could get six children in a seven-floor building replica, you could do a splendid rendition of "The People Upstairs," with each child's head popping out above the one below it and reciting the next two lines.

Picture Books

Don't assume that picture books are only for the young. We can't think of a single picture book that would have no interest to older children and adults. If the plot is too infantile, the pattern might be interesting and worth imitating; the illustrations might be unusual and, therefore, worthy of investigation.

Many picture books are intended for a more mature audience. They have subtle humor or political messages or details that challenge and delight. We have listed a few of our favorites that we have used successfully with upper-grade children. Many other picture books are listed with themes and novels thoughout this book. As with any list in this book or other books, it is not nearly complete.

Aardema, Verna. *Why Mosquitoes Buzz in People's Ears.* Dial, 1975.

See page 17

Ahlberg, Janet and Ahlberg, Allan. *The Jolly Postman.* Little, 1986.

See page 16.

Base, Graeme. *Animalia.* Abrahms, 1987.

In each picture there are objects whose names begin with a target letter. There is also a boy in a striped shirt who is not always easy to find.

Bayer, Jane. *A, My Name Is Alice.* Dial, 1984.

This is the old ball-bouncing game: A my name is Alice and my husband's name is Alex; we come from Alaska where we sell ants. Look at the details Steven Kellogg puts in the illustrations.

Browne, Anthony. *Piggybook.* Knopf, 1986.

See page 82.

Charlip, Remy. *Fortunately.* Macmillan, 1985.

This is wordplay and a story that could serve as the prototype for many more.

Cole, Brock. *The Giant's Toe.* Farrar, 1988.

See page 18.

Cooney, Barbara. *Island Boy.* Viking, 1988.

An island is inhabited by a young man and his family. Gradually the population on the island grows and the changes in the family and the island are beautifully illustrated and beautifully related.

——. *Miss Rumphius.* Viking, 1982.

See page 82.

dePaola, Tomie. *The Legend of the Bluebonnet.* Putnam, 1983.

This story explains that the bluebonnets in Texas are the result of a sacrifice made by an Indian girl.

——. *The Legend of the Indian Paintbrush.* Putnam, 1988.

Here is another beautiful tale of the origin of a beautiful wild flower.

Fair, Sylvia. *The Bedspread.* Morrow, 1982.

Two elderly, bedridden sisters share the same bed and disagree about everything. They decide to change their plain white bedspread into an expression of their memories. Each starts from her own end of the bed. When they meet in the middle, their creations are vastly different.

Fox, Mem. *Wilfrid Gordon McDonald Partridge.* Kane Miller, 1985.

Wilfrid lives next to an old people's home and likes many of the folks who live there, but his favorite is Miss Nancy, who has four names just as he does. When Wilfrid is told that Miss Nancy has lost her memory, he sets about bringing Miss Nancy treasures to help get her memory back.

Gackenbach, Dick. *King Wacky.* Crown, 1984.

See page 14.

Gammell, Stephen. *Once Upon MacDonald's Farm.* Macmillan, 1981.

See page 14.

Griffin, Sandra. *Earth Circles.* Walker, 1989.

A girl and her mother go for a walk in the spring and discover cycles all around them. Each cycle is printed around a circle.

Hall, Donald. *Ox-Cart Man.* Viking, 1979.

See page 38.

Handford, Martin. *Find Waldo Now.* Little, 1988.
  ——. *The Great Waldo Search.* Little, 1989.
  ——. *Where's Waldo?* Little, 1987.

Waldo appears on each page, but so do hundreds of other people and things. The challenge is to find Waldo and to find the items he drops.

Hazen, Barbara Shook. *Tight Times.* Viking, 1979.

The young hero wants a dog, but his father explains that these are tight times and a dog is out of the question. While he's at it, the father explains what else is happening around the house because of tight times. With humor and a light touch, the effects are beautiful.

Heller, Ruth. *A Cache of Jewels and Other Collective Nouns.* Grosset, 1987.

Collective nouns—uncommon and common—are rhythmically presented and beautifully illustrated.

Hoban, Russell. *The Marzipan Pig.* Farrar, 1986.

This is one of those books that's halfway between a picture book and a novel so we've listed it here. The Marzipan Pig is eaten by a mouse early in the story, but his sweetness passes from eater to eater.

Jonas, Ann. *Reflections.* Greenwillow, 1987.

Here is a day near the ocean in full color and, as *Round Trip,* you view the book first one way and then turn it upside down and start again.

———. *Round Trip.* Greenwillow, 1983.

A trip in black and white from a city into the country and back again is told in this ingenious book in which the trip back is the book turned upside down.

Kellogg, Steven. *The Mysterious Tadpole.* Dial, 1977.

See page 14.

Khalsa, Dayal Kaur. *Tales of a Gambling Grandma.* Crown, 1986.

This is not the usual storybook grandmother. This one is ready for everything in life, even the Cossacks. In case they come, she keeps borscht in the refrigerator.

Kimmell, Eric. *Charlie Drives the Stage.* Holiday, 1989.

See page 14.

Lobel, Arnold. *Fables.* Harper, 1980.

These tongue-in-cheek fables are witty and, like all good fables, a mirror to help us see ourselves more clearly. The illustrations are wonderful!

———. *The Rose In My Garden.* Greenwillow, 1984.

Another "This is the House That Jack Built" using the combined skills of Arnold and Anita Lobel tells of a simple incident in a garden. The words will stretch the mind and the illustrations will delight the eye.

Macaulay , David. *Why The Chicken Crossed the Road.* Houghton, 1987.

A chicken crosses the road, precipitating a series of events ending with the chicken crossing the road again. The illustrations are busy with bold colors that make the action seem even more madcap.

McLerran, Alice. *The Mountain That Loved a Bird.* Picture Book, 1985.

No bird can stay on a barren mountain even when there is love. Things do change, however, even mountains.

Mariotti, Mario. *Hanimals.* Green Tiger, 1982.
———. *Humages.* Green Tiger, 1984.
———. *Humands.* Green Tiger, 1982.

Paint and a few props change parts of the body into people and animals. This is one step from shadow-plays and absolutely fascinating.

Marshall, James. *Red Riding Hood.* Dial, 1987.

See page 19.

Moeri, Louise. *Star Mother's Youngest Child.* Houghton, 1975.

This Christmas story is filled with magic and pure joy. It makes a wonderful tale for telling or reading out loud.

Moore, Lilian. *I'll Meet You at the Cucumbers.* Atheneum, 1988.

This is a special and wonderful version of "The Country Mouse and the City Mouse". In this case, Adam, the country mouse, is a poet. He makes up beautiful lyric poems about the country he loves. However, he doesn't know they're poems. The city mouse Adam meets and falls in love with takes him to the library to read the works of other poets and tells Adam that he, too, is a poet who belongs in the country.

Numeroff, Laura. *If You Give a Mouse a Cookie.* Harper, 1985.

Don't give a mouse a cookie. If you do, it's going to want a glass of milk to go with it. Then it's a straw and so on back to the cookie. Catch the action in the pictures as well as in the text.

Pittman, Helena. *The Gift of the Willows.* Carolrhoda, 1988.

In Japan, a young potter sees two willow saplings at the river where he gathers clay. As he marries and has a family, the willows prosper and he incorporates their beauty into his life. When the family nearly drowns, so do the willows; but just in time, they save the lives of the family.

Provensen, Alice and Provensen, Martin. *Shaker Lane.* Viking, 1987.

See page 38.

Rogers, Jean. *King Island Christmas.* Greenwillow, 1985.

See page 73.

———. *Runaway Mittens.* Greenwillow, 1988.

Pica shares a problem with many children: he is always losing his mittens. Pica is an Eskimo child and the book is full of information about his life.

Say, Allen. *The Bicycle Man.* Houghton, 1982.

In 1946, two soldiers appear at a Japanese elementary school. One soldier entertains the children with bicycle tricks. There are nice suggestions of Japanese culture and a timelessness to the story.

Steig, William. *The Amazing Bone.* Farrar, 1976.

Pearl, the pig, finds a talking bone. You'd think this would bring her nothing but pleasure, but there's a fox who isn't put off by a talking bone.

———. *CDB.* Windmill, 1968.
———. *CDC.* Farrar, 1986.

Letter talk is the basis for these books. "A-B, C D B?" "S, I C D B. D B S A B-Z B."

Steptoe, John. *The Story of Jumping Mouse.* Lothrop, 1984.

A mouse looks for the Far Off Place he has heard about from the elders. On the journey he helps many others and, in so doing, loses his senses.

Ungerer, Tomi. *The Beast of Monsieur Racine.* Farrar, 1971.

A very strange beast has been stealing the prize pears of Monsieur Racine. Racine conducts careful scientific observations of this seemingly rare and exotic creature.

Van Laan, Nancy. *Rainbow Crow.* Knopf, 1989.

Before humans came to Earth, a deep snow fell, covering the animals. Eventually, the beautiful rainbow crow offered to go to the Sky Spirit to get help. Sky Spirit gave the crow fire to melt the snow, but the fire blackened the crow's beautiful feathers and ruined its voice.

Viorst, Judith. *Alexander and the Terrible, Horrible, No Good, Very Bad Day.* Atheneum, 1972.

Alexander's day isn't so different from your last bad day; it's just that he tells about it hilariously.

———. *I'll Fix Anthony.* Atheneum, 1969.

Anthony is six, so he can do everything. His younger brother tells us what it's like to have this annoyingly competent sibling. He vows that things will be different when he reaches that exalted age.

———. *My Mama Says There Aren't Any Zombies, Ghosts, Vampires, Creatures, Demons, Monsters, Fiends, Goblins, or Things.* Macmillan, 1973.

This book is really a series of observations about the mistakes even mommies make. Typical Viorst understatement and humor make this one work.

———. *Rosie and Michael.* Atheneum, 1974.

This is an explanation of friendship between a girl and a boy. Each one explains what he or she likes about the other without sentimentality. It's fun.

———. *Sunday Morning.* Aladdin, 1968.

We suspect this book is more for adults than for children. Adults can sympathize with the parents' attempt to get some sleep on Sunday morning.

———. *The Tenth Good Thing About Barney.* Atheneum, 1971.

Barney the cat is dead and his grieving owner tries to think of ten good things to say about Barney for the funeral.

Ward, Lynd. *The Silver Pony.* Houghton, 1973.

Here is a wordless novel of a boy and a flying horse. Even the chapters are indicated wordlessly. This is a beautiful, mythic novel.

Yolen, Jane. *Owl Moon.* Putnam, 1987.

See page 252.

Zimelman, Nathan. *Mean Chickens and Wild Cucumbers.* Macmillan, 1983.

See page 56.

Poetry

Farber, Norma. *How Does It Feel to Be Old?* Dutton, 1979.

An older woman talks frankly and poetically about the advantages and disadvantages of being old.

Time Line of Books

Prehistory
Dyers, T. A. *A Way of His Own.* Houghton, 1981.

■■■■■□□□□□□□□□

Young Shutok has a twisted back and is abandoned by his tribe of Early Americans because he cannot keep up and because they think he is afflicted by evil spirits. Joining ranks with a slave girl, he survives adversity and rejoins his tribe.

Circa 28 A.D.
Speare, Elizabeth George. *The Bronze Bow.* Houghton, 1951.

■■■■■■■■■■■□□□

Daniel Bar Jamin is after revenge for the death of his father and mother at the hands of the Romans in the time of Christ. Aiming for the strength described in a verse from Samuel II "my arms can bend a bow of bronze," he joins a group of outlaws, awaiting his chance for revenge. It is Jesus who allows Daniel to cope with his anger and forgive the Romans.

700
Dickinson, Peter. *The Dancing Bear.* Dell, 1988.

■■■■■■■■■□□□□□

Silvester, a young Greek slave in Byzantium, is in charge of training Bubba the bear to dance. When Huns slaughter his master's family and take the daughter, Adrianne, as captive, Silvester trains Bubba to follow the trail.

Middle Ages
Bulla, Clyde Robert. *The Sword in the Tree.* Crowell, 1956.

■■■■■□□□□□□□□□

See page 35.

De Angeli, Marguerite. *The Door in the Wall.* Doubleday, 1949.

■■■■■■□□□□□□□□

See page 35.

Gray, Elizabeth Janet. *Adam of the Road.* Viking, 1942.

■■■■■■■■■■□□□□□

See page 35.

1100
Bulla, Clyde Robert. *Viking Adventure.* Crowell, 1963.

■■■■■■■■□□□□□□

Young Sigurd joins a Viking crew trying to retrace the voyage Leif Ericson took a hundred years before. When the Captain is murdered, Sigurd escapes and returns home to learn to read and write in order to record the adventure.

1284
Skurzynski, Gloria. *What Happened in Hamelin?* Four Winds, 1979.

■■■■■■■■■□□□□□

See page 35.

1610
Bulla, Clyde Robert. *A Lion to Guard Us.* Crowell, 1981.

■■■■■■■■□□□□□□

See page 194.

1620
Clapp, Patricia. *Constance: A Story of Early Plymouth.* Lothrop, 1968.

■■■■■■■■□□□□□□

This is the imaginary journal of a real person from the time she arrives on the Mayflower until her wedding five years later. It reflects the fears and hopes of many young girls.

1687
Speare, Elizabeth George. *The Witch of Blackbird Pond.* Houghton, 1958.

■■■■■■■■■■□□□□□

See page 262.

1692
Clapp, Patricia. *Witches' Children.* Lothrop, 1982.

■■■■■■■■■■■□□□

Mary Warren tells us of the Salem Witch Trials in a first person narrative that is historically correct and terrifyingly compelling.

1743
Field, Rachel. *Calico Bush.* Macmillan, 1966.

■■■■■■■■■□□□□□

Marguerite Ledoux finds herself in the poor house after the deaths of her only relatives, so she sells herself into bondage for six years in return for board and room. As a young French woman in a land of British colonists, she is subject to prejudice along with her other hardships.

Circa 1750
Fritz, Jean. *The Cabin Faced West.* Coward, 1958.

■■■■■□□□□□□□□□

See page 218.

1756
Edmonds, Walter. *The Matchlock Gun.* Putnam, 1971.

■■■■■■■□□□□□□□

See page 265.

1768
Avi. *Night Journeys.* Pantheon, 1979.

■■■■■■■■■□□□□□

See page 181.

1774
Fritz, Jean. *Early Thunder.* Coward, 1967.

■■■■■■■■■□□□□□

See page 62.

1776
Wibberly, Leonard. *John Treegate's Musket.* Farrar, 1959.

■■■■■■■■■■□□□□□

See page 63.

1777
Collier, James L. and Collier, Christopher. *My Brother Sam Is Dead.* Four Winds, 1974.

■■■■■■■■■■■■■□

See page 62.

1778
Avi. *The Fighting Ground.* Lippincott, 1984.

■■■■■■■■□□□□□□

See page 61.

1793
Fleischman, Paul. *Path of the Pale Horse.* Harper, 1983.

■■■■■■■■■□□□□□

Lep is a doctor's apprentice who, with his mentor Dr. Poole, travels to Philadelphia to purchase medicine. Dr. Poole decides to stay in Philadelphia to help with the yellow fever epidemic. Lep attempts to get his sister to come home with him, because he is convinced that the man she is working for is a charlatan. When Lep's friend Mr. Tweakfield dies of the fever in spite of Lep's medical skills, Lep learns a lesson in humility.

1812
Brady, Esther Wood. *The Toad on Capitol Hill.* Crown, 1978.

■■■■■■■■■□□□□□

See page 267.

Henry, Marguerite. *Justin Morgan Had a Horse.* Rand, 1946.

■■■■■■■□□□□□□□

See page 130.

1830

Blos, Joan. *A Gathering of Days.* Macmillan, 1979.

■■■■■■■■□□□□□□

See page 120.

1835

O'Dell, Scott. *Island of the Blue Dolphins.* Houghton, 1960.

■■■■■■■■□□□□□□

See page 127.

1850

Loeper, John. *The Golden Dragon.* Atheneum, 1978.

■■■■■■■□□□□□□□

A trip is related through the eyes of Jeremy, a ten-year-old boy, on board a ship where another boy is punished for washing his socks in fresh water and the weather turns wild off Cape Horn.

1852

Wiseman, David. *Jeremy Visick.* Houghton, 1981.

■■■■■■■■□□□□□□

When Matthew Clemens becomes intrigued with the life of Jeremy Visick, a boy whose father and two older brothers are killed in a mine disaster in 1852, he is snatched back to that era. Caught in the mine disaster, Matthew attempts to bring Jeremy "to grass."

1860

Harvey, Brett. *Cassie's Journey: Going West in the 1860's.* Holiday, 1988.

■■□□□□□□□□□□□□

See page 57.

Conrad, Pam. *Prairie Songs.* Harper, 1985.

■■■■■■■■□□□□□

See page 147.

1866

Reeder, Carolyn. *Shades of Gray.* Macmillan, 1989.

■■■■■■■■■□□□□□

See page 150.

1872

Talbot, Charlene. *An Orphan for Nebraska.* Atheneum, 1979.

■■■■■■■□□□□□□□

See page 58.

1874

Lasky, Kathryn. *The Bone Wars.* Morrow, 1988.

■■■■■■■■□□□□□

See page 264.

1888

Stevens, Carla. *Anna, Grandpa, and the Big Storm.* Clarion, 1982.

■■■■■■■■□□□□□

See page 73.

1895

Beatty, Patricia. *Sarah and Me and the Lady from the Sea..* Morrow, 1989.

■■■■■■■□□□□□□□

See page 67.

1898

Rappaport, Doreen. *Trouble at the Mines.* Crowell, 1987.

■■■■■■□□□□□□□□

See page 162.

1906

Yep, Laurence. *Dragonwings.* Harper, 1975.

■■■■■■□□□□□□□□

Moon Shadow is eight when his father sends for him to come to San Francisco from China. There Moon Shadow becomes part of Chinatown, makes two non-Chinese friends, and helps with the earthquake's aftermath. His father then pursues his dream of making and flying his own airplane.

1910

Taylor, Sydney. *All-of-a-Kind Family.* Dell, 1966.

■■■■■■□□□□□□□□

Everyday living for five sisters and their parents in a big house in Manhattan comes to life. The family is Jewish and their traditions color much of their existence at the turn of the century.

Sebestyen, Ouida. *Words By Heart.* Little, 1979.

■■■■■■■■□□□□□□

See page 171.

1913

Peck, Richard. *The Ghost Belonged to Me.* Viking, 1975.

■■■■■■■■■■□□□□

See page 22.

1917

Lewis, Claudia. *Long Ago in Oregon.* Harper, 1987.

■■■■■■■■■□□□□□

See page 266.

1927

Peck, Robert Newton. *Arly.* Walker, 1989.

■■■■□□□□□□□□□□

In a migrant camp in Jailtown, Florida, Arly Poole lives with his father in Shack Row. Their lot is not a happy one and Arly would surely have grown up as illiterate as his father and most of the other workers had it not been for Miss Binnie Hoe who,

with her restraint, determination, and humor, decides to set up a school in the camp.

1930

Taylor, Mildred D. *Roll of Thunder, Hear My Cry.* Dial, 1976.

■■■■■■■■■■□□□□

See page 264.

1935

Uchida, Yoshiko. *A Jar of Dreams.* Atheneum, 1981.

■■■■■■■■■■□□□□

Rinko and her Japanese-American family are harassed almost daily by Wilbur Starr and must counter that threat while coping with the Geat Depression. In the process, they rediscover their own tradition.

1936

Hooks, William. *Circle of Fire.* Atheneum, 1982.

■■■■■■■■■□□□□□

See page 265.

1946

Herman, Charlotte. *Millie Cooper, 3B.* Puffin, 1985.

■■■■□□□□□□□□□□

See page 262.

1947

Lord, Bette Bao. *In the Year of the Boar and Jackie Robinson.* Harper, 1984.

■■■■■■■■■□□□□□

See page 125.

1954

Gondosch, Linda. *The Best Bet Gazette.* Dutton, 1989.

■■■■■■■■■□□□□□

See page 265.

1960
Clark, Ann Nolan. *To Stand Against the Wind.* Viking, 1978.

■■■■■■□□□□□□□□

See page 87.

1970
Kehle, Roberta. *The Blooming of the Flame Tree.* Crossway, 1983.

■■■■■■■■■■□□□□□

Tran is a student and expert kite flyer. His father is headmaster of the school. The Communists invade his town in Laos and the family hides in the jungle, hoping to find a boat to take them to safety. Their troubles continue after they reach the refugee camp and, later, America.

Off to a Good Start

The beginning paragraphs of novels can be used in a variety of ways. Obviously, they make a good literary quiz game: can you identify the book? Sometimes, when they are intriguing or exciting enough, the first lines make good teasers, enticing the children to want more of the story. Also, in our attempt to help children learn to read as writers, these beginning lines can be a point of focus for discussion: What do we know about a book from these few lines? What mood has the author established? What do you want to know after this taste?

Because children are apt to skip over what they call description, they often miss these first lines. Although this doesn't usually effect the plot all that much, it means that, when they attempt to write a story, they are reduced to more trite beginnings. Reading and discussing beginnings can give them courage to step out differently in their own writing.

The Dark Is Rising by Susan Cooper
"Too many!" James shouted, and slammed the door behind him.
"What?" said Will.
"Too many kids in this family, that's what. Just too many." James stood fuming on the landing like a small angry locomotive, then stumped across to the windowseat and stared out at the garden. Will put aside his book and pulled up his legs to make room. "I could hear all the yelling," he said, chin on knees.

Did You Carry the Flag Today, Charley? by Rebecca Caudill.
To get to Charley Cornett's house, you turn left off the highway at Main Street, drive to the edge of town, and cross a bridge. There you take another left turn, and you are on your way. You can't get lost because there is only one road to follow. It is a blacktop. It looks like a black ribbon tied around the mountain, sometimes high on the mountainside, sometimes low in the narrow creek bottom.

A Gathering of Days by Joan W. Blos
Sunday, October 17, 1830
I, Catherine Cabot Hall, aged 13 years, 7 months, 8 days, of Meredith in the State of New Hampshire, do begin this book.

Good Night, Mr. Tom by Michelle Magorian
"Yes," said Tom bluntly, on opening the front door, "What d'you want?"

The Indian in the Cupboard by Lynne Reid Banks
It was not that Omri didn't appreciate Patrick's birthday present to him. Far from it. He was really very grateful—sort of. It was, without a doubt, very kind of Patrick to give Omri anything at all, let alone a secondhand plastic Indian that he himself had finished with.

Mr. Popper's Penguins by Florence Atwater and Richard Atwater
It was an afternoon in later September. In the pleasant little city of Stillwater, Mr. Popper, the house painter was going home from work. He was carrying his buckets, his ladders, and his boards so that he had rather a hard time moving along. He was spattered here and there with paint and calcimine, and there were bits of wallpaper clinging to his hair and whiskers, for he was rather an untidy man.

The Peppermint Pig by Nina Bawden
Old Granny Greengrass had her finger chopped off in the butcher's when she was buying half a leg of lamb. She had pointed to the place where she wanted her joint to be cut but then she decided she needed a bigger piece and pointed again. Unfortunately, Mr. Grummett, the butcher, was already bringing his sharp chopper down.

The Secret Garden by Frances Hodgson Burnett
When Mary Lennox was sent to Misselthwaite Manor to live with her uncle everybody said she was the most disagreeable-looking child ever seen. It was true, too. She had a little thin face and a little thin body, thin light hair and a sour expression. Her hair was yellow and her face was yellow because she had been born in India and had always been ill in one way or another.

Stone Fox by John Gardiner
One day Grandfather wouldn't get out of bed. He just lay there and stared at the ceiling and looked sad.

Thank You, Jackie Robinson by Barbara Cohen
Listen. When I was a kid, I was crazy. Nuttier than a fruitcake. Madder than a hatter. Out of my head. You see, I had this obsession. This hang-up. It was all that mattered to me. I was in love with the Brooklyn Dodgers.

Tuck Everlasting by Natalie Babbitt
The first week in August hangs at the very top of summer, the top of the live-long year, like the highest seat of a Ferris wheel when it pauses in its turning. The weeks that come before are only a climb from the balmy spring, and those that follow a drop to the chill of autumn, but the first week of August is motionless, and hot. It is curiously silent, too, with blank white dawns and glaring noons, and sunsets smeared with too much color. Often at night there is lightning, but it quivers all alone. There is no thunder, no relieving rain. These are strange and breathless dog days, when people are led to do things they are sure to be sorry for after.

The Winter Room by Gary Paulsen
If books could be more, could show more, could own more, this book would have smells... It would have the smells of old farms; the sweet smell of new-mown hay as it falls off the oiled sickle blade when the horses pull the mower through the field, and the sour smell of manure steaming in a winter barn. It would have the sticky-slick smell of birth when the calves come and they suck for the first time on the rich, new milk; the dusty smell of winter hay dried and storied in the loft waiting to be dropped down to the cattle; the pungent fermented smell of the chopped corn silage when it is brought into the manger on the silage fork. This book would have the smell of new potatoes sliced and frying in light pepper on a woodstove burning dry pine, the damp smell of leather mittens steaming on the back of the stovetop, and the acrid smell of the slop bucket by the door when the lid is lifted and the potato peelings are dumped in—but it can't.

The Wolves of Willoughby Chase by Joan Aiken
It was dusk—winter dusk. Snow lay white and shining over the pleated hills, and icicles hung from the forest trees. Snow lay piled on the dark road across Willoughby Wold, but from dawn men had been clearing it with brooms and shovels. There were hundreds of them at work, wrapped in sacking because of the bitter cold, and keeping together in groups for fear of the wolves, grown savage and reckless from hunger.

A Wrinkle in Time by Madeleine L'Engle
It was a dark and stormy night. In her attic bedroom Margaret Murry, wrapped in an old patchwork quilt, sat on the foot of her bed and watched the trees tossing in the frenzied lashing of the wind. Behind the trees clouds scudded frantically across the sky. Every few moments the moon ripped through them, creating wraith-like shadows that raced along the ground.

Writer's Techniques

To help children become more skillful writers, it is sometimes useful to point out techniques used by professional writers. Such literary techniques as foreshadowing, point of view, and flashback are often overlooked by readers intent on the plot of a good story. Therefore, we have listed a few of the books in which such techniques are used. Check the Index for story summaries.

Flashback
Banks, Lynne Reid. *The Fairy Rebel.* Doubleday, 1988. ✔

Bawden, Nina. *Carrie's War.* Lippincott, 1973. ✔

Jacobs, Paul. *Born Into Light.* Scholastic, 1988.

Lister, Robin. *The Legend of King Arthur.* Doubleday, 1990. ✔

Magorian, Michelle. *Good Night, Mr. Tom.* Harper, 1982. ✔

O'Brien, Robert. *Mrs. Frisby and the Rats Of NIMH.* Atheneum, 1971. ✔

Paulsen, Gary. *The Voyage of the Frog.* Orchard, 1988. ✔

Foreshadowing
Babbit, Natalie. *Tuck Everlasting.* Farrar, 1975. ✔

Conrad, Pam. *Prairie Songs.* Harper, 1985. ✔

Cooper, Susan. *Dawn of Fear.* Harcourt, 1970. ✔

Dunlop, Eileen. *The Valley of Deer.* Holiday, 1989. ✔

Holman, Felice. *Slake's Limbo.* Scribner, 1974. ✔

Hunter, Mollie. *A Stranger Came Ashore.* Harper, 1975. ✔

Lister, Robin. *The Legend of King Arthur.* Doubleday, 1990. ✔

Paulsen, Gary. *Popcorn Days and Buttermilk Nights.* Lodestar, 1983. ✔

Pearce, Philippa. *Tom's Midnight Garden.* Harper, 1984. ✔

Slepian, Jan. *The Night of the Bozos.* Dutton, 1983. ✔

Exaggeration
Salassi, Otto R. *On the Ropes.* Greenwillow, 1981.

Allegory
Heide, Florence Parry. *The Shrinking of Treehorn.* Holiday, 1971. ✔

Saint-Exupery, Antoine de. *The Little Prince.* Harcourt, 1943.

Present Tense
Holman, Felice. *Secret City, USA.* Scribners, 1990.

First Person Diaries or Journals
See pages 31–33.

Alternating Points of View
Byars, Betsy. *The Animal, the Vegetable and John D. Jones.* Deleacorte, 1982. ✔

Sharmat, Marjorie. *Chasing After Annie.* Harper, 1981. ✔

Wiseman, David. *Adam's Common.* Houghton, 1984.

Cliff Hangers
Byars, Betsy. *The Two-Thousand-Pound Goldfish.* Harper, 1982. ✔

Reading Aloud

☐ Is there any one left who doesn't know that reading aloud is a necessary and vital part of every reading program through all the grades? The research is so convincing and the publicity so prevalent that no one can consider it a frill any longer. If you need further persuasion, Jim Trelease's book *The New Read-Aloud Handbook* (Penguin, 1989) will bring you to your senses immediately. Besides citing the research and giving you all the arguments you'll ever need for reading aloud to children, Jim's book gives an excellent annotated bibiliography.

☐ Let's assume, then, that you are convinced and that you've been reading aloud to your class every day for years. Have you considered that your read aloud program should be as carefully planned as every other program in your class? Your purpose in reading a book aloud is to entice the kids into better literature, new genres, and more difficult reading than they might otherwise choose. There is no point in reading aloud all of the books in a series or even more than the first one. Therefore, read the first of a series like the Narnia books, the Prydain Cycle, the Ramona books, the Indian in the Cupboard series, or the Bunnicula books and let the kids read the others on their own.

☐ Books read aloud by the teacher should usually be a little bit harder than those the majority of the class is ready to read independently. The most popular book with a class is usually the one the teacher is currently reading aloud or has just finished. Because the meaning of the book is clear, the reader can linger over the scenes he or she liked best or figure out a part that was murky.

☐ Be sure that your read-aloud choices don't leave emergent readers thinking that all good books are fantasies or here-and-now books. In the course of a school year, your read-aloud choices should come from every genre. The books you read aloud in class become a point of reference for all the other reading and writing done by the class. The characters, themes, moods, and plots of such books can be compared to others at every juncture. It's a way to explore feelings together and to discuss the techniques of the author. These book discussions might be the only ones in which the whole class can participate. Literary themes, such as we've outlined in the first section of this book, are much more apt to catch fire if you are reading aloud from a novel relevant to that theme each day.

☐ Choose from a variety of authors. Keep broadening the scope of available and desirable books. Be sure, of course, that you've read the book yourself before reading aloud. Many a teacher has been caught red-faced by a section that is embarassing or objectionable or better enjoyed by a silent reader.

☐ Don't read aloud a book that you yourself don't like. It doesn't matter how many critics tell you it's a wonderful book; if you don't like it, it won't take your listeners long to figure that out. One of the main reasons for reading aloud is to show readers how wonderful a good book can be. The reader should be moved to tears, laughter, fear, or wonder as much as the listeners.

Instead of a Book Report

☐ Sometimes in an effort to make sure kids are reading, teachers assign book reports. Such activities are usually self-defeating. If enjoying reading is the desired outcome, the surest way to kill all interest in it is to require it. If writing about their reading is the goal, book reports don't do that very well either. The writing for such an assignment is apt to be stilted and cursory. If good book discussion is the aim, few children have ever been known to get so excited after hearing a book reported upon that they want to continue the discussion. If the reason for the required report is to check on whether or not the child has really read and understood the book, a book report is an inefficient and chancy way to do it.

Book reports do send children scurrying to the library to find, in this order: a book they already had to read for another assignment, a book another teacher read aloud to them, a book they read last year, the thinnest book permitted, a book with enough information on the book jacket to suffice for the assignment. So, book reports, however well-intentioned, often drive out leisure reading, book discussion, and good critical writing.

☐ Book contests, another motivational scheme, usually fail because they reward the number of books read instead of thoughtful reading. Again, children choose books that fall into the same categories as the ones they use for book reports. Slower, thoughtful readers are penalized, as are children who choose books for content rather than speed.

☐ The best way to get reading going in a classroom is to treasure reading, to model it, to discuss it, to make it the center of your curriculum and your classroom. If you read a book tonight that is suitable reading for your children, take it in tomorrow and hand it to a child saying, "I read this last night. I laughed/cried/was so excited that I couldn't put it down. I thought of you because you like . . . Let me know what you think of it." If you meant those words, that child will probably read the book and will want to talk to you about it and so will several other children within earshot of your conversation. Within a month you could have thirty such books circulating in the classroom, you will know thirty more books, and the conversations you have with the children and that they have with each other will be more in depth than from any book report.

☐ Add to that technique a classroom readers' newspaper and/or television or radio show that contains book reviews, analyses of a specific writer's work, poems and songs that extend the books, and you've got more interest.

☐ Posters made by your reading population and placed around the school will help; so will opportunities for book talking. In Jim Yvon's fourth grade classroom, children sit in two concentric circles after a silent reading session. They talk to the person sitting closest in the other circle about what they had been reading. Then the outside circle moves one space. Again the conversations and then one more move. Such a set-up only lasts fifteen minutes or so each day, but the books that children find and like are passed on to others.

☐ Reading groups formed around single themes or single authors or even around one book will allow for the discussion and sharing of ideas and questions about the reading.

☐ Colorful events such as literature fairs, slide shows, video tapes, costume days, author/illustrator/poet visits and telephone interviews add spark to a flagging program and give the children a chance to celebrate what they've learned.

☐ Think of activities that create interest rather than test details or reward speed. Make your classroom shout "Reading Lives Here!" and you won't need "The name of the book I read is _____ . It is about a _____ . The part I liked best is _____ ."

Literary Pursuit

Directions

□ Announce the Literary Pursuit in advance with posters hung around the school, making clear that children can choose to try it on their own, with a group of friends, or as a whole class.

□ Set a date when the entries must be in. Prepare a lot of copies of questions for the hunt. This is the kind of thing that starts off slowly and gains momentum as other kids hear it being discussed. I've also used a Literary Pursuit as an ice breaker with gifted students from many different classes who don't know or trust each other yet. If you use it with a smaller group, the rules should be altered to include this one: No one's paper will be accepted until everyone's is complete. That way those playing individually will be needed eventually for their information and vice versa.

□ No matter what, entrants should be encouraged to ask for help from friends, neighbors, and family. The point is to get kids' books talked about in school and at home. Oh, and don't look at the answers until you've tried it yourself.

Part 1: Mother Goose

1. What did the fiddling cat hold under her arm as she came out of the barn?
2. What is true about the wise old owl who lived in an oak?
3. Who ran off with a dish?
4. When Sleepy Head says it's time for bed, what does Greedy Gut say?
5. Where's Peter Peter Pumpkineater's wife?
6. Who went to bed with his stockings on?
7. Where is Little Boy Blue?
8. Most of the beggars come in rags and tags but one of them wears something else. What is it?
9. Who says, "When nobody's with me, I'm all alone"?
10. What happened to the old man who wouldn't say his prayers?
11. Why doesn't Doctor Foster go to Gloucester any more?
12. Higgledy, Piggledy Pop! Who ate the mop?
13. What did all the king's horses and all the king's men fail to do?

14. Why did the King of Spain's daughter come to visit me?
15. If all the boys lived across the sea, what would the girls become good at?

Part 2: Street Rhymes and Songs

Add the next line.

1. One potato, two potato, three potato, four.
2. Last night as I lay on my pillow,
   Last night as I lay on my bed,
   I stuck my feet out of the window. . .
3. I love coffee, I love tea. . .
4. Marguerite, go wash your feet. . .
5. Roses are red, Violets are blue. . .
6. Yours till the . . . River
   Wears. . .
7. Red Rover, Red Rover. . .
8. It was midnight on the ocean,
   Not a streetcar was in sight,
   The sun was shining brightly,
   For it rained all day that night,
   'Twas a summer day in winter,
   And the snow was raining fast,
   As a barefoot boy with shoes on. . .
9. It's raining, it's pouring,
   The old man is snoring,
   He bumped his head. . .
10. First comes love, then comes marriage. . .
11. No more pencils!
    No more books. . .
12. Ask me no questions. . .
13. What's your name? Puddintane. . .
14. Johnny over the ocean,
    Johnny over the sea. . .
15. See my finger! See my thumb. . .

Part 3: Characters and Chants from Folk and Fairy Tales

Name the chanter and the tale.

1. Mirror, mirror, on the wall,
   Who is fairest of us all?
2. Let down your hair,
   That I may climb the golden stair.
3. I ran away from the old woman,
   I ran away from the old man,
   And I can run away from you,
   I can, I can!

4. Nibble, nibble like a mouse,
   Who is nibbling at my house?
5. Bleat, my little goat, bleat.
   Cover the table with something to eat!
6. Today I brew, today I bake,
   Tomorrow I shall the Queen's child take.
7. Not by the hair of my chinny chin chin!
8. Somebody's been sitting in my chair!
9. Then I'll huff and I'll puff,
   And I'll blow your house in.
10. Nimmy, nimmy not!
    My name is. . .

Part 4: Places
1. Lucy gets there through a door in the back of a closet.
2. The first thing she sees there is a White Rabbit.
3. Owl lives there and so does Piglet.
4. He was found there wearing a hat given him by his great-aunt Lucy. The tag said, "Please take care of this bear."
5. Hazel leads them there with a lot of help from Fiver's foresight.
6. Scarecrow, the Tin Woodman, and the Lion go there with Dorothy.
7. There you can find the Foothills of Confusion, the Mountains of Ignorance, the Doldrums, and the Sea of Knowledge.
8. Tom can get there through the back door of the house only when the clock strikes thirteen.
9. Susan Oldknow lived there once.
10. Bilbo Baggins kills a dragon there.

Part 5: Songs
Add the next line.
1. There's a hole, there's a hole. . .
2. Can't you hear the Captain shoutin'. . .
3. I love thy rocks and rills. . .
4. Ate a peanut, ate a peanut. . .
5. The fox went out on a chilly night. . .
6. The tree was in the wood
   And the. . .
7. Dunderbeck, oh Dunderbeck,
   How could you be so mean. . .
8. The wheels on the bus go round and round
   Round and round, round and round.
   The wheels on the bus go round and round. . .
9. There was a farmer had a dog. . .
10. Oh, we'll all go out to meet her. . .

Part 6: People
1. He finally allows his chair to be painted pink.
2. He is so mad that he says, "I'LL EAT YOU UP!"
3. By getting the fish to act as one, he saves them all.
4. He found "cats here, cats there, cats and kittens everywhere."
5. He couldn't take off his hat.
6. Because Monkey killed one of her children, she will not let the sun come up.
7. He finds two strange bumps at the foot of his bed.
8. He can't sing, but he saves the town celebration when he plays the harmonica.
9. She and her mother and Little Bear and its mother get all mixed up on a hillside.
10. Because the last one in line gets spanked, he is in for a frightening experience.

Part 7: Authors and Illustrators
1. As a young child growing up in Brooklyn, the illustrator painted a picture in the middle of the kitchen table. His father was furious; his mother bought a piece of clear oil cloth to preserve it. Although he was not black, most of the children in his illustrations are.
2. One of his books is a sentimental journey into his childhood: the buildings are containers from his pantry shelves. The main character is named after a Disney creation. The only other characters are from childhood movies. A street in the book is named after his favorite dog.
3. Now he lives in a huge Victorian house in Northampton, Massachusetts. Once he lived in Nazi Germany where, as a child, he was not allowed to see any art produced after that of Wagner's time and only that done by Germans. His thinking and learning was very rigid and was highly structured by the Nazis. When he first came to this country, he was befriended by Leo Lionni. Now his very successful books involve a free use of colored tissue paper and vivid colors.
4. The husband/illustrator of this husband/wife team often uses real models for the characters in his pictures. They live in Santa Barbara, California, where the entrance of their house looks very much like the entrance to the title house in one of their books.

5. This husband and wife team live on Martha's Vineyard off the coast of Massachusetts. They do picture book stories about real incidents that are often inspired by their son, Christopher.

6. In each of his books there is an English bull terrier somewhere. He is a sculptor turned author/illustrator who likes mingling fantasy with reality.

Answers to Literary Pursuit 1:

Part 1: 1. Bagpipes. 2. The more he heard, the less he spoke. 3. The spoon. 4. "put on the pot, we'll sup before we go." 5. In the pumpkin shell. 6. My Son John. 7. Under the haystack. 8. A velvet gown. 9. Little Jumping Joan. 10. They took him by his left leg and threw him down the stairs. 11. He stepped in a puddle up to his middle. 12. The dog. 13. Put Humpty together again. 14. For the sake of my little nut tree. 15. Swimming.

Part 2: 1. Five potato, six potato, seven potato, more. 2. Next morning the neighbors were dead 3. I like the boys and the boys like me. 4. The board of health's across the street. 5. Sugar is sweet and so are you. 6. Westfield River wears rubber pants to keep its bottom dry. 7. Let (Joan) come over. 8. Stood sitting in the grass. 9. And went to bed and won't get up till morning. 10. Then comes (Tom) with a baby carriage. 11. No more teachers' dirty looks. 12. I'll tell you no lies. 13. Ask me again and I'll tell you the same. 14. Johnny broke the telephone and blamed it on to me. 15. See my fist! You better run!

Part 3: 1. Queen Tale, "Snow White" 2. Witch, "Rapunzel" 3. Gingerbread Boy, "The Gingerbread Boy" 4. Witch, "Hansel and Gretel" 5. Little Two Eyes, "One Eye, Two Eyes and Three Eyes" 6. Rumplestiltskin, "Rumplestiltskin" 7. Three Pigs, "The Three Pigs" 8. Three bears, "Goldilocks and The Three Bears" 9. Big Bad Wolf, "The Three Pigs" 10. Tom Tit Tot, "Tom Tit Tot"

Part 4: 1. Narnia 2. Wonderland 3. Hundred Acre Wood 4. Paddington Station 5. Watership Down 6. Oz 7. Phantom Tollbooth 8. Midnight Garden 9. Green Knowe 10. Long Mountain

Part 5: 1. In the bottom of the sea. 2. Dinah, blow your horn. 3. Thy woods and templed hills. 4. Ate a peanut just now. 5. Prayed for the moon for to give him light. 6. Green grass grew all around, around, around. 7. To ever have invented the sausage meat machine. 8. All through the town. 9. And Bingo was his name, oh. 10. When she comes.

Part 6: 1. Peter 2. Max 3. Swimmy 4. Little Old Man 5. Bartholomew Cubbins 6. Mother Owl 7. Owl 8. Lentil 9. Sal 10. Ping

Part 7: 1. Ezra Jack Keats 2. Maurice Sendak 3. Eric Carle 4. Don and Audrey Wood 5. Donald and Carol Carrick 6. Chris Van Allsburg

Literary Pursuit 2

Rules:
1. You can get help from any source.
2. Spelling counts.

Part 1: Mother Goose
1. Who was Taffy?
2. What will poor robin do when the north wind blows?
3. What does the lady at Banbury Cross have on her toes?
4. What is Wednesday's child full of?
5. Why don't we like Dr. Fell?
6. What does Tommy Tucker eat for supper?
7. How much do hot cross buns cost?
8. Why did Polly Flinders get spanked?
9. What could happen to Jerry Hall who is so small?
10. How many were going to St. Ives?

Part 2: Rhymes, Riddles, and Songs
Write the next line to each rhyme, riddle, or song.
1. Mabel, Mabel,
   Strong and able. . .
2. Do you have Prince Albert in the can?
3. Cinderella, dressed in yella. . .
4. In came the doctor,
   In came the nurse. . .
5. Finders keepers. . .
6. Nobody loves me,
   Everybody hates me. . .
7. I had a little brother and his name was Tiny Tim. . .
8. Hello, Hello, Hello, Sir. . .
9. Latin is a language,
   As old as it can be.
   First it killed the Ancient Romans. . .
10. Step on a crack. . .

Part 3: Folk and Fairy Tales

1. It pricked the finger of Sleeping Beauty.
2. It lives under a bridge between the Three Billy Goats Gruff and the green, green grass.
3. These are the four ways the wicked queen tries to kill Snow White.
4. This is the last thing Red Riding Hood says to the Big Bad Wolf.
5. This is how the third pig escapes the wolf at the fair.
6. This wakens Sleeping Beauty and Snow White.
7. This is what Rumplestiltskin does when the Queen guesses his name.
8. This is what Bluebeard's last wife did that made him angry.
9. This is how Hansel fools the witch into thinking he is still skinny.
10. This is Rapunzel's prison.

Part 4: Places

1. Mrs. Mallard and her ducklings cross it.
2. The Polar Express goes there.
3. Claudia and her younger brother hide there and uncover a mystery.
4. It's where Karana lived alone for many years.
5. It's where the letters are going in *Chicka Chicka Boom Boom.*
6. It's where they love Max so much, they threaten to eat him up.
7. Rob Mallory witnesses a murder from there.
8. It's where Brian survives alone for a year after the plane crash.
9. Wilfred Gordon MacDonald Partridge has many friends there.
10. The Song and Dance Man keeps his memories there.

Part 5: Songs

Add the next line.

1. The horse was lean and lank. . .
2. Can't you hear the Captain shoutin'. . .
3. On the shore dimly seen. . .
4. Ate a peanut, ate a peanut. . .
5. The fox went out on a chilly night. . .
6. If you're happy and you know it. . .
7. I know an old woman
Who swallowed a cow. . .
8. There was a farmer had a dog. . .
9. The bear went over the mountain,
The bear went over the mountain,
The bear went over the mountain. . .
10. I went to the animal fair. . .

Part 6: Things

1. Sarah brought it from the sea for Caleb.
2. A robin shows Mary Lennox where to find it in a hole that a dog had dug.
3. According to Byrd Baylor, everybody needs one.
4. In it, there's a cozy bed on which is a snoring granny, a dreaming child, and much, much, more.
5. The Great Big Hungry Bear is after it.
6. This is how Abel measures his island.
7. Mr. Popper gives them to Admiral Drake.
8. Dr. DeSoto uses it to outwit the fox.
9. It is Julie's Eskimo name.
10. It's what Alexander must find to become a wind-up mouse.

Part 7: Authors and Illustrators

1. He lives in St. Paul, Minnesota, and often uses himself and family members in his illustrations. He's also especially fond of red sneakers. He won the Caldecott Award in 1989.
2. He lives in an old farmhouse in Wilmot Flats, New Hampshire. He loves Christmas, decorating his house elaborately every year and producing one Christmas book each year. He's written several books about a character whose name means Grandmother Witch and her not-very-bright servant.
3. This author/illustrator was born in Augusta, Georgia. Many of her books are about feelings and several have an imaginary, chalk-drawn bear as one of the main characters.
4. This poet and collector of poetry was born in Brooklyn, New York, and now lives in Albuquerque, New Mexico. He's been a cab driver, bus boy, photographer, furniture mover, potter, folksinger, and actor.
5. This author/illustrator was born in San Antonio, Texas, and was going to be a concert violinist until his hand was injured in a plane crash. He drew himself as Lamar J. Spurgle in one of his books. Often his characters have pin-point eyes. He usually has fat cats in his illustrations, no matter what the subject is.

6. His books are often set in Maine, where he now lives on an island. He used his own daughters, Sal and Jane, as characters in some of his books.

7. This author/illustrator was born in Bunbury in Western Australia. She uses her daughters as models and inspirations for her books, many of which are about babies.

8. One of his books is a sentimental journey into his childhood. The buildings are containers from his pantry shelves. The main character is named after a Disney creation. The only other characters are from childhood movies. A street in the book is named after his favorite dog.

9. This author was born in South Carolina, but taught school in Oklahoma, Kentucky, and New York City, before returning to South Carolina, where she wrote many books which starred a literal, well-meaning maid for the Rogers family.

10. This two-time Caldecott Award winner was born in Brooklyn, New York, in a hotel her grandfather owned. She grew up on Long Island, lived in Littleton, Massachusetts, but now lives in South Bristol, Maine. Her last two books are about the area where she now lives.

Answers to Literary Pursuit 2:

Part 1: 1. A Welshman and a thief. 2. He'll sit in the barn to keep himself warm and put his head under his wing. 3. Bells. 4. Woe. 5. The reason why I cannot tell. 6. Bread and butter. 7. One a penny, two a penny. 8. For spoiling her nice new clothes. 9. A rat could eat him, tail and all. 10. One.

Part 2: (Answers may vary according to neighborhood.) 1. Get your elbows off the table. 2. Then let him out. 3. Went upstairs to kiss her fella. 4. In came the lady with the alligator purse. 5. Losers weepers. 6. Going in the garden to eat worms. 7. I put him in the bathtub to teach him how to swim. 8. Are you coming out, Sir? 9. And now it's killing me. 10. You break your mother's back.

Part 3: 1. A spindle. 2. A troll. 3. A hunter, a poisoned comb, a girdle, a poisoned apple. 4. But Grandma, what big teeth you have. 5. He rolls away in a butter churn. 6. A kiss. 7. He stamps his foot and breaks in two. 8. Opened the secret closet. 9. He sticks out a chicken bone for her to feel. 10. A tower.

Part 4: 1. Boston Common 2. North Pole 3. Metropolitan Museum of Art 4. Island of the Blue Dolphins 5. Up the coconut tree 6. Where the Wild Things Are 7. The cherry tree. 8. Northern Canada 9. Old People's Home 10. A trunk in the attic

Part 5: 1. Misfortune seemed his lot, 2. Dinah, blow your horn. 3. In the mists of the deep. 4. Ate a peanut just now. 5. Prayed for the moon to give him light. 6. Clap your hands. 7. I don't know how she swallowed a cow. 8. And Bingo was his name, oh. 9. To see what he could see. 10. The birds and the beasts were there.

Part 6: 1. A shell 2. The key to the Secret Garden 3. A rock 4. The Napping House 5. The Red, Ripe Strawberry 6. By tail lengths 7. Penguins 8. Glue 9. Miyax 10. A purple pebble

Part 7: 1. Stephen Gammell 2. Tomie de Paola 3. Martha Alexander 4. Jack Prelutsky 5. James Marshall 6. Robert McCloskey 7. Jan Ormerod 8. Maurice Sendak 9. Peggy Parish 10. Barbara Cooney

Literature Source Books

Baskwill, Jane and Whitman, Paulette. *Moving On.* Scholastic, 1988.

This book follows the wonderful *The Whole Language Sourcebook Grades K-2* (Scholastic, 1985). It focuses on the upper grades with the same format: what to do, why to do it, and how to do it.

Bauer, Caroline. *Celebrations.* Wilson, 1985.
———. *Presenting Reader's Theater.* Wilson, 1987.
———. *This Way to Books.* Wilson, 1983.

Ms. Bauer's approach to books is outrageous and perfect for those times when things are bogging down. Ideas for storytelling programs, special programs, and poetry and book activities abound.

Heald-Taylor, Gail. *The Administrator's Guide to Whole Language.* Richard C. Owens, 1989.

Don't let this book fool you. Every administrator should read it, but so should all practitioners. This book gives a concise overview of whole language, cites its research, and gives thought and space to community relations and support for the program.

Holdaway, Don. *The Foundations of Literacy.* Heinemann, 1979.

This is one of the books that started the current use of literature as part of the curriculum. Mr. Holdaway writes about the literacy experience clearly and compellingly.

Huck, Charlotte S. *Children's Literature in the Elementary School.* Fourth Edition. Holt, 1987.

An excellent textbook on children's literature, this book also contains suggestions for classroom activities. It has a strong whole language component.

Hurst, Carol Otis et al. *Once Upon a Time: An Encyclopedia for Successfully Using Literature with Young Children.* DLM, 1990.

This is the first volume of the present work. Although directed at early elementary students and teachers, the book contains a great deal of information on picture books and ways to use them that is relevant to upper-grade classrooms.

Isaacson, Richard et al. *Children's Catalog.* Wilson, 1986.

This is a categorized bibliography that is updated each year. If you're looking for books on a specific topic, this is the place to go.

Johnson, Terry D. and Louis, Daphne R. *Literacy Through Literature.* Heinemann, 1987.

This is a practical book of specifics for using literature in the classroom: what to do and how to do it.

Kimmell, Margaret Mary. *For Reading Out Loud!* Delacorte, 1988.

An excellent resource for read-alouds, this one gives approximate reading time, number of sittings, summaries, and recommended levels.

Kobrin, Beverly. *Eyeopeners! How to Choose and Use Children's Books About Real People, Places, and Things.* Penguin, 1988.

This is an excellent guide to nonfiction with annotated book lists by subject. Great for planning thematic units.

Moss, Joy F. *Focus on Literature, a Context for Literacy Learning.* Owen, 1990.

Here are some good practical suggestions, the theory behind them, and ten strong focus units.

Stewig, John Warren. *Read to Write: Using Children's Literature as a Springboard for Teaching Writing.* Owen, 1990.

Mr. Stewig believes that to be able to write clearly and creatively, students need the kind of direction that comes from literature. He uses it as a background and as the focus of directed writing activities. There is a scope and sequence for his literature-based program, which gives structure to those of us uncomfortable with less-formal programs.

Trelease, Jim. *The New Read-Aloud Handbook.* Penguin, 1989.

If you need to convince anybody that reading aloud is a vital and necessary part of the curriculum and homelife, this book is the one that will do it. In addition to the well-thought-out arguments, Mr. Trelease provides an excellent annotated bibliography.

Weaver, Constance. *Reading Process and Practice.* Heinemann, 1988.

Ms. Weaver first analyzes the reading process and then shows ways that whole language techniques apply to the process.

Book Information Sources

□ Because increasing numbers of bookstores are part of large chains that stock mainly best sellers, it is sometimes difficult for people to obtain specific children's books. Of course, almost any bookstore will order a book that is in print at the time. If the book is temporarily out-of-stock at the publishers, the bookstore is reluctant or unable to keep trying for you, and they sometimes wait to order until they have several orders so that they get better rates and faster service.

□ You can almost always order directly from the publisher. A list of publishers with their addresses and phone numbers follows. If you order on school stationery, you can usually be billed. Otherwise, if you call the publisher's customer service department, they will tell you the price, including shipping of a book. Many have 800 numbers for toll-free calling. Be prepared to wait—many trade publishers are slow filling small orders.

□ Librarians often use jobbers to obtain books for the library. Jobbers are wholesale distributors who stock and order books from many publishers. These jobbers are often willing to supply individual books for teachers or the librarian can attach individual orders to the main book order.

□ Children's book stores are, for the most part, thriving throughout the country. Because of their specialization, they are able to stock more titles than the all-purpose bookstore. Most large cities have at least one such bookstore and often they maintain a mail order business. Besides offering books, such enterprises often distribute book posters and author information and they provide special opportunities to meet children's authors and illustrators. Make sure you're on the mailing list of at least one good children's bookstore.

□ Most teachers and librarians have added to their book collections through book clubs and book sales. Many good titles are available this way. Remember, however, that all such sources are not alike. Some have more interest in television-related titles and paraphernalia than in good literature. The best of them offer good titles at reasonable prices and as premiums.

□ There are also some mail order catalogs and telephone services available for children's books.

Check *The New York Times* or other large newspaper's book review section for this information.

□ Also in such book review sections there are advertisements for dealers in out-of-print books and remainders. Don't assume that such books are beyond your reach or pocketbook. Although some rare books demand large prices, many that are only recently out-of-print are available for a few dollars, often for less than the list price of a new book. Most dealers will search for your title at no charge and then tell you the condition and price of the volume they were able to locate. You can then decide whether the price is worth it.

□ Most publishers offer extensive paperback listings, so a book that is currently out-of-print and unavailable may be returned to current status at any time. So keep a wish list. You will notice that our book references are to the earliest publication of a title. There are several reasons for that: We want you to be able to recognize a classic immediately. A book that was originally printed in 1932 and is still in publication is worth looking at. With the growth in the children's book market and the buying, selling, and trading of publishing houses going on, new editions come out monthly.

□ Make sure that people who might shop for gifts for you know about your list. Suggest they purchase books for the classroom instead of gifts for you or members of the class. A birthday gift for the class with that child's name in it is usually met with approval on all sides.

□ Of course, don't forget garage sales, flea markets, and moving sales. For some strange reason, a few people don't keep books they've read.

□ Although we've tried to be as current as possible while composing this book, more children's books are coming off the presses even as we speak. Keeping up-to-date is an endless task. Consult periodicals such as *The Hornbook Magazine, The School Library Journal, Teaching K-8, Instructor, Learning, Booklist, Publishers' Weekly,* and the children's book review sections in major newspapers. The most important source of books, however, is your fellow teachers. Set up a time when you and your colleagues can share your finds in the field of children's literature.

Publishers' Addresses

A. Whitman
5747 W. Howard Street
Niles, IL 60648
(800) 255-7675

ABC CLIO
PO Box 1911
Santa Barabar, CA 93116-1911
(800) 422-2546

Abingdon Press
PO Box 801
201 Eighth Ave. S.
Nashville, TN 37202
(800) 251-3320

Abrams
100 Fifth Ave.
New York, NY 10011
(800) 345-1359

Acadia Publishing
PO Box 170
Bar Harbor, ME 04609
(207) 288-9025

Addison Wesley
1 Jacob Way
Reading, MA 01867
(800) 447-2226

Aladdin Books
See Macmillan.

Andre Deutsch
c/o Penguin USA
PO Box 120
Bergenfield, NJ 07621
(800) 526-0275

Apple Paperbacks
See Scholastic.

Astor-Honor, Inc.
48 E. 43rd St.
New York, NY 10017
(212) 687-6190

Atheneum
See Macmillan.

Atlantic Monthly Press
8 Arlington St.
Boston, MA 02116
(617) 536-9500
Distributed by Little, Brown

Avon Books
105 Madison Ave.
New York, NY 10016
(800) 223-0690

Bantam Books
666 Fifth Ave.
New York, NY 10103
(800) 223-6834

Barron Educational Series
PO Box 8040
250 Wireless Blvd.
Hauppauge, NY 11788
(800) 645-3476

Beacon Press
See HarperCollins.

Blue Ribbon Press
See Scholastic.

Peter Bedrick Bks
2112 Broadway, Rm. 318
New York, NY 10023
(212) 496-0751

Bradbury Press
Affiliate of Macmillan
866 Third Ave.
New York, NY 10022
(212) 702-3598

Camelot
See Avon.

Carolrhoda Bks, Inc.
241 First Avenue N.
Minneapolis, MN 55401
(800) 328-4929

Child's Play
550 Harrow Ct.
Rochester Hills, MI 46063
(313) 852-9242

Children's Press
5440 N. Cumberland Ave.
Chicago, Il 60656
(800) 621-1115

Clarion
See Houghton Mifflin.

Cobblestone Publishers
30 Grove Street.
Peterborough, NH 03458
(603) 924-7209

Collier Books
See Macmillan.

David C. Cook
850 N. Grove Ave.
Elgin, IL 60120
(800) 323-7543

Coward
See Putnam.

Creative Arts Book Company
833 Bancroft Way
Berkeley, CA 94710

Creative Education, Inc
123 S. Broad St.
PO Box 227
Mankato, MN 56001
(800) 445-6209

Crestwood House
See Macmillan.

Thomas Y. Crowell
See HarperCollins.

Crown Publishers
225 Park Ave. S.
New York, NY 10003
(212) 254-1600

Delacorte Press
1 Dag Hammarskjold Plaza
245 E. 47th St.
New York, NY 10017
(800) 221-4676

Dell Publishing
See Doubleday.

Dial Books
See Dutton.

DLM
1 DLM Park
Allen, TX 75002
(800) 527-4747

Dodd, Mead & Co.
71 Fifth Ave.
New York, NY 10003
(800) 237-3255

Doubleday & Co
245 Park Ave.
New York, NY 10017
(800) 223-6834

E. P. Dutton
2 Park Ave.
New York, NY 10016
(212) 725-1818

Faber & Faber
50 Cross St.
Winchester, MA 01890
(617) 721-1427

Fawcett Book Group
See Random House.

Four Winds
see Macmillan.

Farrar, Straus & Girroux
19 Union Sq. W.
New York, NY 10003
(212) 741-6900

Garrard Publishing Co.
1607 N. Market St.
Champaign, IL 61820
(217) 352-7685

David R. Godine
300 Massachusetts Ave.
Horticulture Hall
Boston, MA 02115
(617) 536-0761

Green Tiger Press
435 E. Carmel St
San Marcos, CA 92069-4362
(800) 424-2443

Greenwillow Books
See William Morrow.

Harcourt Brace Jovanovich, Inc.
1250 Sixth Ave.
San Diego, CA 92101
(800) 543-1918

HarperCollins
10 E. 53rd St.
New York, NY 10022
(800) 242-7737

Hastings House
Div. of Gallen Fund, Inc.
260 Fifth Ave.
New York, NY 10001

Heinemann Educational Books
70 Court St.
Portsmouth, NH 03801
(603) 431-7894

Holiday House
18 E. 53rd St.
New York, NY 10022
(212) 688-0085

Henry Holt & Co.
521 Fifth Ave.
New York, NY 10175
(800) 247-3912

Houghton Mifflin
1 Beacon St.
Boston, MA 02108
(617) 725-5000

Jamestown Publishers Inc.
P. O. Box 9168
Providence, RI 02940
(800) 872-7323

Alfred A. Knopf Inc
See Random House.

Lerner Publishing
241 First Ave. N.
Minneapolis, MN 55401
(800) 328-4929

J. B. Lippincott Bks
See HarperCollins.

Little, Brown & Co.
Div. of Time Inc.
34 Beacon St.
Boston, MA 02108
(800) 343-9204

Lodestar Books
See E. P. Dutton.

Lothrop, Lee and Shepard Books
See William Morrow.

McElderry
See Macmillan.

McGraw Hill Book Co.
1221 Avenue of the Americas
New York, NY 10020
(800) 722-4726

David McKay Co.
2 Park Avenue
New York, NY 10016
(212) 340-9800

Macmillan Publishing Co.
866 Third Avenue
New York, NY 10022
(800) 257-5755

Julian Messner
See Simon & Schuster.

William Morrow & Co.
105 Madison Ave.
New York, NY 10016
(800) 237-0657

North-South Books
See Picture Book Studio.

Oxford University Press
200 Madison Ave.
New York, NY 10016
(800) 334-4249

Pantheon Books
See Random House.

Parents Magazine Press
685 Third Ave.
New York, NY 10017
(212) 878-8700

Penguin Books
40 W. 23rd St.
New York, NY 10010
(800) 631-3577

Philomel Books
See Putnam.

Picture Book Studio
60 N. Main St.
Natick, MA 01760
(617) 655-9696

Prentice Hall Inc.
See Simon & Schuster.

Putnam Publishing Group
200 Madison Ave.
New York, NY 10016
(800) 631-8571

Raintree Publishers
310 W. Wisconsin Ave.
Milwaukee, WI 53203
(800) 558-7264

Rand McNally & Co.
P. O. Box 7600
Chicago, IL 60680
(312) 673-9100

Random House Inc
201 E. 50th St., 31st Floor
New York, NY 10022
(800) 726-0600

St. Martin's Press
See Macmillan.

Scholastic Inc.
730 Broadway
New York, NY 10003
(800) 392-2179

Scribners
See Macmillan.

Sierra Club
See Random House.

Silver Burdette
See Simon & Schuster.

Simon & Schuster Inc.
1230 Ave. of the Americas
New York, NY 10020
(800) 223-2348

Sterling Publishing Co., Inc.
2 Park Ave.
New York, NY 10016
(800) 367-9692

Time-Life Books
Div. of Time, Inc.
777 Duke St.
Alexandria, VA 22314
(800) 621-7026
Dis. by Little Brown

Tundra Books
Affiliate of Tundra Books Canada
P.O. Box 1030
Plattsburgh, NY 12901
Dist. by Univ of Toronto Press
33 E. Tupper St.
Buffalo, NY 14225
(716) 683-4547

Viking
See Penguin.

Wanderer Books
See Simon & Schuster.

Franklin Watts, Inc.
Subsidiary of Grolier, Inc.
387 Park Ave. S.
New York, NY 10016
(800) 672-6672

Authors and Illustrators in Your School

It's a wonderful idea to bring someone from the field of children's books into your school to work with and/or talk to the children. Such an experience can provide a focus for a great deal of reading and writing activity. It can help children see that real people write the books they're reading, but it's important to have the right person for your situation.

Choosing a Guest

Talk to publicity directors at children's publishers and to children's bookstore proprietors to find out who might come to your area. Make sure you know the fees and what expenses you're going to be responsible for. Ask for the names of other schools that person has been to recently. Talk to librarians and teachers at those schools. Encourage them to be frank with you about the success of the visit. Just because people write or draw well doesn't mean that they are especially good with large groups of children. Many of them chose the work they do because they are shy or prefer to work away from people. Make sure that the author or illustrator experience is pleasant for both the presenter and the audience. Choose someone whose work is appropriate for the age level in your building. Most of them are booked far in advance, so plan ahead.

Scheduling a Guest

When you have decided on the right person, talk to him/her on the phone, if possible. Find out what he/she expects from the visit. Follow up the phone call with a letter in which you state the terms you agreed on. Include the schedule for the day, and be sure to tell the guest the age level of the audience.

When setting up the schedule, you want to get your money's worth of course, but remember that you're dealing with real humans here. They need breaks, too. If you are in a very conservative or difficult area, make sure the author knows that. Those who work in schools don't expect perfection, but they need to know what to expect. Make sure you tell the artist when he or she can expect payment and then make sure you have it ready. If you are going to offer the artist's books for autographing that day, be sure the books arrive several days early and that a system is in place for selling the books and autographing. Remember that autographing books is exhausting, as is performing, for most people. Allow ample recuperation time.

Preparing the Audience

Make sure that the audience is prepared. There is little point in listening to the author or illustrator unless the books are very familiar to almost everyone. Also prepare the audience for the fact that this person is probably not going to be doing a "show" as such. A few authors are real performers but most will not be capable of doing more than talking to the children about their work. Most authors and illustrators respond best to children who are well prepared.

Making Accommodations

Ask whether the artist prefers to stay in a private home or at a hotel or motel. Usually they like the privacy of a commercial establishment, but not always. Check out the motel or hotel where the artist will be housed. You probably haven't stayed there and you do want it to be pleasant. If possible, choose a place where someone you know has had a pleasant experience. Find out about such things as whether or not there is an in-house restaurant and whether the person will have access to a car. Will breakfast be served there? If not, be sure someone reliable is responsible for taking the guest out for each meal. At any rate, ask whether the artist prefers to be left alone or prefers company and, if so, when. Remember that if you take that person out for dinner with some of the staff, it may well be a very enjoyable experience, but the artist is always "on" to some degree on such occasions. He or she is expected to be pleasant company. Some of them are very gregarious and enjoy such situations. Others would much prefer a quiet dinner on their own. Ask! Give them a choice.

Ask someone with a pleasant personality who is familiar with the artist's work to meet him/her at the airport. Remember that if they've been traveling very far, they are probably exhausted and may be hungry or thirsty. Make sure you ask what they need or want. Don't assume anything. Make sure that before you drop them off to rest and refresh, they have phone numbers where you or others can be reached. If the guest is arriving under her/his own power, call after the scheduled arrival to welcome the guest and find out preferences for the evening before the school day.

Also, some artists like to travel to the schools around the country because they are inveterate sightseers.

Have a list of possible side trips prepared and offer to have someone take the guest on a tour before he/she leaves town. Have a bowl of fruit or a small bouquet of flowers with a welcome note delivered to the room in advance of the guest's arrival, if possible. Such touches make a lot of difference in the attitude your guest will have by the time he or she gets to your school. After the time with the children and/or staff, make sure that the artist gets to the airport in time for departure. If the guest is staying in the area, make sure the same choices are offered as to company or lack of company for dinner or sight seeing. No one is immune to appreciation. Make sure your author or illustrator hears yours.

Following Through
The chances are that this will be a wonderful experience for everyone. Be sure to send thank you notes to the guest and those responsible for arranging the visit. If, heaven forbid, the experience was not pleasant, if the author or illustrator was not well received, let other librarians and teachers know what happened. And pass the word back to the publisher or publicist that the visit didn't work out and be frank as to why. Such experiences don't help anyone much and should not be repeated, but do try again with a different artist.

Author/Illustrator Birthday Calendar

January
1 Jacqueline Chwast
2 Crosby Bonsall
3 Joan Walsh Anglund
   Carolyn Haywood
5 Celestino Piatti
7 Eleanor Clymer
9 Clyde Robert Bulla
10 Remy Charlip
13 Michael Bond
14 Hugh Lofting
   Thornton Burgess
18 Alan Alexander Milne
   Raymond Briggs
22 Blair Lent
   Brian Wildsmith
27 Julius Lester
28 Ferdinand Monjo
29 Bill Peet

February
2 Rebecca Caudill
   Patricia Lauber
4 Russell Hoban
7 Laura Ingalls Wilder
11 Jane Yolen
16 Nancy Ekholm Burkert
22 Edward Gorey
27 Uri Shulevitz

March
2 Dr. Seuss
3 Erik Blegvad
11 Ezra Jack Keats
   Wanda Gag
13 Ellen Raskin
14 Marguerite de Angeli
17 Kate Greenaway
20 Mitsumasa Anno
22 Randolph Caldecott
31 Beni Montresor

April
1 Jan Wahl
2 Hans Christian Andersen
4 Glen Rounds
8 Trina Schart Hyman
12 Beverly Cleary
   Hardie Gramatky
   C. W. Anderson
13 Jan Berenstain
15 Eleanor Schick
16 Garth Williams
22 Kurt Wiese
24 Evaline Ness
25 Walter de la Mare
27 Ludwig Bemelmans
   John Burningham

May
5 Leo Lionni
6 Randall Jarrell
7 Nonny Hogrogian
8 Helen Griffiths
9 Eleanor Estes
18 Lillian Hoban
19 Tom Feelings
22 Arnold Lobel
23 Margaret Wise Brown
   Peter Parnall
25 Martha Alexander
31 Jay Williams

June
1 James Daugherty
2 Paul Galdone
   Helen Oxenbury
   George Mendoza
   Anita Lobel
5 Richard Scarry
   Irene Haas
6 Peter Spier
7 Nikki Giovanni
10 Maurice Sendak
12 James Houston
14 Janice Udry
21 Robert Kraus
24 John Ciardi
   Leonard Everett Fisher
26 Lynd Ward
27 Lucille Clifton

July
1 Emily McCully
10 Martin Provensen
13 Marcia Brown
17 Karla Kuskin
19 Eve Merriam
22 Margery Williams Bianco
23 Robert Quackenbush
25 Clyde Watson
27 Scott Corbett
28 Natalie Babbitt

August
2 Holling C. Holling
3 Mary Calhoun
5 Robert Bright
6 Barbara Cooney
10 Margot Tomes
11 Don Freeman
14 Alice Provensen
15 Brinton Turkle
16 Beatrice de Regniers
17 Myra Cohn Livingston
18 Louise Fatio
28 Roger Duvoisin
   Tasha Tudor
30 Virginia Lee Burton
   Laurent de Brunhoff

September
3 Aliki (Aliki L. Brandenberg)
4 Syd Hoff
   Richard Kennedy
9 Aileen Fisher
10 Robert McClung
13 Roald Dahl
   Else Minarik
14 John Steptoe
15 Robert McCloskey
   Tomie dePaola
16 H. A. Rey
19 Arthur Rackham
21 Taro Yashima
22 Charles Keeping
   Esphyr Slobodkina
24 Harry Behn
27 Bernard Waber
29 Stanley Berenstain
30 Edgar d'Aulaire
   Alvin Tresselt

October
3 Natalie Savage Carlson
4 Robert Lawson
   Donald Sobol
5 Gene Zion
6 Crockett Johnson
7 Alice Dalgliesh
8 Edward Ormondroyd
14 Lois Lenski
16 Edward Ardizzone
19 Ed Emberley
23 Marjorie Flack
24 Felice Holman
   Bruno Munari
28 Leonard Kessler

November
1 Hilary Knight
2 Margaret Bloy Graham
4 Gail Haley
13 Nathaniel Benchley
14 Miska Miles
   William Steig
15 David McCord
16 Jean Fritz
21 Leo Politi
25 Crescent Dragonwagon
26 Charles Schultz
27 Katherine Milhous
28 Tomi Ungerer
30 Margot Zemach

December
4 Munro Leaf
8 James Thurber
10 Rumer Godden
   Ernest Shepard
12 Barbara Emberley
13 Leonard Weisgard
16 Marie Hall Ets
   Quentin Blake
21 Feodor Rojankovsky
27 Ingri d'Aulaire
30 Rudyard Kipling

Caldecott and Newbery Medal Winners

Caldecott Medal Winners

The Caldecott Medal, in honor of nineteenth-century English illustrator Randolph Caldecott, has been given annually since 1938 by the American Library Association to the illustrator of the most outstanding picture book published in the United States during the previous year.

1938 *Animals of the Bible.*
Illustrated by Dorothy Lathrop. Written by Helen Dean Fish. Lippincott.
1939 *Mei Li.*
Illustrated and written by Thomas Handforth. Doubleday.
1940 *Abraham Lincoln.*
Illustrated and written by Ingri and Edgar d'Aulaire. Doubleday.
1941 *They Were Strong and Good.*
Illustrated and written by Robert Lawson. Viking.
1942 *Make Way for Ducklings.*
Illustrated and written by Robert McCloskey. Viking.
1943 *The Little House.*
Illustrated and written by Virginia Lee Burton. Houghton.
1944 *Many Moons.*
Illustrated by Louis Slobodkin. Written by James Thurber. Harcourt.
1945 *Prayer for a Child.*
Illustrated by Elizabeth Orton Jones. Written by Rachel Field. Macmillan.
1946 *The Rooster Crows.*
Illustrated and written by Maude and Miska Petersham. Macmillan.
1947 *The Little Island.*
Illustrated by Leonard Weisgard. Written by Golden MacDonald. Doubleday.
1948 *White Snow, Bright Snow.*
Illustrated by Roger Duvoisin. Written by Alvin Tresselt. Lothrop.
1949 *The Big Snow.*
Illustrated and written by Berta and Elmer Hader. Macmillan.
1950 *Song of the Swallows.*
Illustrated and written by Leo Politi. Scribner.
1951 *The Egg Tree.*
Illustrated and written by Katherine Milhous. Scribner.

1952 *Finders Keepers.*
Illustrated by Nicolas Mordvinoff. Written by Will Lipkind. Harcourt.
1953 *The Biggest Bear.*
Illustrated and written by Lynd Ward. Houghton.
1954 *Madeline's Rescue.*
Illustrated and written by Ludwig Bemelmens. Viking.
1955 *Cinderella.*
Illustrated and retold from Perrault by Marcia Brown. Scribner.
1956 *Frog Went a-Courtin'.*
Illustrated by Feodor Rojankovsky. Retold by John Langstaff. Harcourt.
1957 *A Tree Is Nice.*
Illustrated by Marc Simont. Written by Janice Udry. Harper.
1958 *Time of Wonder.*
Illustrated and written by Robert McCloskey. Viking.
1959 *Chanticleer and the Fox.*
Illustrated and retold by Barbara Cooney. Crowell.
1960 *Nine Days to Christmas.*
Illustrated and written by Marie Hall Ets and Aurora Labastida. Viking.
1961 *Baboushka and the Three Kings.*
Illustrated by Nicholas Sidjakov. Written by Ruth Robbins. Parnassus.
1962 *Once a Mouse.*
Illustrated and written by Marcia Brown. Scribner.
1963 *The Snowy Day.*
Illustrated and written by Ezra Jack Keats. Viking.
1964 *Where the Wild Things.*
Illustrated and written by Maurice Sendak. Harper.
1965 *May I Bring a Friend.*
Illustrated by Beni Montresor. Written by Beatrice Schenk de Regniers. Atheneum.
1966 *Always Room for One More.*
Illustrated by Nonny Hogrogian. Written by Sorche Nic Leodhas. Holt.
1967 *Sam, Bangs and Moonshine.*
Illustrated and written by Evaline Ness. Holt.
1968 *Drummer Hoff.*
Illustrated by Ed Emberley. Adapted by Barbara Emberley. Prentice.
1969 *The Fool of the World and the Flying Ship.*
Illustrated by Uri Shulevitz. Retold by Arthur Ransome. Farrar.

1970 *Sylvester and the Magic Pebble.*
Illustrated and written by Willilam Steig. Windmill.
1971 *A Story, A Story.*
Illustrated and written by Gail Haley. Atheneum.
1972 *One Fine Day.*
Illustrated and written by Nonny Hogrogian. Macmillan.
1973 *The Funny Little Woman.*
Illustrated by Blair Lent. Written by Lafcadio Hern, retold by Arlene Mosel. Dutton.
1974 *Duffy and the Devil.*
Illustrated by Margot Zemach. Retold by Harve Zemach. Farrar.
1975 *Arrow to the Sun.*
Illustrated and written by Gerald McDermott. Viking.
1976 *Why Mosquitoes Buzz in People's Ears.*
Illustrated by Leo and Diane Dillon. Retold by Verna Aardema. Dial.
1977 *Ashanti to Zulu.*
Illustrated by Leo and Diane Dillon. Written by Margaret Musgrove. Dial.
1978 *Noah's Ark.*
Illustrated and written by Peter Spier. Doubleday.
1979 *The Girl Who Loved Wild Horses.*
Illustrated and written by Paul Goble. Bradbury.
1980 *Ox-Cart Man.*
Illustrated by Barbara Cooney. Written by Donald Hall. Viking.
1981 *Fables.*
Illustrated and written by Arnold Lobel. Harper.
1982 *Jumanji.*
Illustrated and written by Chris Van Allsburg. Houghton.
1983 *Shadow.*
Illustrated and translated by Marcia Brown. Written by Blaise Cendrars. Scribner.
1984 *The Glorious Flight.*
Illustrated and written by Alice and Martin Provensen. Viking.
1985 *Saint George and the Dragon.*
Illustrated by Trina Schart Hyman. Retold by Margaret Hodges. Little.
1986 *Polar Express.*
Illustrated and written by Chris Van Allsburg. Houghton.
1987 *Hey, Al.*
Illustrated by Richard Egielski. Written by Arthur Yorinks. Farrar.

1988 *Owl Moon.*
Illustrated by John Schoenherr. Written by Jane Yolen. Philomel.
1989 *Song and Dance Man.*
Illustrated by Stephen Gammell. Written by Karen Ackerman. Knopf.
1990 *Lon Po Po.*
Illustrated and written by Ed Young. Philomel.

Newbery Medal Winners
The Newbery Medal has been given since 1922 by the American Library Association to the author of a book deemed to make the most outstanding contribution to children's literature. The award is named for John Newbery, an eighteenth-century British bookseller.

Not all great books have received a Newbery Medal and not all of the books that did receive it are of equal merit. The number of worthwhile books varies greatly from year to year because some years there are fewer books from which to choose and some years the field is so large that great books are passed by. Remember that audience age varies widely and some award-winning books are really for the young adult audience.

1922 *The Story of Mankind.*
Written by Henrik Van Loon. Liveright.
1923 *The Voyages of Doctor Dolittle.*
Written by Hugh Lofting. Lippincott.
1924 *The Dark Frigate.*
Written by Charles Hawes. Little.
1925 *Tales from Silver Lands.*
Written by Charles Finger. Doubleday.
1926 *Shen of the Sea.*
Written by Arthur Chrisman. Dutton.
1927 *Smoky, the Cowhorse.*
Written by Will James. Scribner.
1928 *Gay Neck, the Story of a Pigeon.*
Written by Dhan Mukerji. Dutton.
1929 *Trumpeter of Krakow.*
Written by Eric P. Kelly. Macmillan.
1930 *Hitty, Her First Hundred Years.*
Written by Rachel Field. Macmillan.
1931 *The Cat Who Went to Heaven.*
Written by Elizabeth Coatsworth. Macmillan.
1932 *Waterless Mountain.*
Written by Laura Armer. Longmans.

1933 *Young Fu of the Upper Yangtze.*
Written by Elizabeth Lewis. Winston.

1934 *Invincible Louisa.*
Written by Cornelia Meigs. Little.

1935 *Dobry.*
Written by Monica Shannon. Viking.

1936 *Caddie Woodlawn.*
Written by Carol Brink. Macmillan.

1937 *Roller Skates.*
Written by Ruth Sawyer. Viking.

1938 *The White Stag.*
Written by Kate Seredy. Viking.

1939 *Thimble Summer.*
Written by Elizabeth Enright. Rinehart.

1940 *Daniel Boone.*
Written by James Daugherty. Viking.

1941 *Call It Courage.*
Written by Armstrong Sperry. Macmillan.

1942 *The Matchlock Gun.*
Written by Walter Edmonds. Dodd.

1943 *Adam of the Road.*
Written by Elizabeth Gray. Viking.

1944 *Johnny Tremain.*
Written by Esther Forbes. Houghton.

1945 *Rabbit Hill.*
Written by Robert Lawson. Viking.

1946 *Strawberry Girl.*
Written by Lois Lenski. Lippincott.

1947 *Miss Hickory.*
Written by Carolyn Bailey. Viking.

1948 *The Twenty-One Balloons.*
Written by William Pene du Bois. Viking.

1949 *King of the Wind.*
Written by Marguerite Henry. Rand.

1950 *The Door in the Wall.*
Written by Marguerite de Angeli. Doubleday.

1951 *Amos Fortune, Free Man.*
Written by Elizabeth Yates. Dutton.

1952 *Ginger Pye.*
Written by Eleanor Estes. Harcourt.

1953 *Secret of the Andes.*
Written by Ann Nolan Clark. Viking.

1954 *.. And Now Miguel.*
Written by Joseph Krumgold. Crowell.

1955 *The Wheel on the School.*
Written by Meindert DeJong. Harper.

1956 *Carry On, Mr. Bowditch.*
Written by Jean Lee Latham. Houghton.

1957 *Miracles on Maple Hill.*
Written by Virginia Sorensen. Harcourt.

1958 *Rifles for Watie.*
Written by Harold Keith. Crowell.

1959 *The Witch of Blackbird Pond.*
Written by Elizabeth George Speare. Houghton.

1960 *Onion John.*
Written by Joseph Krumgold. Crowell.

1961 *Island of the Blue Dolphins.*
Written by Scott O'Dell. Houghton.

1962 *The Bronze Bow.*
Written by Elizabeth George Speare. Houghton.

1963 *A Wrinkle in Time.*
Written by Madeline L'Engle. Farrar.

1964 *It's Like This, Cat.*
Written by Emily Neville. Harper.

1965 *Shadow of a Bull.*
Written by Maia Wojciechowska. Atheneum.

1966 *I, Juan de Pareja.*
Written by Elizabeth Borton de Trevino. Farrar.

1967 *Up a Road Slowly.*
Written by Irene Hunt. Follett.

1968 *From the Mixed-Up Files of Mrs. Basil E. Frank-weiler.*
Written by E. L. Konigsburg. Atheneum.

1969 *The High King.*
Written by Lloyd Alexander. Holt.

1970 *Sounder.*
Written by William H. Armstrong. Harper.

1971 *Summer of the Swans.*
Written by Betsy Byars. Viking.

1972 *Mrs. Frisby and the Rats of NIMH.*
Written by Robert C. O'Brien. Atheneum.

1973 *Julie of the Wolves.*
Written by Jean Craighead George. Harper.

1974 *The Slave Dancer.*
Written by Paula Fox. Bradbury.

1975 *M.C. Higgins, the Great.*
Written by Virginia Hamilton. Macmillan.

1976 *The Grey King.*
Written by Susan Cooper. Atheneum.

1977 *Roll of Thunder, Hear My Cry.*
Written by Mildred D. Taylor. Dial.

1978 *Bridge to Terabithia.*
Written by Katherine Paterson. Crowell.

1979 *The Westing Game.*
Written by Ellen Raskin. Dutton.

1980 *A Gathering of Days.*
Written by Joan W. Blos. Scribner.

1981 *Jacob Have I Loved.*
Written by Katherine Paterson. Harper.
1982 *A Visit to William Blake's Inn.*
Written by Nancy Willard. Harcourt.
1983 *Dicey's Song.*
Written by Cynthia Voigt. Atheneum.
1984 *Dear Mr. Henshaw.*
Written by Beverly Cleary. Morrow.
1985 *The Hero and the Crown.*
Written by Robin McKinley. Greenwillow.
1986 *Sarah, Plain and Tall.*
Written by Patricia MacLachlan. Harper.
1987 *The Whipping Boy.*
Written by Sid Fleischman. Greenwillow.
1988 *Lincoln: A Photobiography*
Written by Russell Freedman. Houghton.
1989 *Joyful Noise.*
Written by Paul Fleischman. Harper.
1990 *Number the Stars.*
Written by Lois Lowry. Houghton.

Index

Boldfaced numerals refer to pages with summaries. Superscript 1 indicates coverage in *Once Upon a Time.*